I love the Moomins, so I made
an impulse buy. I especially
like the Groke.

—*Yūki Tabata, 2019*

YŪKI TABATA
was born in Fukuoka Prefecture
and got his big break in the 2011
Shonen Jump Golden Future Cup
with his winning entry, *Hungry
Joker*. He started the magical fantasy
series *Black Clover* in 2015.

BLACK CLOVER
VOLUME 21
SHONEN JUMP Manga Edition

Story and Art by YŪKI TABATA

Translation ✽ TAYLOR ENGEL, HC LANGUAGE SOLUTIONS, INC.

Touch-Up Art & Lettering ✽ ANNALIESE CHRISTMAN

Design ✽ KAM LI

Editor ✽ ALEXIS KIRSCH

First published in Japan in 2015 by SHUEISHA Inc., Tokyo.
English translation rights arranged by SHUEISHA Inc.

Printed in the U.S.A.

Published by VIZ Media, LLC
P.O. Box 77010
San Francisco, CA 94107

10 9 8 7 6 5 4 3 2 1
First printing, June 2020

RATED T TEEN ratings.viz.com

PARENTAL ADVISORY
BLACK CLOVER is rated T for Teen and is recommended for ages 13 and up. This volume contains realistic and fantasy violence.

VIZ MEDIA
viz.com

SHONEN JUMP
shonenjump.com

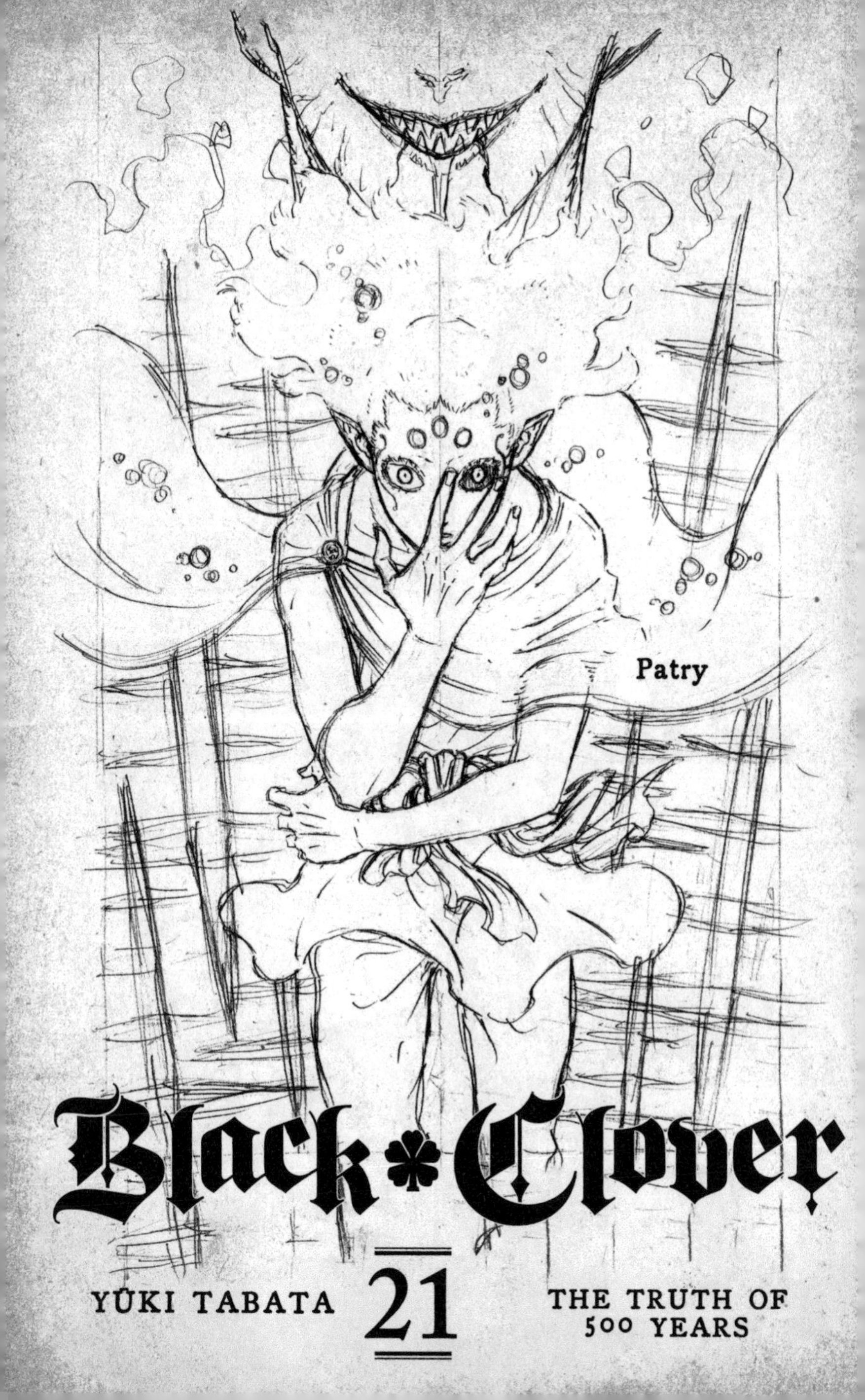
Patry

Black Clover

21

YŪKI TABATA

THE TRUTH OF 500 YEARS

Characters

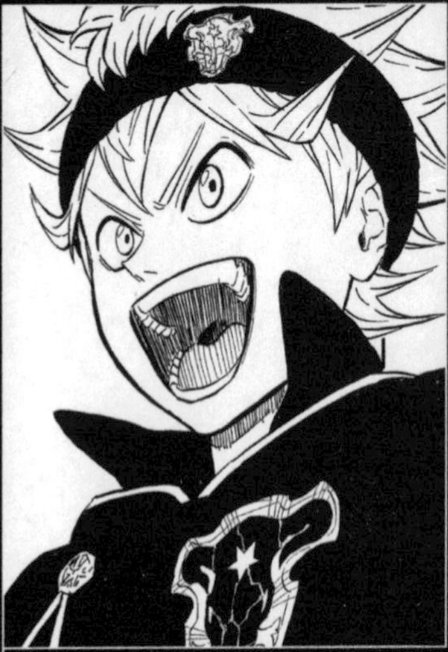

Asta

Member of: The Black Bulls
Magic: None (Anti-Magic)

He has no magic, but he's working to become the Wizard King through sheer guts and his well-trained body. He fights with anti-magic swords.

Yuno

Member of: The Golden Dawn
Magic: Wind

Asta's best friend, and a good rival who's also been working to become the Wizard King. He controls Sylph, the spirit of wind.

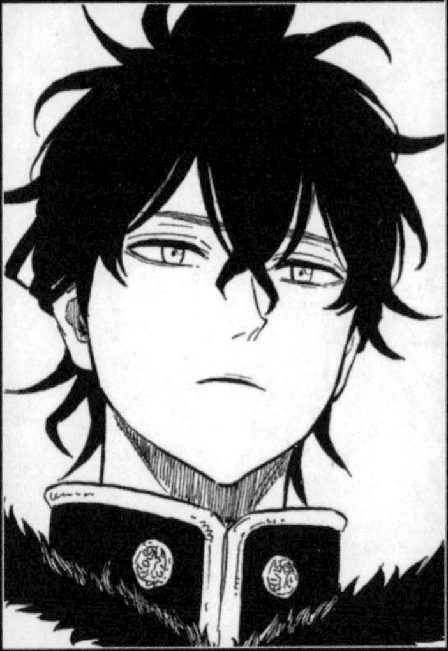

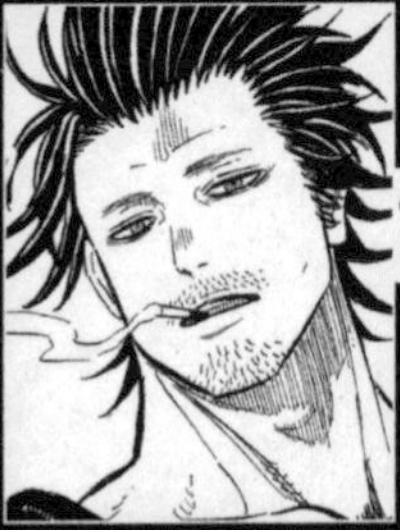

Yami Sukehiro

Member of: The Black Bulls
Magic: Dark

A captain who looks fierce, but is very popular with his brigade, which has a deep-rooted confidence in him. Heavy smoker.

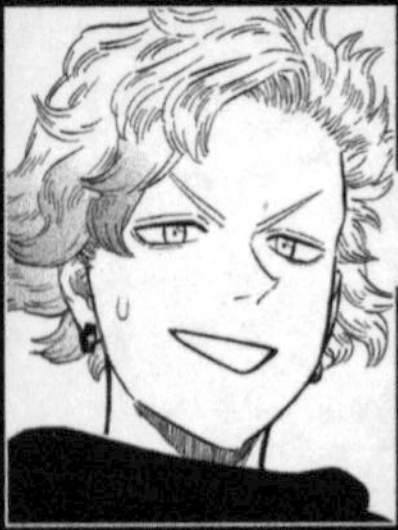

Finral Roulacase

Member of: The Black Bulls
Magic: Spatial

A playboy who immediately chats up any woman he sees. He can't attack, but he has high-level abilities.

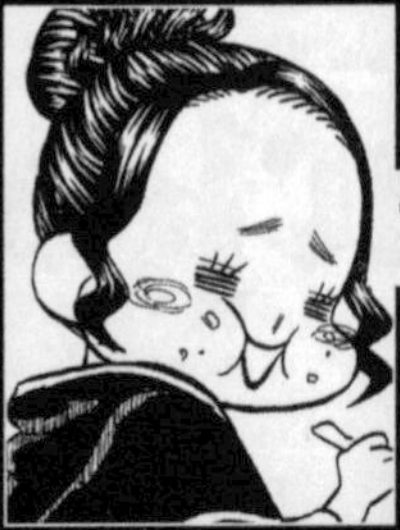

Charmy Pappitson

Member of: The Black Bulls
Magic: Cotton and Food

She eats like a maniac, and prizes food above all else. She's half dwarf. She has a big crush on Yuno.

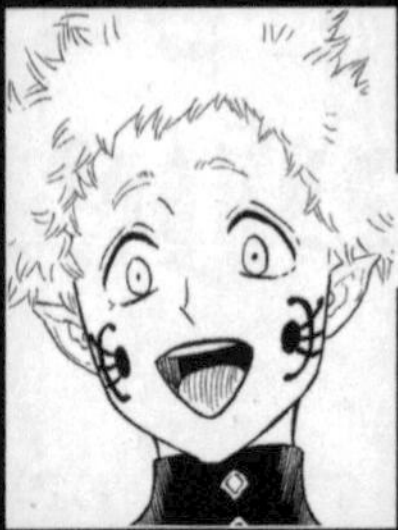

Rill Boismortier

Member of: The Aqua Deer
Magic: Picture

A young captain with outstanding talent. His body has been taken over by an elf named Lira.

Noelle Silva

Member of:
The Black Bulls
Magic: Water

A royal. She feels inferior to her brilliant siblings. Her latent abilities are an unknown quantity.

Nozel Silva

Member of:
The Silver Eagles
Magic: Mercury

Noelle's older brothe[r], captain who values h[is] pride as a royal. Con[siders] Fuegoleon a friendly [rival.]

Raia

Magic: Copy

Once he touches his opponent's grimoire, he's able to copy their magic. He's regained powerful mana through the reincarnation spell.

Mimosa Vermillion

Member of:
The Golden Dawn
Magic: Plant

Noelle's cousin. She's ladylike and a bit of an airhead, but she can be rude. She just might like Asta…

Licht

Magic: Sword

The leader of the elves. He was resurrected by the reincarnation spell, but his mind hasn't returned yet, and he's unstable.

Patry

Magic: Light

He monopolized the body he'd shared wit[h] William and comple[ted] the reincarnation. Hi[s] temporary form look[s] exactly like Licht.

STORY

In a world where magic is everything, Asta and Yuno are both found abandoned on the same day at a church in the remote village of Hage. Both dream of becoming the Wizard King, the highest of all mages, and they spend their days working toward that dream.

The year they turn 15, both receive grimoires, magic books that amplify their bearer's magic. They take the entrance exam for the Magic Knights, nine groups of mages under the direct control of the Wizard King. Yuno, whose magic is strong, joins the Golden Dawn, an elite group, while Asta, who has no magic at all, joins the Black Bulls, a group of misfits. With this, the two finally take their first step toward becoming the Wizard King…

In an attempt to keep the elves from completing their reincarnation, Asta and members of the other Magic Knight brigades follow Yami's group into the Shadow Palace. While the Magic Knights and the Apostles of Sephira fight all through the palace, Asta and Mimosa face off against Lira. Then, suddenly, Charmy awakens!!

CONTENTS

BLACK ❀ CLOVER

21

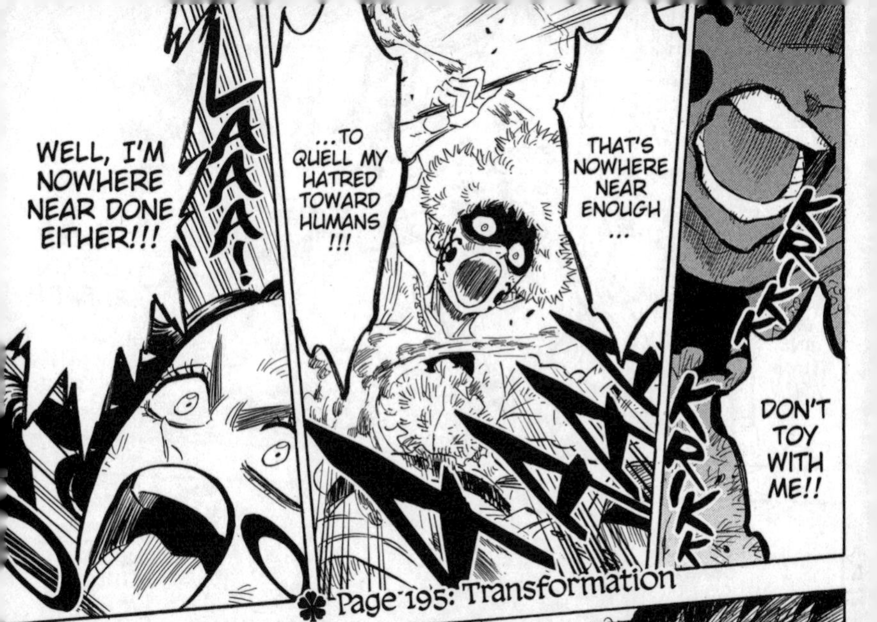
DON'T TOY WITH ME!!
KRIKK KRIKK
THAT'S NOWHERE NEAR ENOUGH...
...TO QUELL MY HATRED TOWARD HUMANS!!!
LAAAA!
WELL, I'M NOWHERE NEAR DONE EITHER!!!

Page 195: Transformation

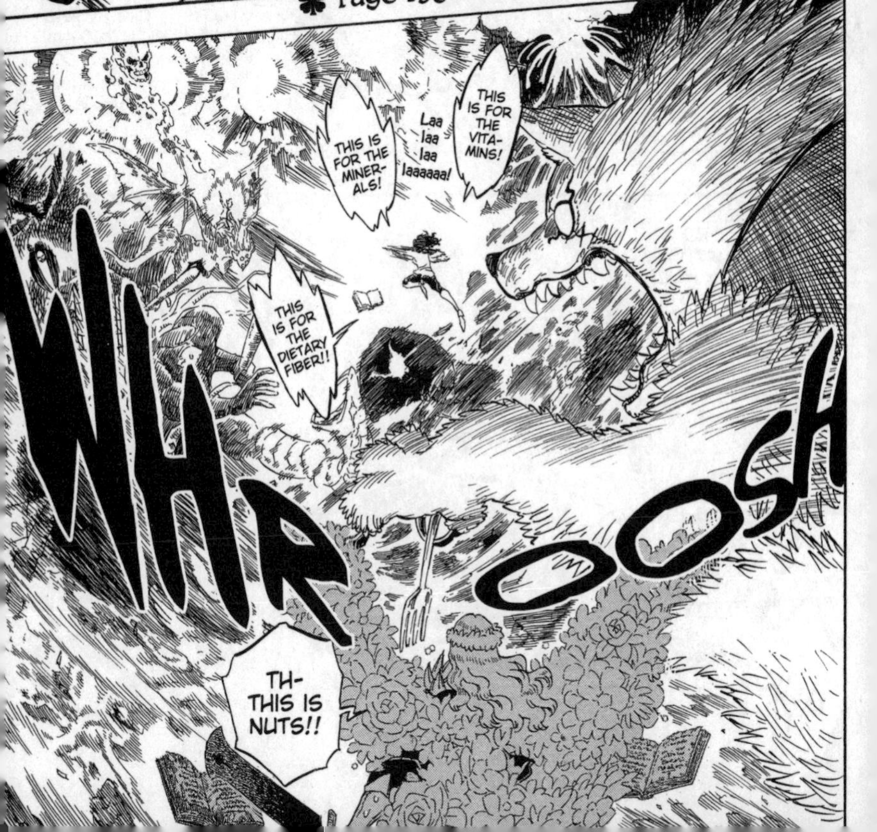
THIS IS FOR THE VITAMINS!
Laa laa laa laaaaaa!
THIS IS FOR THE MINERALS!
THIS IS FOR THE DIETARY FIBER!!
WHROOOSH
TH-THIS IS NUTS!!

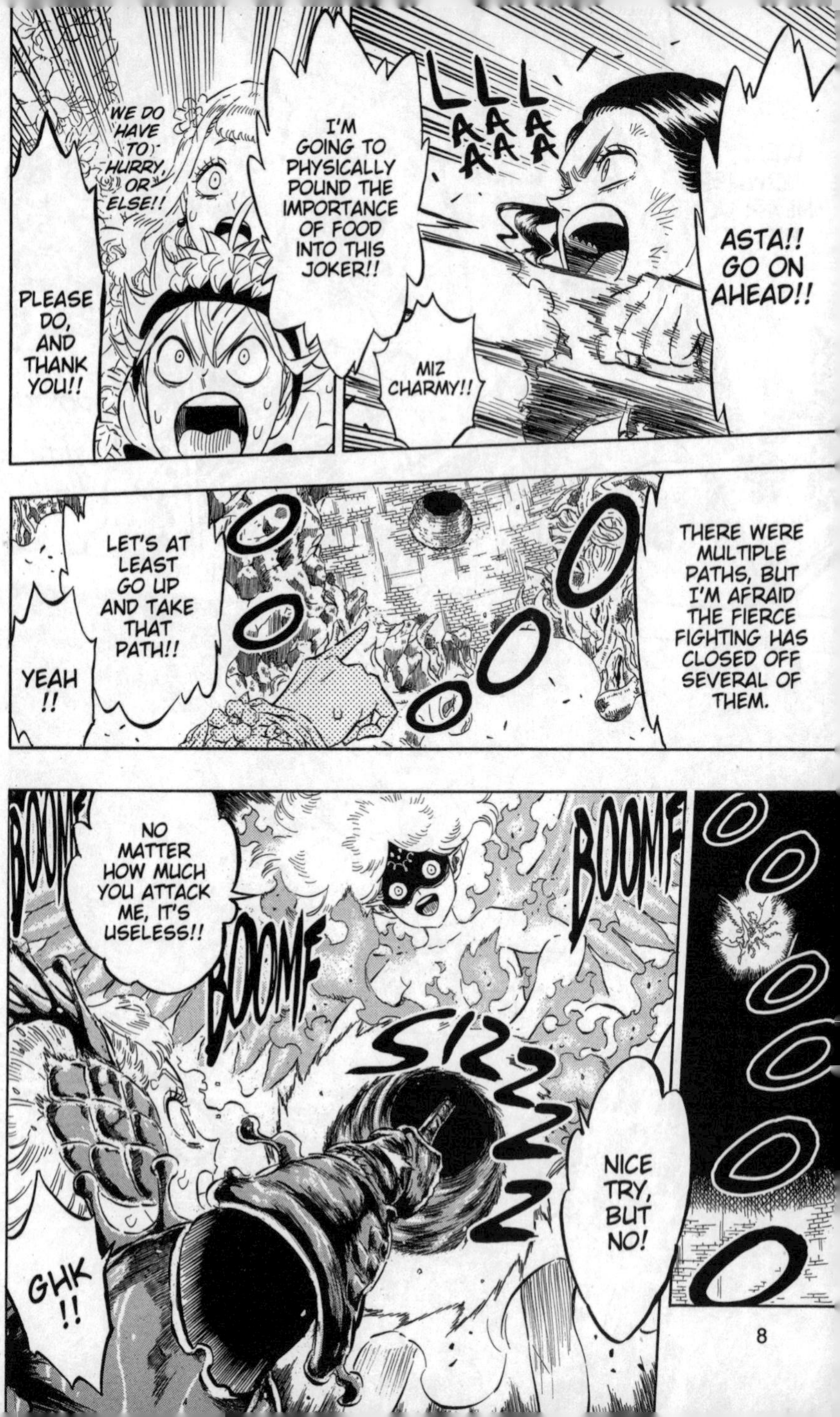
ASTA!! GO ON AHEAD!!
LLLAAAAAA
I'M GOING TO PHYSICALLY POUND THE IMPORTANCE OF FOOD INTO THIS JOKER!!
MIZ CHARMY!!
WE DO HAVE TO HURRY, OR ELSE!!
PLEASE DO, AND THANK YOU!!
THERE WERE MULTIPLE PATHS, BUT I'M AFRAID THE FIERCE FIGHTING HAS CLOSED OFF SEVERAL OF THEM.
OOOOOO
LET'S AT LEAST GO UP AND TAKE THAT PATH!!
YEAH!!
OOOOOOOO
NICE TRY, BUT NO!
SIZZZ
BOOMF
NO MATTER HOW MUCH YOU ATTACK ME, IT'S USELESS!!
BOOMF
BOOMF
GHK!!

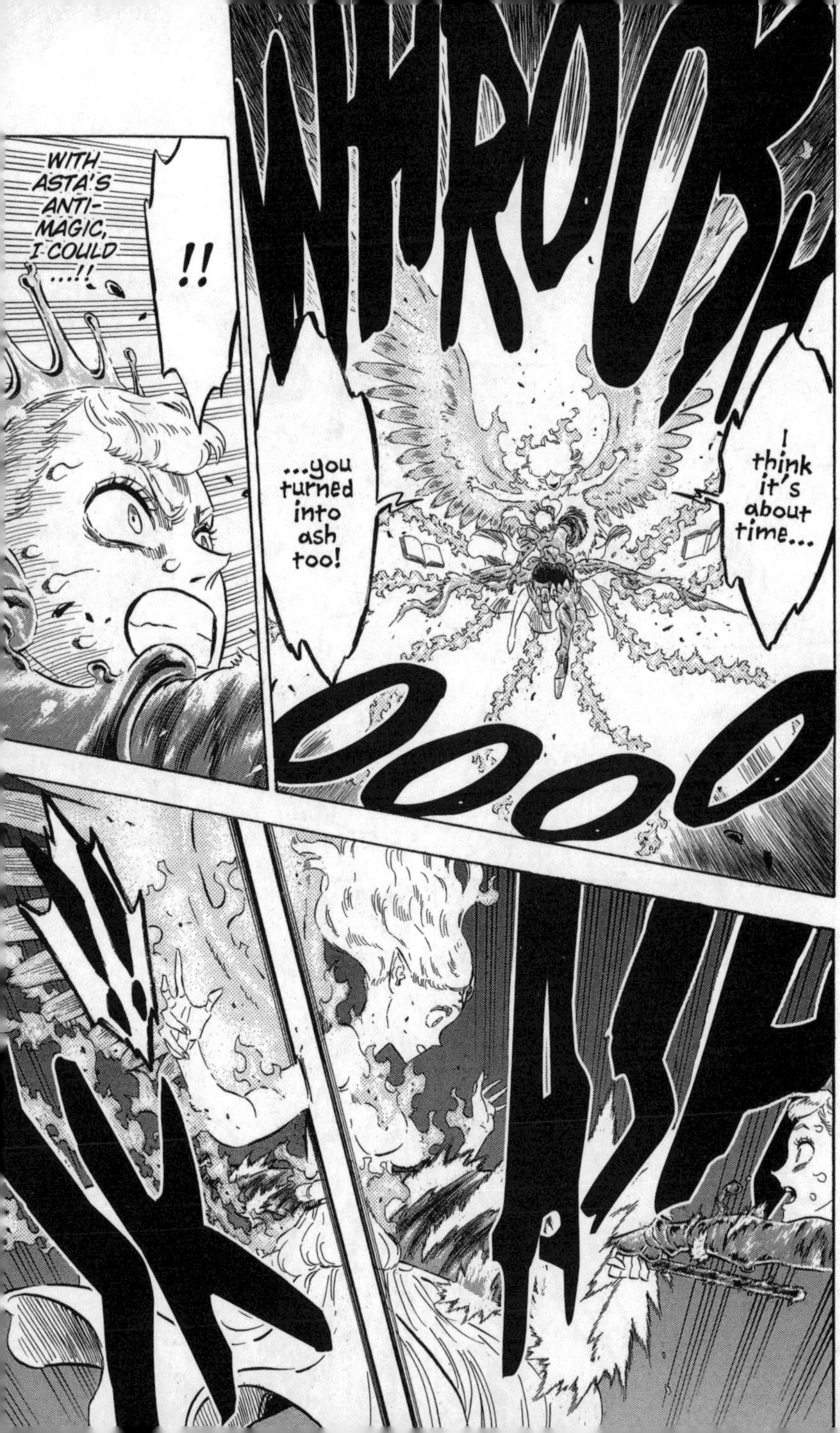
I think it's about time...
...you turned into ash too!
WITH ASTA'S ANTI-MAGIC, I COULD ...!!
!!
!!

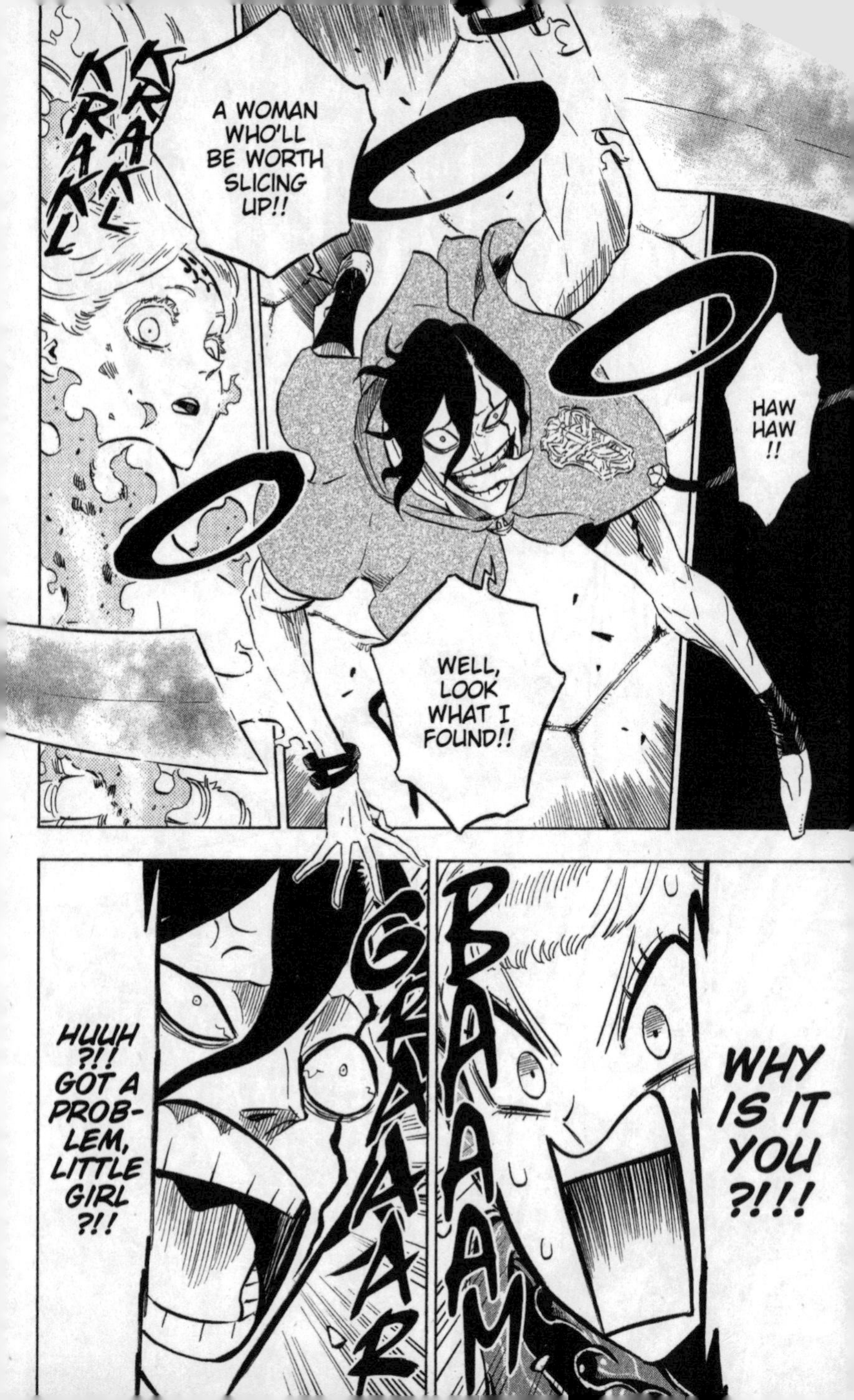
KRAKL KRAKL
A WOMAN WHO'LL BE WORTH SLICING UP!!
HAW HAW!!
WELL, LOOK WHAT I FOUND!!
WHY IS IT YOU?!!!
BRAAAAM
GRAAAAR
HUUH?!! GOT A PROB-LEM, LITTLE GIRL?!!

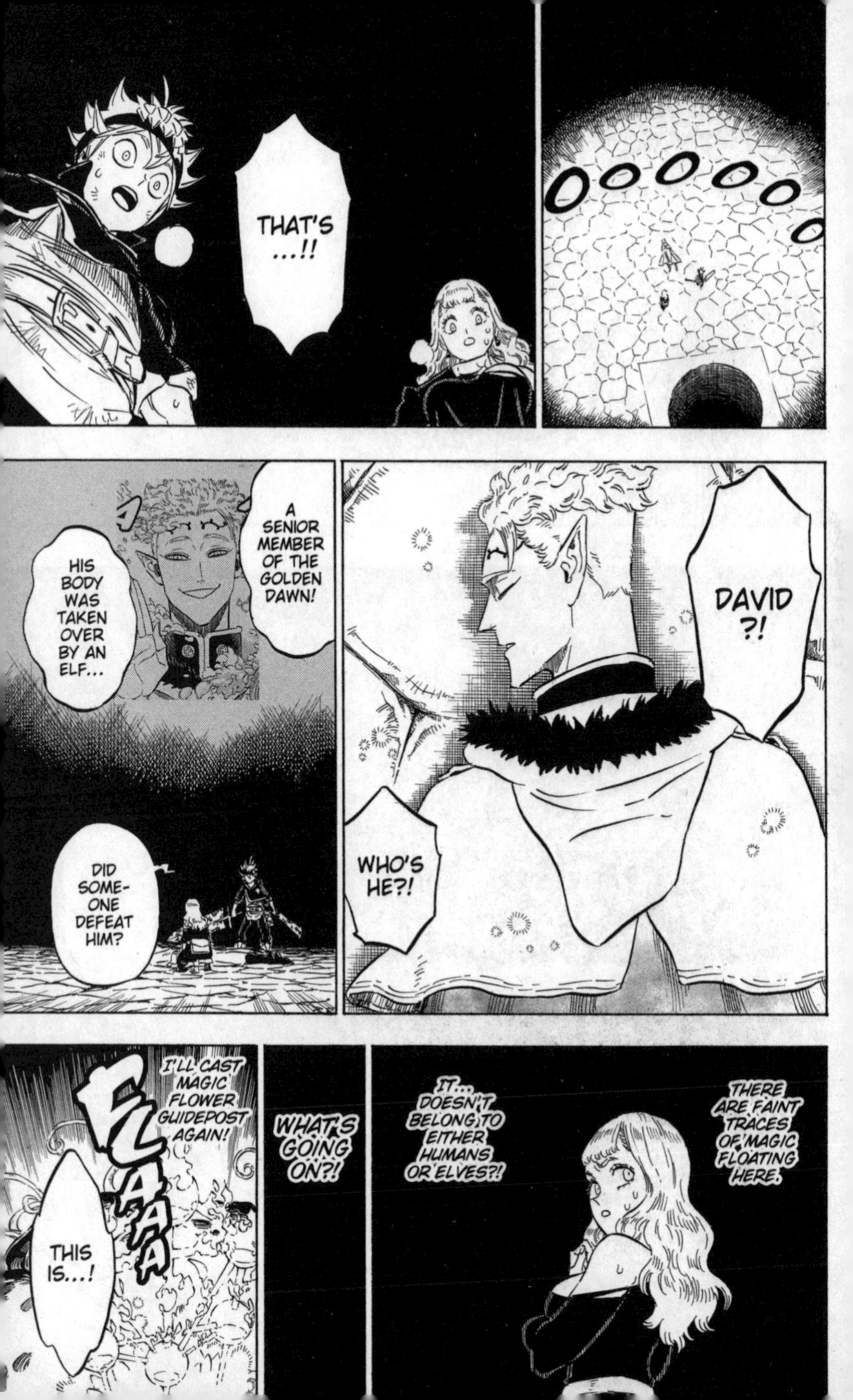
OOOOOOO
THAT'S ...!!
DAVID ?!
WHO'S HE?!
A SENIOR MEMBER OF THE GOLDEN DAWN!
HIS BODY WAS TAKEN OVER BY AN ELF...
DID SOME-ONE DEFEAT HIM?
THERE ARE FAINT TRACES OF MAGIC FLOATING HERE.
IT... DOESN'T BELONG TO EITHER HUMANS OR ELVES?!
WHAT'S GOING ON?!
I'LL CAST MAGIC FLOWER GUIDEPOST AGAIN!
THIS IS...!

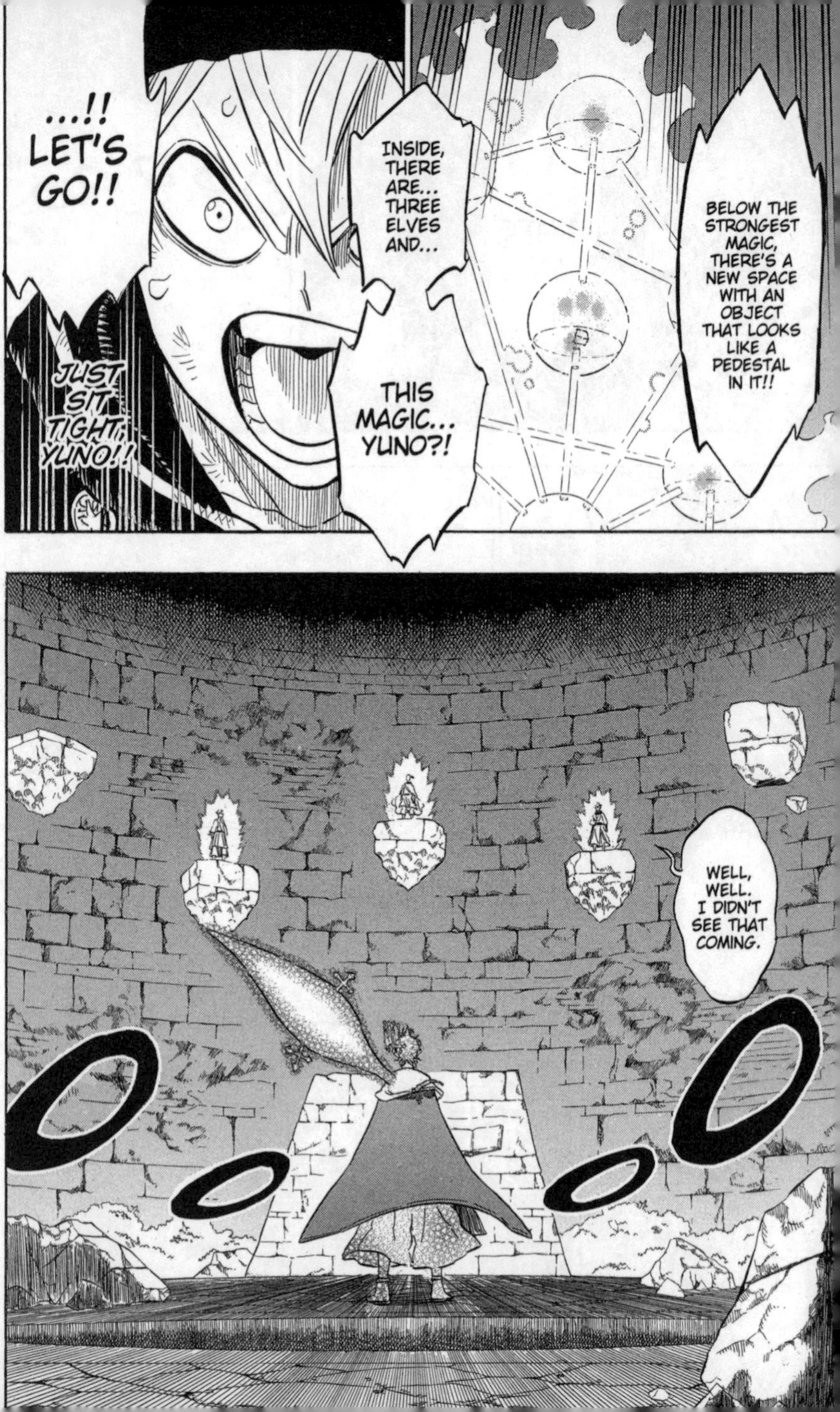
BELOW THE STRONGEST MAGIC, THERE'S A NEW SPACE WITH AN OBJECT THAT LOOKS LIKE A PEDESTAL IN IT!!
INSIDE, THERE ARE... THREE ELVES AND...
THIS MAGIC... YUNO?!
...!! LET'S GO!!
JUST SIT TIGHT, YUNO!!
WELL, WELL. I DIDN'T SEE THAT COMING.

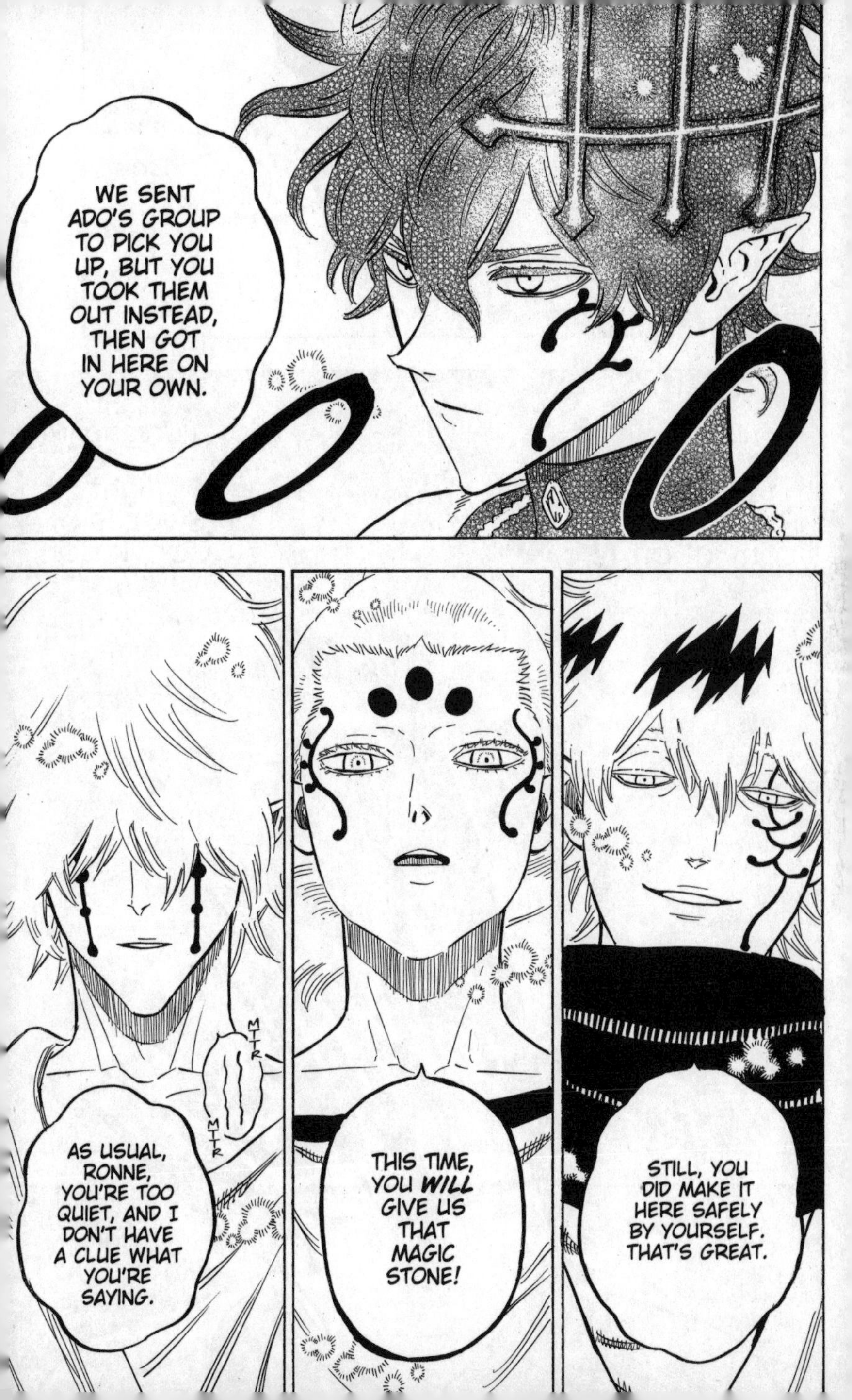
WE SENT ADO'S GROUP TO PICK YOU UP, BUT YOU TOOK THEM OUT INSTEAD, THEN GOT IN HERE ON YOUR OWN.
STILL, YOU DID MAKE IT HERE SAFELY BY YOURSELF. THAT'S GREAT.
THIS TIME, YOU ***WILL*** GIVE US THAT MAGIC STONE!
MTTR
MTTR
AS USUAL, RONNE, YOU'RE TOO QUIET, AND I DON'T HAVE A CLUE WHAT YOU'RE SAYING.

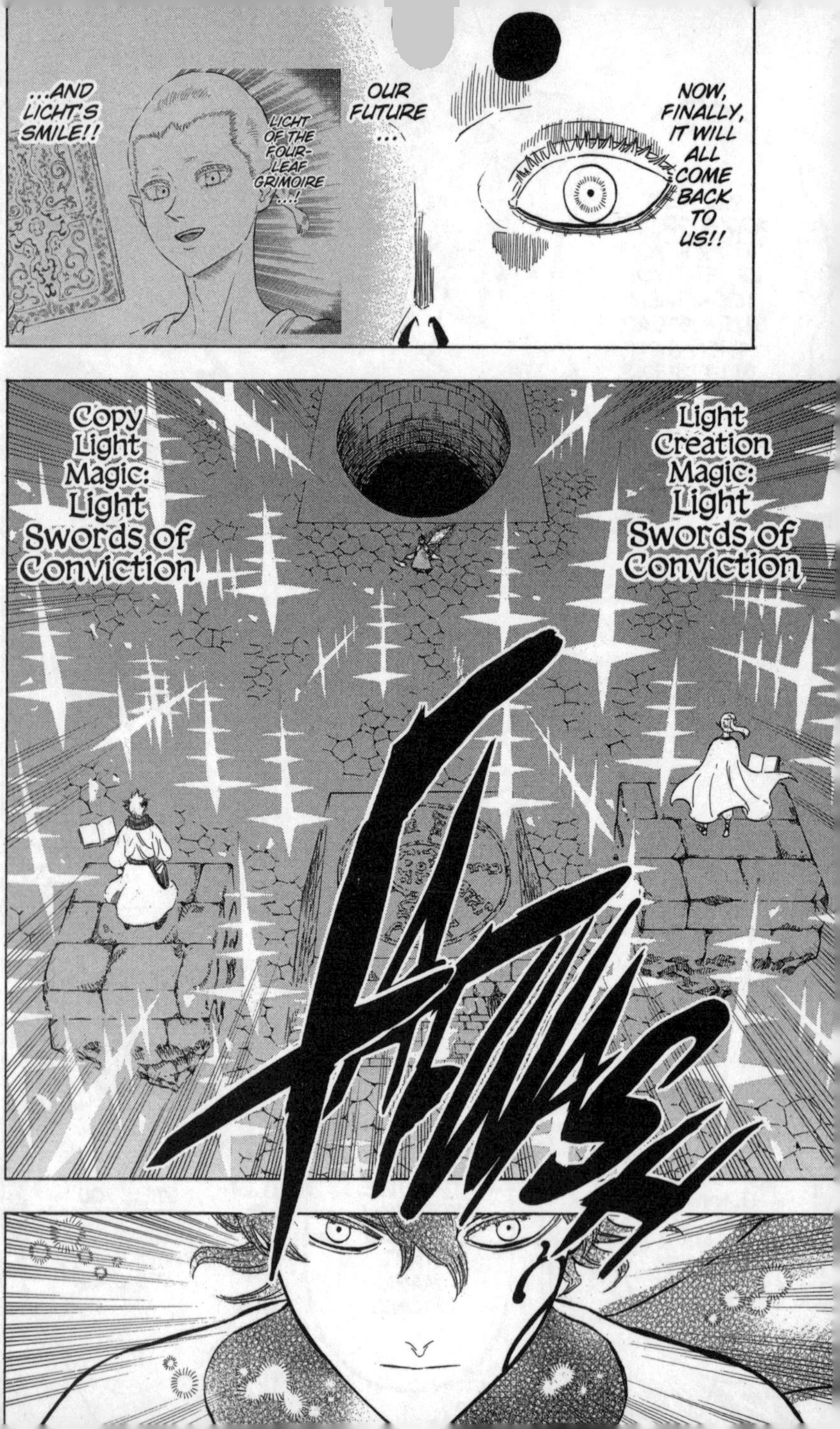
NOW, FINALLY, IT WILL ALL COME BACK TO US!!
OUR FUTURE...
LICHT OF THE FOUR-LEAF GRIMOIRE...!
...AND LICHT'S SMILE!!
Light Creation Magic: Light Swords of Conviction
Copy Light Magic: Light Swords of Conviction

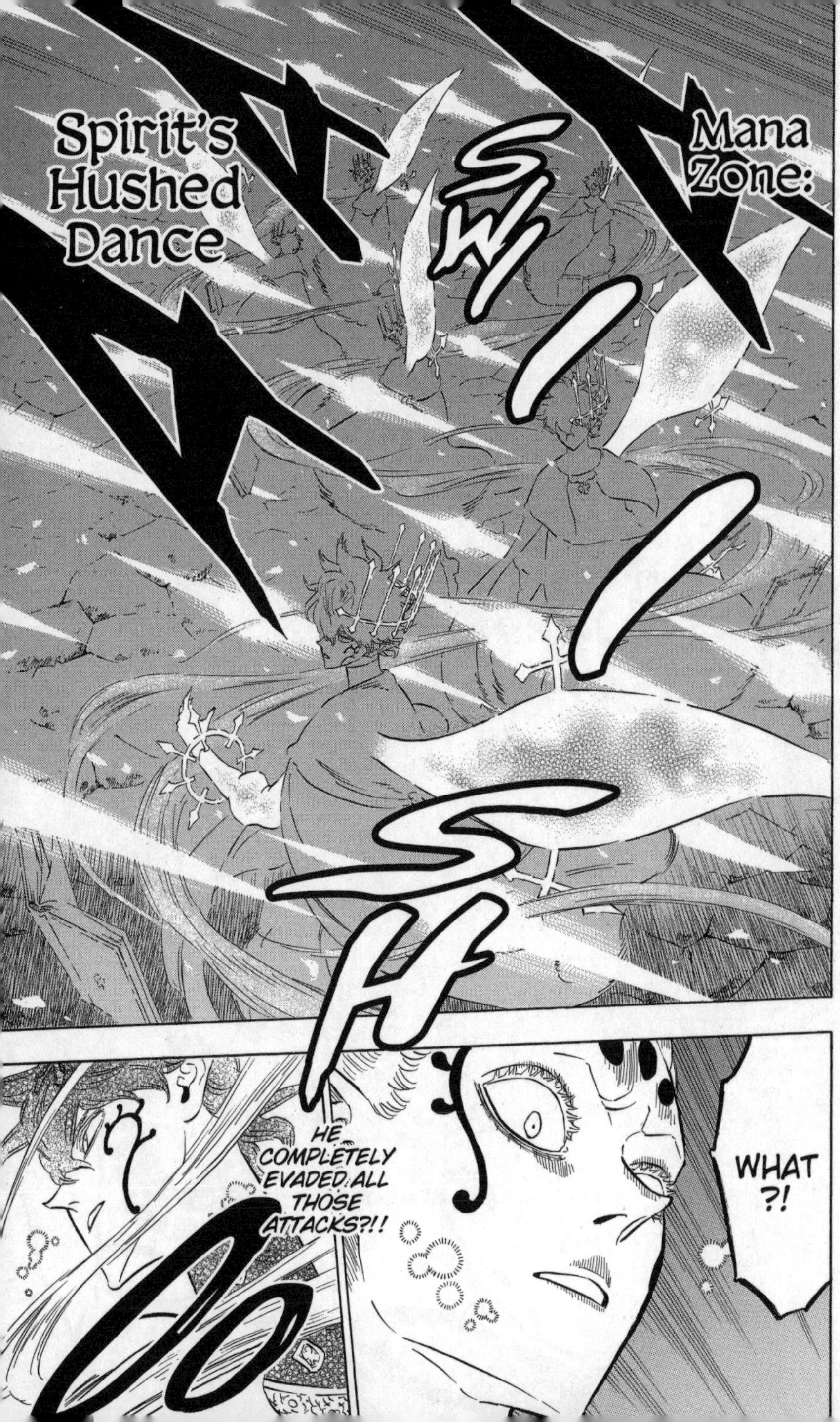

Mana Zone:
Spirit's Hushed Dance
SWISH
WHAT?!
HE COMPLETELY EVADED ALL THOSE ATTACKS?!!

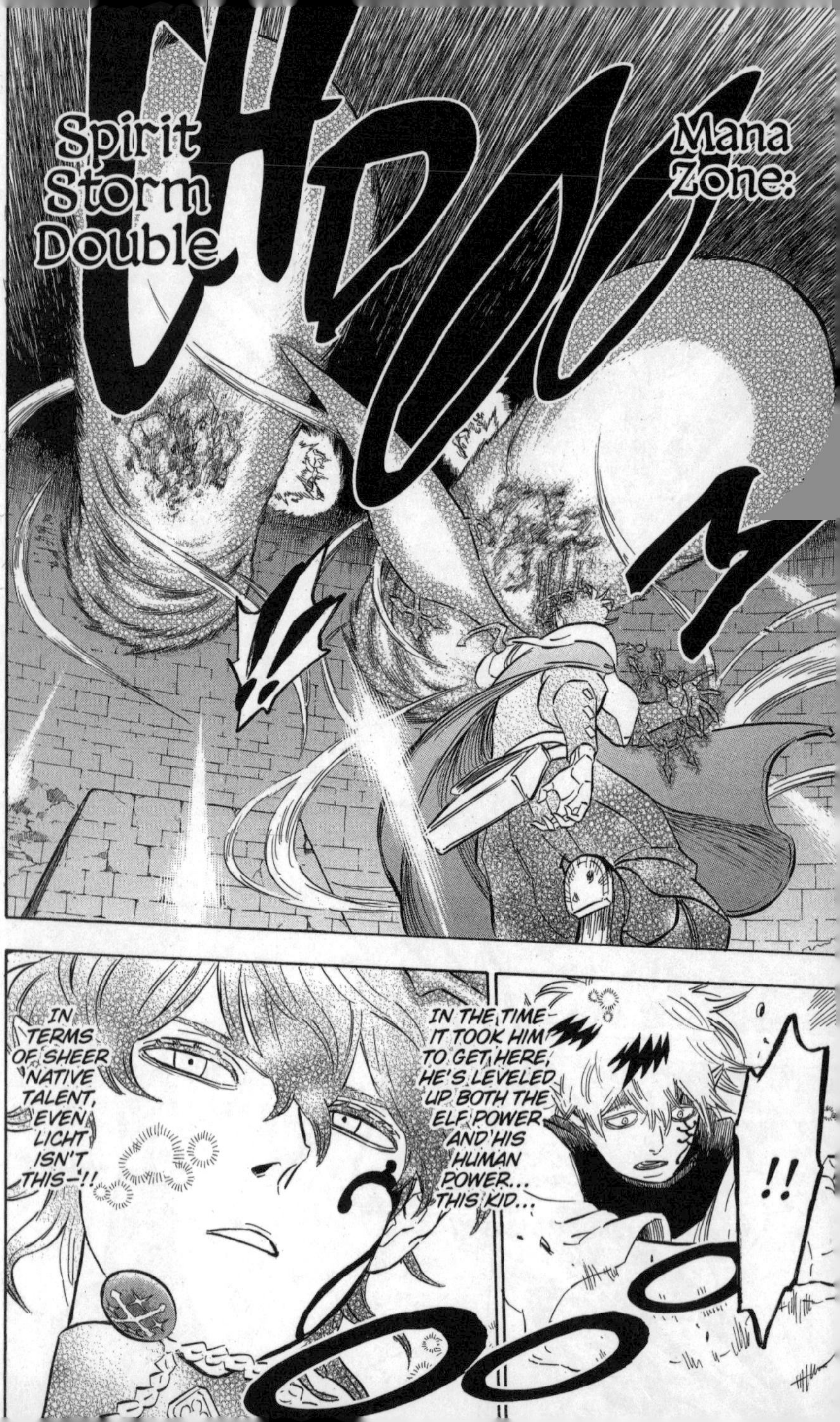
Mana Zone:
Spirit Storm Double
!!
IN THE TIME IT TOOK HIM TO GET HERE, HE'S LEVELED UP BOTH THE ELF POWER AND HIS HUMAN POWER... THIS KID...
IN TERMS OF SHEER NATIVE TALENT, EVEN LICHT ISN'T THIS--!!

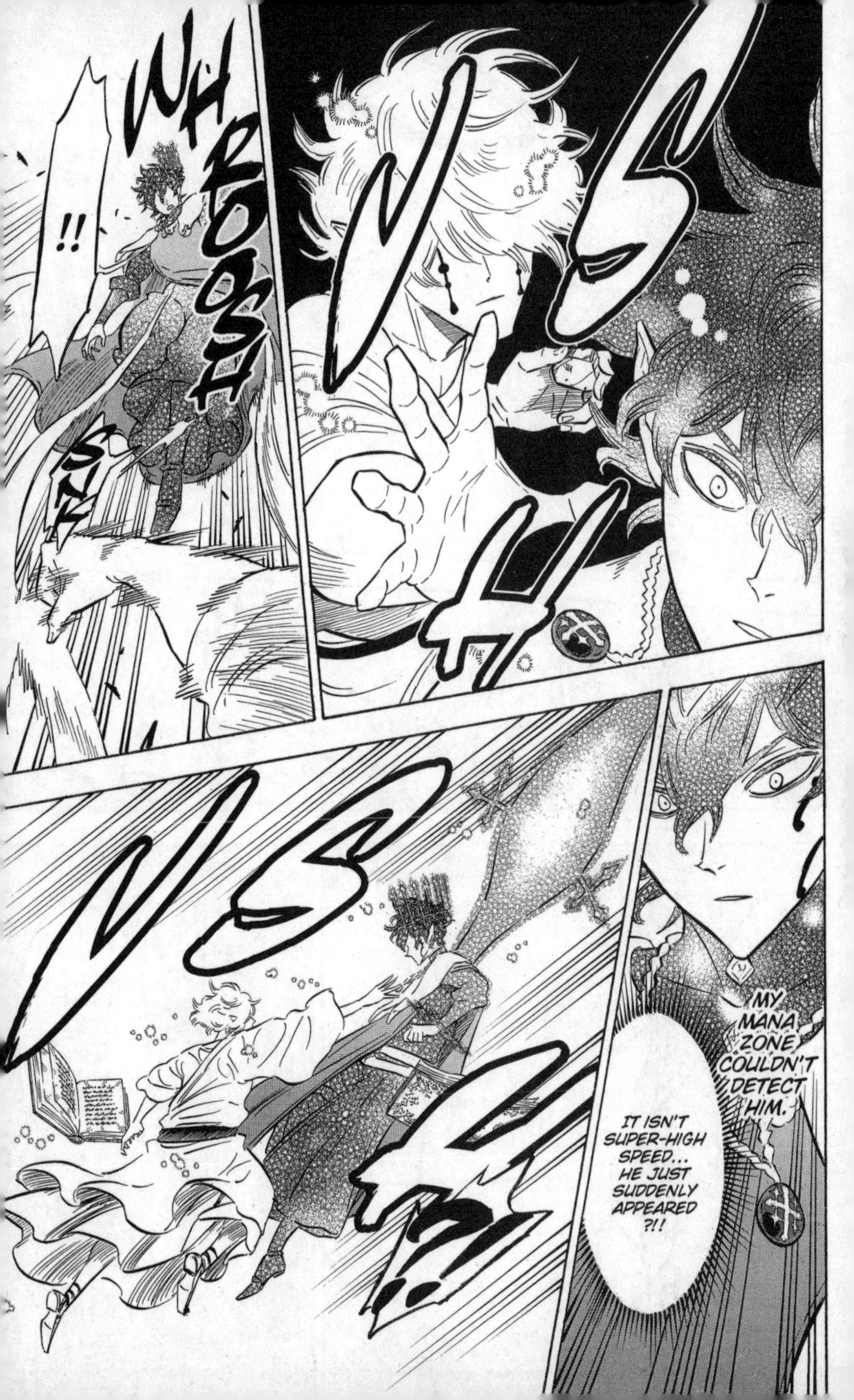
WHOOSH
!!
MY MANA ZONE COULDN'T DETECT HIM.
IT ISN'T SUPER-HIGH SPEED... HE JUST SUDDENLY APPEARED ?!!

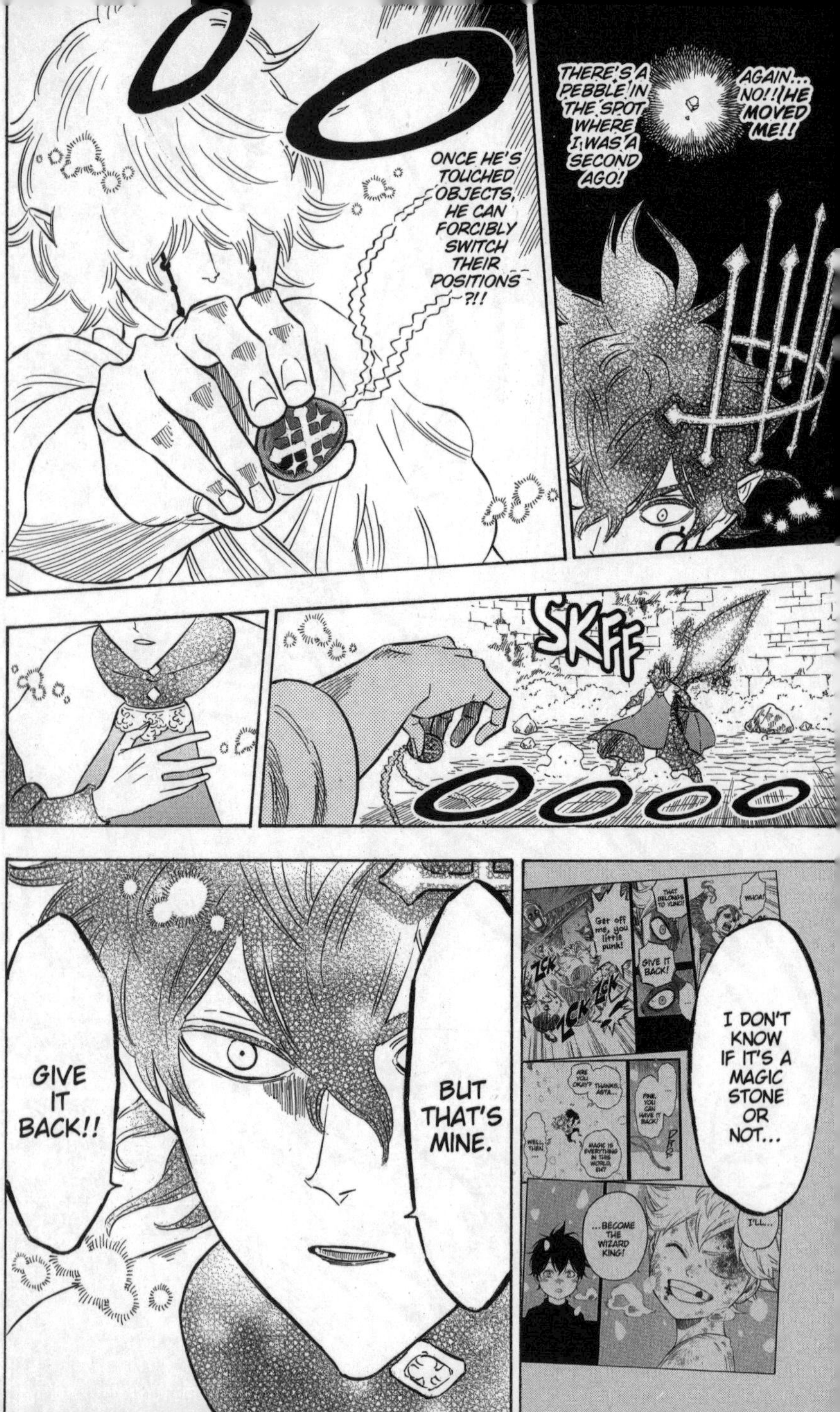
AGAIN... NO!! HE MOVED ME!!
THERE'S A PEBBLE IN THE SPOT WHERE I WAS A SECOND AGO!
ONCE HE'S TOUCHED OBJECTS, HE CAN FORCIBLY SWITCH THEIR POSITIONS?!!
SKFF
WHOA!
THAT BELONGS TO YUNO!
Get off me, you little punk!
GIVE IT BACK!
ZCK
ZCK ZCK
FINE, YOU CAN HAVE IT BACK!
ARE YOU OKAY?
THANKS, ASTA...
MAGIC IS EVERYTHING IN THIS WORLD, EH?
WELL, THEN...
I'LL...
...BECOME THE WIZARD KING!
I DON'T KNOW IF IT'S A MAGIC STONE OR NOT...
BUT THAT'S MINE.
GIVE IT BACK!!

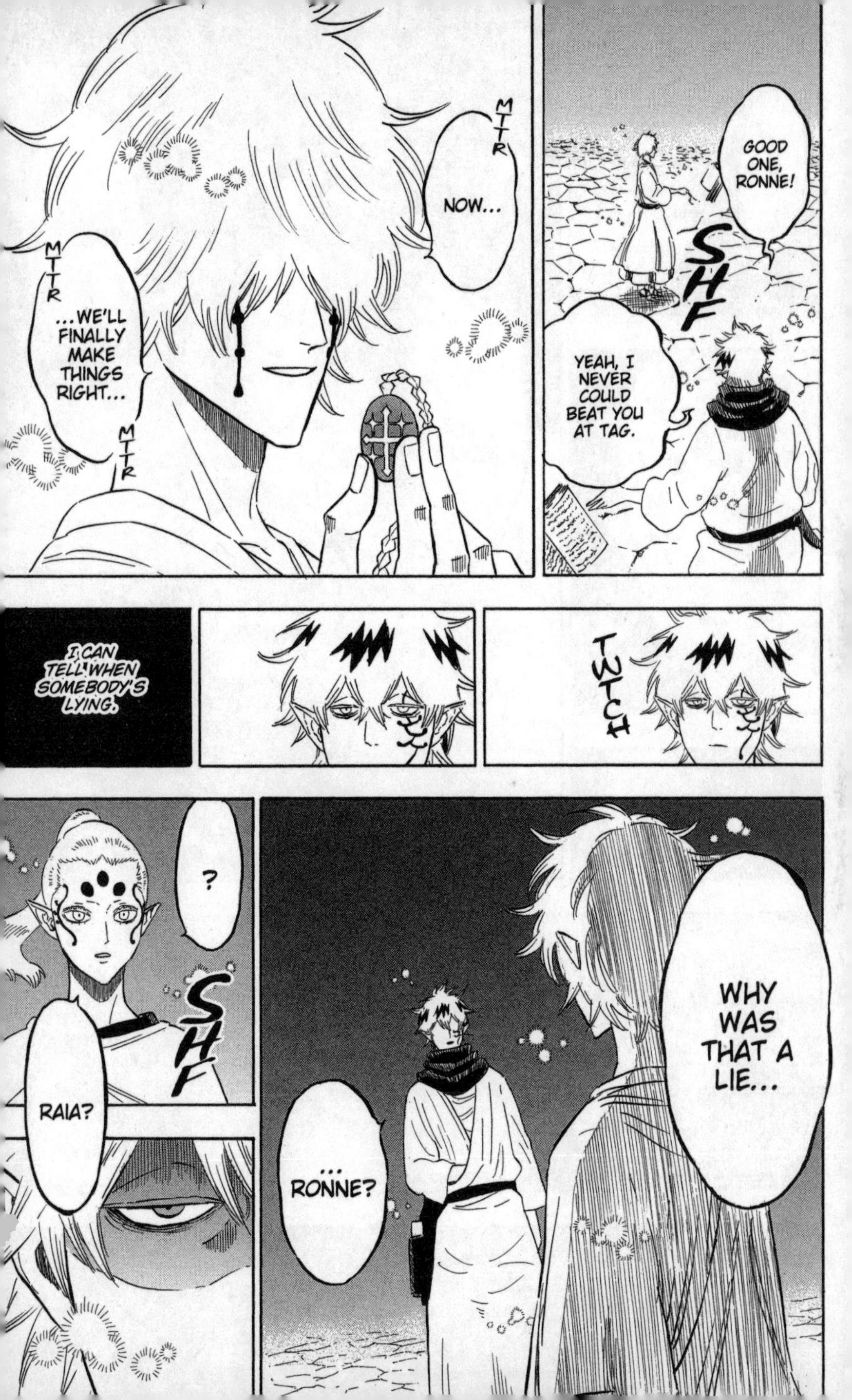
GOOD ONE, RONNE!
SHF
YEAH, I NEVER COULD BEAT YOU AT TAG.
MTTR
NOW...
MTTR
...WE'LL FINALLY MAKE THINGS RIGHT...
MTTR
TWITCH
I CAN TELL WHEN SOMEBODY'S LYING.
WHY WAS THAT A LIE...
...RONNE?
?
SHF
RAIA?

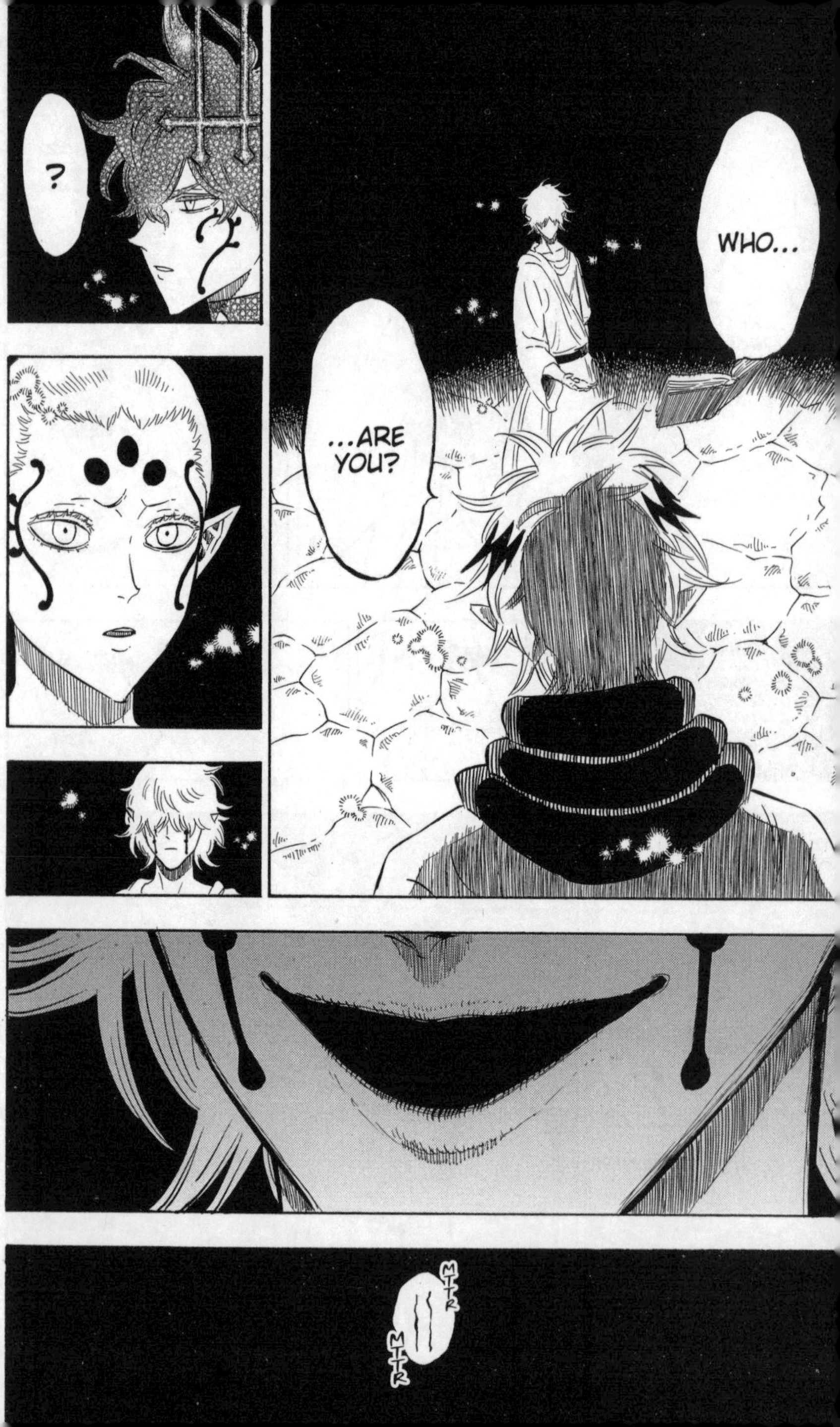
WHO...
...ARE YOU?
?
MTTR
MTTR

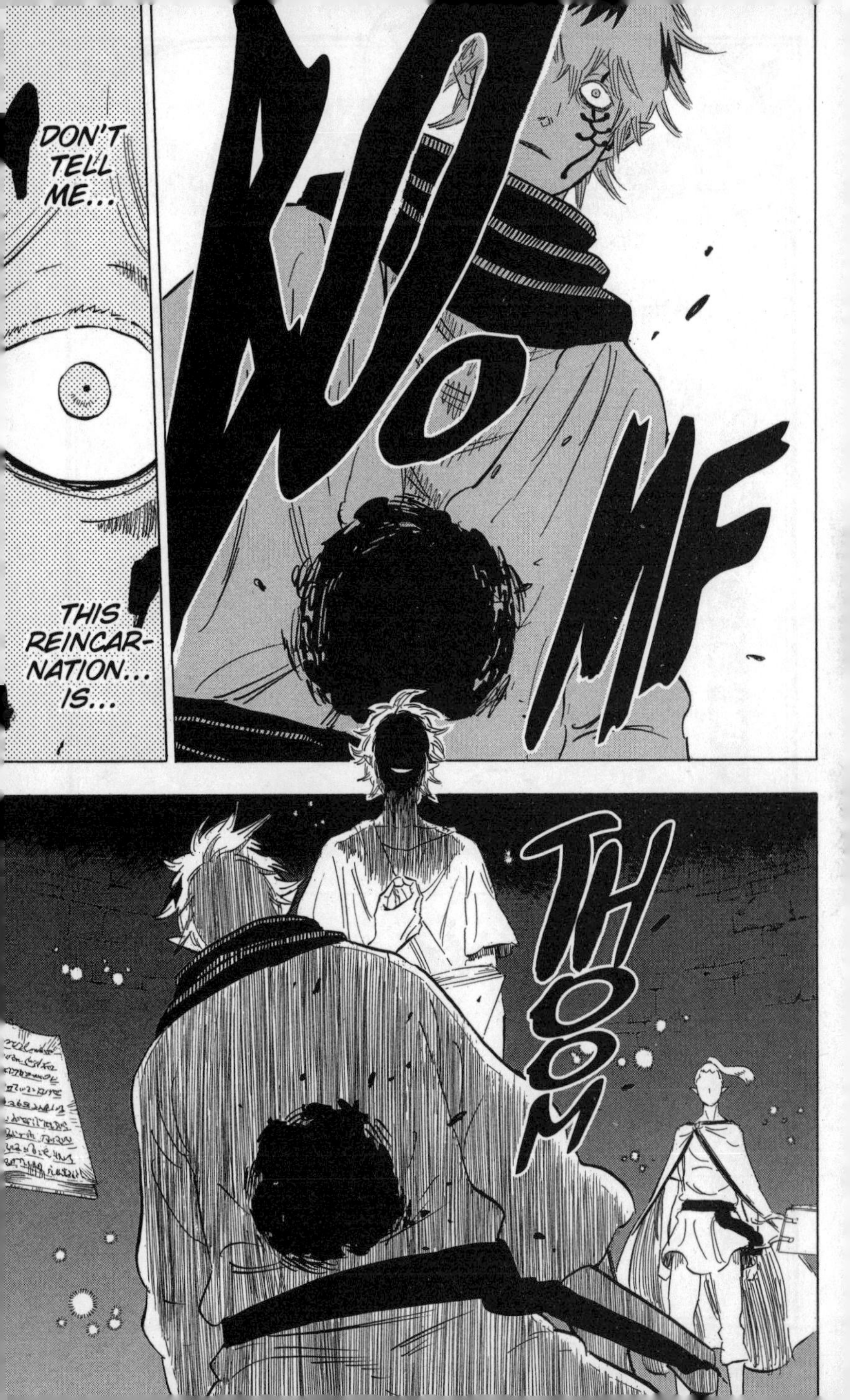
BWOMF
DON'T TELL ME...
THIS REINCAR-NATION... IS...
THOOM

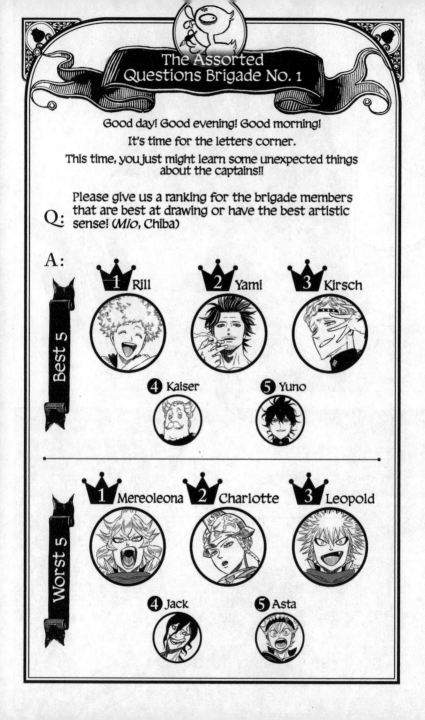

The Assorted Questions Brigade No. 1

Good day! Good evening! Good morning!

It's time for the letters corner.

This time, you just might learn some unexpected things about the captains!!

Q: Please give us a ranking for the brigade members that are best at drawing or have the best artistic sense! (*Mio*, Chiba)

A:

Best 5

1 Rill

2 Yami

3 Kirsch

4 Kaiser

5 Yuno

Worst 5

1 Mereoleona

2 Charlotte

3 Leopold

4 Jack

5 Asta

Page 196: Mastermind

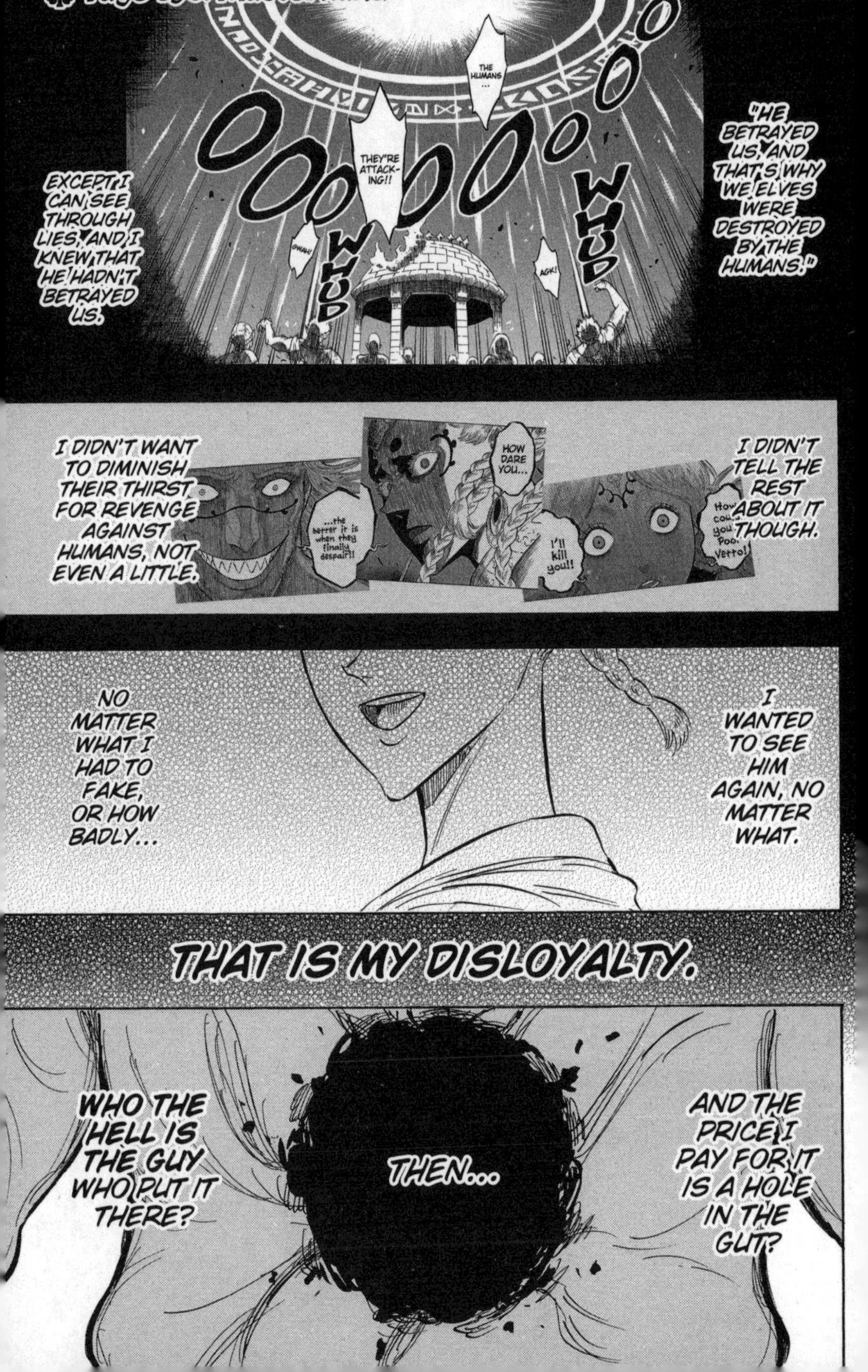
"HE BETRAYED US, AND THAT'S WHY WE ELVES WERE DESTROYED BY THE HUMANS."
THE HUMANS...
WHUD
OOOOOOOO
THEY'RE ATTACKING!!
AGK!
GWAH!
WHUD
EXCEPT I CAN SEE THROUGH LIES, AND I KNEW THAT HE HADN'T BETRAYED US.
I DIDN'T TELL THE REST ABOUT IT THOUGH.
HOW DARE YOU...
I'll kill you!!
...the better it is when they finally despair!!
I DIDN'T WANT TO DIMINISH THEIR THIRST FOR REVENGE AGAINST HUMANS, NOT EVEN A LITTLE.
I WANTED TO SEE HIM AGAIN, NO MATTER WHAT.
NO MATTER WHAT I HAD TO FAKE, OR HOW BADLY...
THAT IS MY DISLOYALTY.
AND THE PRICE I PAY FOR IT IS A HOLE IN THE GUT?
THEN...
WHO THE HELL IS THE GUY WHO PUT IT THERE?

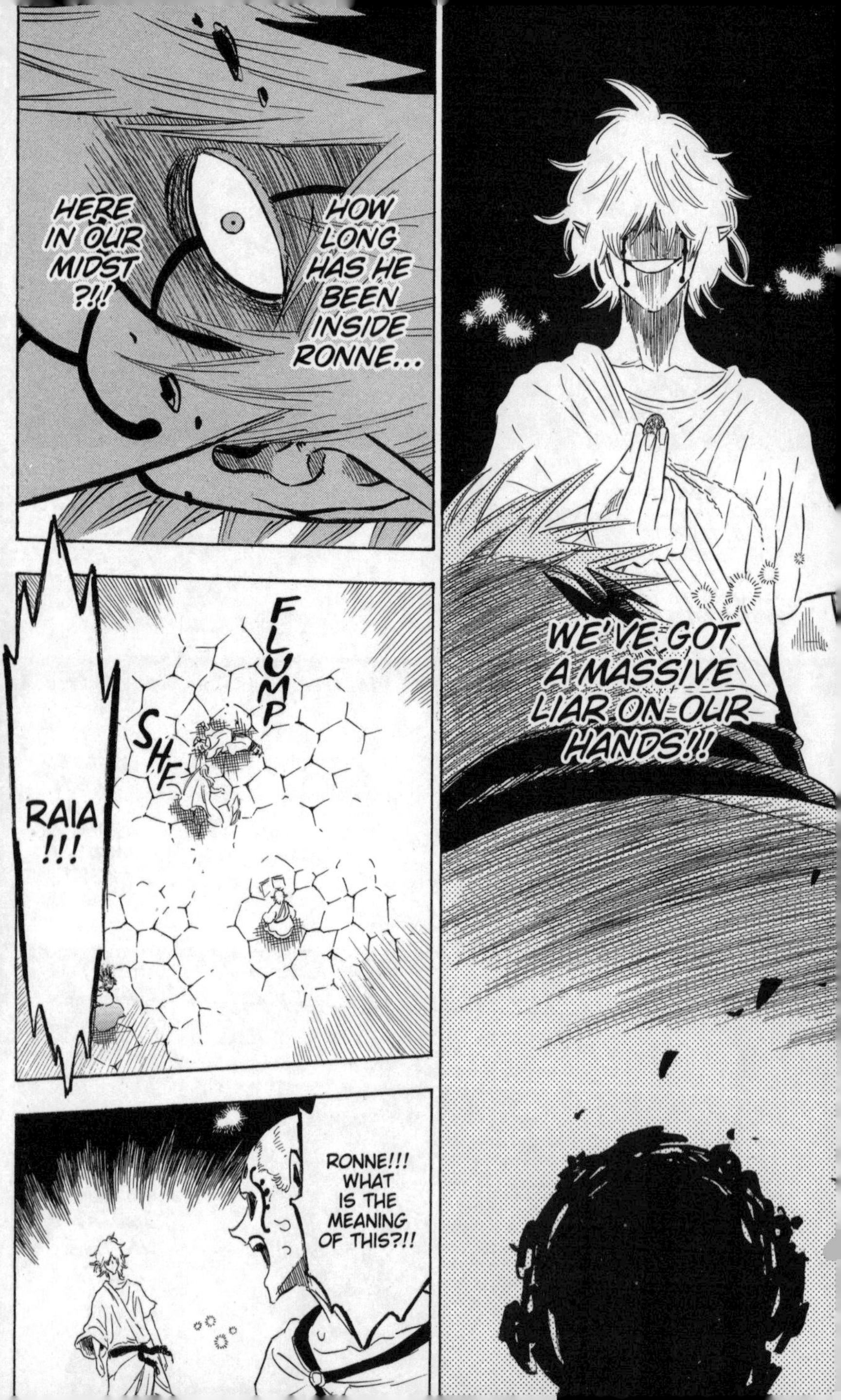
WE'VE GOT A MASSIVE LIAR ON OUR HANDS!!!
HOW LONG HAS HE BEEN INSIDE RONNE...
HERE IN OUR MIDST ?!!
FLUMP
SHF
RAIA !!!
RONNE!!! WHAT IS THE MEANING OF THIS?!!

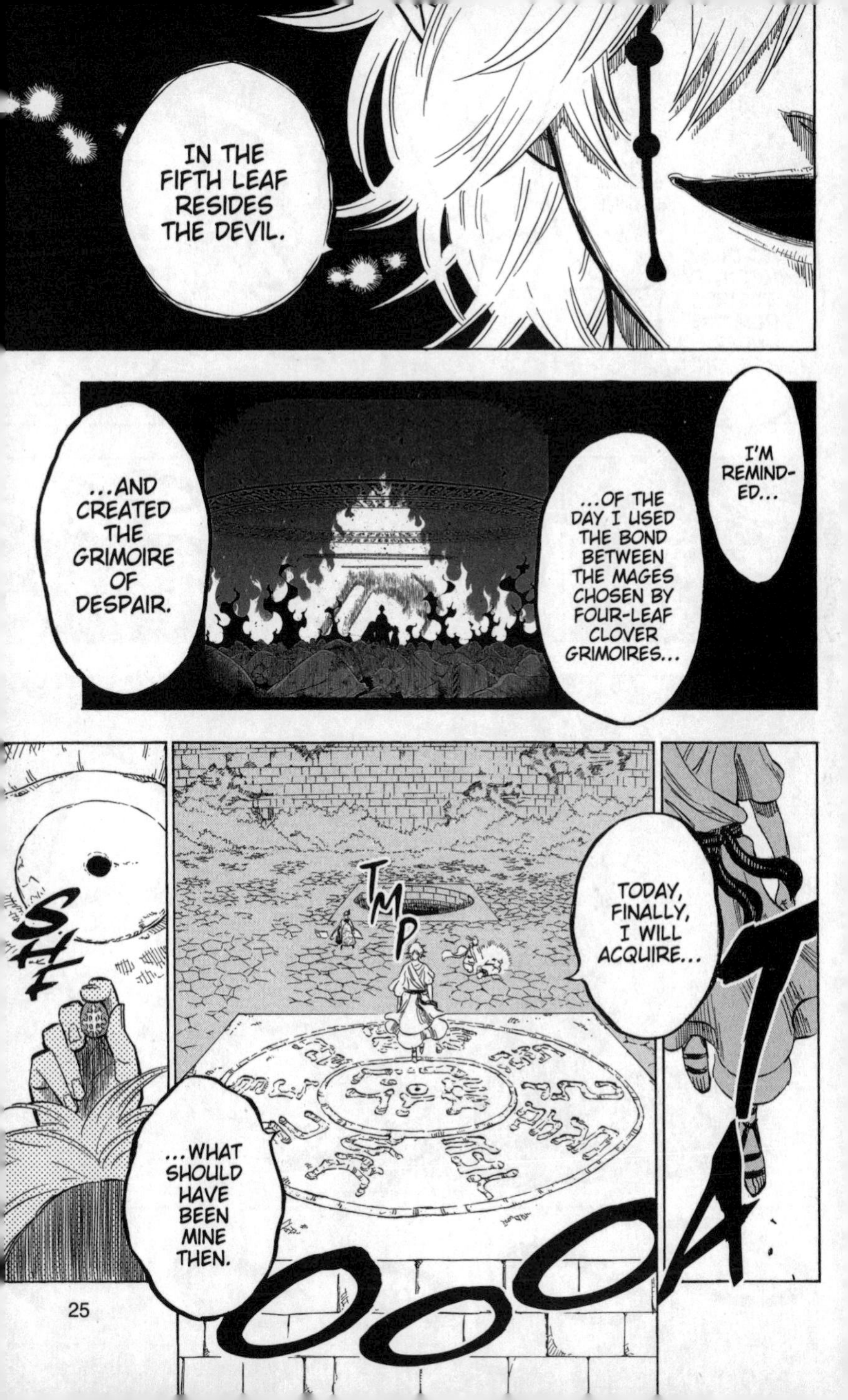
IN THE FIFTH LEAF RESIDES THE DEVIL.
I'M REMIND-ED...
...OF THE DAY I USED THE BOND BETWEEN THE MAGES CHOSEN BY FOUR-LEAF CLOVER GRIMOIRES...
...AND CREATED THE GRIMOIRE OF DESPAIR.
TODAY, FINALLY, I WILL ACQUIRE...
OOOA
TMP
...WHAT SHOULD HAVE BEEN MINE THEN.
SHF

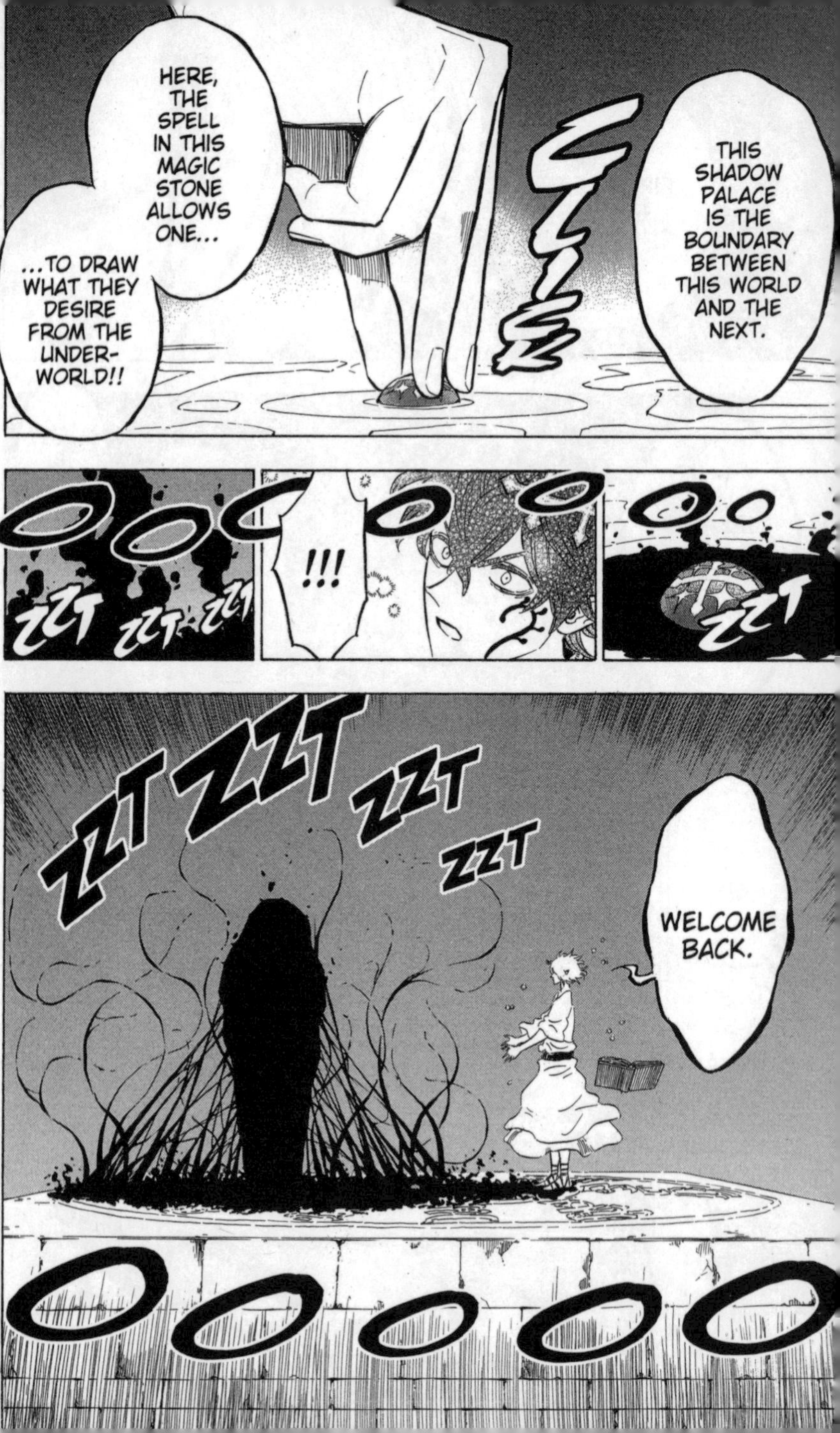
THIS SHADOW PALACE IS THE BOUNDARY BETWEEN THIS WORLD AND THE NEXT.
CLICK
HERE, THE SPELL IN THIS MAGIC STONE ALLOWS ONE...
...TO DRAW WHAT THEY DESIRE FROM THE UNDER-WORLD!!
OOOOOO
ZZT
!!!
ZZT ZZT ZZT
ZZT ZZT ZZT ZZT
WELCOME BACK.
OOOOOOO

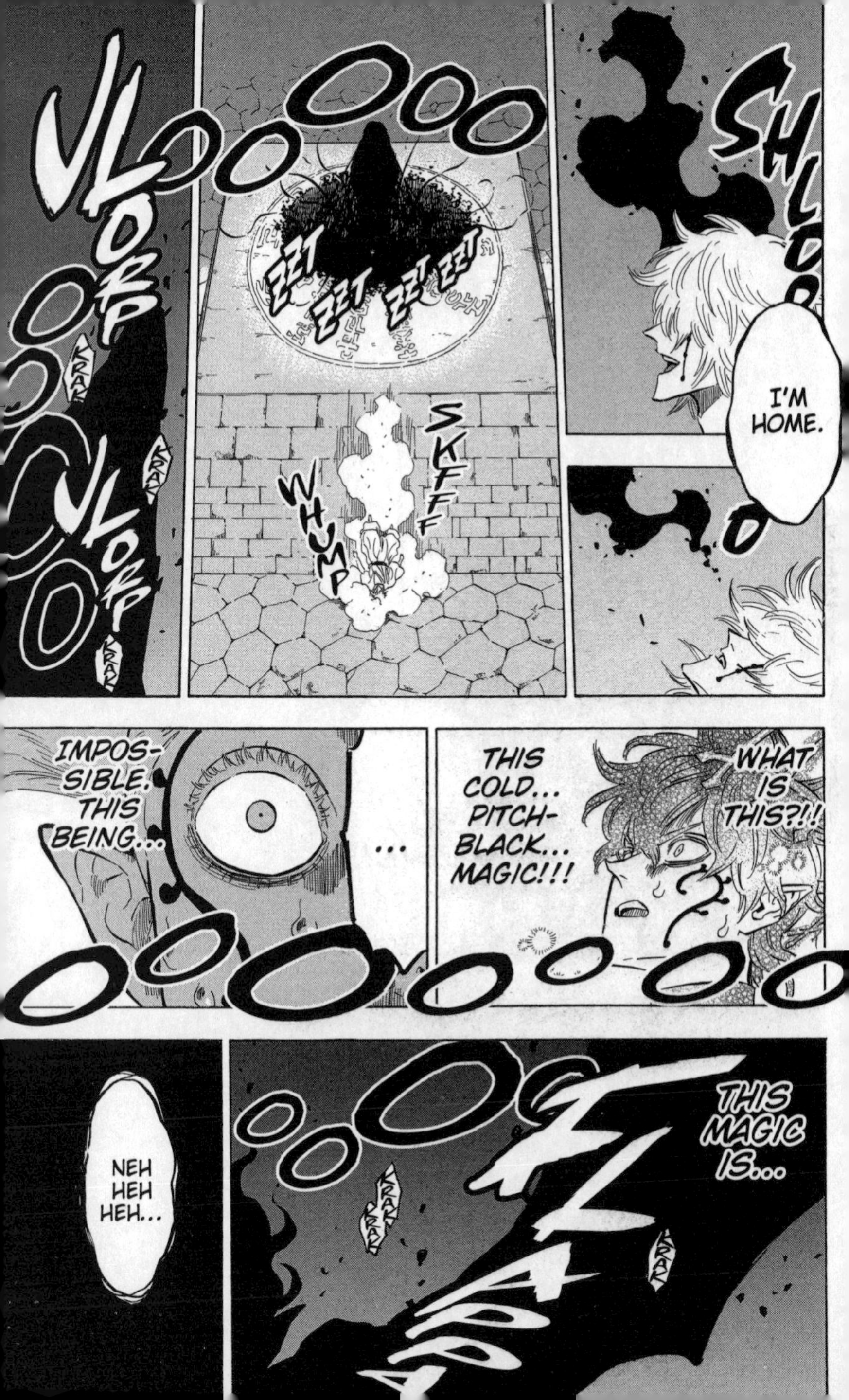
I'M HOME.
ZZZT ZZZT ZZZT ZZZT
SKFFF
WHUMP
VLOOOOOOO
WORP
KRAK
WHAT IS THIS?!!
THIS COLD... PITCH-BLACK... MAGIC!!!
...
IMPOS-SIBLE. THIS BEING...
OOOOOOOOO
THIS MAGIC IS...
KRAK
NEH HEH HEH...

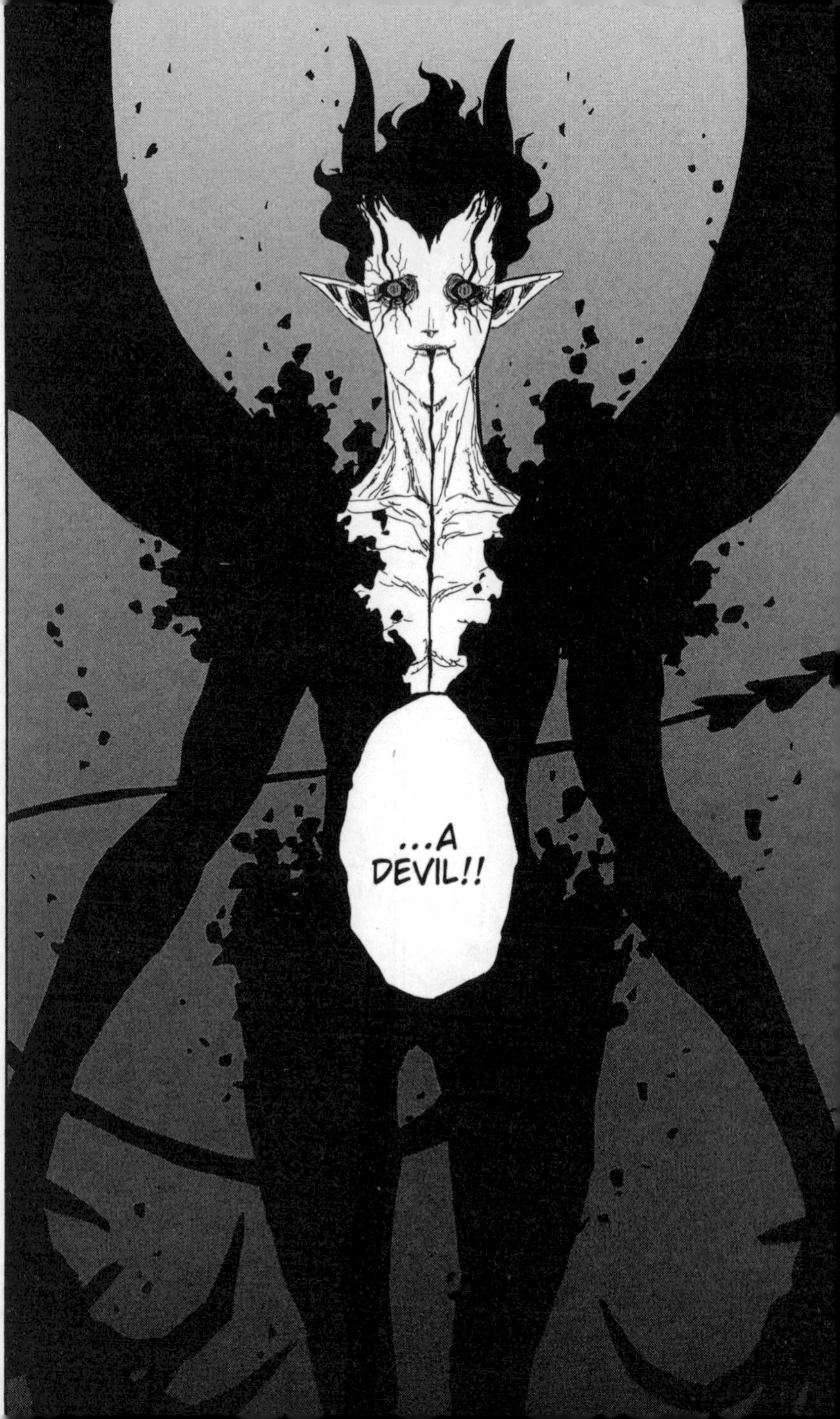
...A DEVIL!!

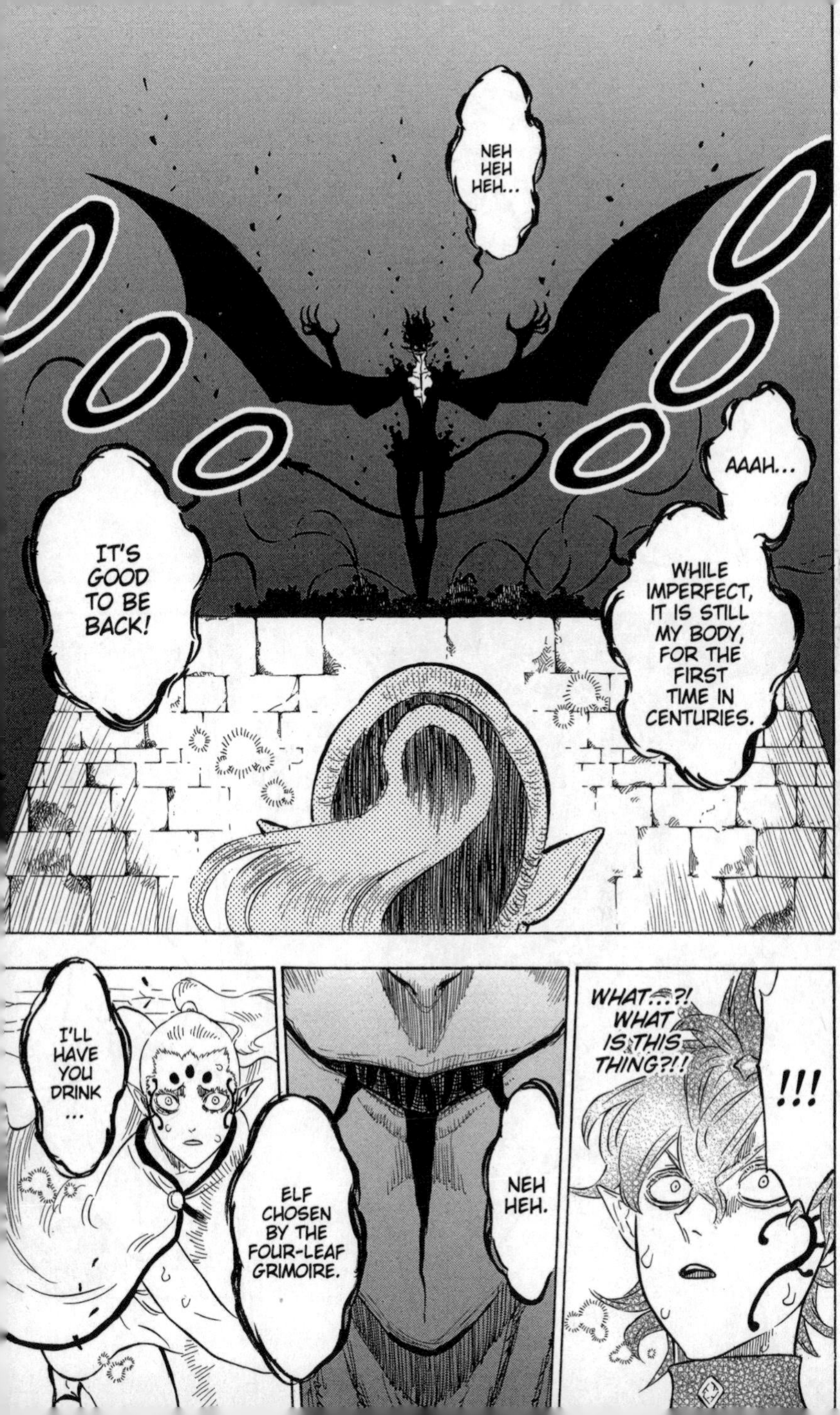
NEH HEH HEH...
AAAH...
WHILE IMPERFECT, IT IS STILL MY BODY, FOR THE FIRST TIME IN CENTURIES.
IT'S GOOD TO BE BACK!
WHAT...?! WHAT IS THIS THING?!!
!!!
NEH HEH.
ELF CHOSEN BY THE FOUR-LEAF GRIMOIRE.
I'LL HAVE YOU DRINK ...

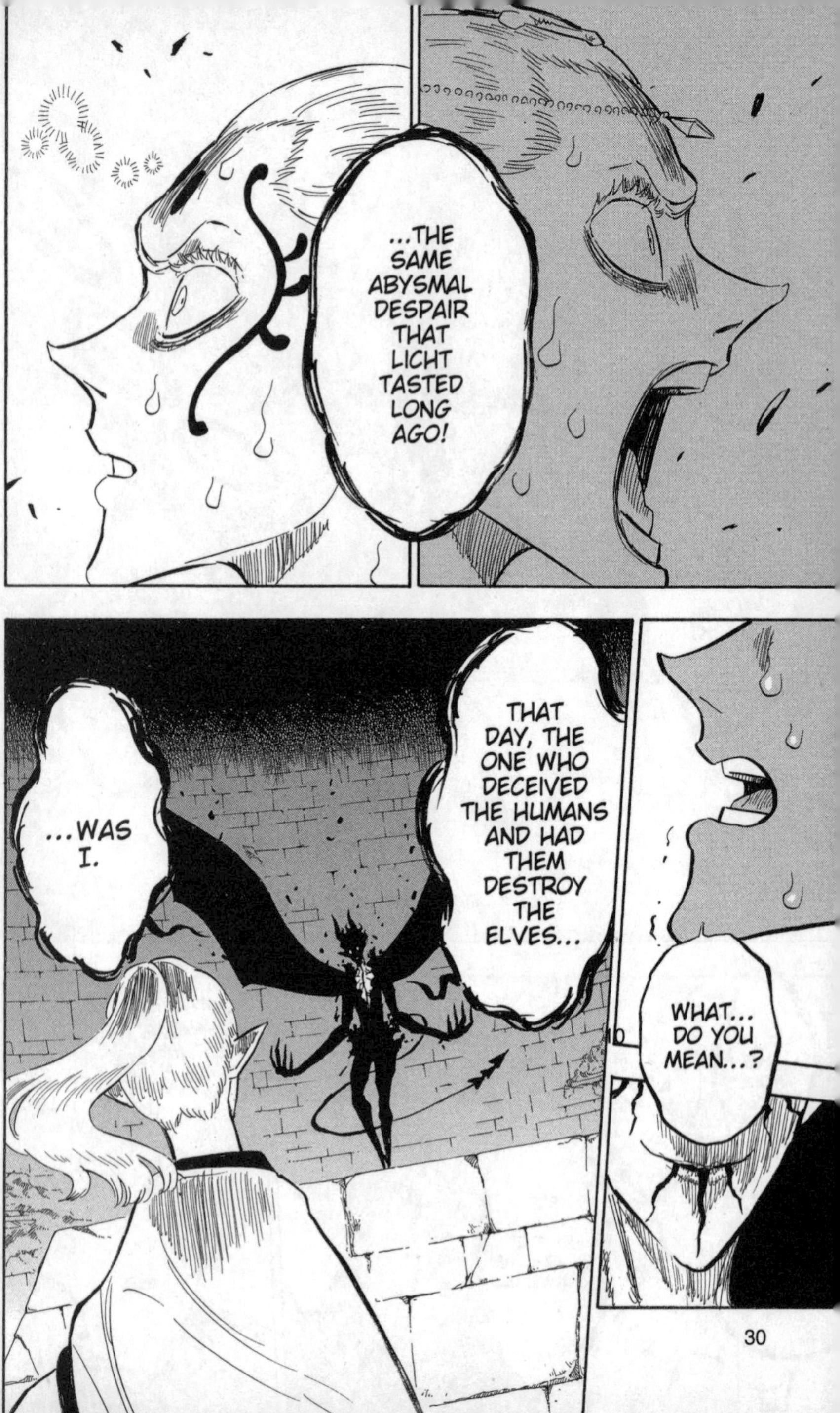
...THE SAME ABYSMAL DESPAIR THAT LICHT TASTED LONG AGO!
WHAT... DO YOU MEAN...?
THAT DAY, THE ONE WHO DECEIVED THE HUMANS AND HAD THEM DESTROY THE ELVES...
...WAS I.

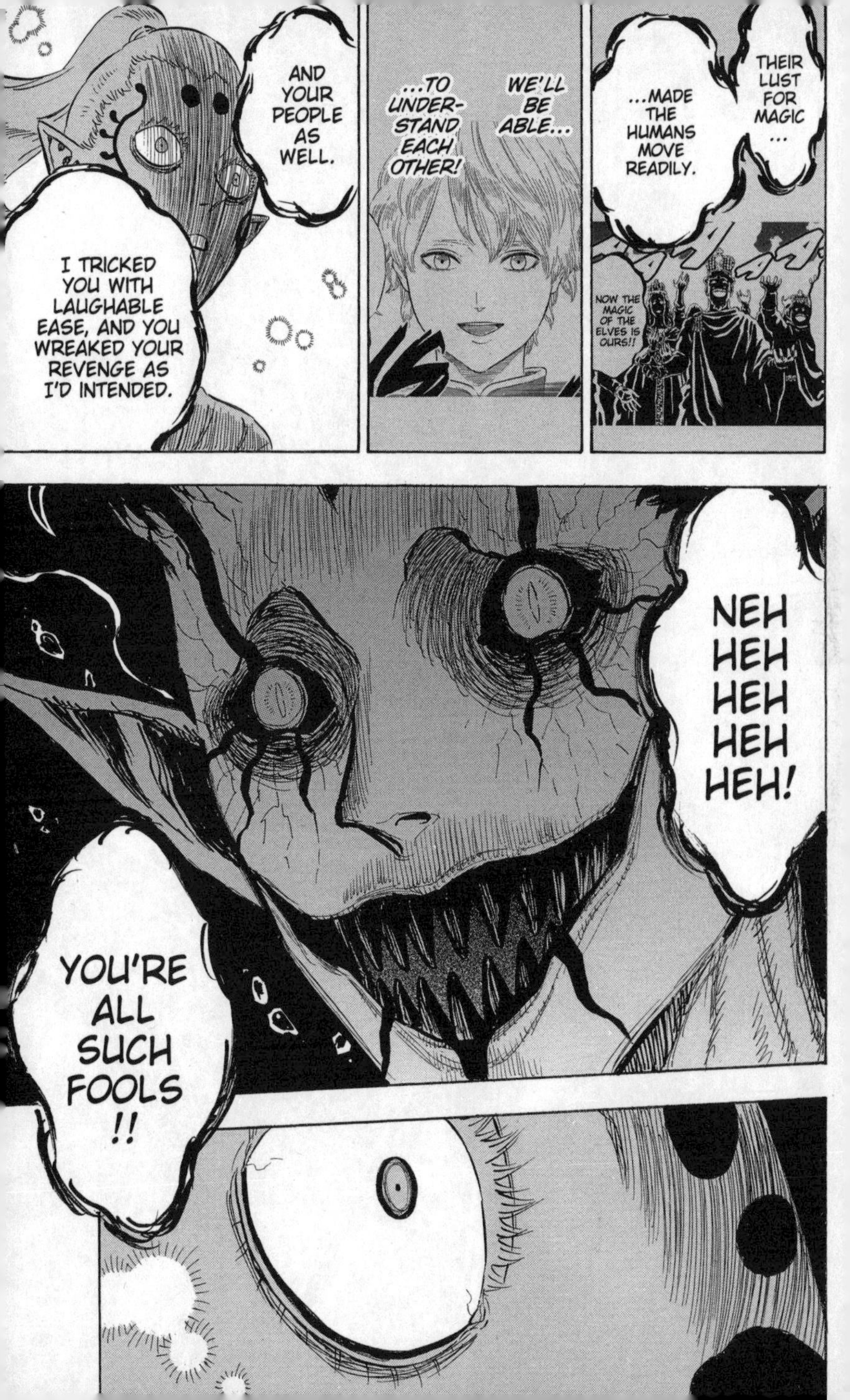
THEIR LUST FOR MAGIC...
...MADE THE HUMANS MOVE READILY.
NOW THE MAGIC OF THE ELVES IS OURS!!
WE'LL BE ABLE...
...TO UNDER-STAND EACH OTHER!
AND YOUR PEOPLE AS WELL.
I TRICKED YOU WITH LAUGHABLE EASE, AND YOU WREAKED YOUR REVENGE AS I'D INTENDED.
NEH HEH HEH HEH HEH!
YOU'RE ALL SUCH FOOLS!!

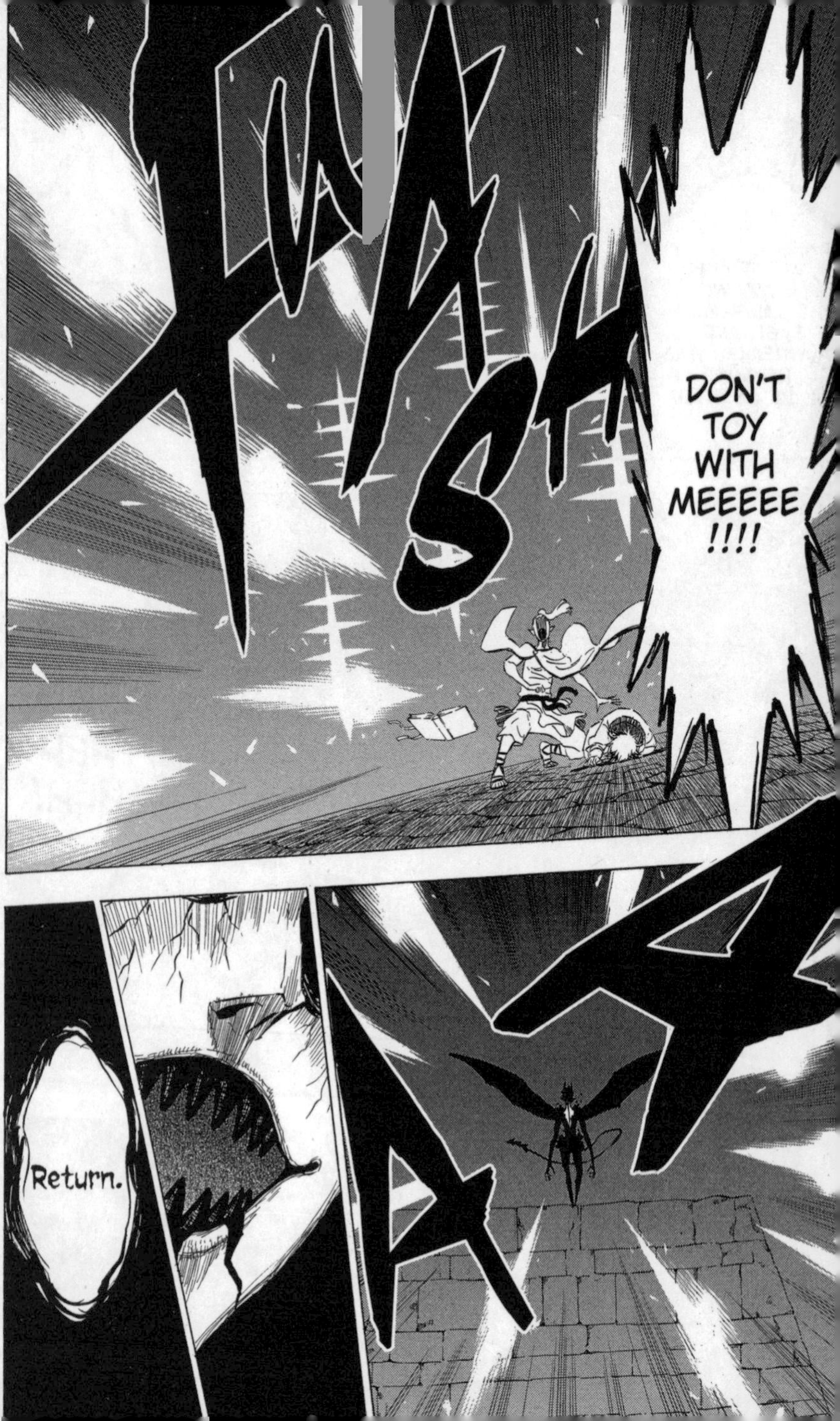
DON'T TOY WITH MEEEEE !!!!
Return.

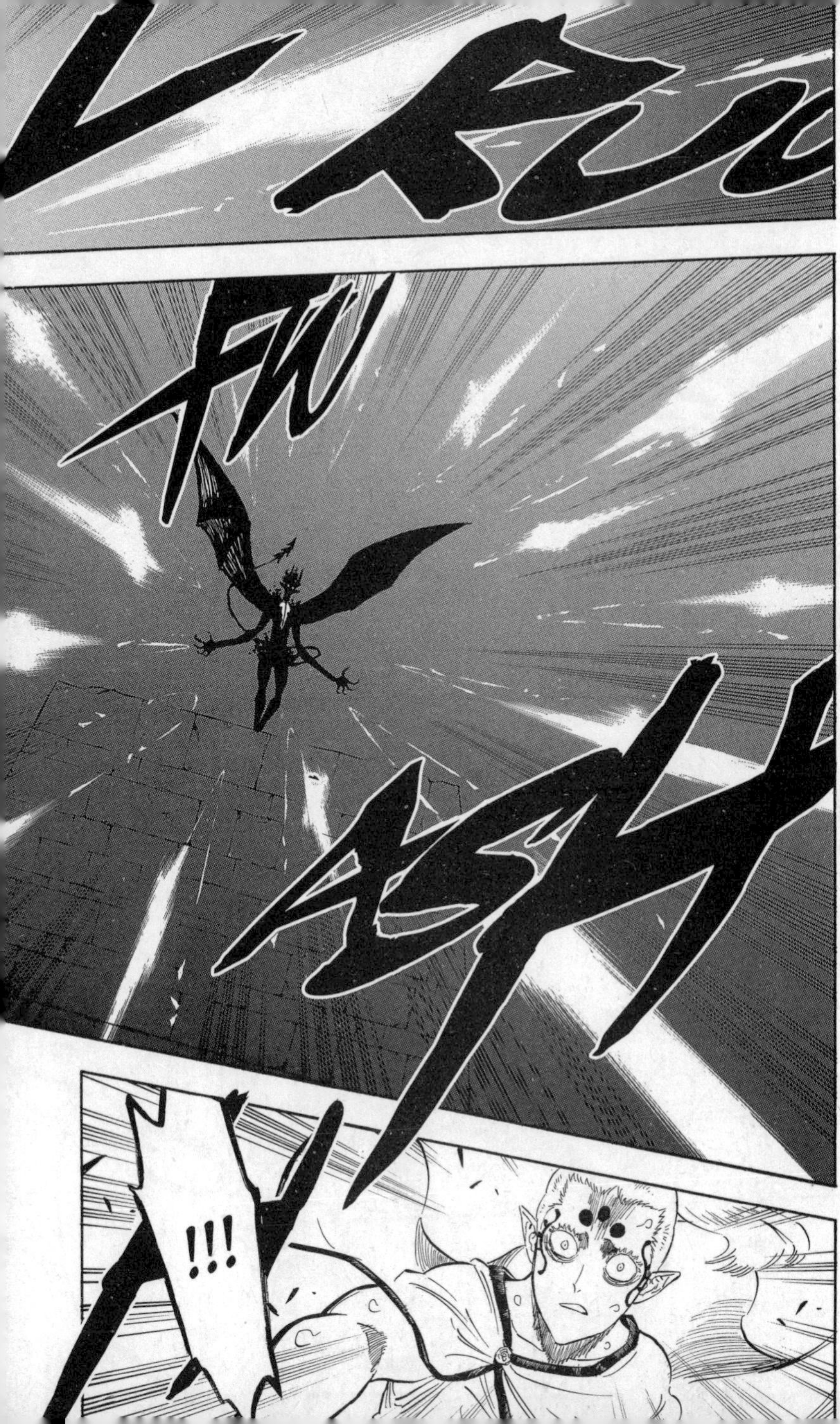
!!!

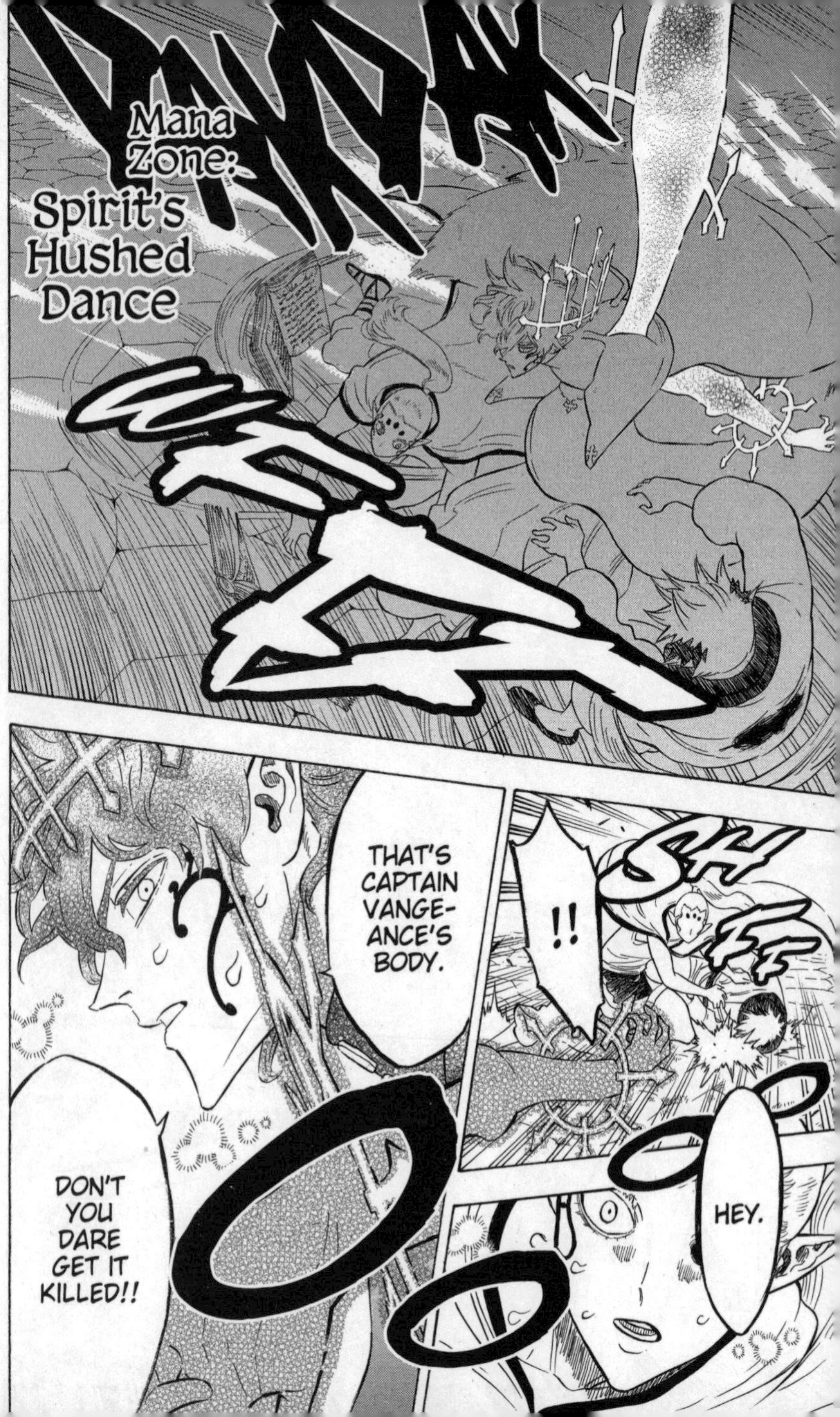
Mana Zone: Spirit's Hushed Dance
!!
HEY.
THAT'S CAPTAIN VANGE-ANCE'S BODY.
DON'T YOU DARE GET IT KILLED!!

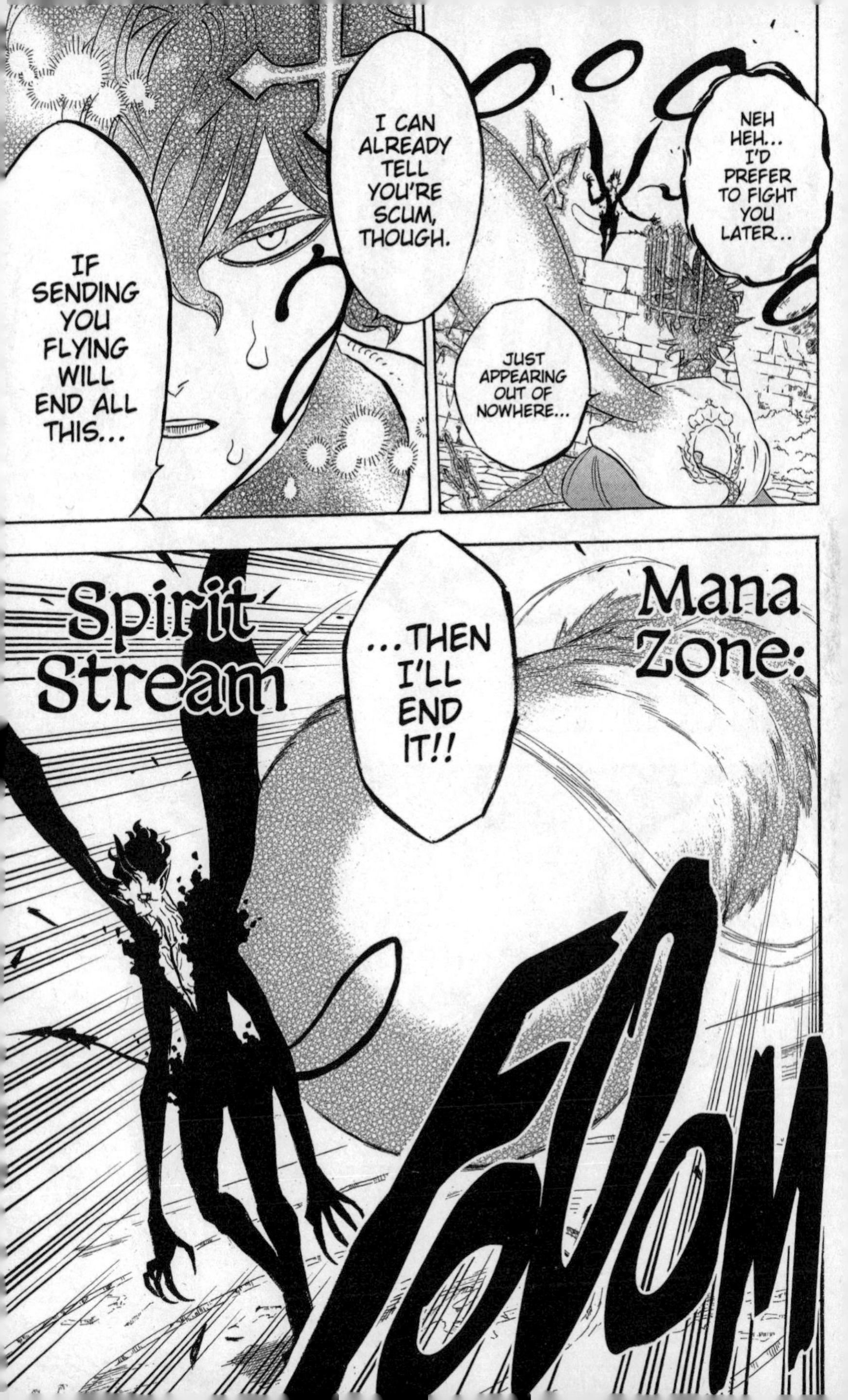
NEH HEH... I'D PREFER TO FIGHT YOU LATER...
JUST APPEARING OUT OF NOWHERE...
I CAN ALREADY TELL YOU'RE SCUM, THOUGH.
IF SENDING YOU FLYING WILL END ALL THIS...
...THEN I'LL END IT!!
Mana Zone:
Spirit Stream

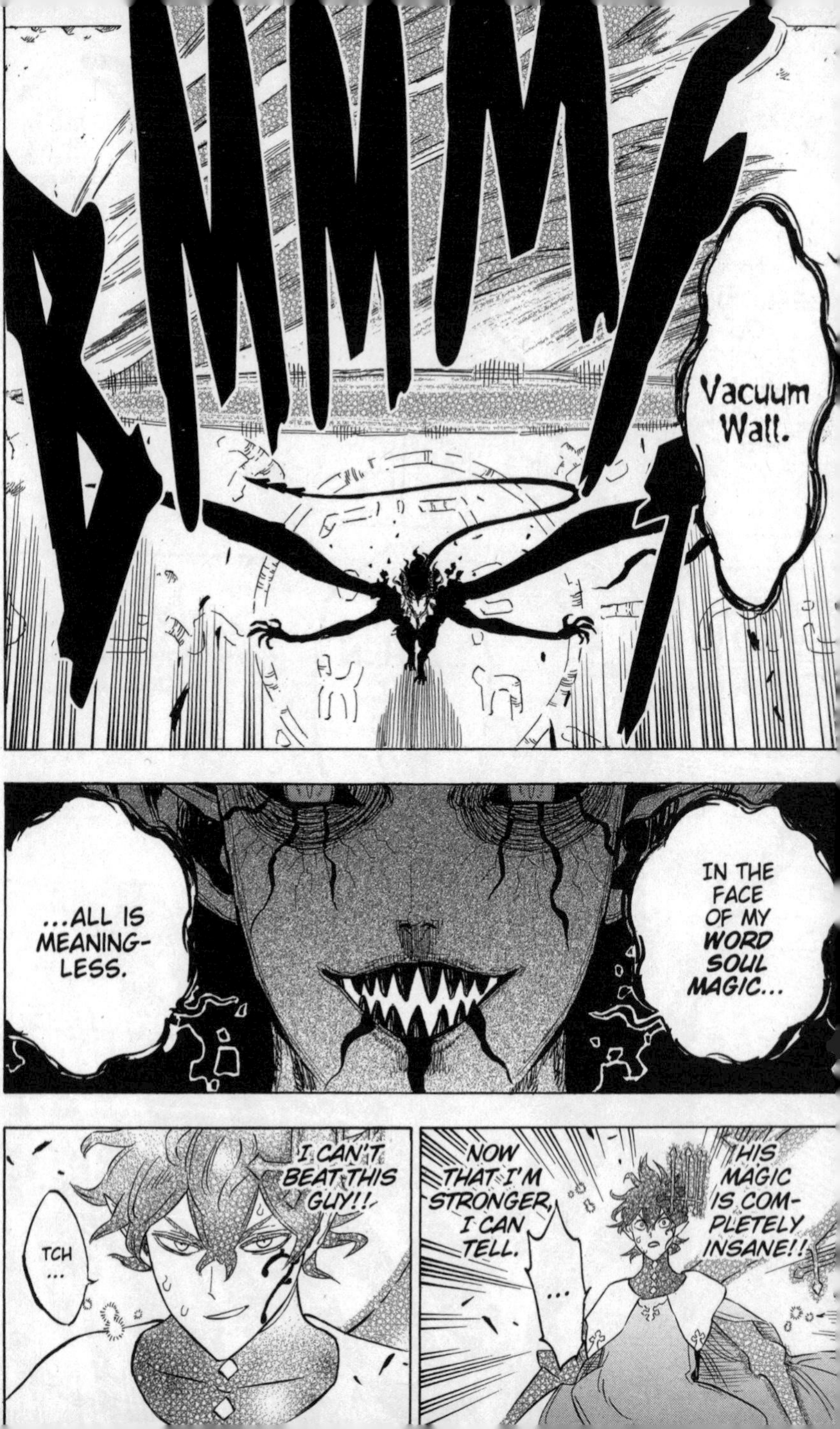
Vacuum Wall.
IN THE FACE OF MY WORD SOUL MAGIC...
...ALL IS MEANING-LESS.
HIS MAGIC IS COMPLETELY INSANE!!
NOW THAT I'M STRONGER, I CAN TELL.
...
I CAN'T BEAT THIS GUY!!
TCH...

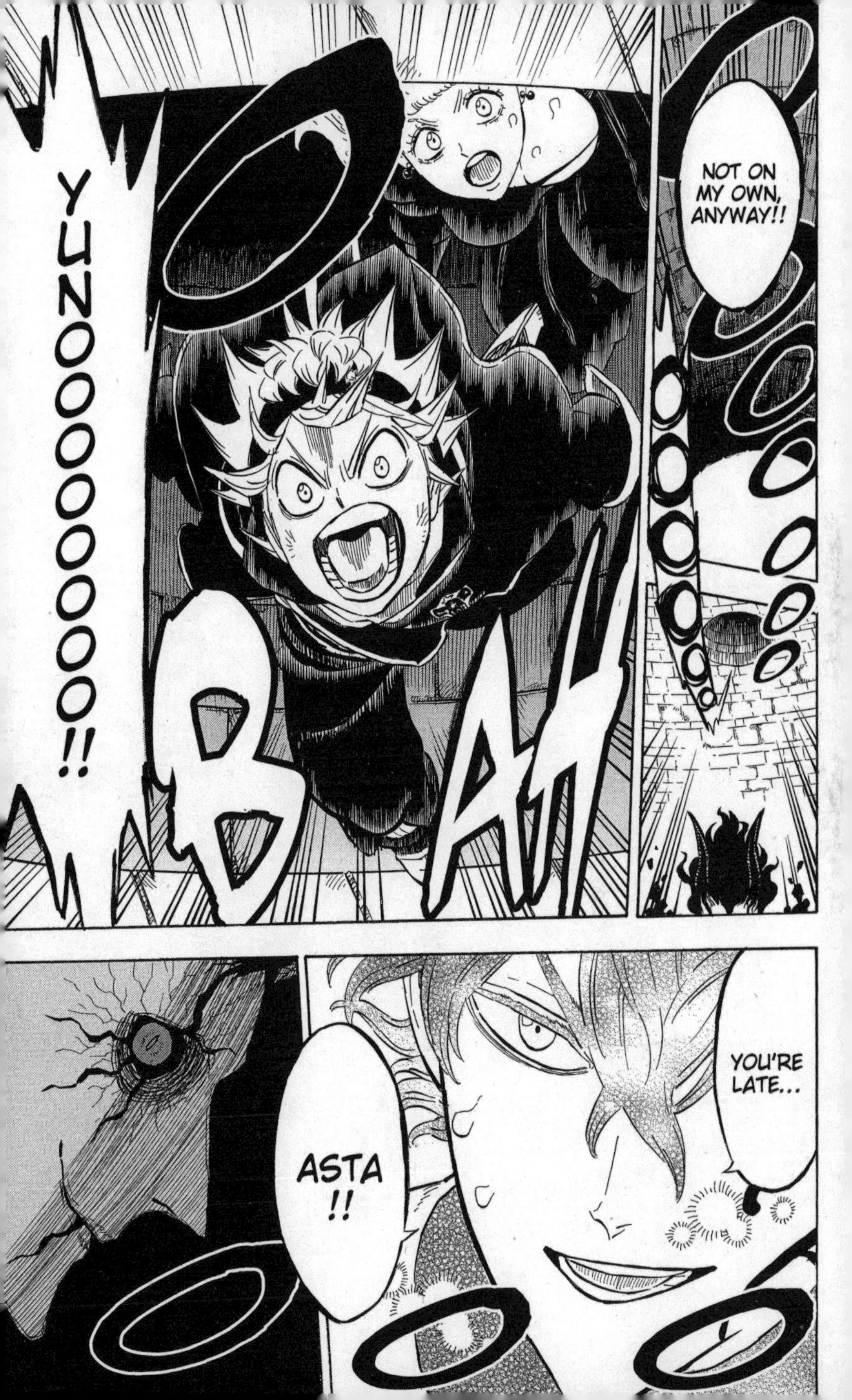
NOT ON MY OWN, ANYWAY!!
YUNOOOOOOOOOO!!
BAM
YOU'RE LATE...
ASTA!!

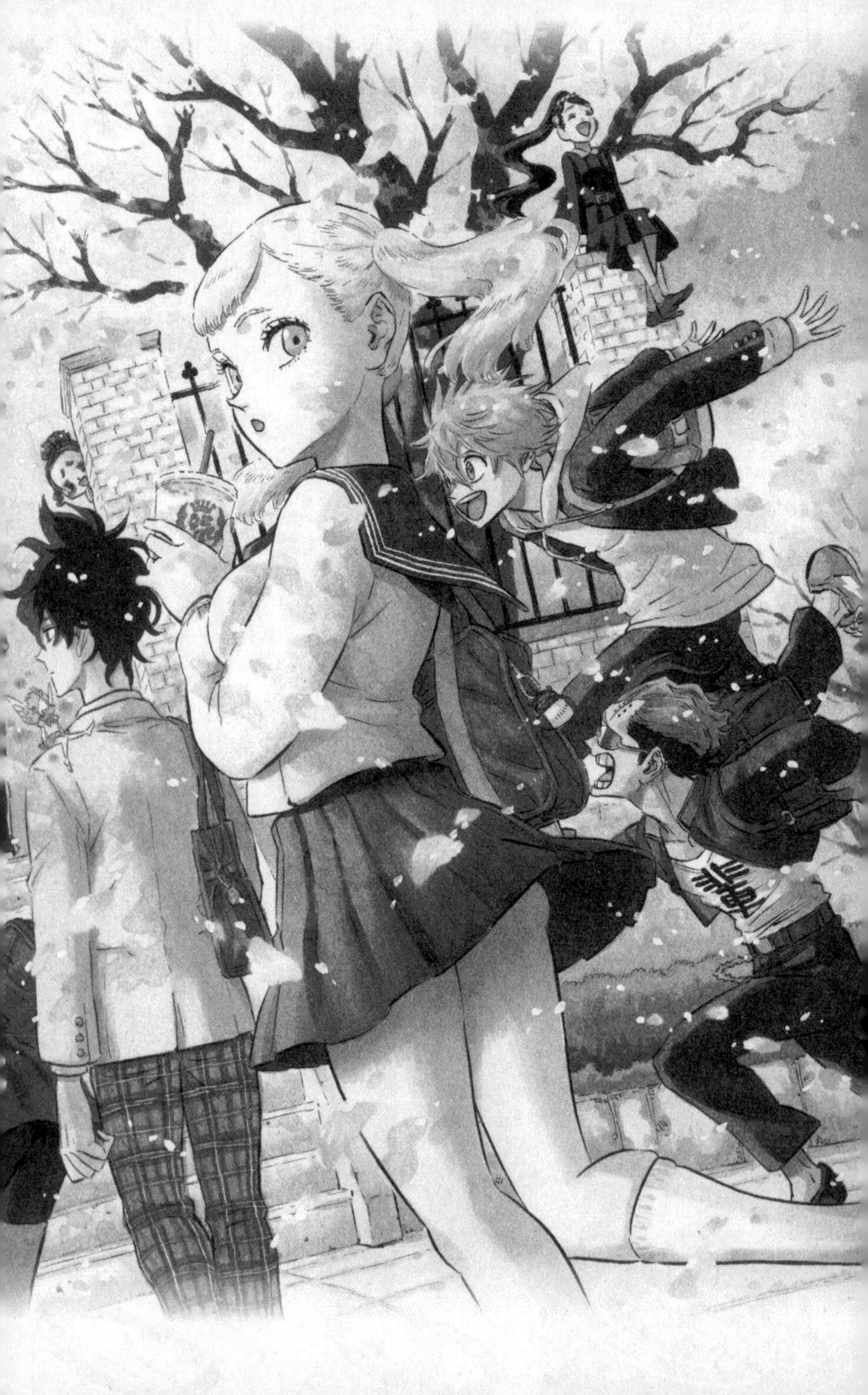

Page 198: False Hope

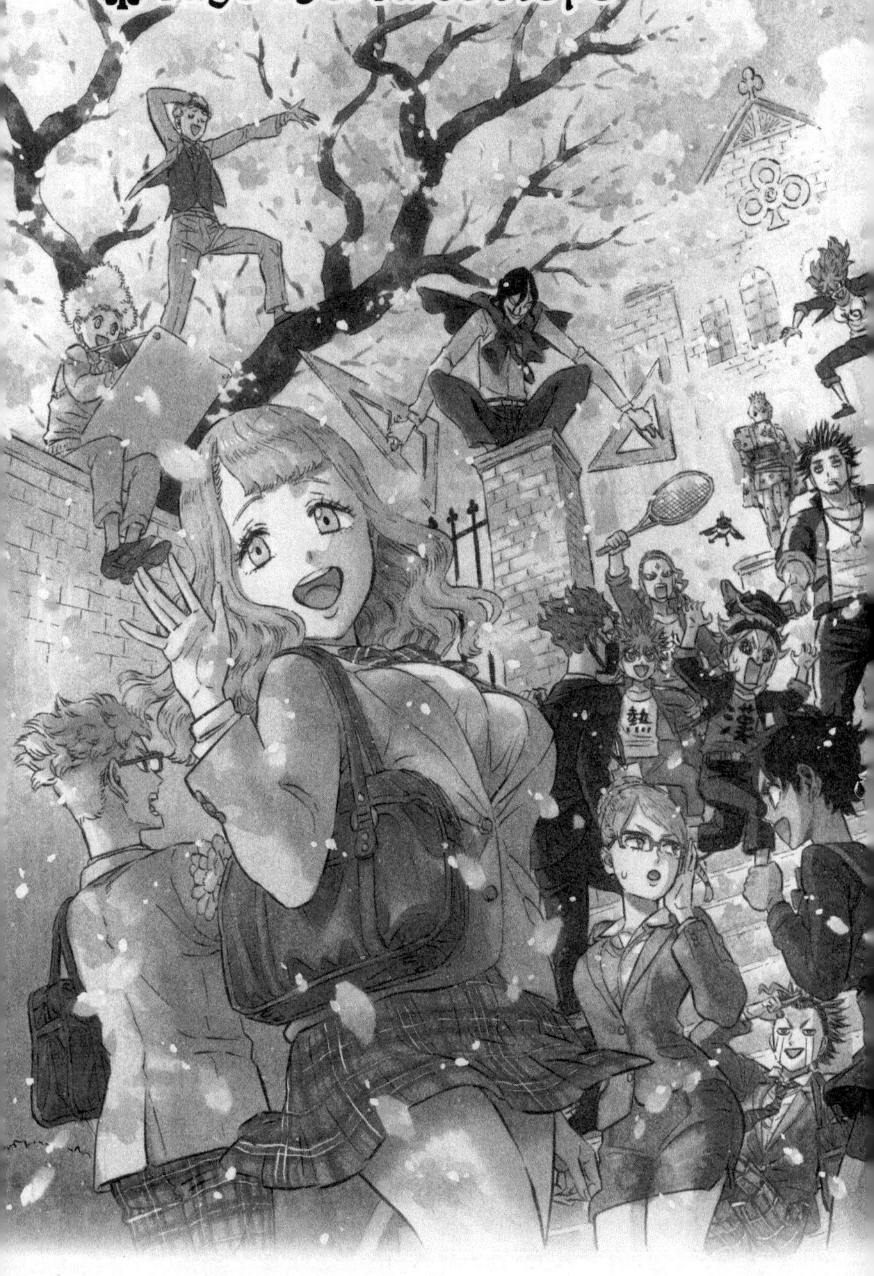

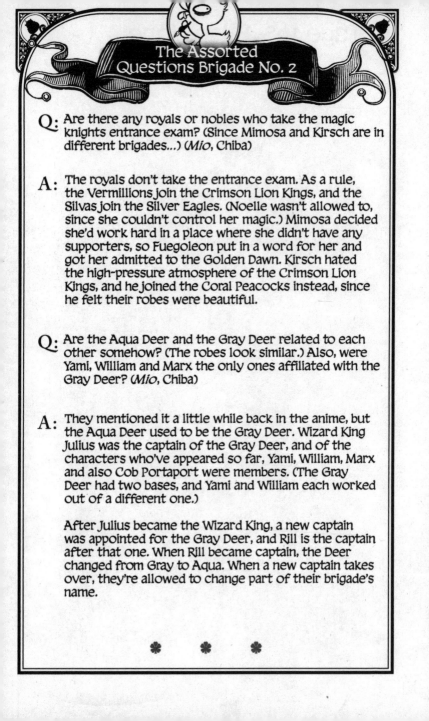

The Assorted Questions Brigade No. 2

Q: Are there any royals or nobles who take the magic knights entrance exam? (Since Mimosa and Kirsch are in different brigades...) (*Mio*, Chiba)

A: The royals don't take the entrance exam. As a rule, the Vermillions join the Crimson Lion Kings, and the Silvas join the Silver Eagles. (Noelle wasn't allowed to, since she couldn't control her magic.) Mimosa decided she'd work hard in a place where she didn't have any supporters, so Fuegoleon put in a word for her and got her admitted to the Golden Dawn. Kirsch hated the high-pressure atmosphere of the Crimson Lion Kings, and he joined the Coral Peacocks instead, since he felt their robes were beautiful.

Q: Are the Aqua Deer and the Gray Deer related to each other somehow? (The robes look similar.) Also, were Yami, William and Marx the only ones affiliated with the Gray Deer? (*Mio*, Chiba)

A: They mentioned it a little while back in the anime, but the Aqua Deer used to be the Gray Deer. Wizard King Julius was the captain of the Gray Deer, and of the characters who've appeared so far, Yami, William, Marx and also Cob Portaport were members. (The Gray Deer had two bases, and Yami and William each worked out of a different one.)

After Julius became the Wizard King, a new captain was appointed for the Gray Deer, and Rill is the captain after that one. When Rill became captain, the Deer changed from Gray to Aqua. When a new captain takes over, they're allowed to change part of their brigade's name.

✽ ✽ ✽

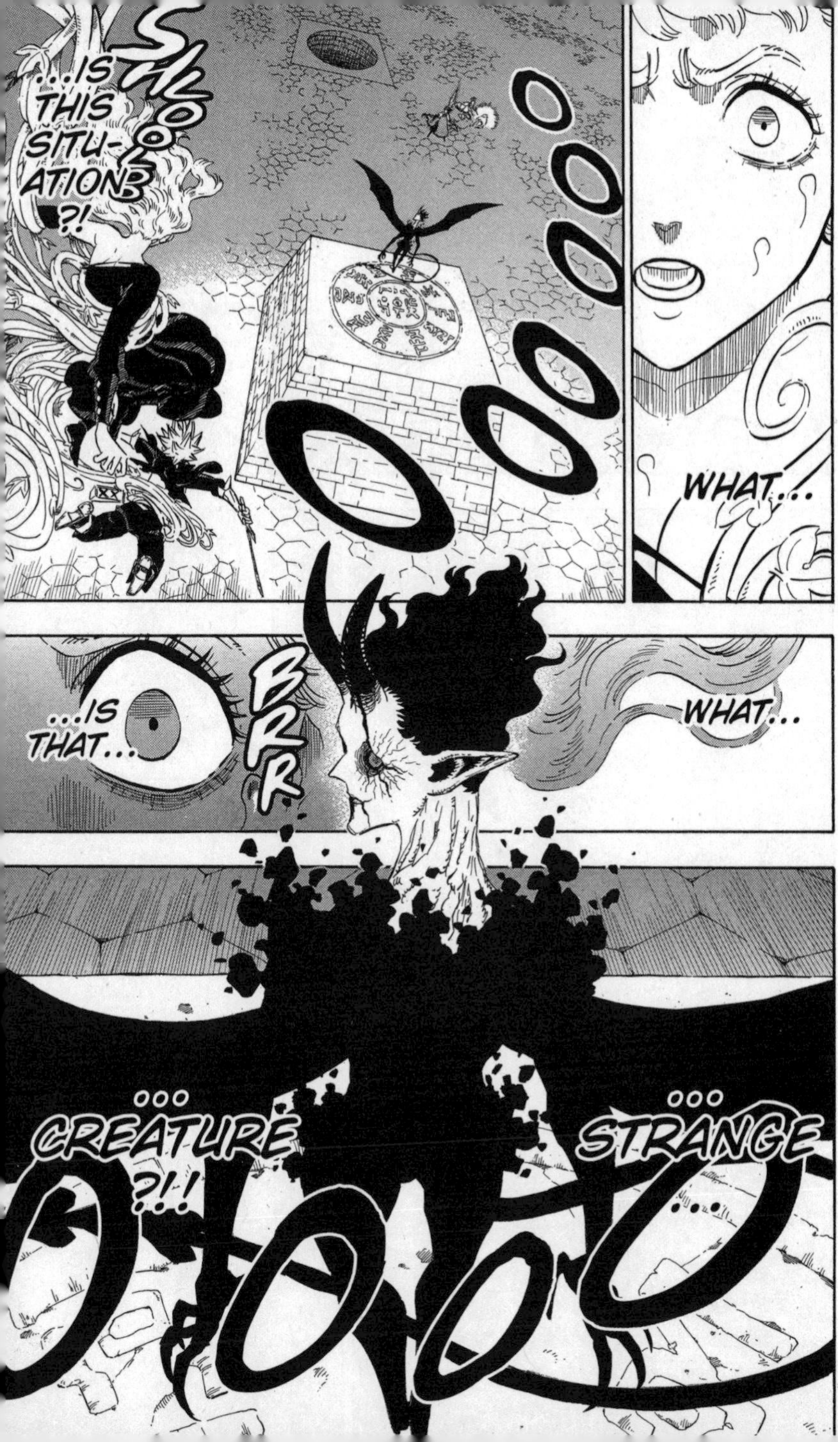
WHAT...
...IS THIS SITUATION?!
WHAT...
BRR
...IS THAT...
...STRANGE...
...CREATURE?!!

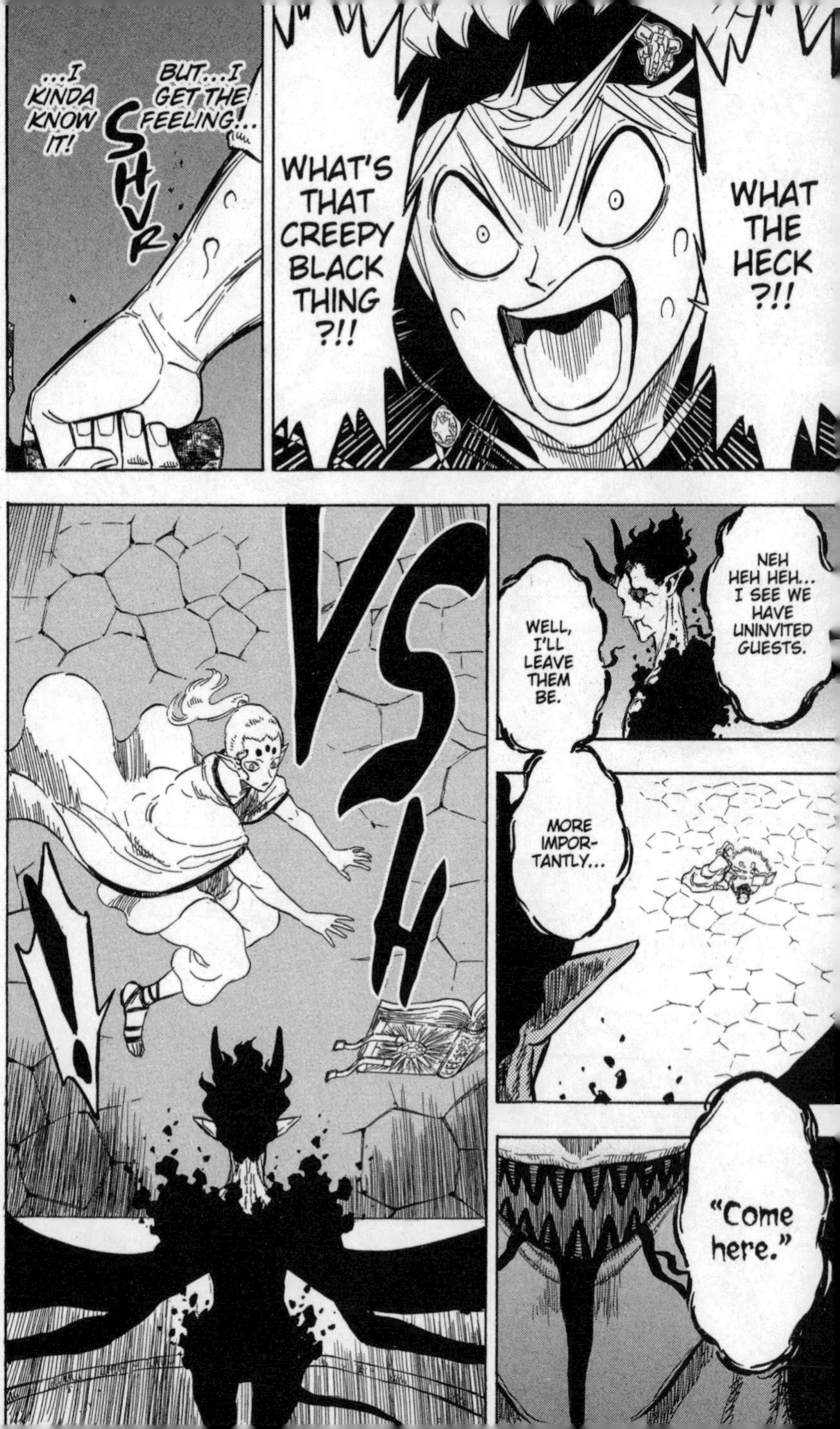
WHAT THE HECK ?!!
WHAT'S THAT CREEPY BLACK THING ?!!
BUT...I GET THE FEELING...
...I KINDA KNOW IT!
SHVR
NEH HEH HEH... I SEE WE HAVE UNINVITED GUESTS.
WELL, I'LL LEAVE THEM BE.
MORE IMPOR-TANTLY...
“Come here.”
VSH
!

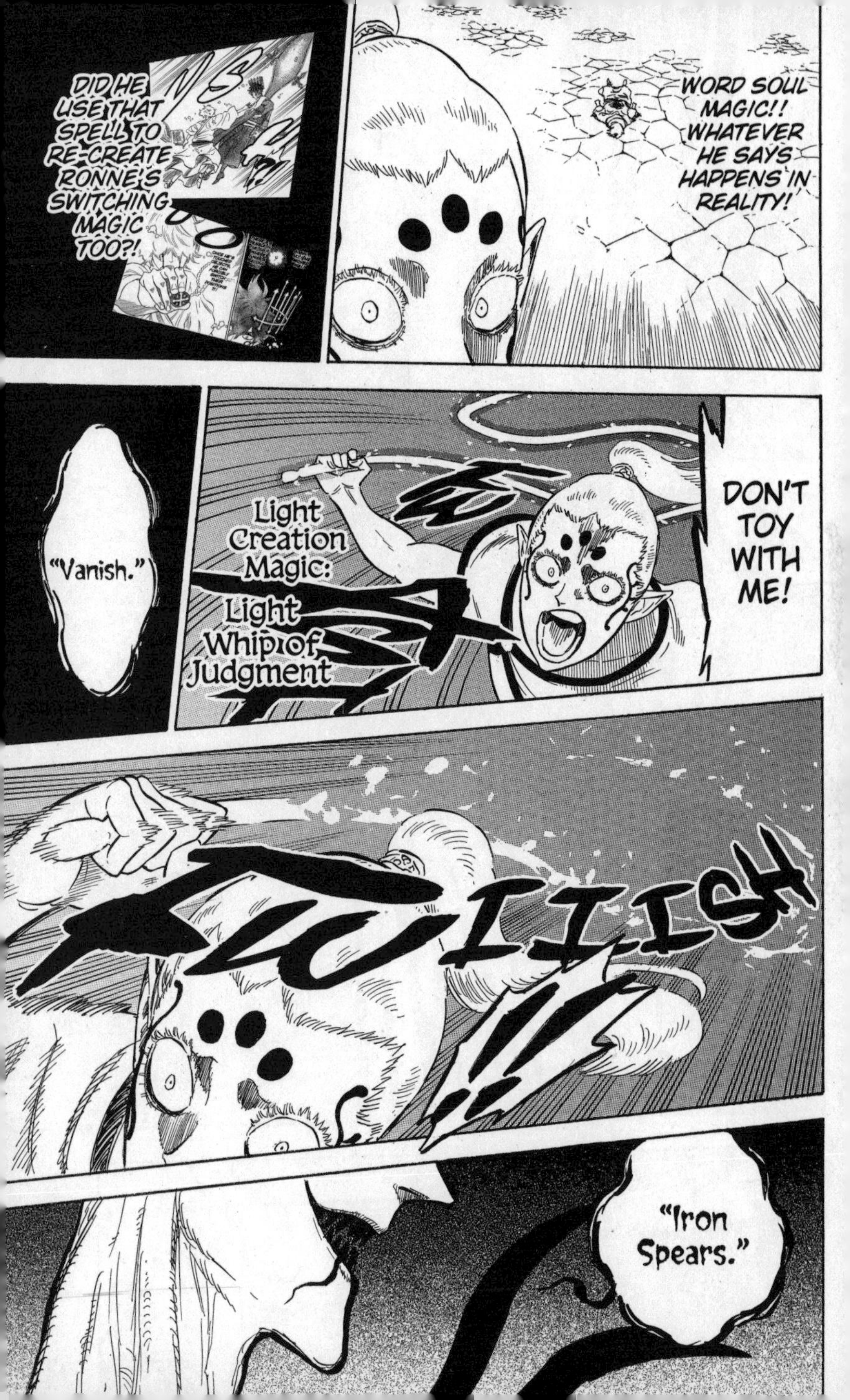
WORD SOUL MAGIC!! WHATEVER HE SAYS HAPPENS IN REALITY!
DID HE USE THAT SPELL TO RE-CREATE RONNE'S SWITCHING MAGIC TOO?!
DON'T TOY WITH ME!
Light Creation Magic: Light Whip of Judgment
"Vanish."
FWIIISH
"Iron Spears."

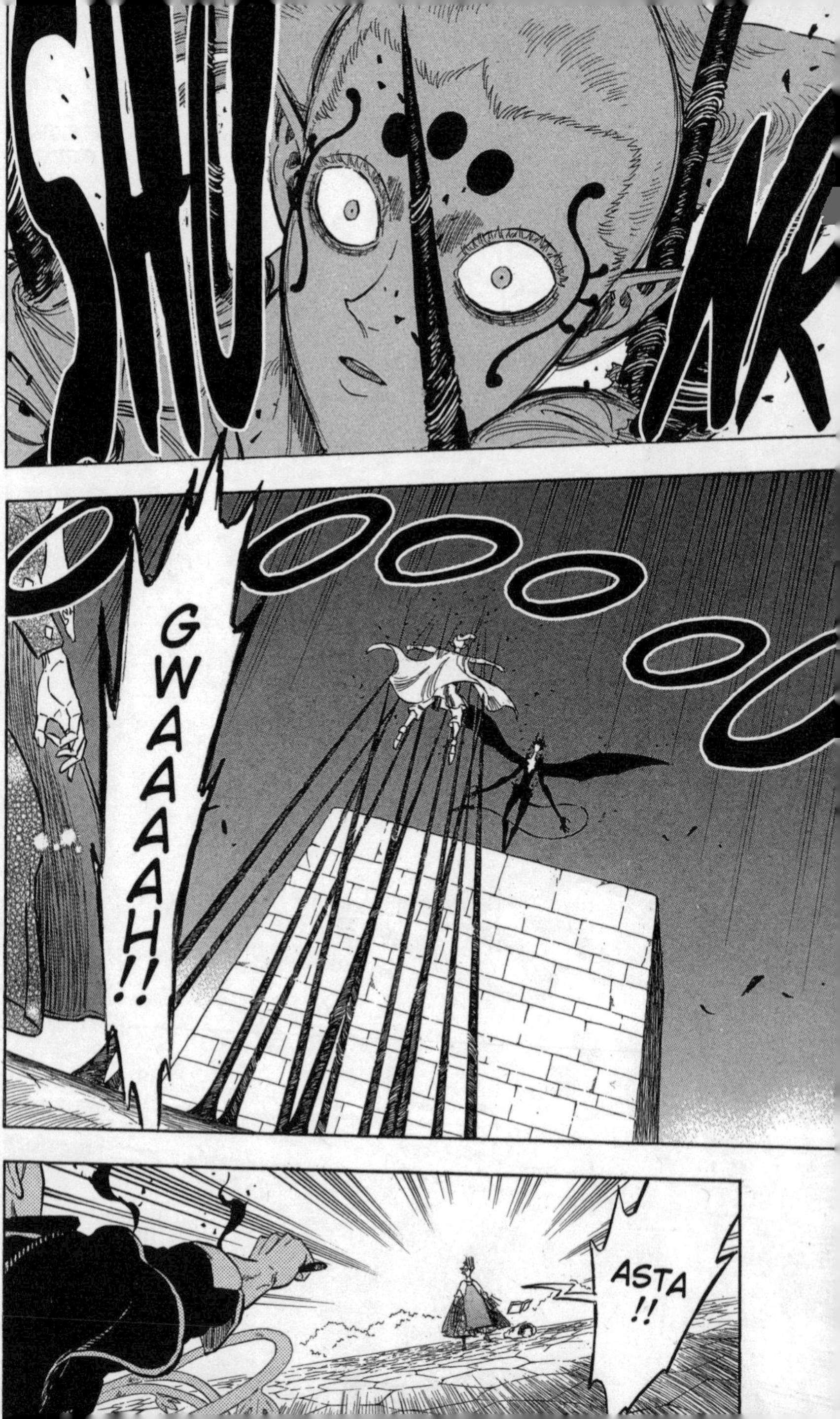
SHUNK
GWAAAAAH!!
OOOOOOO
ASTA!!

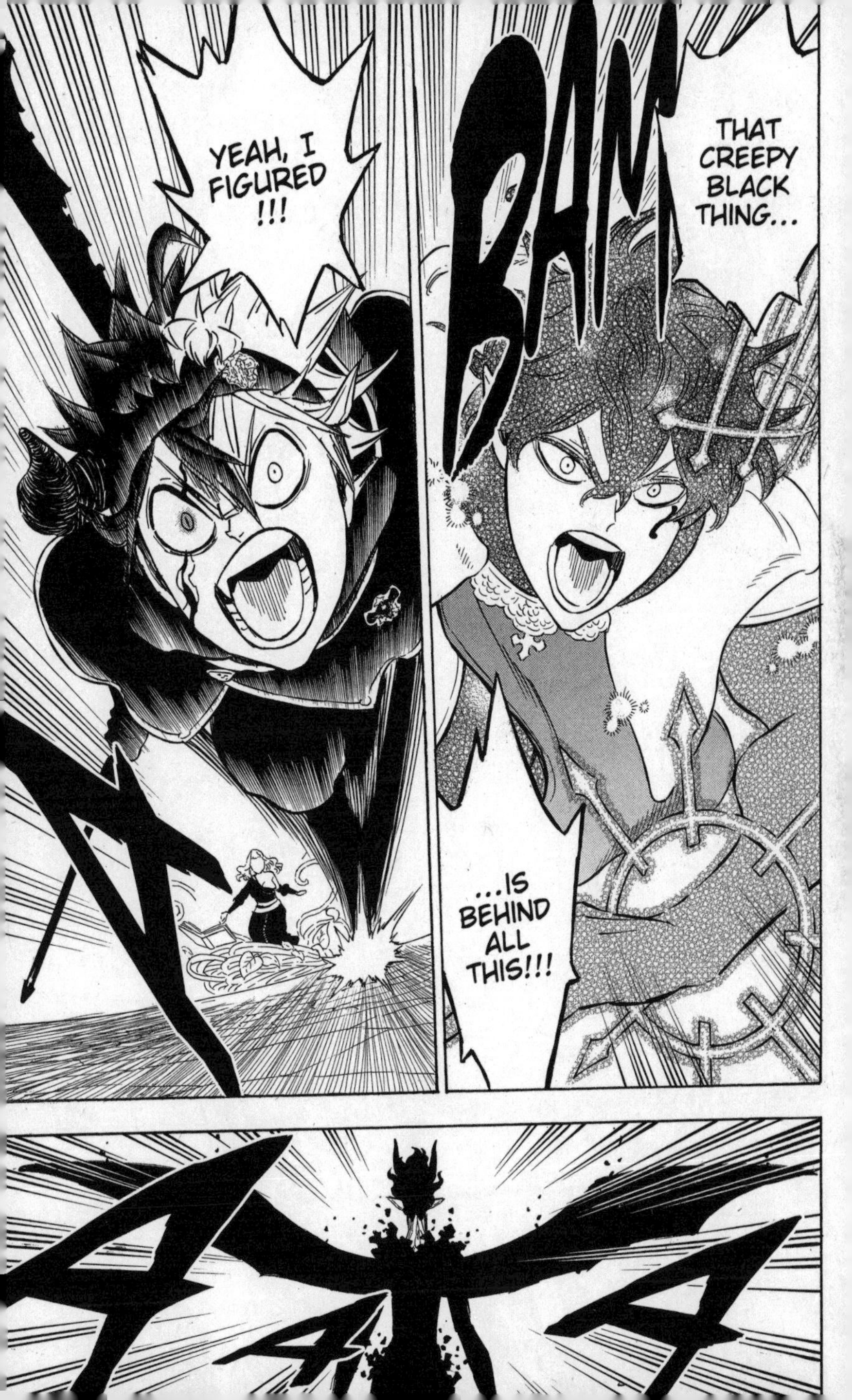
THAT CREEPY BLACK THING...
BAM
...IS BEHIND ALL THIS!!!
YEAH, I FIGURED!!!

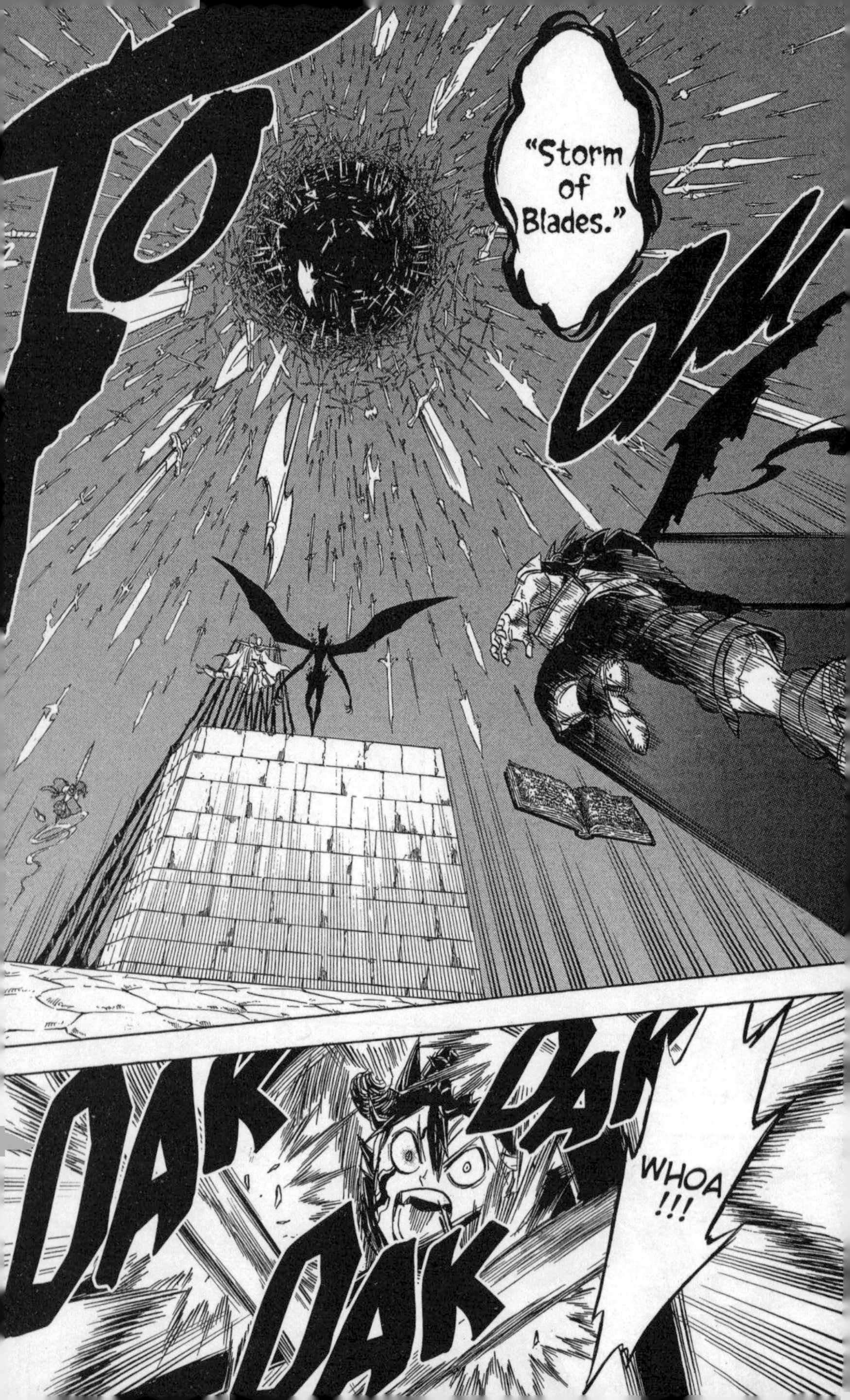
"Storm of Blades."
WHOA!!!
DAK
DAK

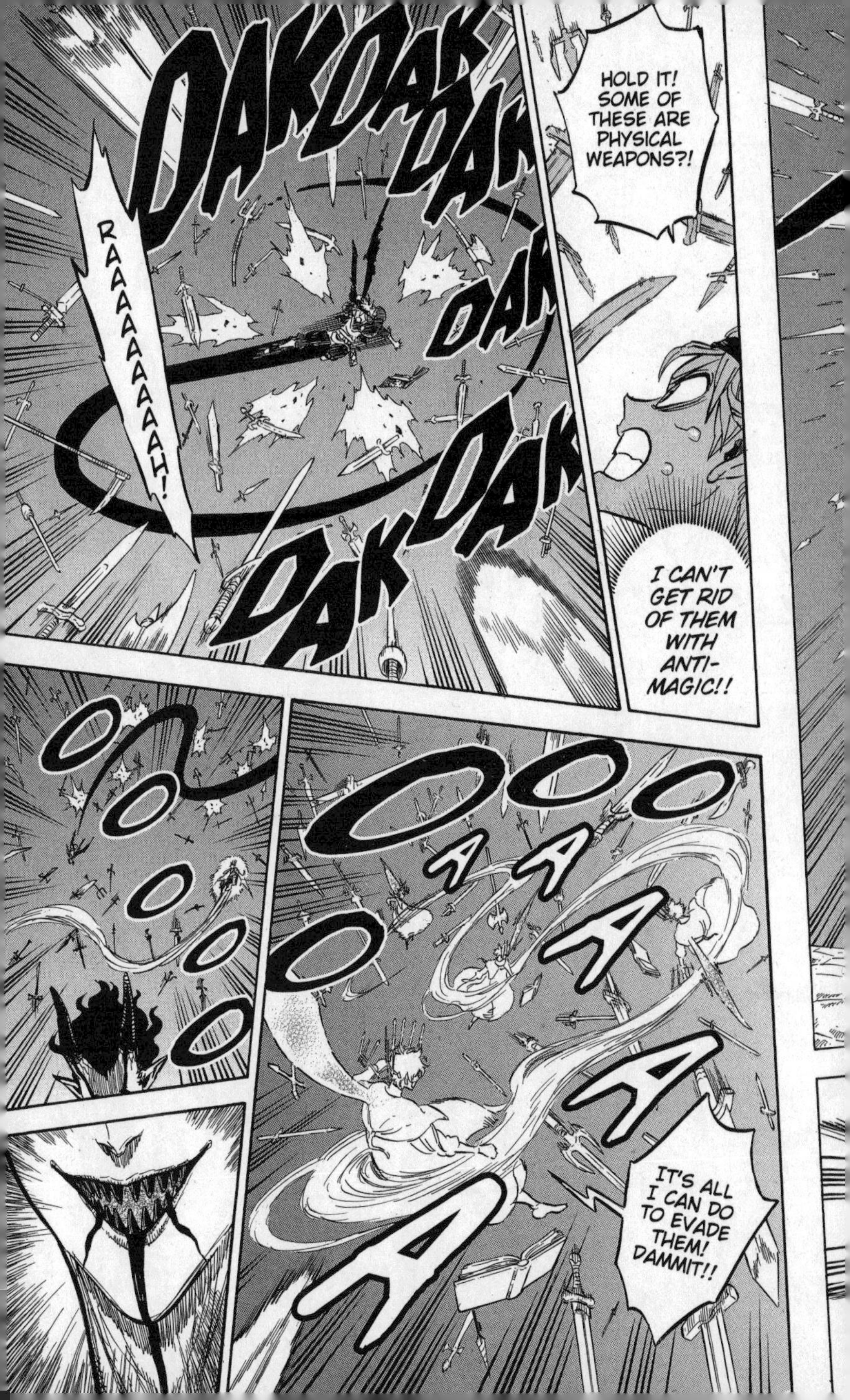
HOLD IT! SOME OF THESE ARE PHYSICAL WEAPONS?!
I CAN'T GET RID OF THEM WITH ANTI-MAGIC!!
DAKDAKDAKDAKDAKDAKDAK
RAAAAAAAAAAAAH!
OOOOAAAAAA
IT'S ALL I CAN DO TO EVADE THEM! DAMMIT!!
OOOOOOOO

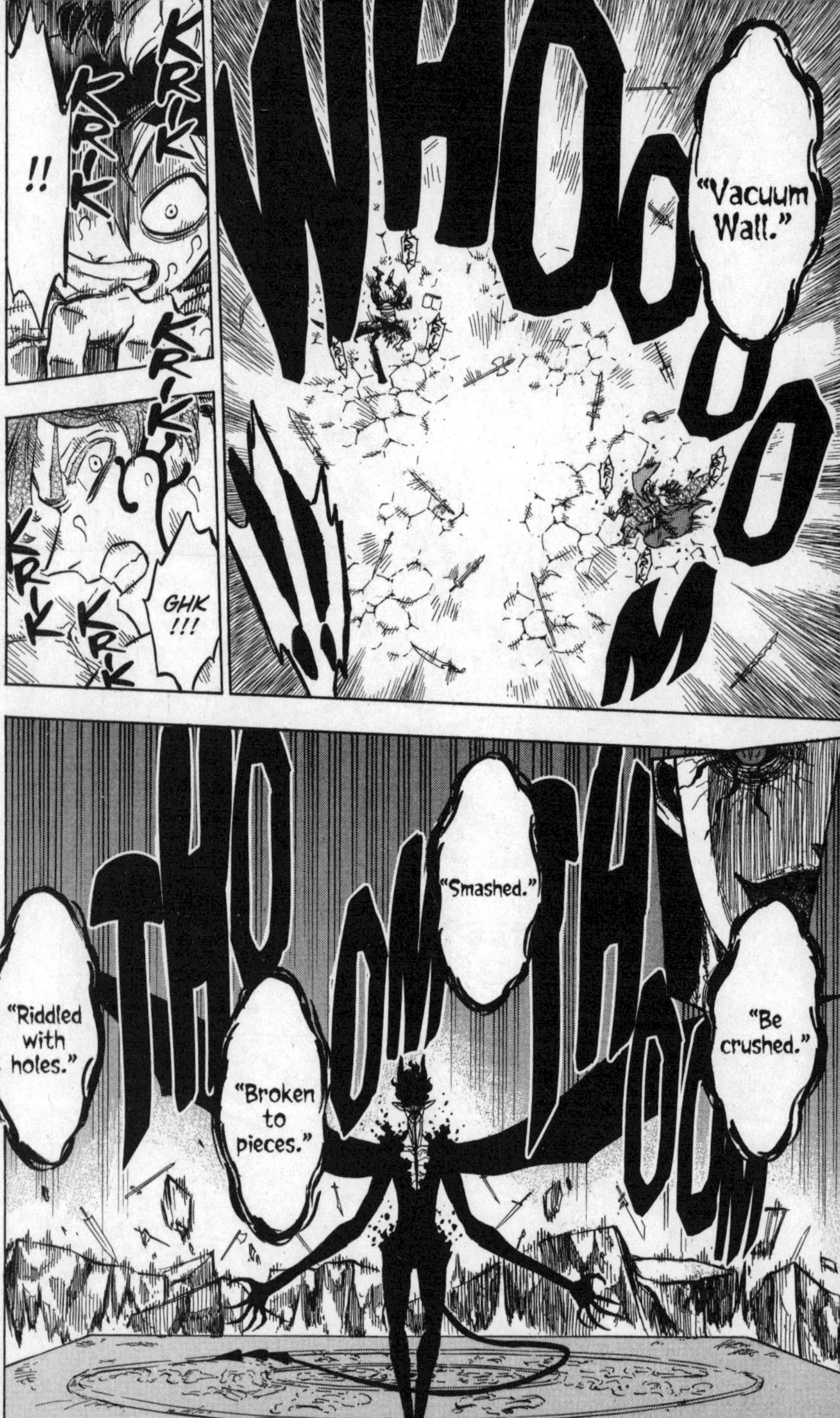
WHOOOOOM
"Vacuum Wall."
KRIK KRIK
!!
KRIK
KRIK KRIK
GHK !!!
THOOM THOOOM
"Smashed."
"Be crushed."
"Broken to pieces."
"Riddled with holes."

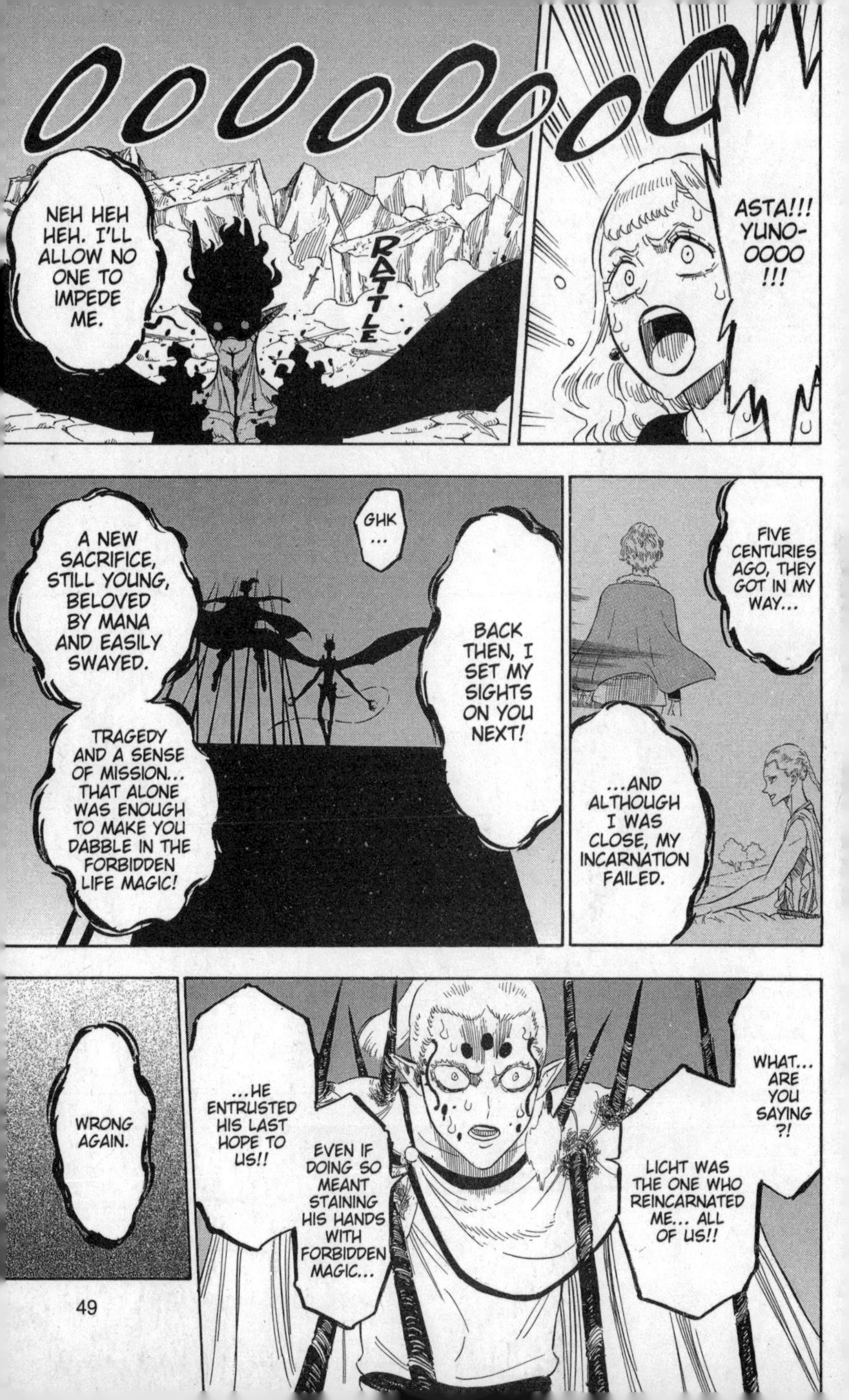
ASTA!!! YUNO-OOOO !!!
OOOOOOOOO
NEH HEH HEH. I'LL ALLOW NO ONE TO IMPEDE ME.
RATTLE
FIVE CENTURIES AGO, THEY GOT IN MY WAY...
...AND ALTHOUGH I WAS CLOSE, MY INCARNATION FAILED.
A NEW SACRIFICE, STILL YOUNG, BELOVED BY MANA AND EASILY SWAYED.
TRAGEDY AND A SENSE OF MISSION... THAT ALONE WAS ENOUGH TO MAKE YOU DABBLE IN THE FORBIDDEN LIFE MAGIC!
BACK THEN, I SET MY SIGHTS ON YOU NEXT!
GHK ...
WHAT... ARE YOU SAYING ?!
LICHT WAS THE ONE WHO REINCARNATED ME... ALL OF US!!
EVEN IF DOING SO MEANT STAINING HIS HANDS WITH FORBIDDEN MAGIC...
...HE ENTRUSTED HIS LAST HOPE TO US!!
WRONG AGAIN.

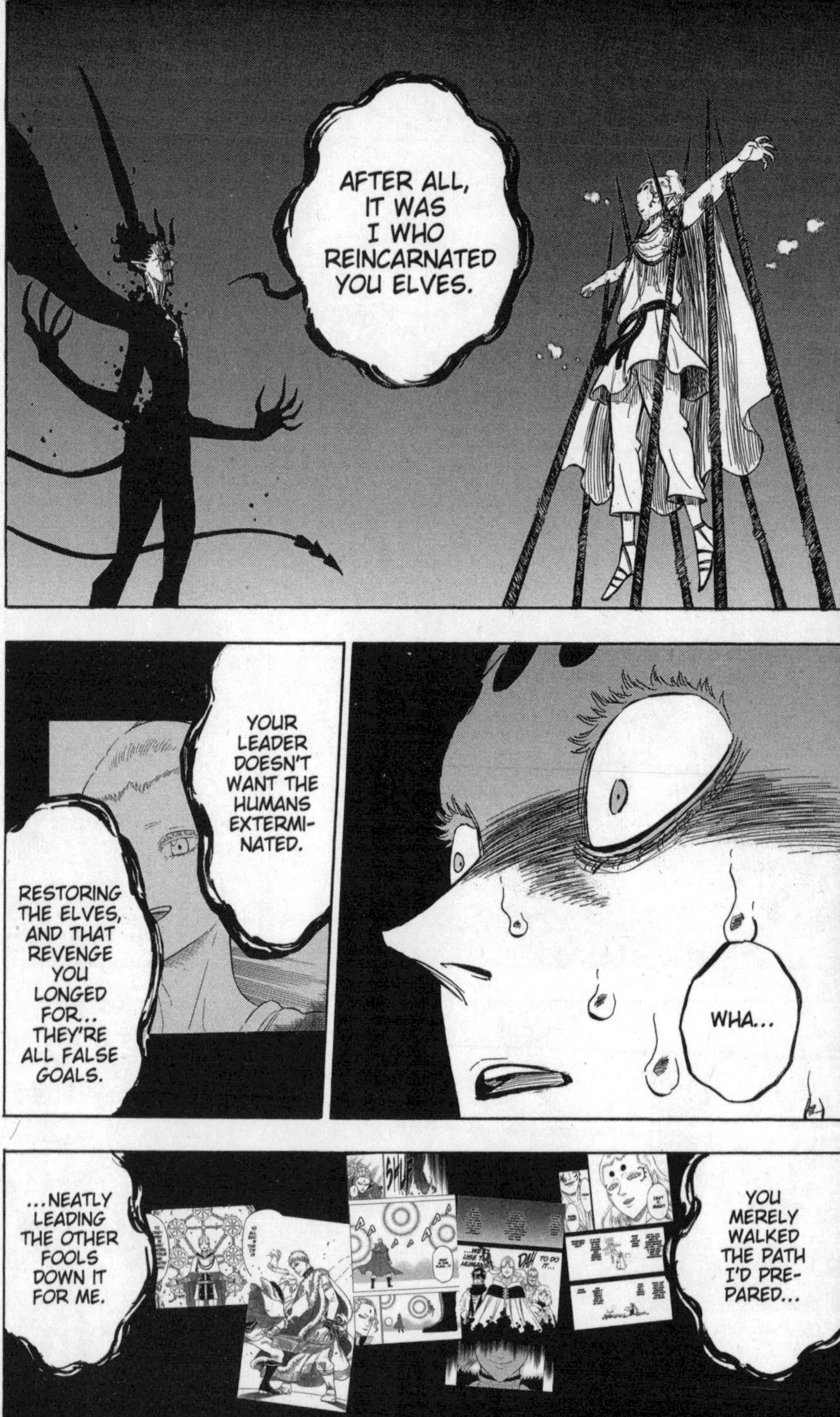
AFTER ALL, IT WAS I WHO REINCARNATED YOU ELVES.
WHA...
YOUR LEADER DOESN'T WANT THE HUMANS EXTERMINATED.
RESTORING THE ELVES, AND THAT REVENGE YOU LONGED FOR... THEY'RE ALL FALSE GOALS.
YOU MERELY WALKED THE PATH I'D PREPARED...
...NEATLY LEADING THE OTHER FOOLS DOWN IT FOR ME.

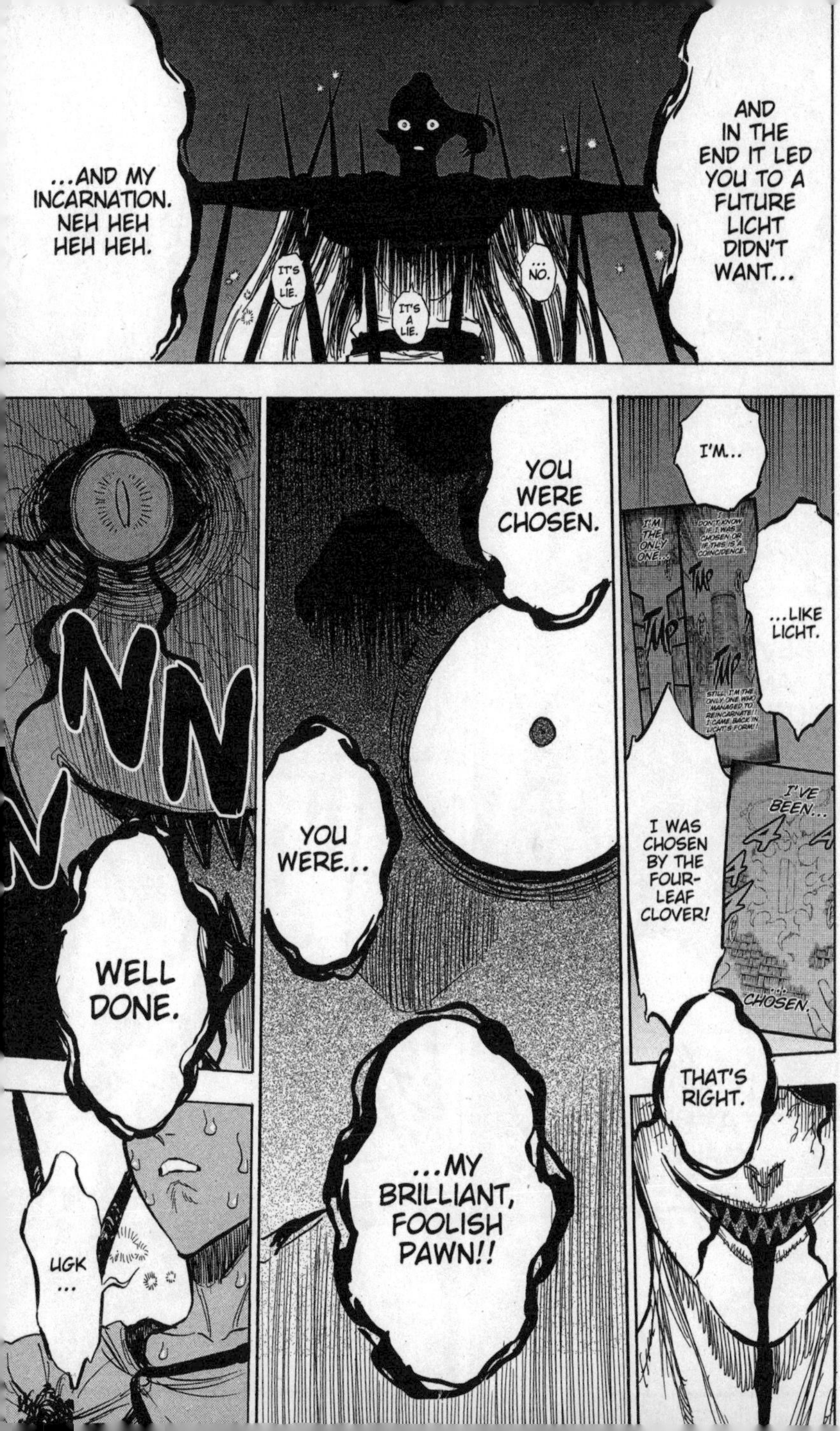
AND IN THE END IT LED YOU TO A FUTURE LICHT DIDN'T WANT...
...NO.
IT'S A LIE.
IT'S A LIE.
...AND MY INCARNATION. NEH HEH HEH HEH.
I'M...
I'M THE ONLY ONE...
I DON'T KNOW IF I WAS CHOSEN OR IF THIS IS A COINCIDENCE.
TMP
TMP
TMP
...LIKE LICHT.
STILL, I'M THE ONLY ONE WHO MANAGED TO REINCARNATE! I CAME BACK IN LICHT'S FORM!
I'VE BEEN...
I WAS CHOSEN BY THE FOUR-LEAF CLOVER!
...CHOSEN.
YOU WERE CHOSEN.
YOU WERE...
NNN
WELL DONE.
THAT'S RIGHT.
...MY BRILLIANT, FOOLISH PAWN!!
UGK...

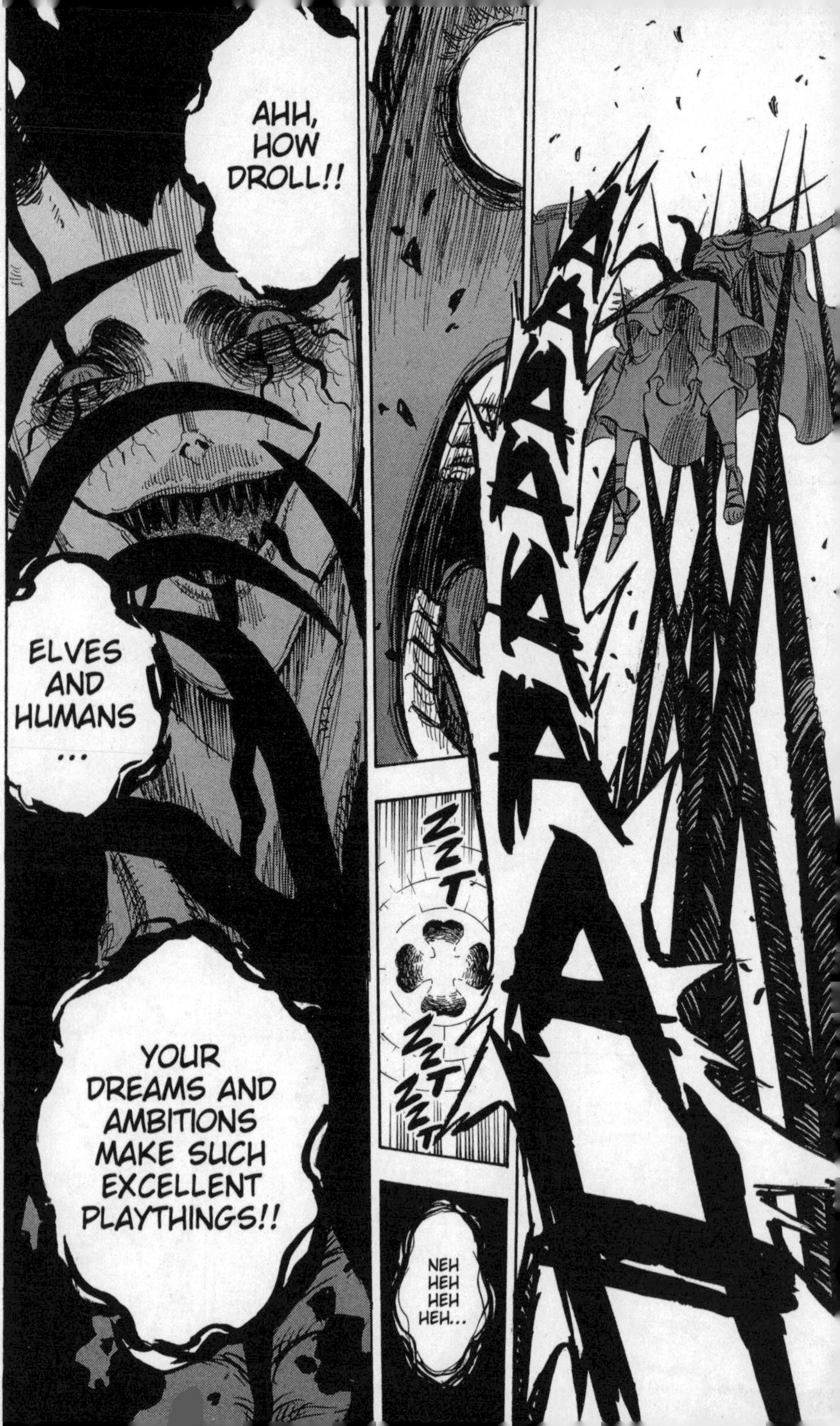
AAAAAAAAAH
ZZZT
ZZZT ZZZT
NEH HEH HEH HEH...
AHH, HOW DROLL!!
ELVES AND HUMANS...
YOUR DREAMS AND AMBITIONS MAKE SUCH EXCELLENT PLAYTHINGS!!

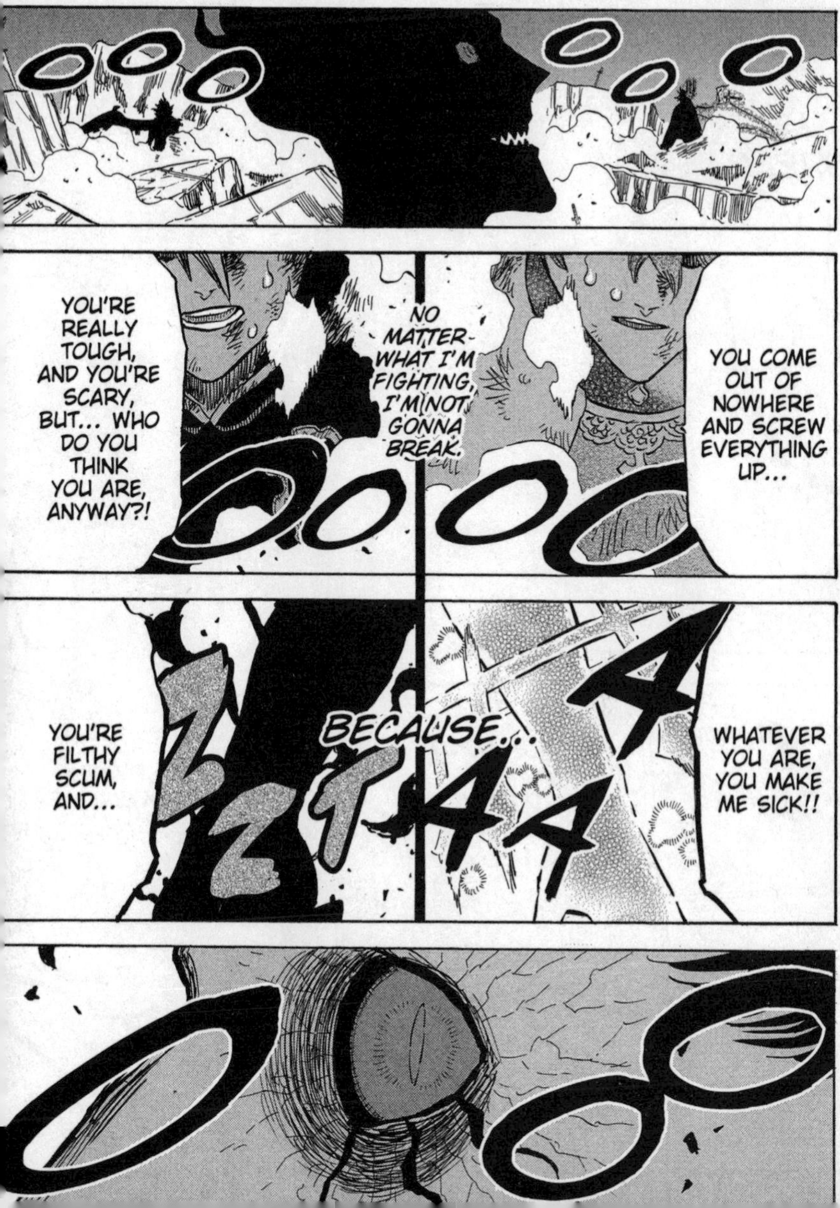
YOU COME OUT OF NOWHERE AND SCREW EVERYTHING UP...
YOU'RE REALLY TOUGH, AND YOU'RE SCARY, BUT... WHO DO YOU THINK YOU ARE, ANYWAY?!
NO MATTER WHAT I'M FIGHTING, I'M NOT GONNA BREAK.
WHATEVER YOU ARE, YOU MAKE ME SICK!!
YOU'RE FILTHY SCUM, AND...
BECAUSE...

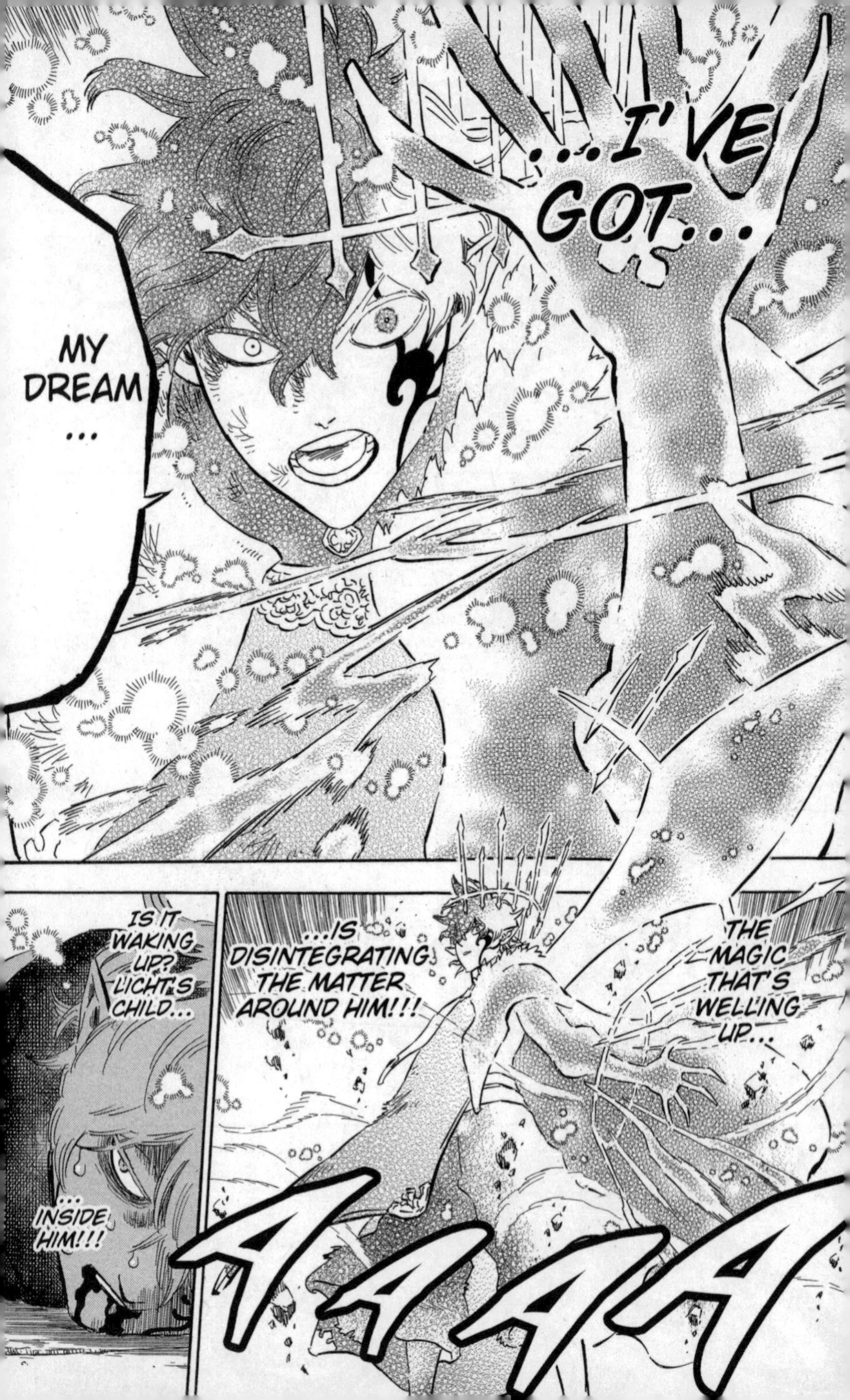
...I'VE GOT...
MY DREAM ...
THE MAGIC THAT'S WELLING UP...
...IS DISINTEGRATING THE MATTER AROUND HIM!!!
IS IT WAKING UP? LICHT'S CHILD...
...INSIDE HIM!!!

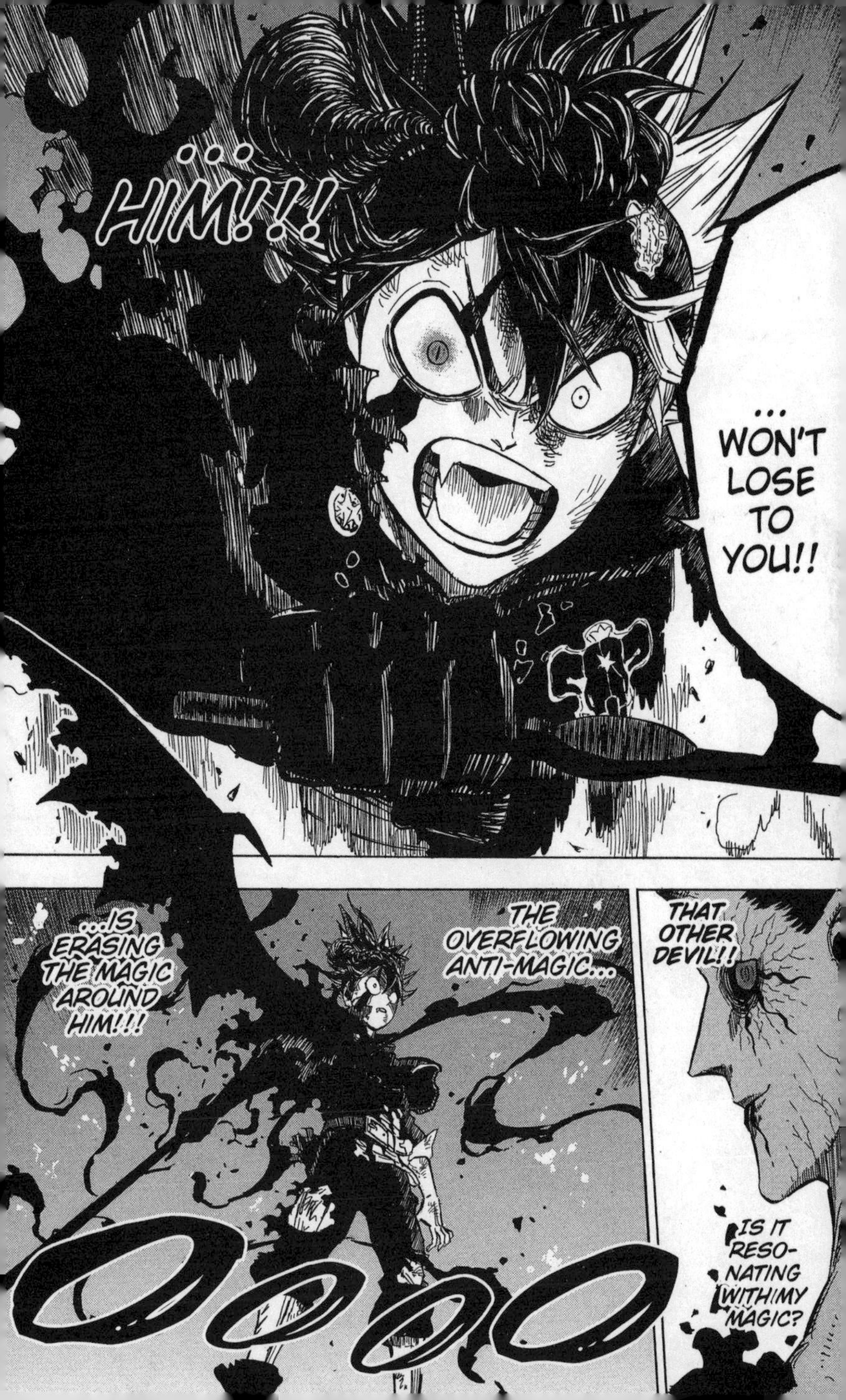
...WON'T LOSE TO YOU!!
...HIM!!!
THAT OTHER DEVIL!!
IS IT RESONATING WITH MY MAGIC?
THE OVERFLOWING ANTI-MAGIC...
...IS ERASING THE MAGIC AROUND HIM!!!

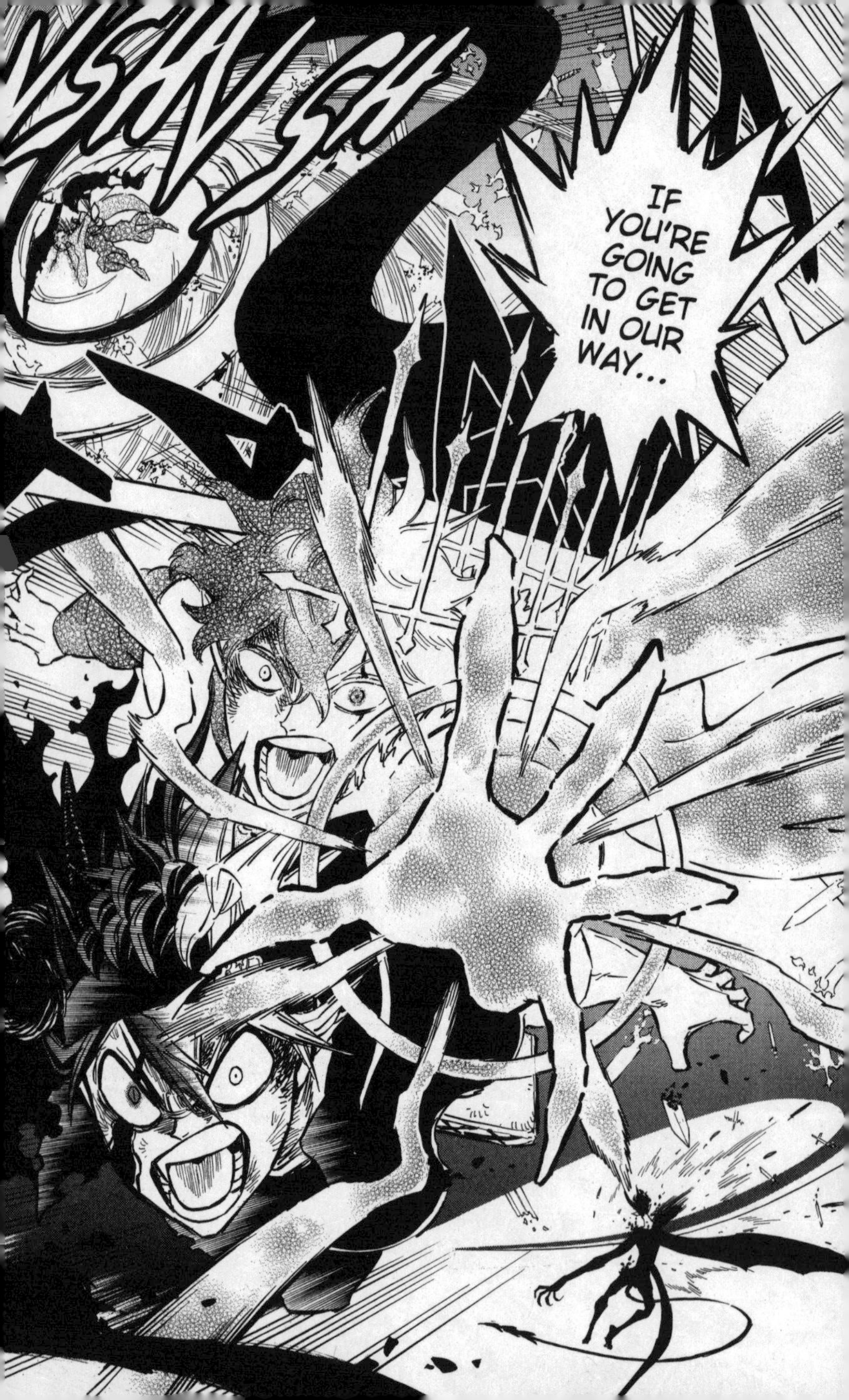
SHH SHH
IF YOU'RE GOING TO GET IN OUR WAY...

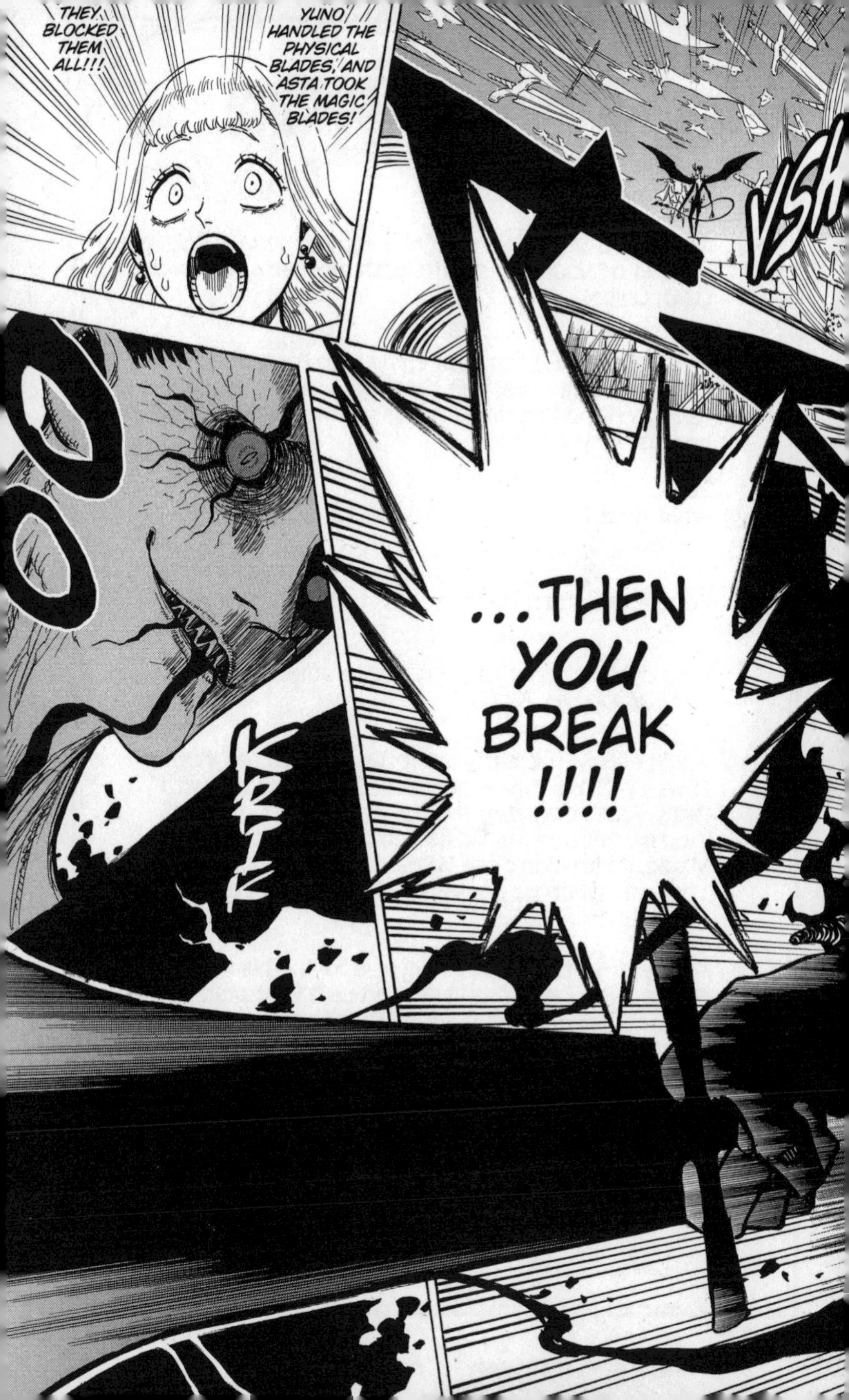
VSH
YUNO HANDLED THE PHYSICAL BLADES, AND ASTA TOOK THE MAGIC BLADES!
THEY BLOCKED THEM ALL!!!
...THEN YOU BREAK!!!!
KRIK

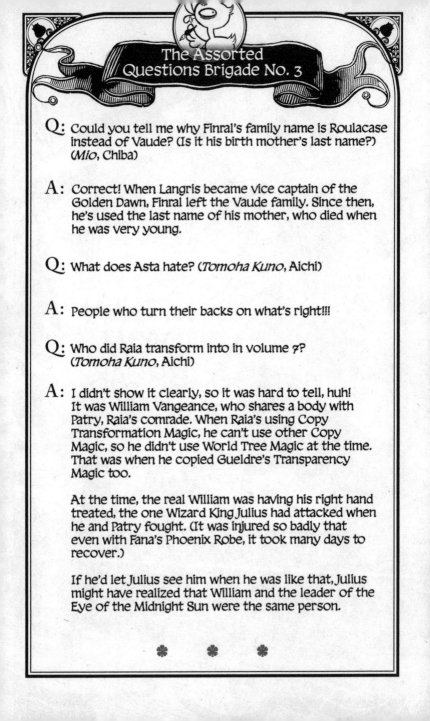

The Assorted Questions Brigade No. 3

Q: Could you tell me why Finral's family name is Roulacase instead of Vaude? (Is it his birth mother's last name?) (*Mio*, Chiba)

A: Correct! When Langris became vice captain of the Golden Dawn, Finral left the Vaude family. Since then, he's used the last name of his mother, who died when he was very young.

Q: What does Asta hate? (*Tomoha Kuno*, Aichi)

A: People who turn their backs on what's right!!!

Q: Who did Raia transform into in volume 7? (*Tomoha Kuno*, Aichi)

A: I didn't show it clearly, so it was hard to tell, huh! It was William Vangeance, who shares a body with Patry, Raia's comrade. When Raia's using Copy Transformation Magic, he can't use other Copy Magic, so he didn't use World Tree Magic at the time. That was when he copied Gueldre's Transparency Magic too.

At the time, the real William was having his right hand treated, the one Wizard King Julius had attacked when he and Patry fought. (It was injured so badly that even with Fana's Phoenix Robe, it took many days to recover.)

If he'd let Julius see him when he was like that, Julius might have realized that William and the leader of the Eye of the Midnight Sun were the same person.

❋　　❋　　❋

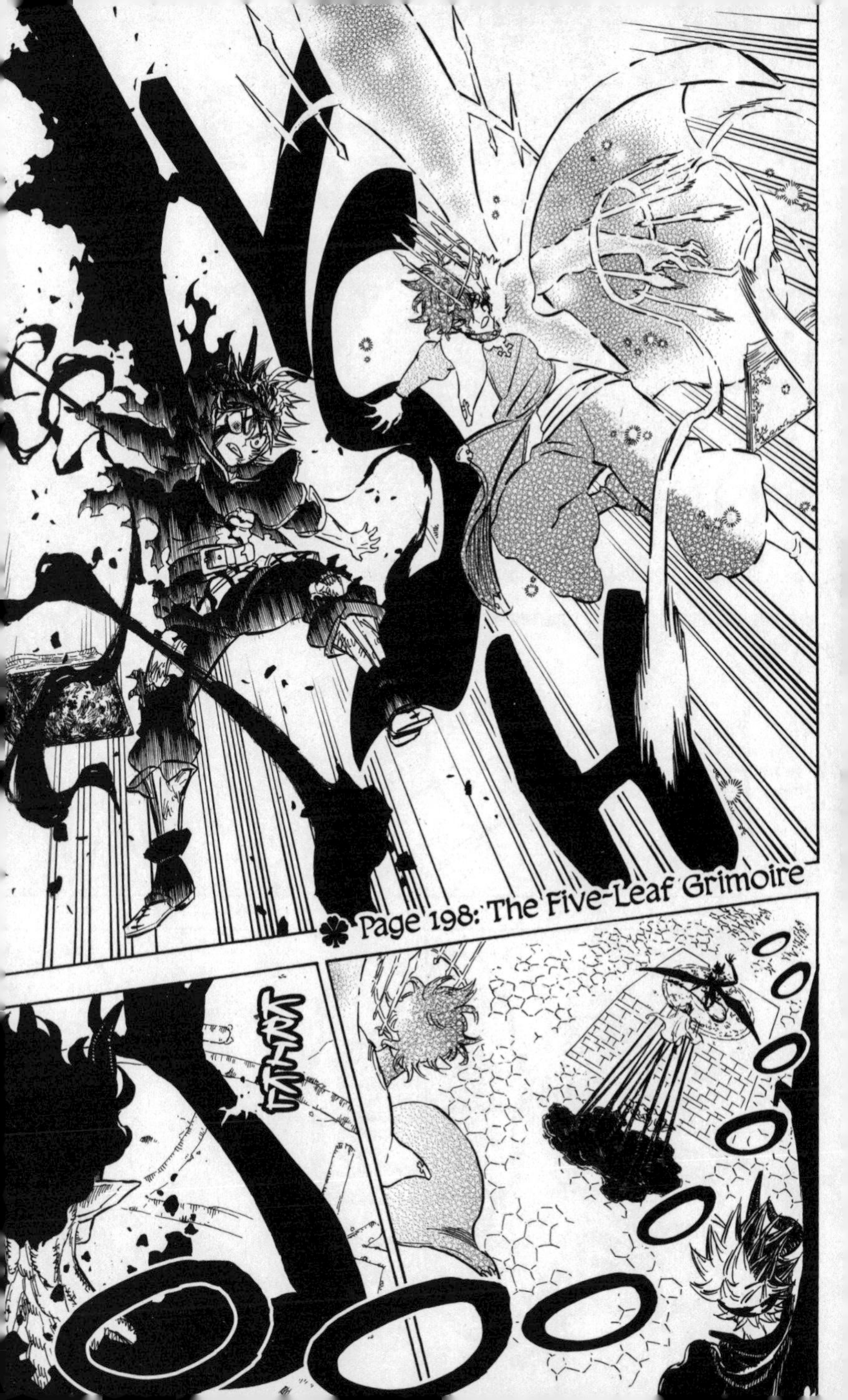
Page 198: The Five-Leaf Grimoire

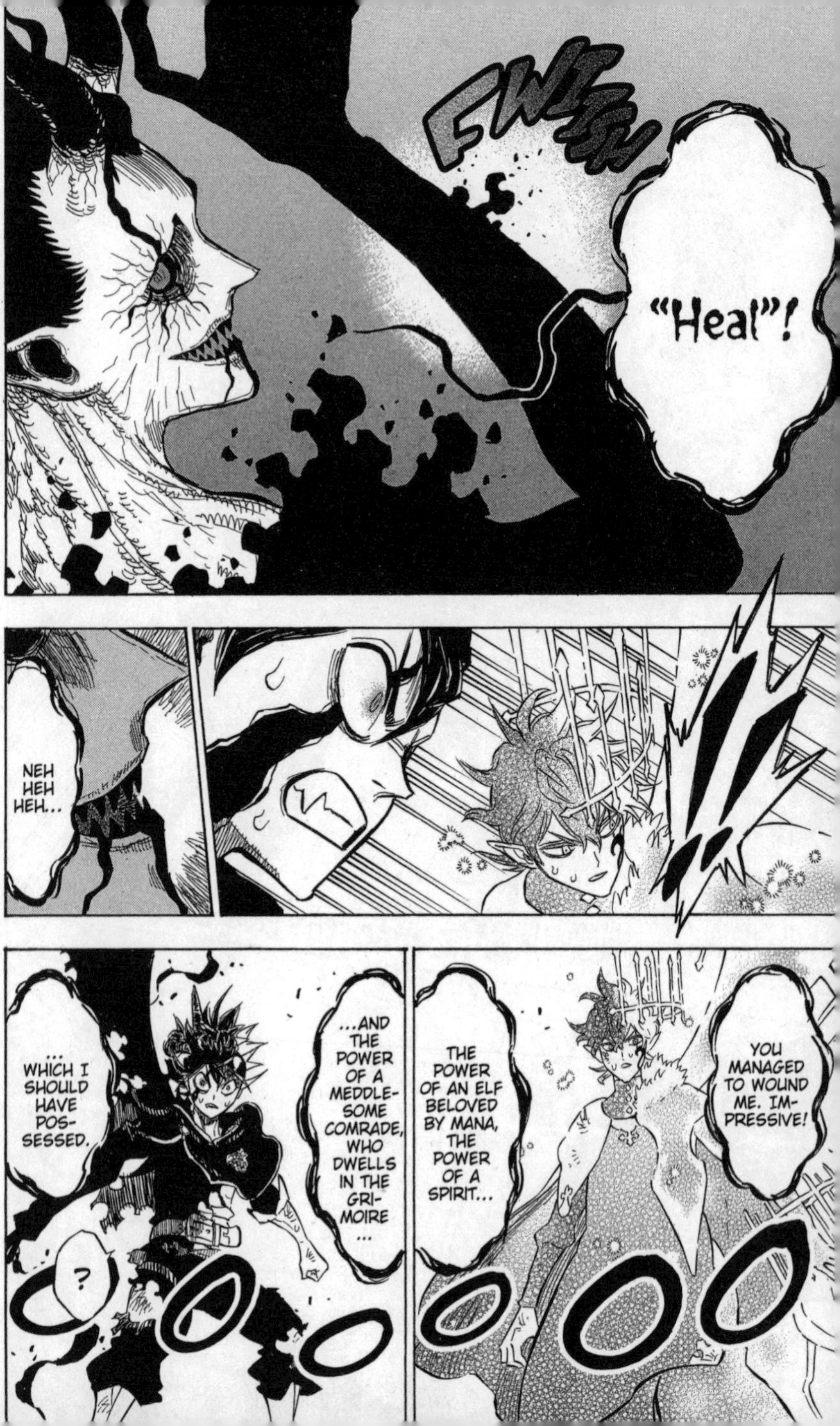
FWISH
"Heal"!
NEH HEH HEH...
YOU MANAGED TO WOUND ME. IMPRESSIVE!
THE POWER OF AN ELF BELOVED BY MANA, THE POWER OF A SPIRIT...
...AND THE POWER OF A MEDDLESOME COMRADE, WHO DWELLS IN THE GRIMOIRE...
...WHICH I SHOULD HAVE POSSESSED.
?

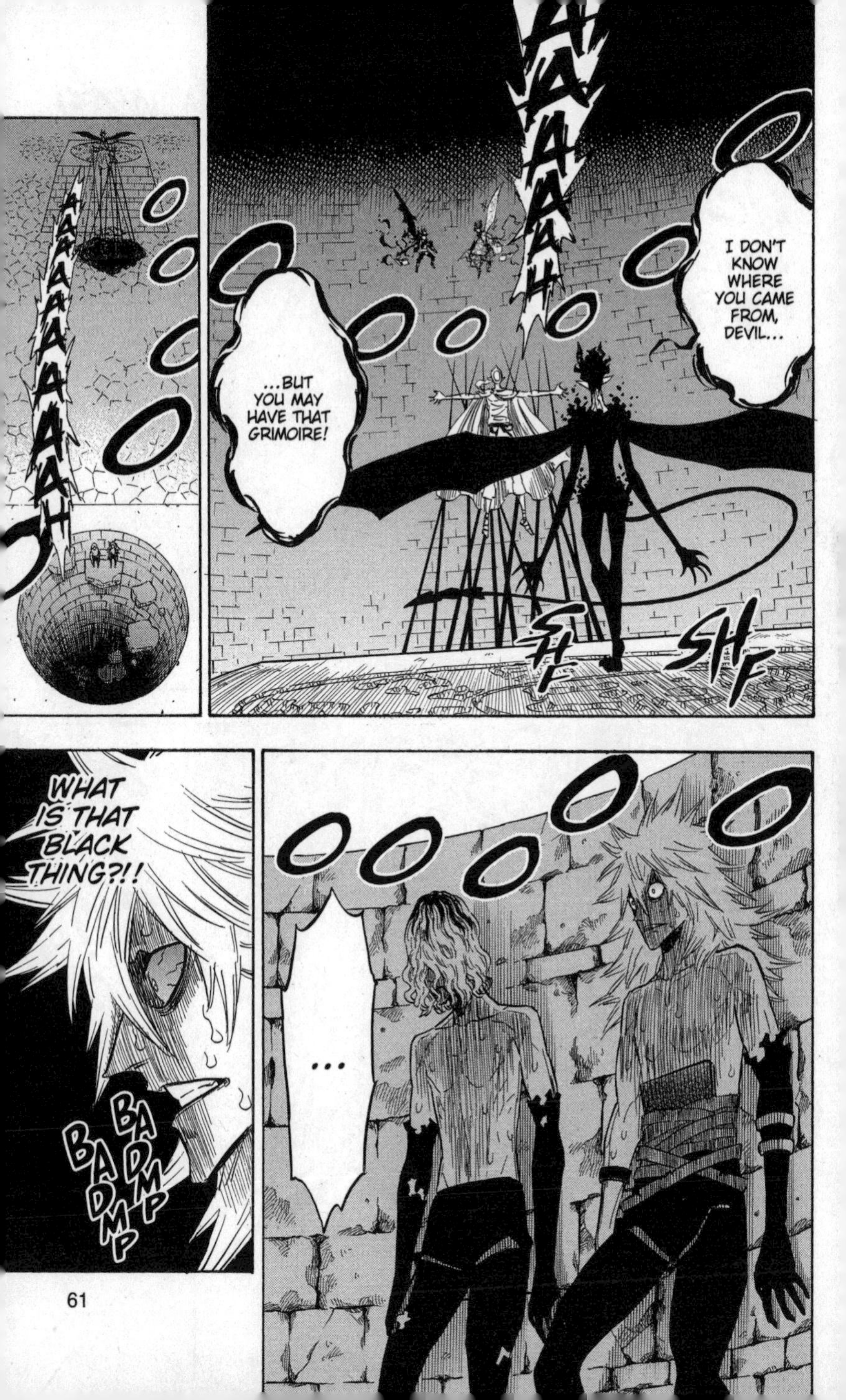
I DON'T KNOW WHERE YOU CAME FROM, DEVIL...
...BUT YOU MAY HAVE THAT GRIMOIRE!
SHF
SHF
...
WHAT IS THAT BLACK THING?!!
BA DMP
BA DMP

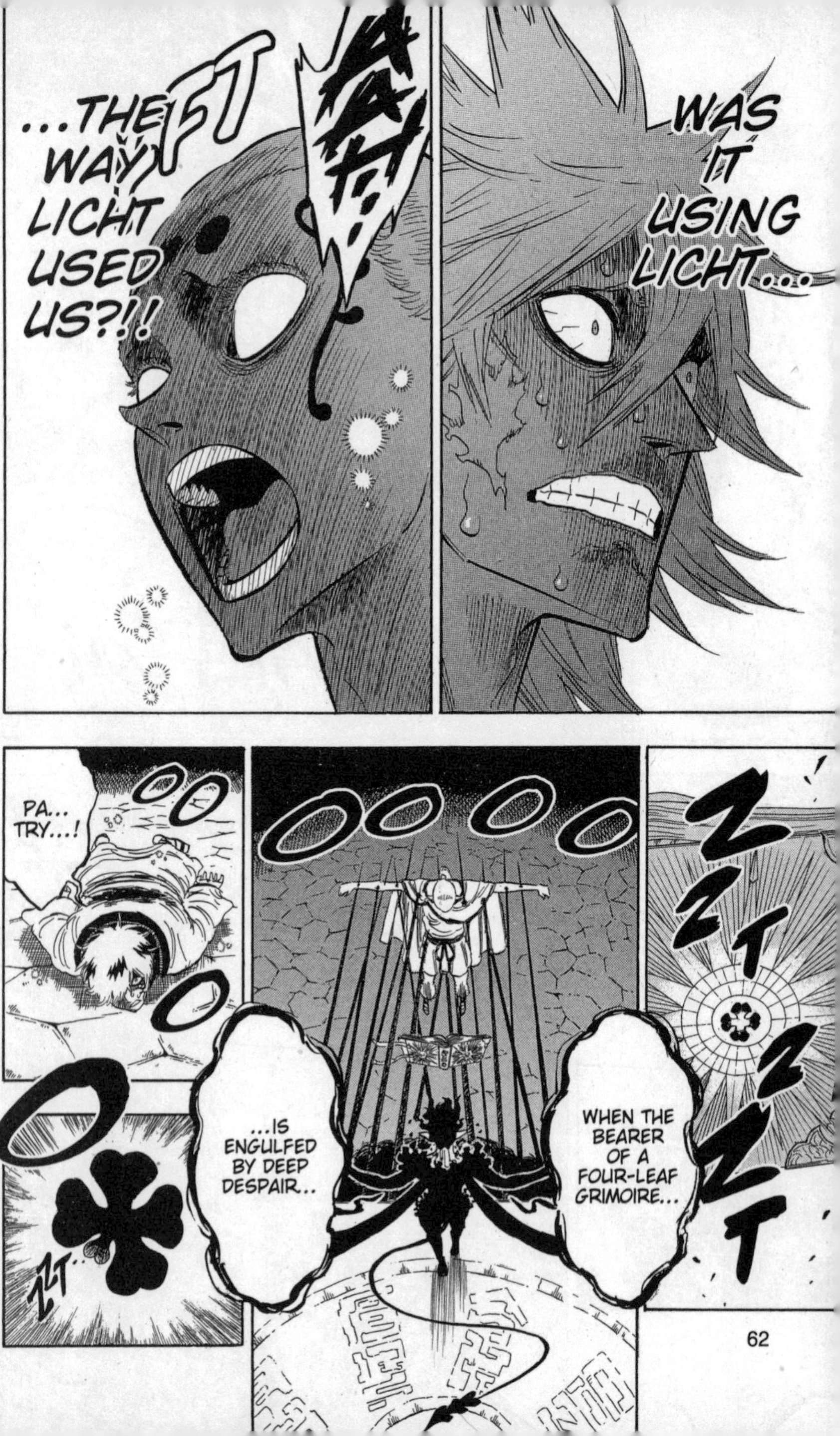
WAS IT USING LICHT...
...THE WAY LICHT USED US?!!
FT
ZZZZT
OOOO
WHEN THE BEARER OF A FOUR-LEAF GRIMOIRE...
...IS ENGULFED BY DEEP DESPAIR...
OO
PA... TRY...!
OO
ZZT...

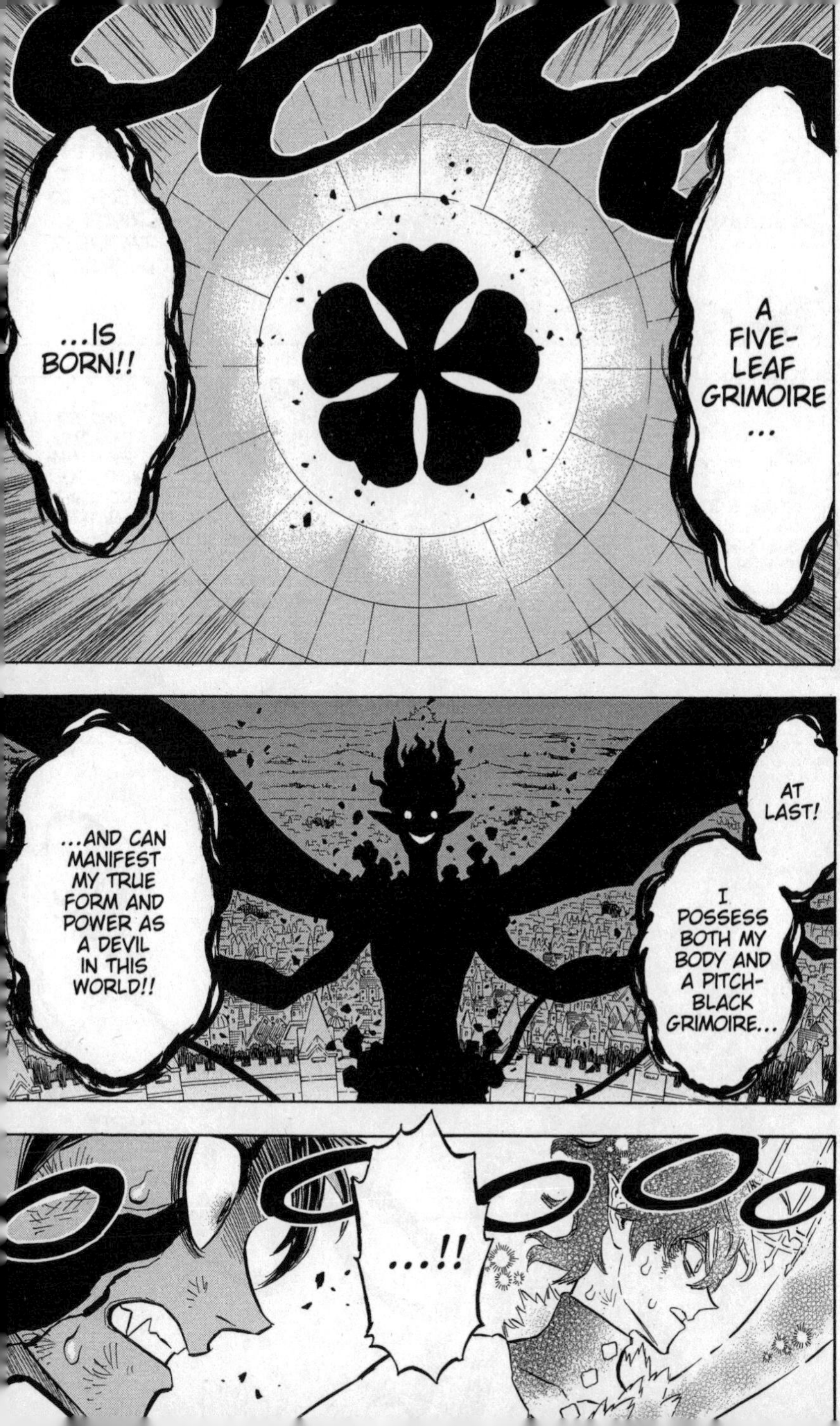
A FIVE-LEAF GRIMOIRE...
...IS BORN!!
AT LAST!
I POSSESS BOTH MY BODY AND A PITCH-BLACK GRIMOIRE...
...AND CAN MANIFEST MY TRUE FORM AND POWER AS A DEVIL IN THIS WORLD!!
...!!

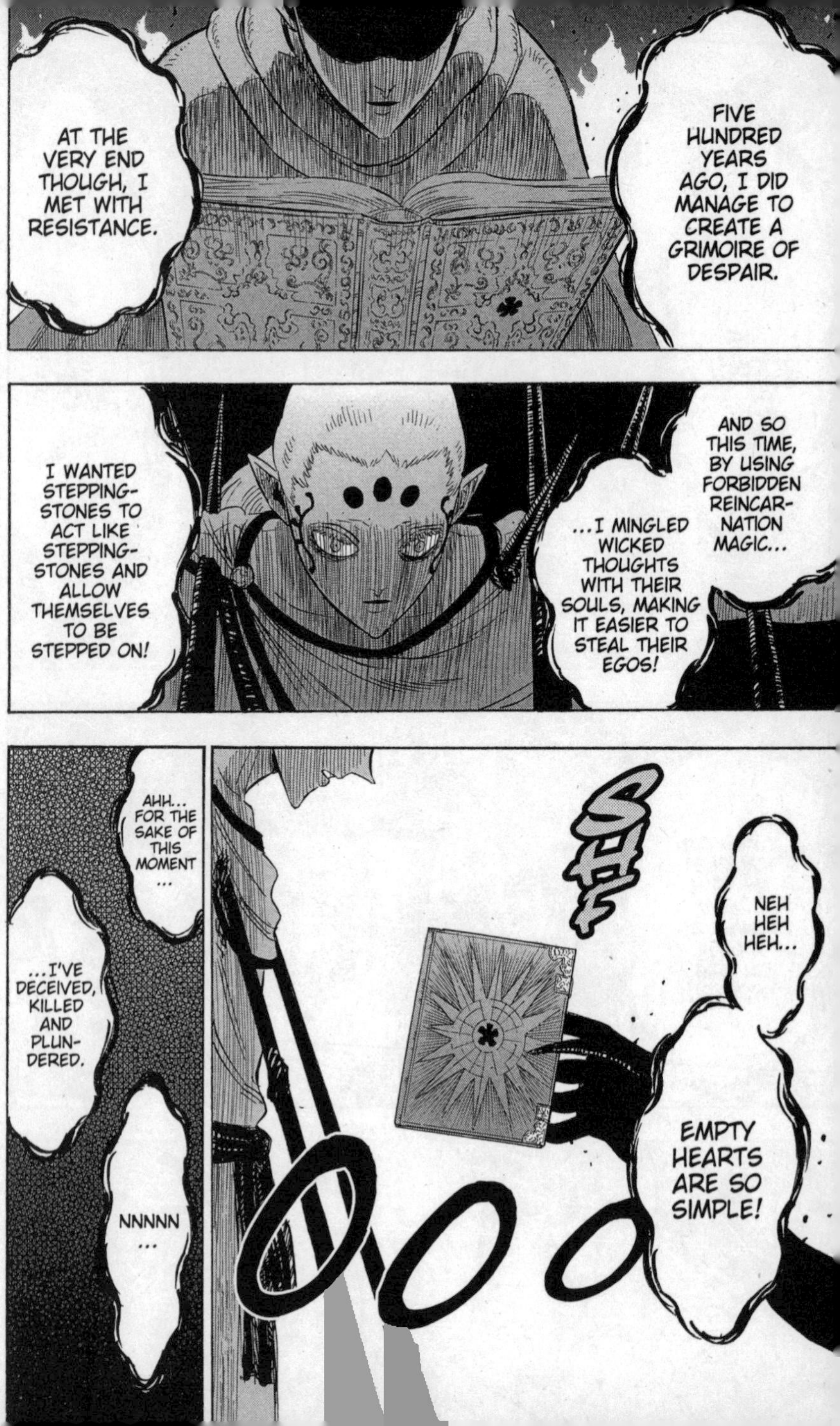
FIVE HUNDRED YEARS AGO, I DID MANAGE TO CREATE A GRIMOIRE OF DESPAIR.
AT THE VERY END THOUGH, I MET WITH RESISTANCE.
AND SO THIS TIME, BY USING FORBIDDEN REINCARNATION MAGIC...
...I MINGLED WICKED THOUGHTS WITH THEIR SOULS, MAKING IT EASIER TO STEAL THEIR EGOS!
I WANTED STEPPING-STONES TO ACT LIKE STEPPING-STONES AND ALLOW THEMSELVES TO BE STEPPED ON!
SHF
NEH HEH HEH...
EMPTY HEARTS ARE SO SIMPLE!
AHH... FOR THE SAKE OF THIS MOMENT ...
...I'VE DECEIVED, KILLED AND PLUNDERED.
NNNNN ...

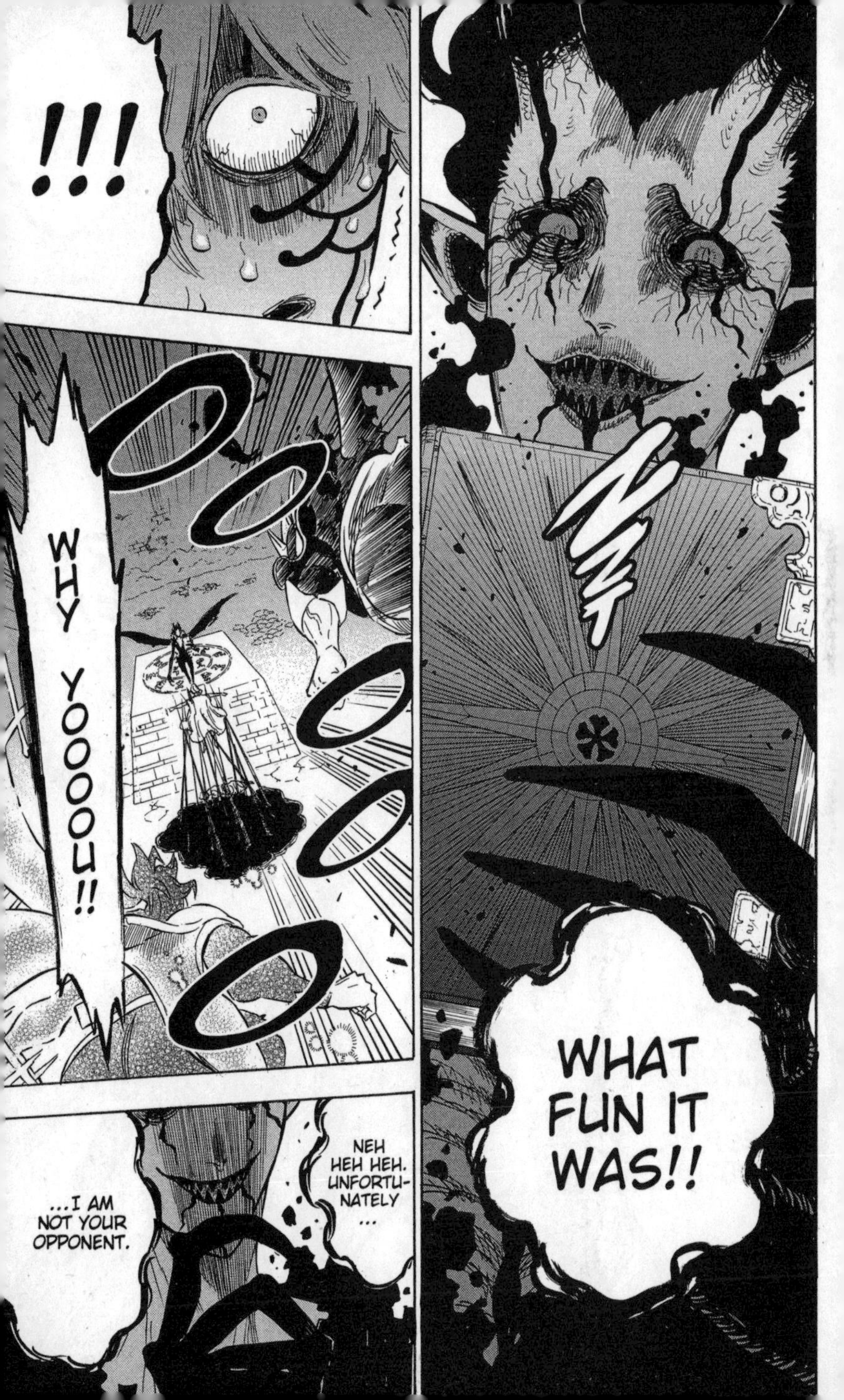
WHAT FUN IT WAS!!
!!!
WHY YOOOOU!!
NEH HEH HEH. UNFORTUNATELY ...
...I AM NOT YOUR OPPONENT.

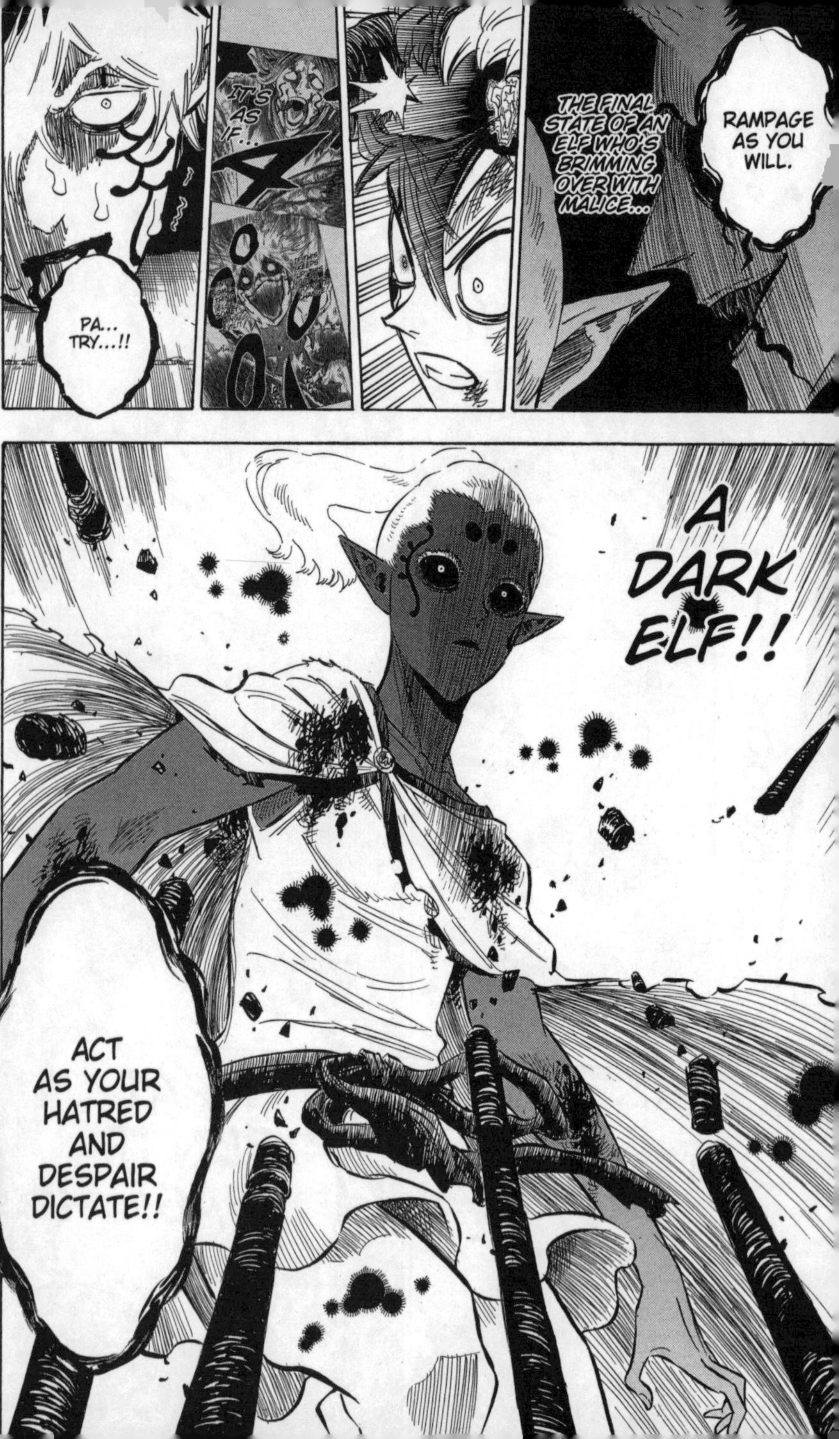
RAMPAGE AS YOU WILL.
THE FINAL STATE OF AN ELF WHO'S BRIMMING OVER WITH MALICE...
IT'S AS IF...
PA... TRY...!!
A DARK ELF!!
ACT AS YOUR HATRED AND DESPAIR DICTATE!!

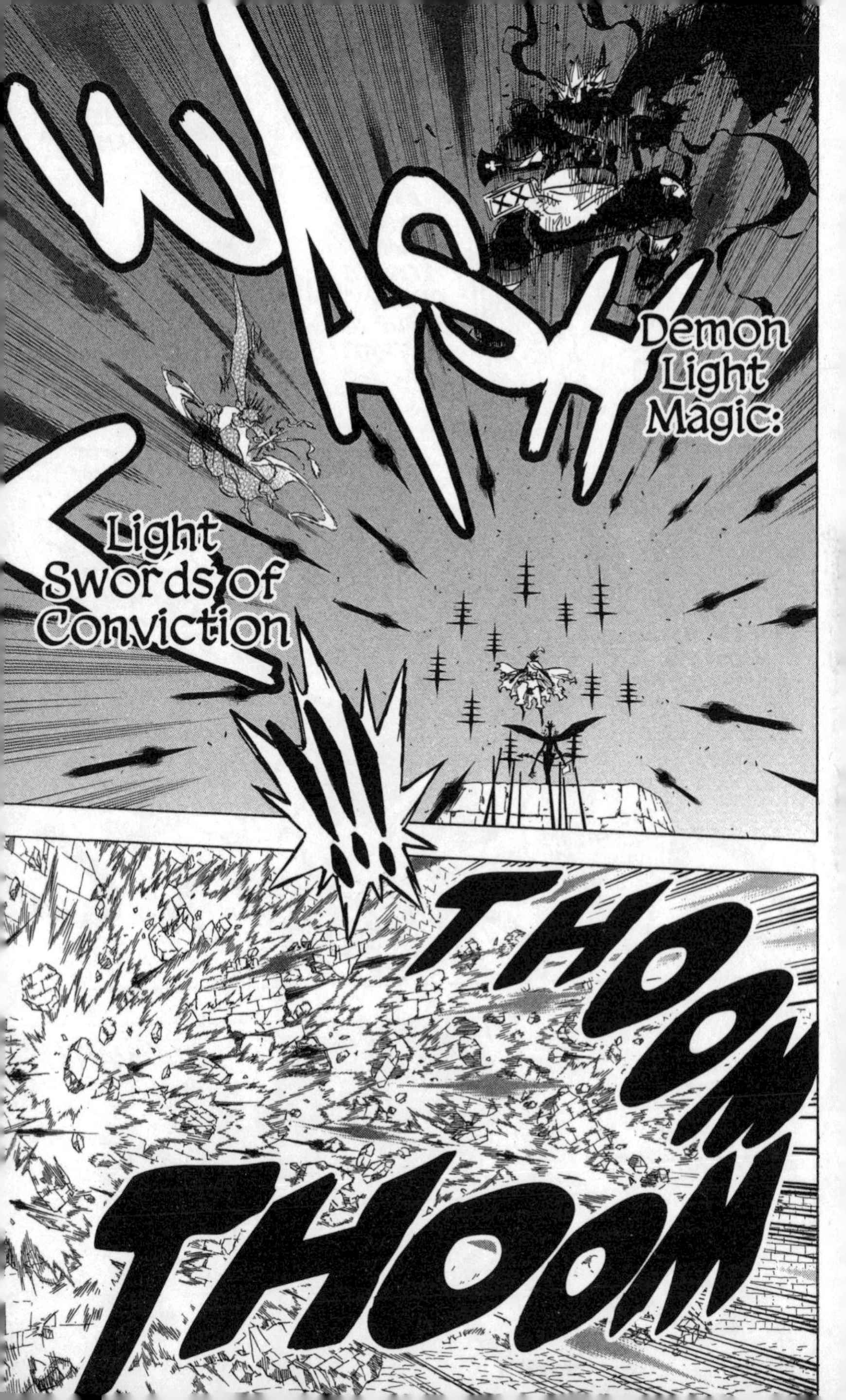
Demon Light Magic:
Light Swords of Conviction
THOOM
THOOM

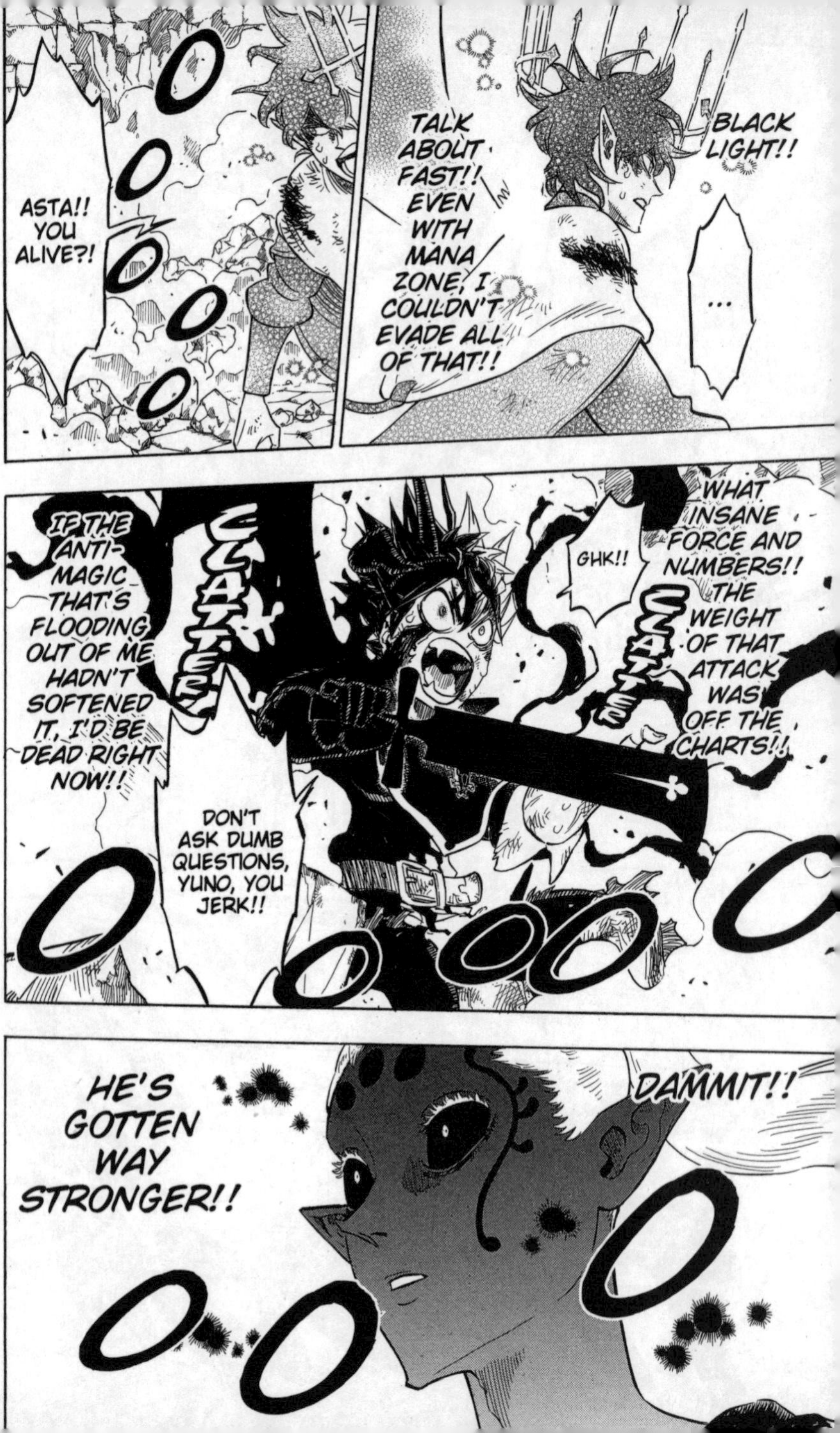
BLACK LIGHT!!
...
TALK ABOUT FAST!! EVEN WITH MANA ZONE, I COULDN'T EVADE ALL OF THAT!!
ASTA!! YOU ALIVE?!
WHAT INSANE FORCE AND NUMBERS!! THE WEIGHT OF THAT ATTACK WAS OFF THE CHARTS!!
GHK!!
CLATTER
CLATTER
IF THE ANTI-MAGIC THAT'S FLOODING OUT OF ME HADN'T SOFTENED IT, I'D BE DEAD RIGHT NOW!!
DON'T ASK DUMB QUESTIONS, YUNO, YOU JERK!!
DAMMIT!!
HE'S GOTTEN WAY STRONGER!!

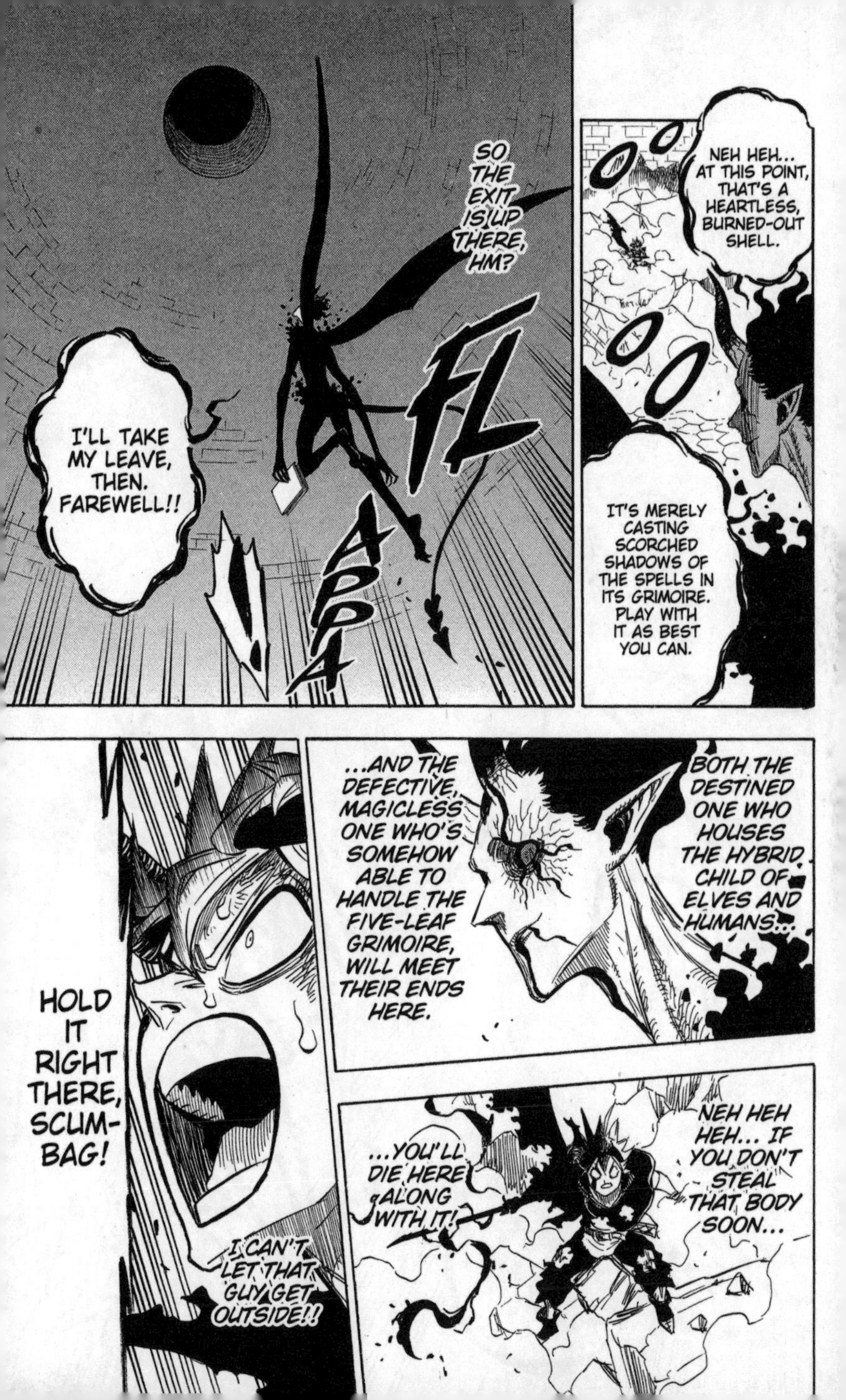
NEH HEH... AT THIS POINT, THAT'S A HEARTLESS, BURNED-OUT SHELL.
IT'S MERELY CASTING SCORCHED SHADOWS OF THE SPELLS IN ITS GRIMOIRE. PLAY WITH IT AS BEST YOU CAN.
SO THE EXIT IS UP THERE, HM?
FLAPPA
I'LL TAKE MY LEAVE, THEN. FAREWELL!!
!
BOTH THE DESTINED ONE WHO HOUSES THE HYBRID CHILD OF ELVES AND HUMANS...
...AND THE DEFECTIVE, MAGICLESS ONE WHO'S SOMEHOW ABLE TO HANDLE THE FIVE-LEAF GRIMOIRE, WILL MEET THEIR ENDS HERE.
NEH HEH HEH... IF YOU DON'T STEAL THAT BODY SOON...
...YOU'LL DIE HERE ALONG WITH IT!
HOLD IT RIGHT THERE, SCUM-BAG!
I CAN'T LET THAT GUY GET OUTSIDE!!

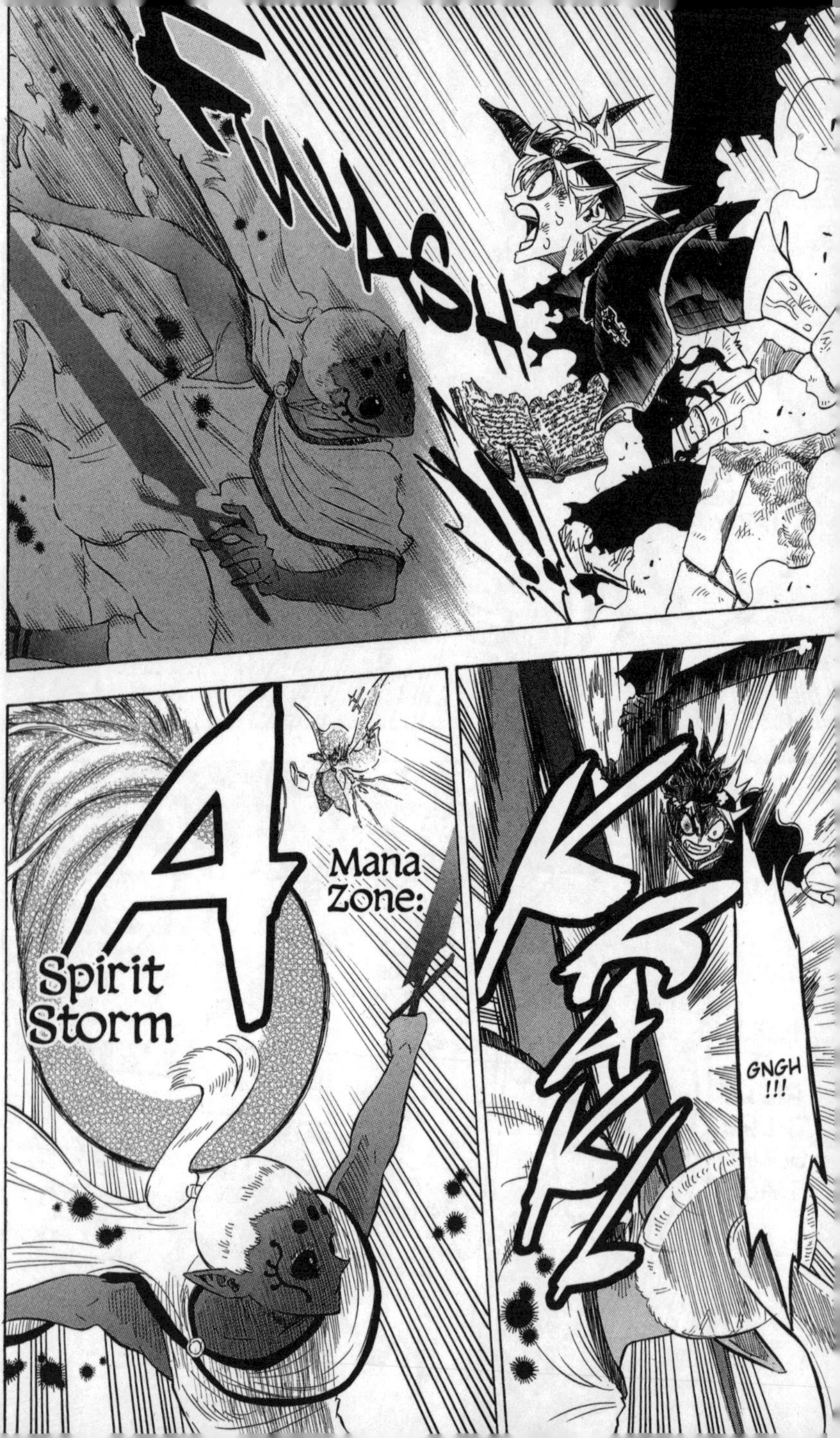
KWASH!!!
GNGH!!!
Mana Zone:
Spirit Storm

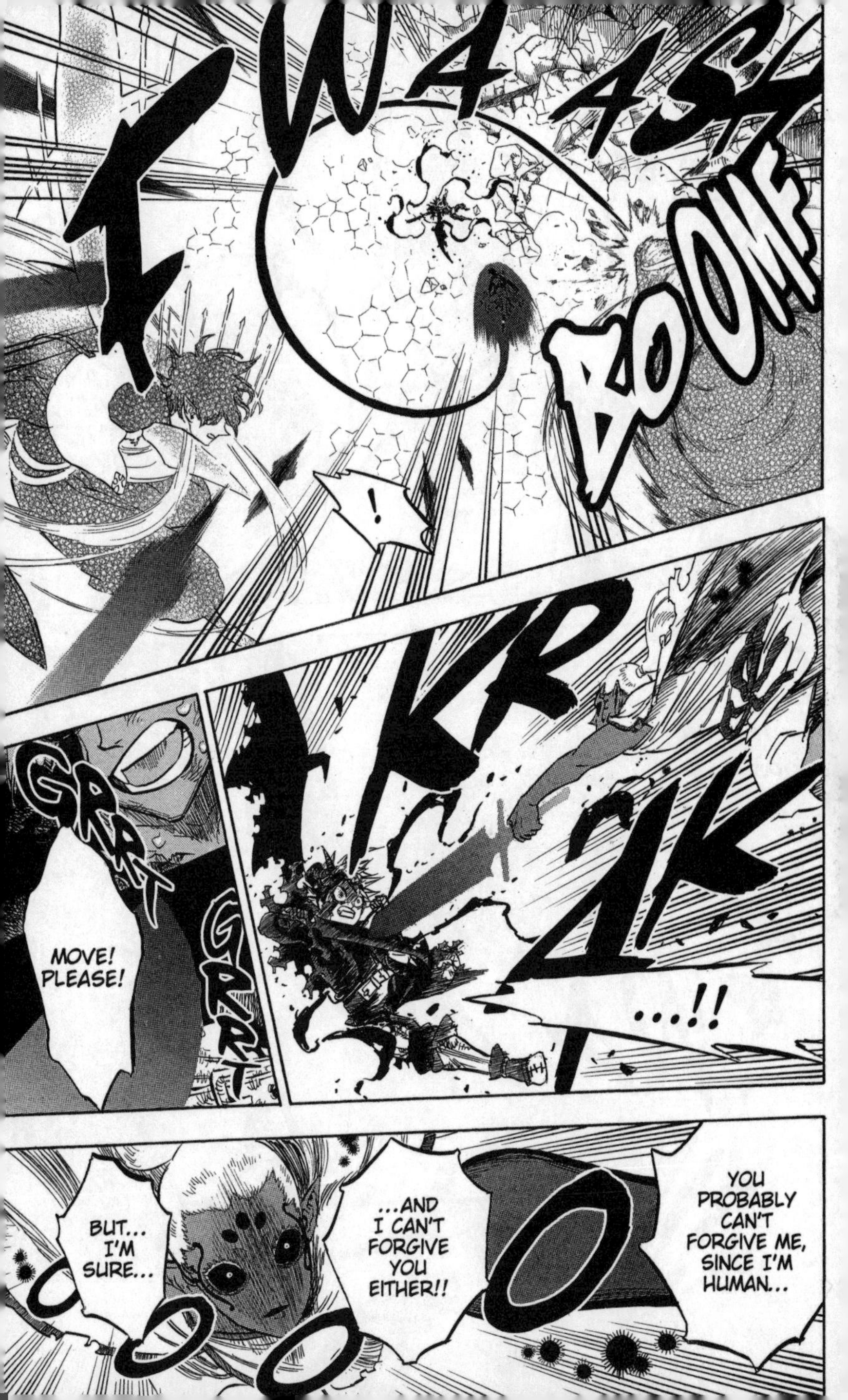
FWASH
BOOMF
!
KRAK
...!!
GRRRT
GRRRT
MOVE! PLEASE!
YOU PROBABLY CAN'T FORGIVE ME, SINCE I'M HUMAN...
...AND I CAN'T FORGIVE YOU EITHER!!
BUT... I'M SURE...

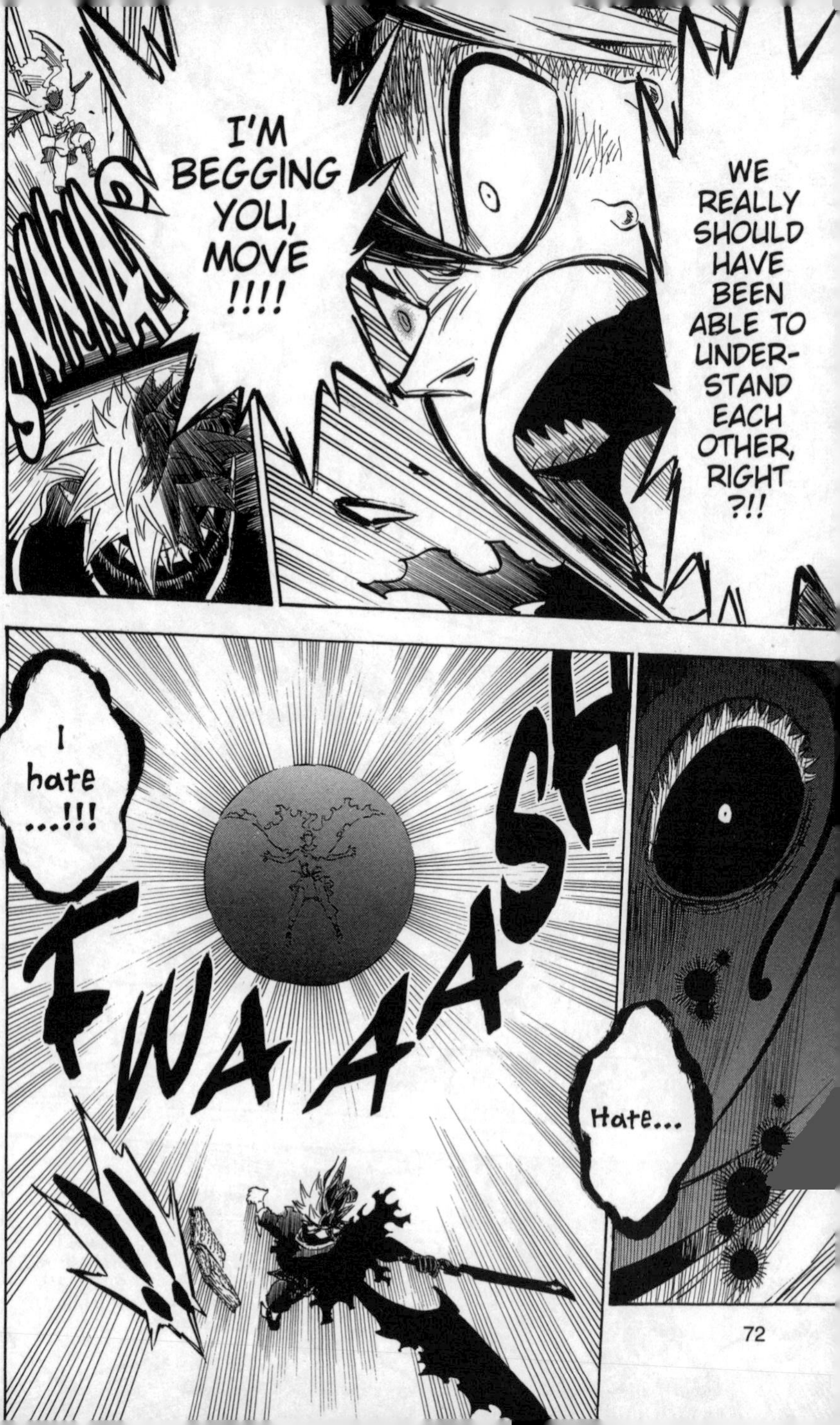
WE REALLY SHOULD HAVE BEEN ABLE TO UNDER-STAND EACH OTHER, RIGHT ?!!
I'M BEGGING YOU, MOVE !!!!
Hate...
I hate ...!!!
FWAASH

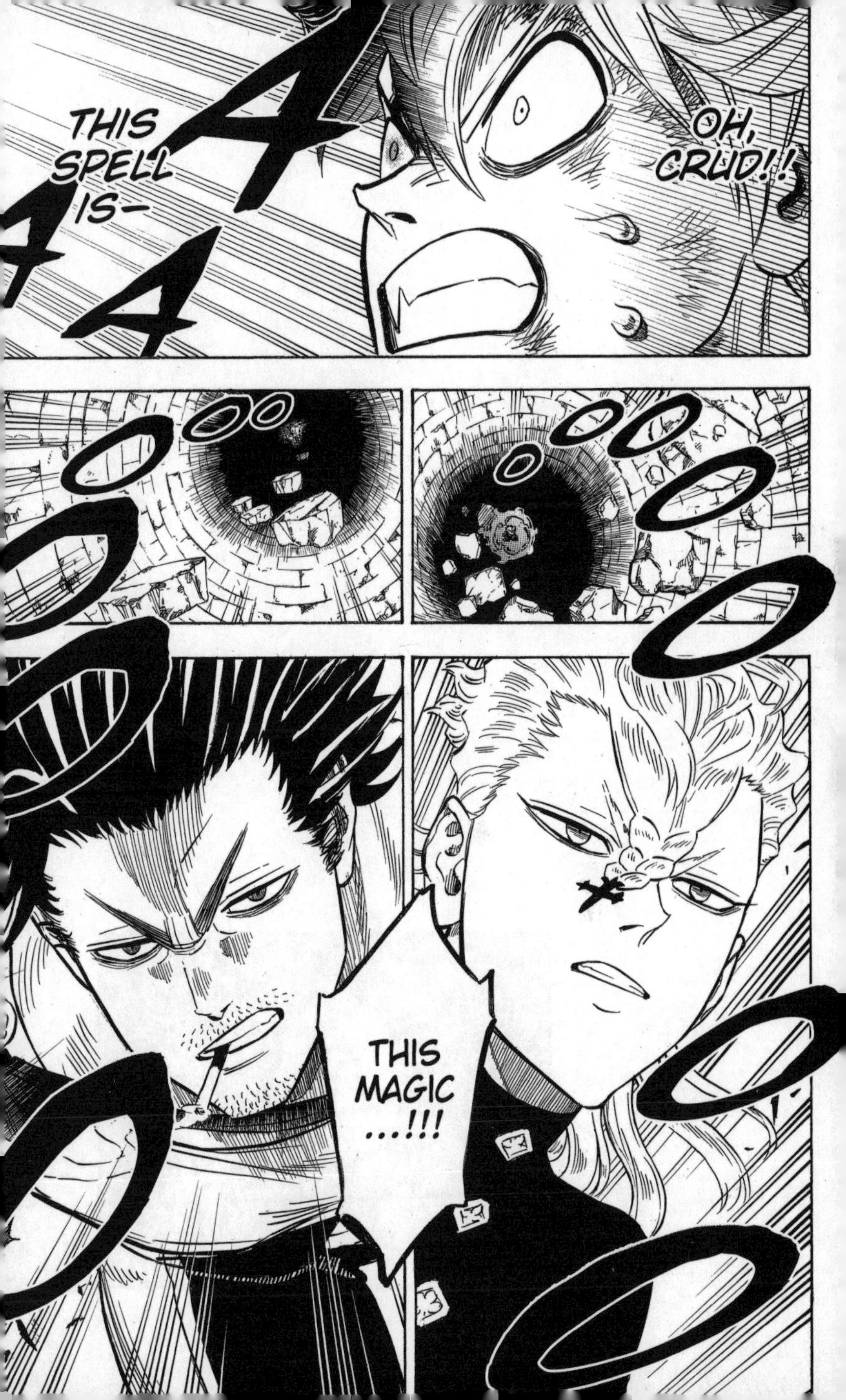
OH, CRUD!!
THIS SPELL IS–
THIS MAGIC ...!!!

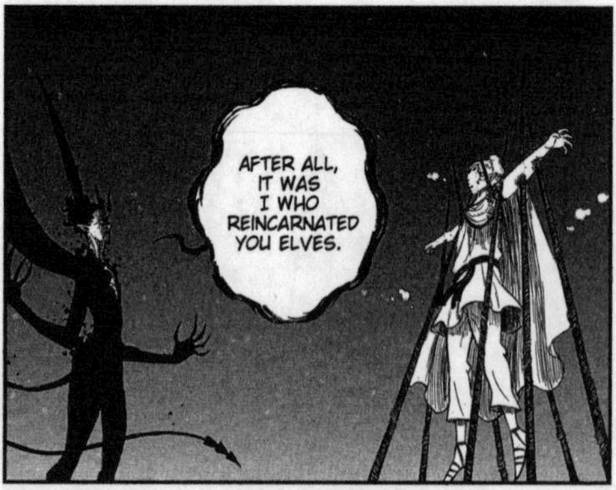
AFTER ALL, IT WAS I WHO REINCARNATED YOU ELVES.

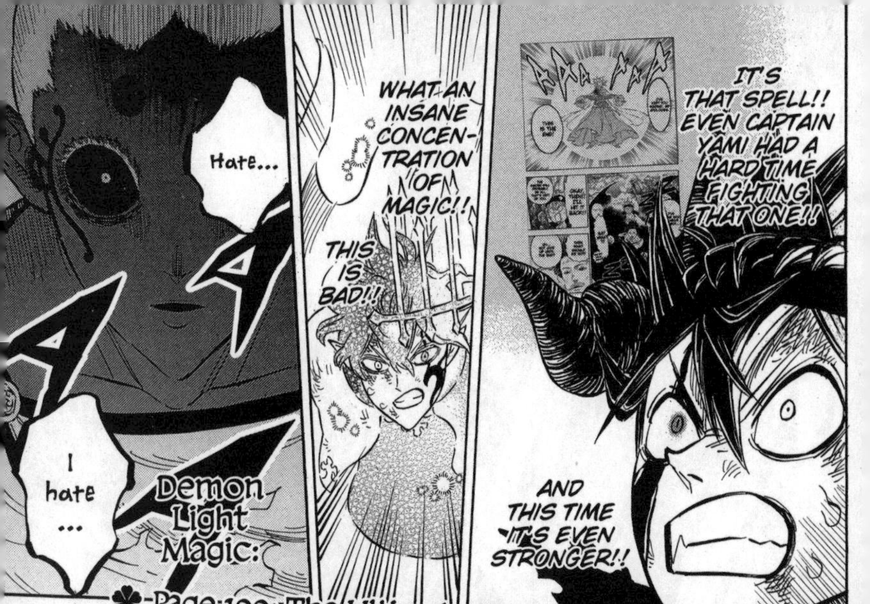
IT'S THAT SPELL!! EVEN CAPTAIN YAMI HAD A HARD TIME FIGHTING THAT ONE!!
AND THIS TIME IT'S EVEN STRONGER!!
WHAT AN INSANE CONCENTRATION OF MAGIC!!
THIS IS BAD!!
Hate...
I hate...
Demon Light Magic:

Page 199: The Ultimate Natural Enemy

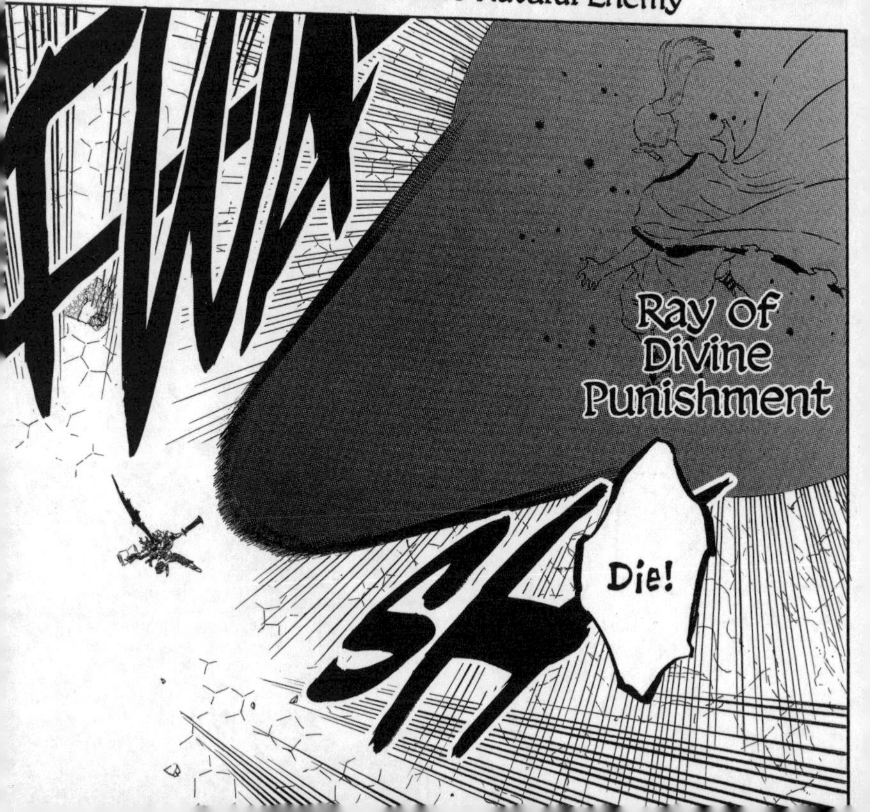
Ray of Divine Punishment
Die!

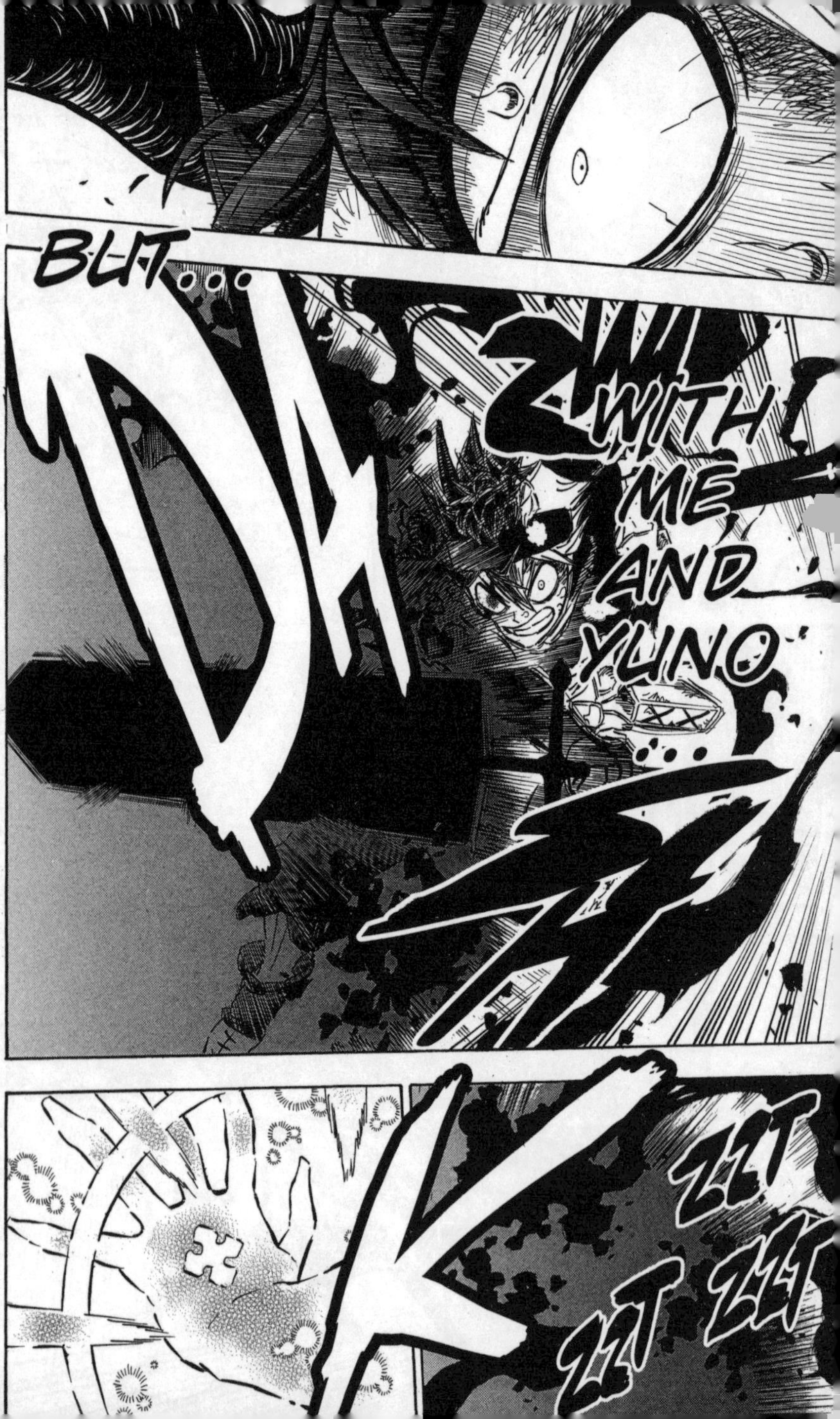
BUT...
WITH ME AND YUNO...
ZZT
ZZT ZZT

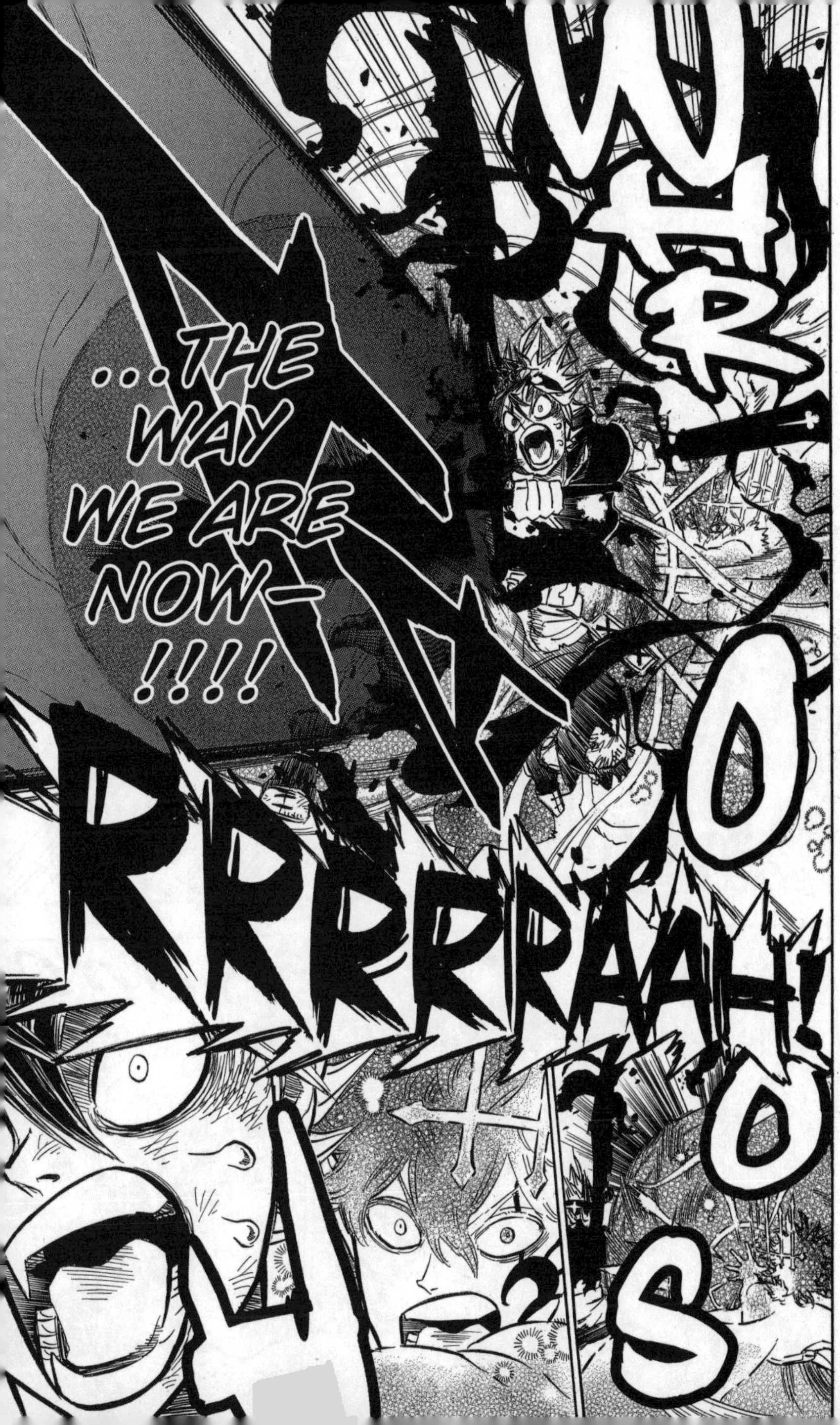

...THE WAY WE ARE NOW-!!!!
RRRRRAAH!

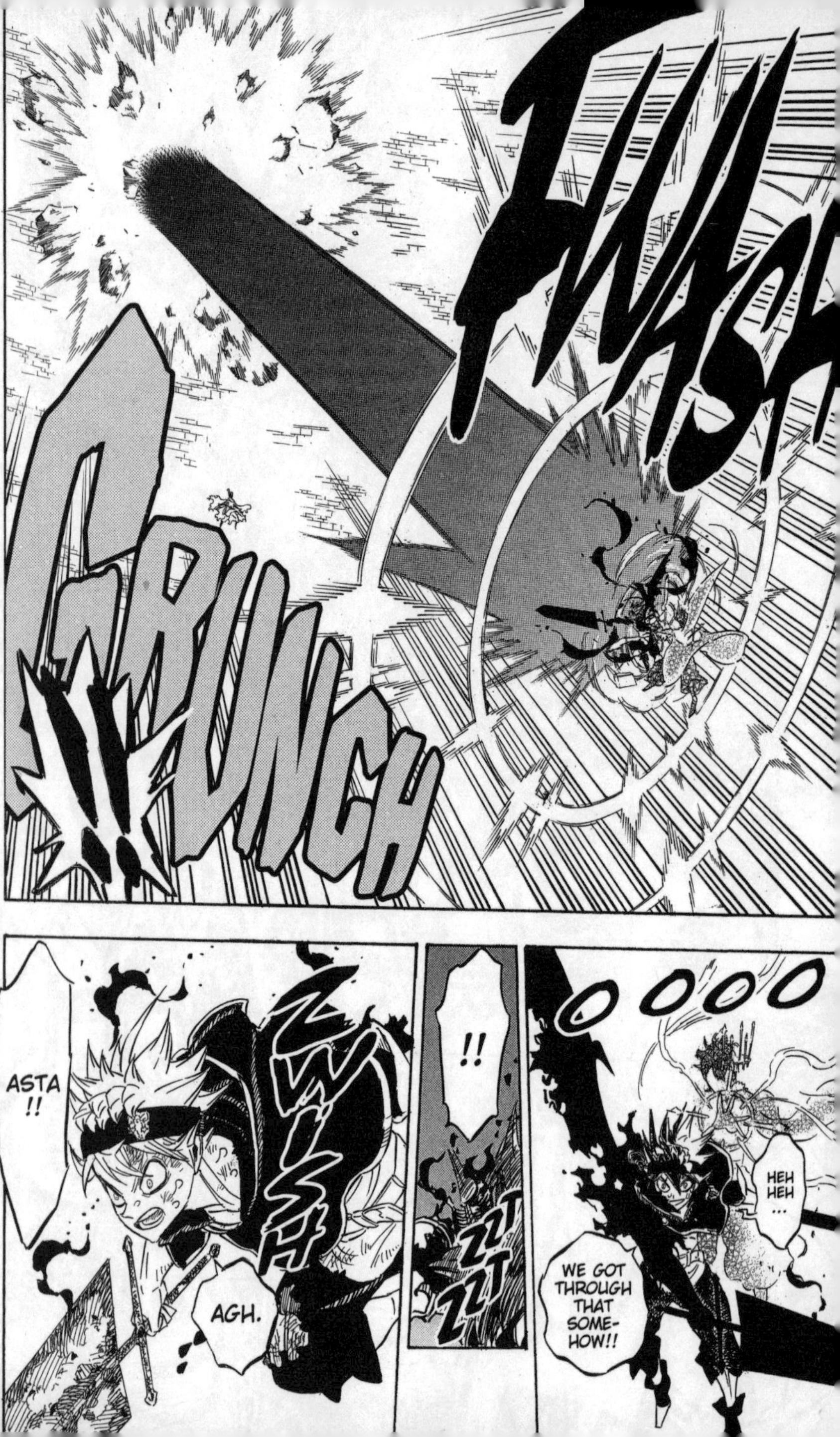
FWASH
CRUNCH
OOOO
HEH HEH ...
WE GOT THROUGH THAT SOME-HOW!!
!!
ASTA !!
AGH.

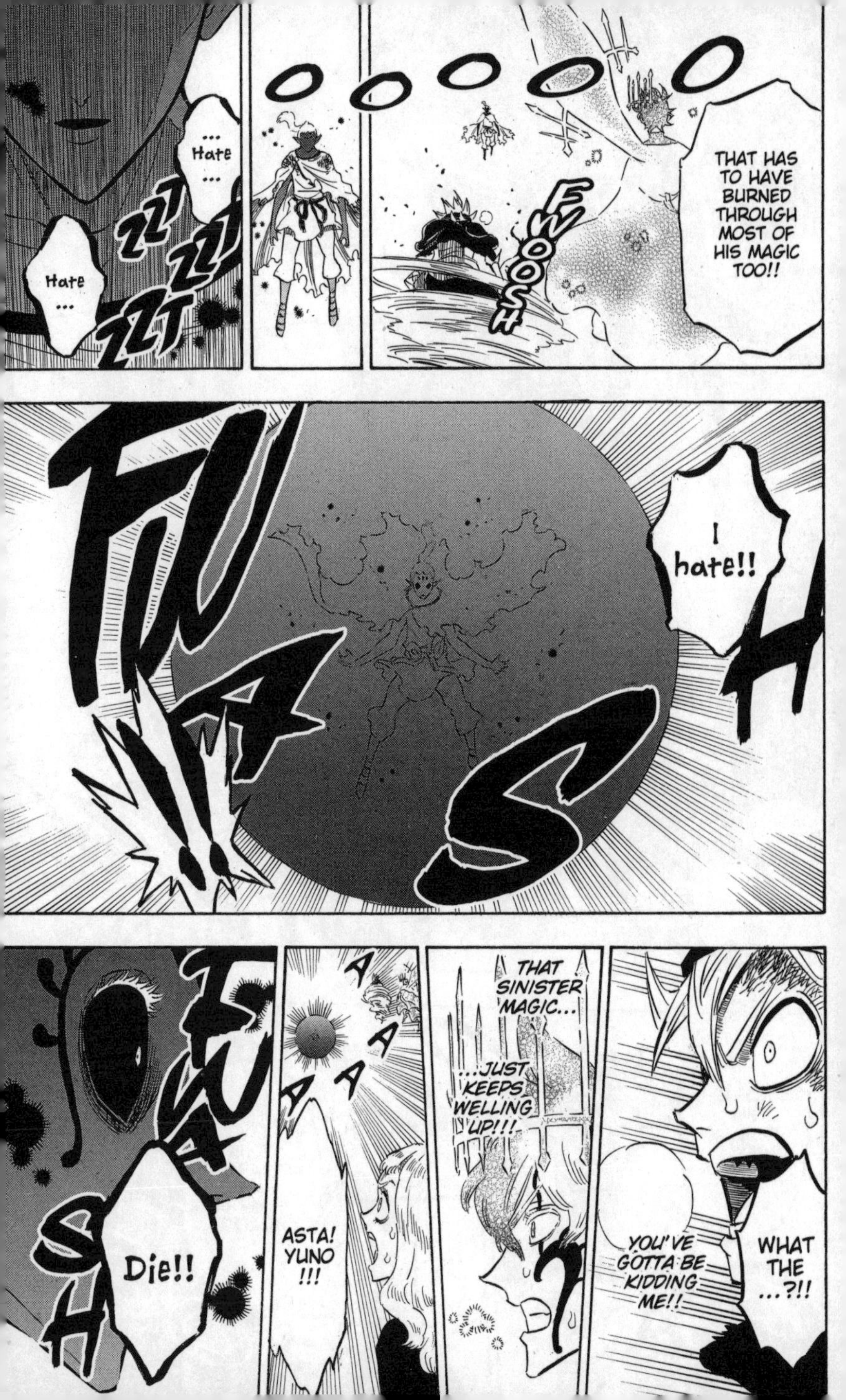
OOOOOO
THAT HAS TO HAVE BURNED THROUGH MOST OF HIS MAGIC TOO!!
FWOOSH
... Hate ...
Hate ...
ZZZT ZZZT ZZZT
I hate!!
FWASH
WHAT THE ...?!!
YOU'VE GOTTA BE KIDDING ME!!
THAT SINISTER MAGIC...
...JUST KEEPS WELLING UP!!!
AAAAA
ASTA! YUNO !!!
FWASH
Die!!

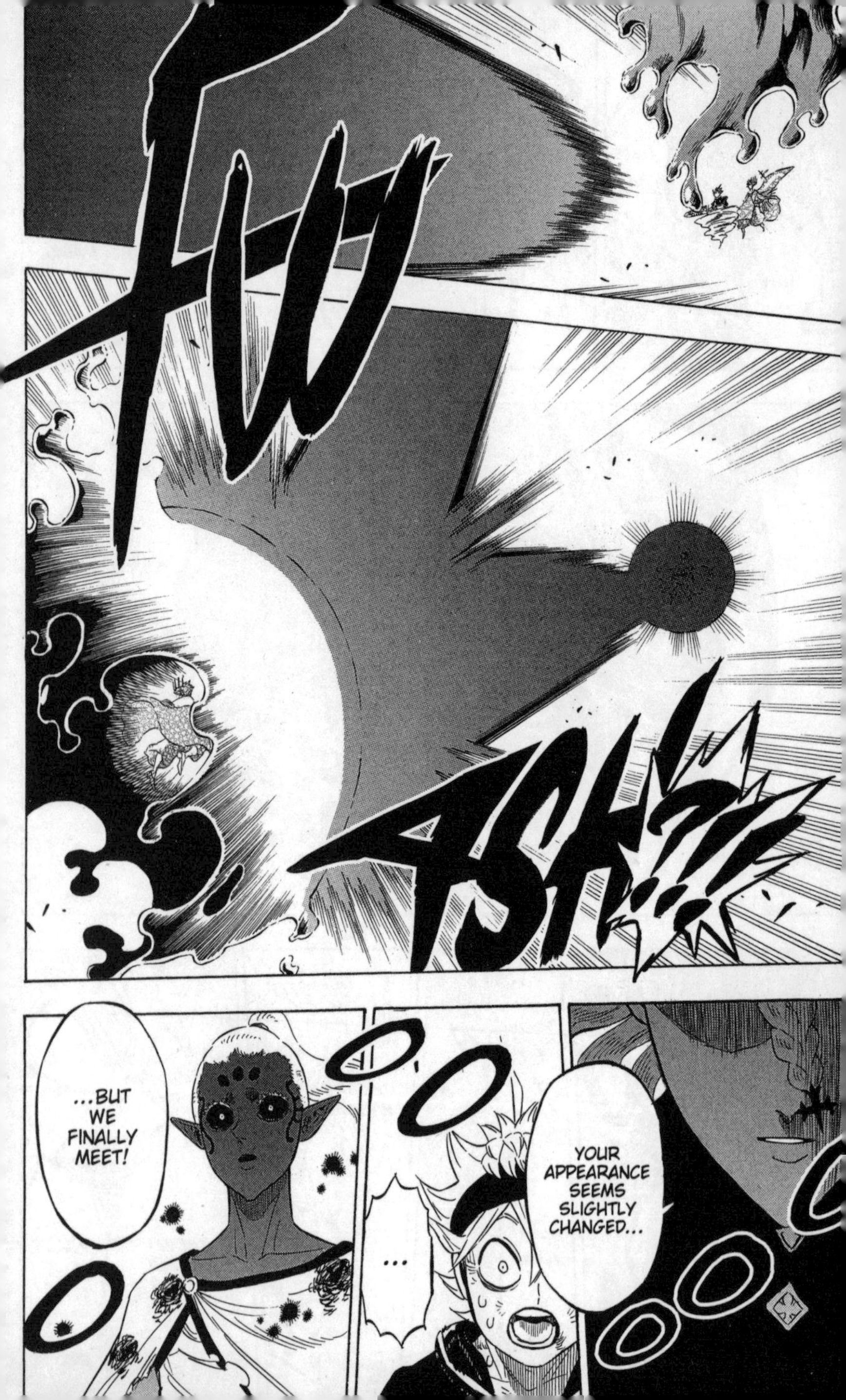
YOUR APPEARANCE SEEMS SLIGHTLY CHANGED...
...
...BUT WE FINALLY MEET!

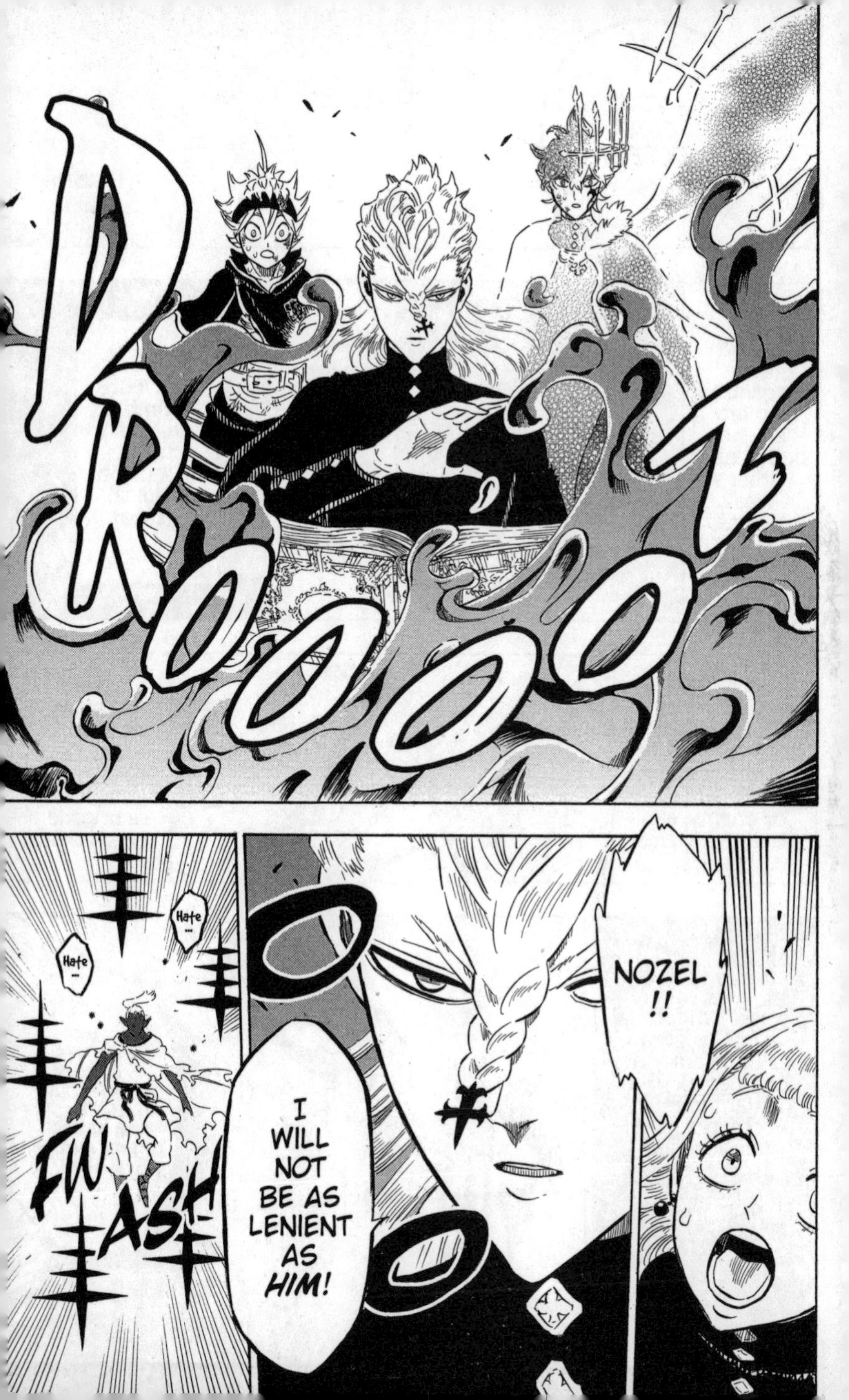
NOZEL!!
I WILL NOT BE AS LENIENT AS HIM!
Hate...
Hate...
FWASH

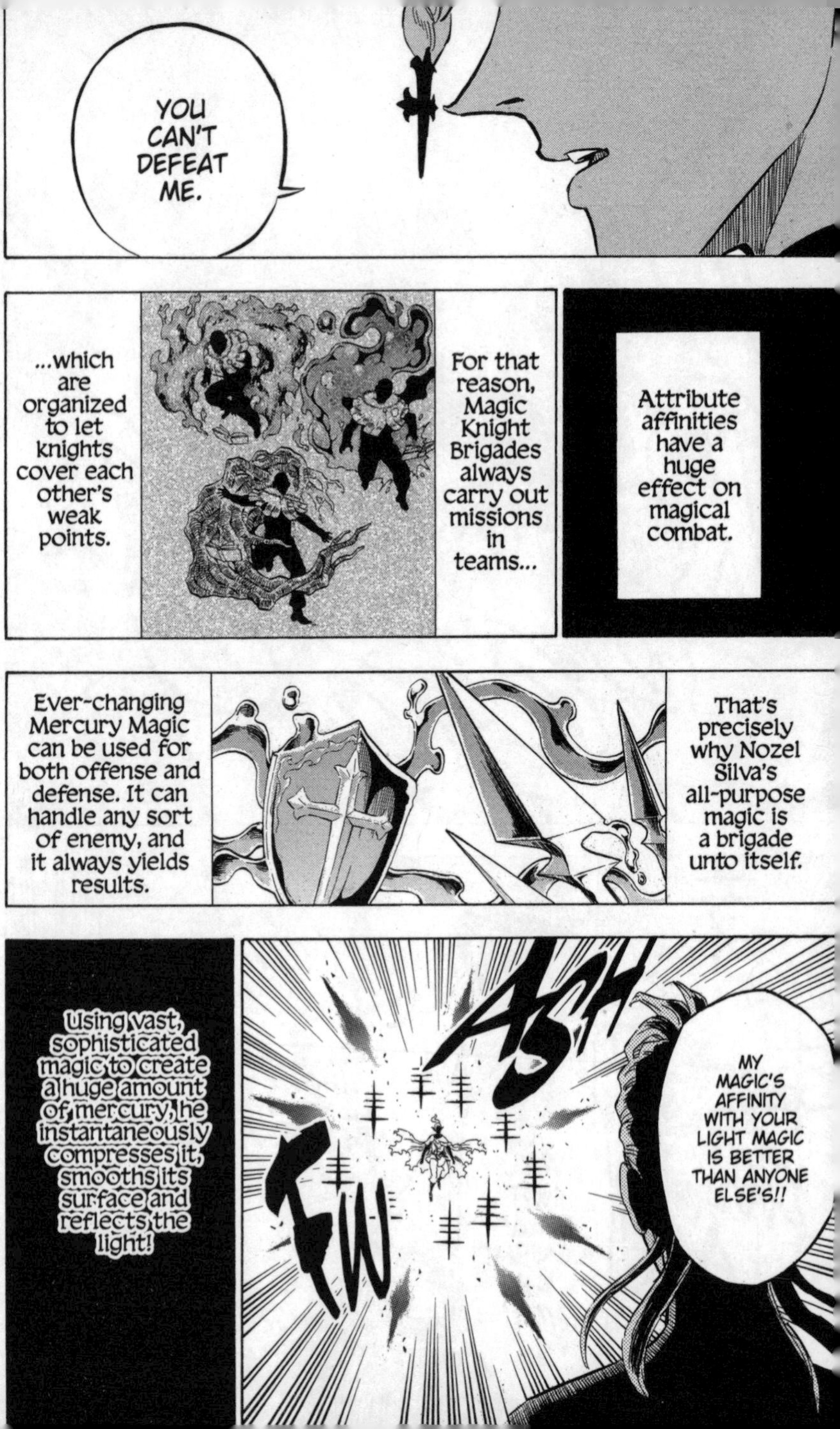
YOU CAN'T DEFEAT ME.
Attribute affinities have a huge effect on magical combat.
For that reason, Magic Knight Brigades always carry out missions in teams...
...which are organized to let knights cover each other's weak points.
That's precisely why Nozel Silva's all-purpose magic is a brigade unto itself.
Ever-changing Mercury Magic can be used for both offense and defense. It can handle any sort of enemy, and it always yields results.
FW
ASH
MY MAGIC'S AFFINITY WITH YOUR LIGHT MAGIC IS BETTER THAN ANYONE ELSE'S!!
Using vast, sophisticated magic to create a huge amount of mercury, he instantaneously compresses it, smooths its surface and reflects the light!

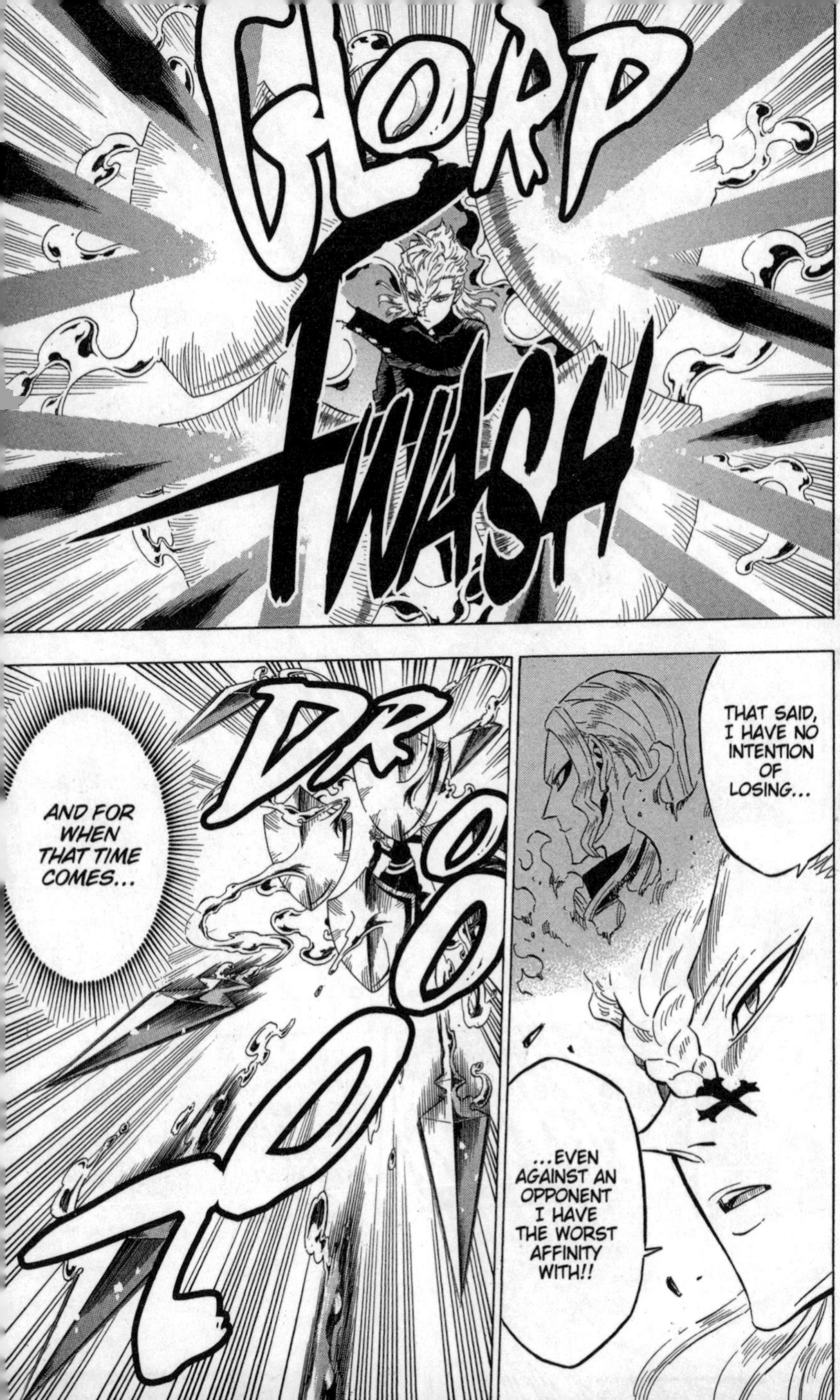
GLORP
FWASH
THAT SAID, I HAVE NO INTENTION OF LOSING...
...EVEN AGAINST AN OPPONENT I HAVE THE WORST AFFINITY WITH!!
AND FOR WHEN THAT TIME COMES...

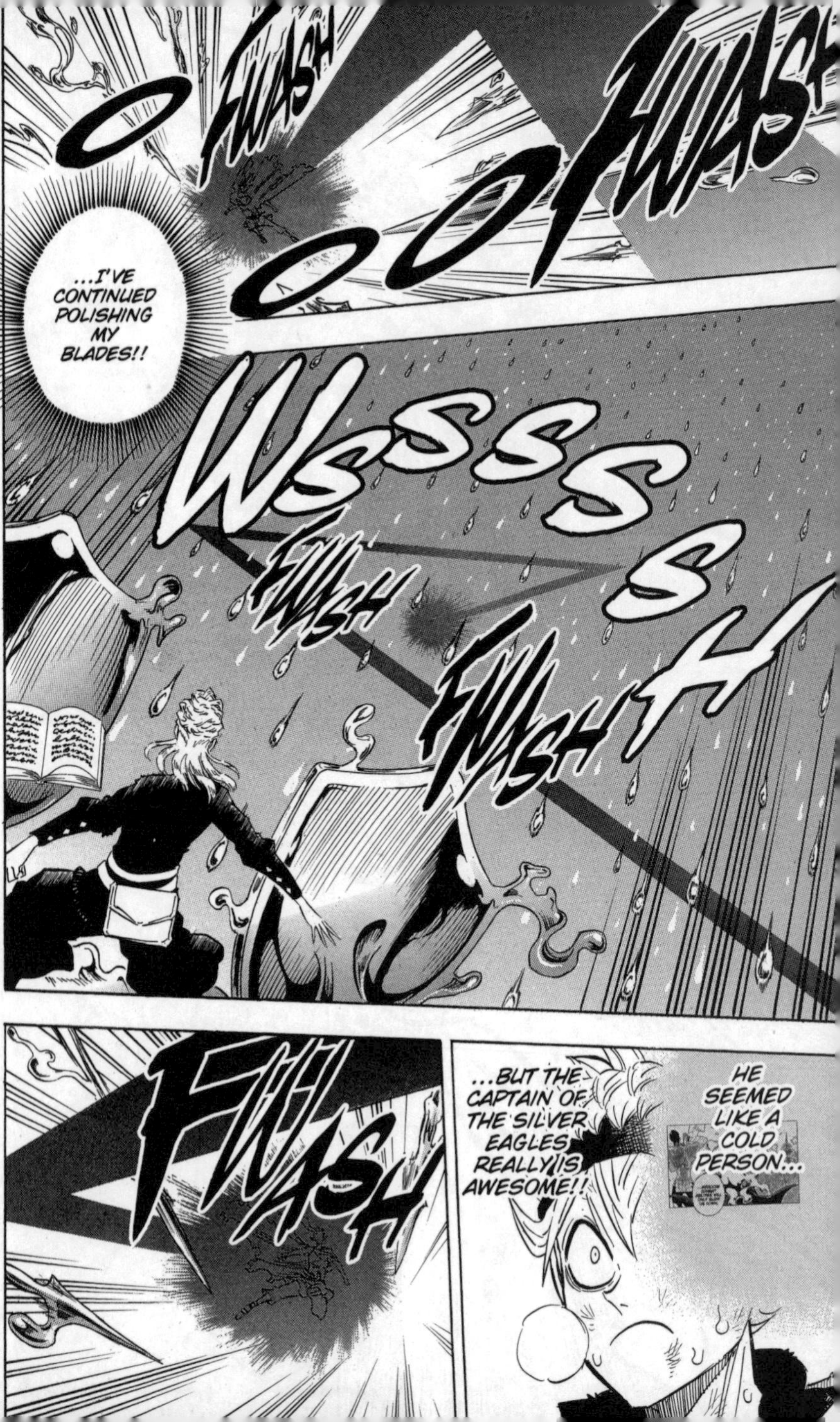
FWASH
FWASH
...I'VE CONTINUED POLISHING MY BLADES!!
WSSSSSH
FWASH
FWASH
HE SEEMED LIKE A COLD PERSON...
...BUT THE CAPTAIN OF THE SILVER EAGLES REALLY IS AWESOME!!
FWASH

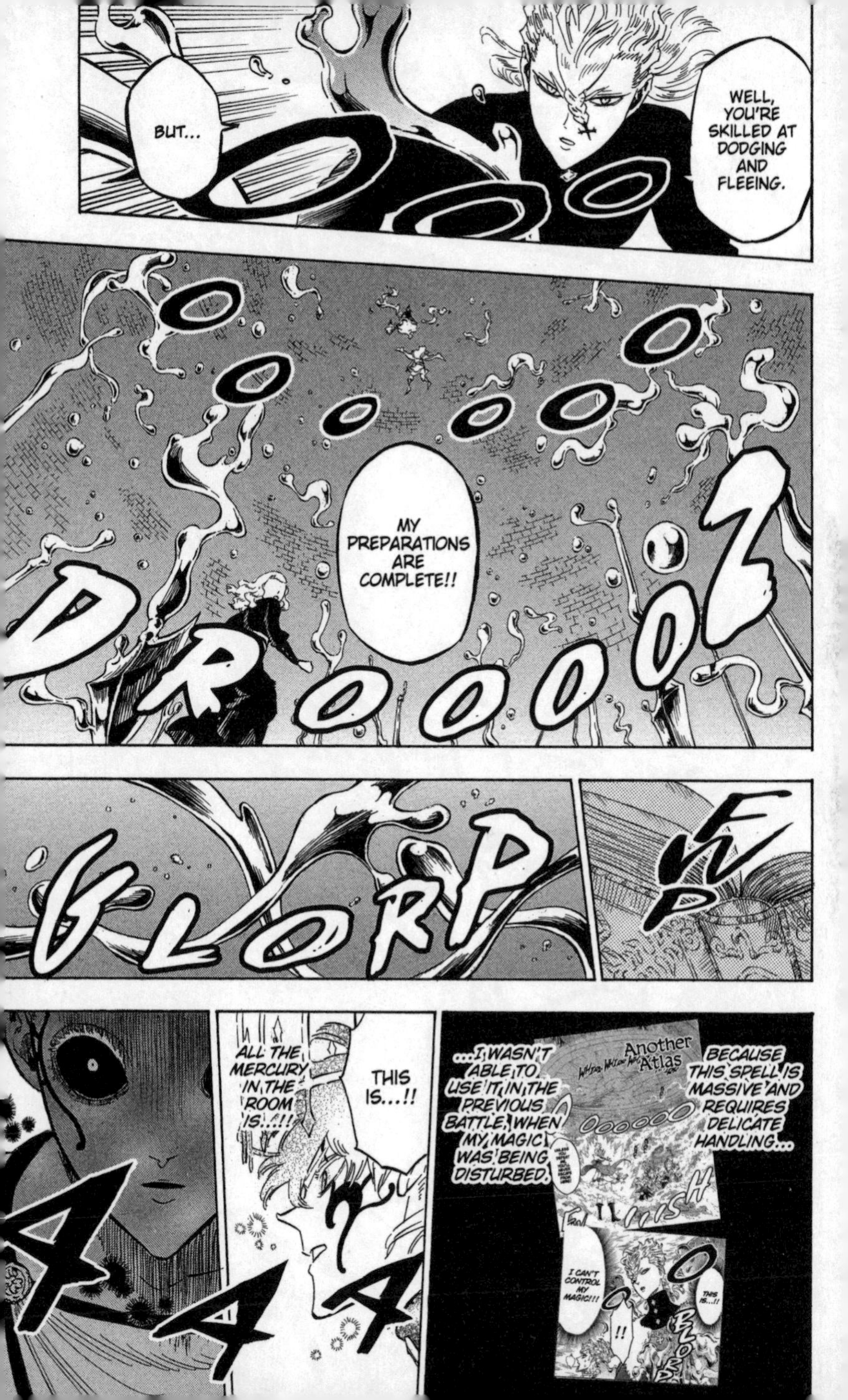
WELL, YOU'RE SKILLED AT DODGING AND FLEEING.
BUT...
MY PREPARATIONS ARE COMPLETE!!
GLORP
BECAUSE THIS SPELL IS MASSIVE AND REQUIRES DELICATE HANDLING...
...I WASN'T ABLE TO USE IT IN THE PREVIOUS BATTLE, WHEN MY MAGIC WAS BEING DISTURBED.
Another Atlas
THIS IS...!!
I CAN'T CONTROL MY MAGIC!!!
!!
THIS IS...!!
ALL THE MERCURY IN THE ROOM IS...!!

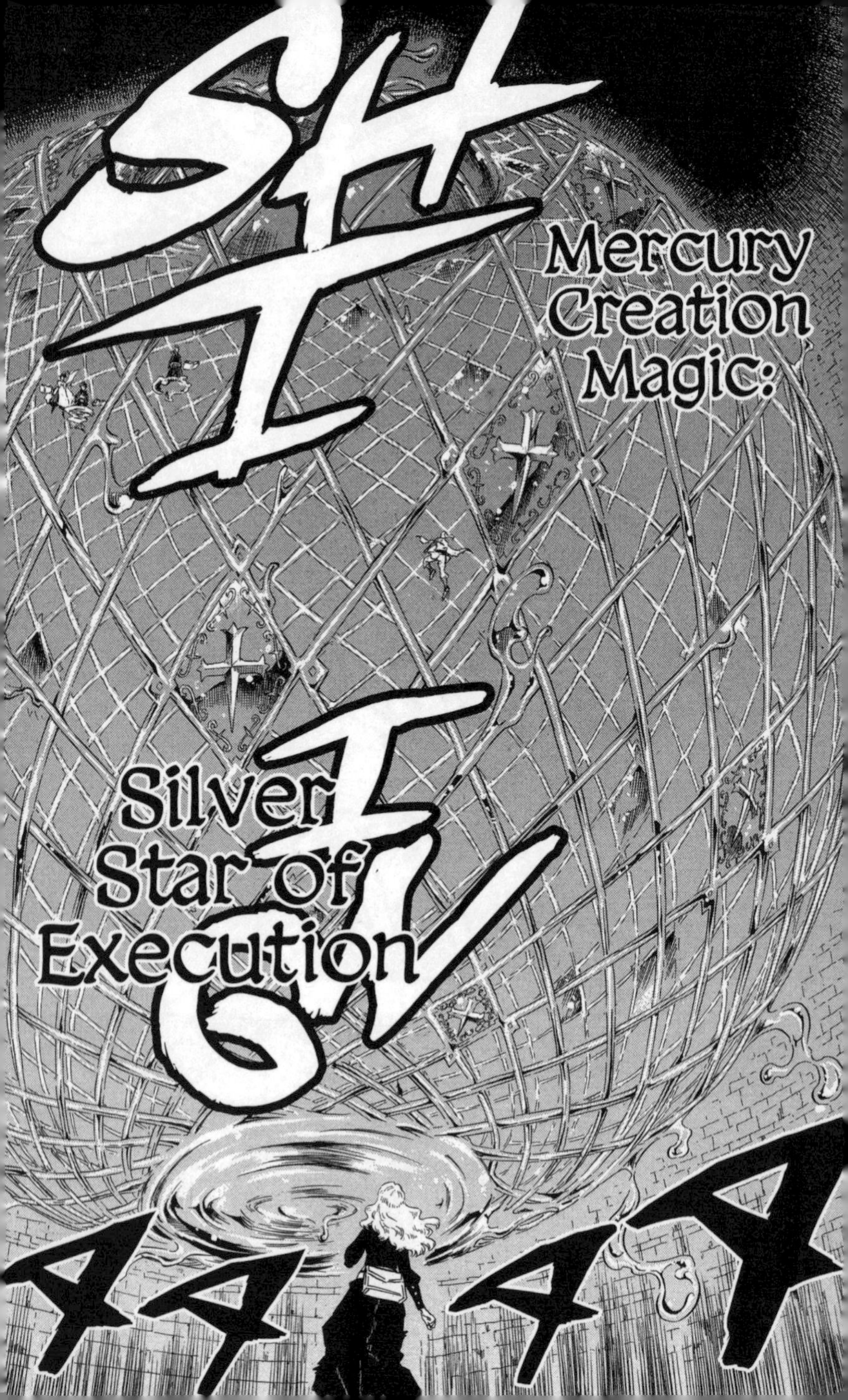
Mercury Creation Magic:
Silver Star of Execution

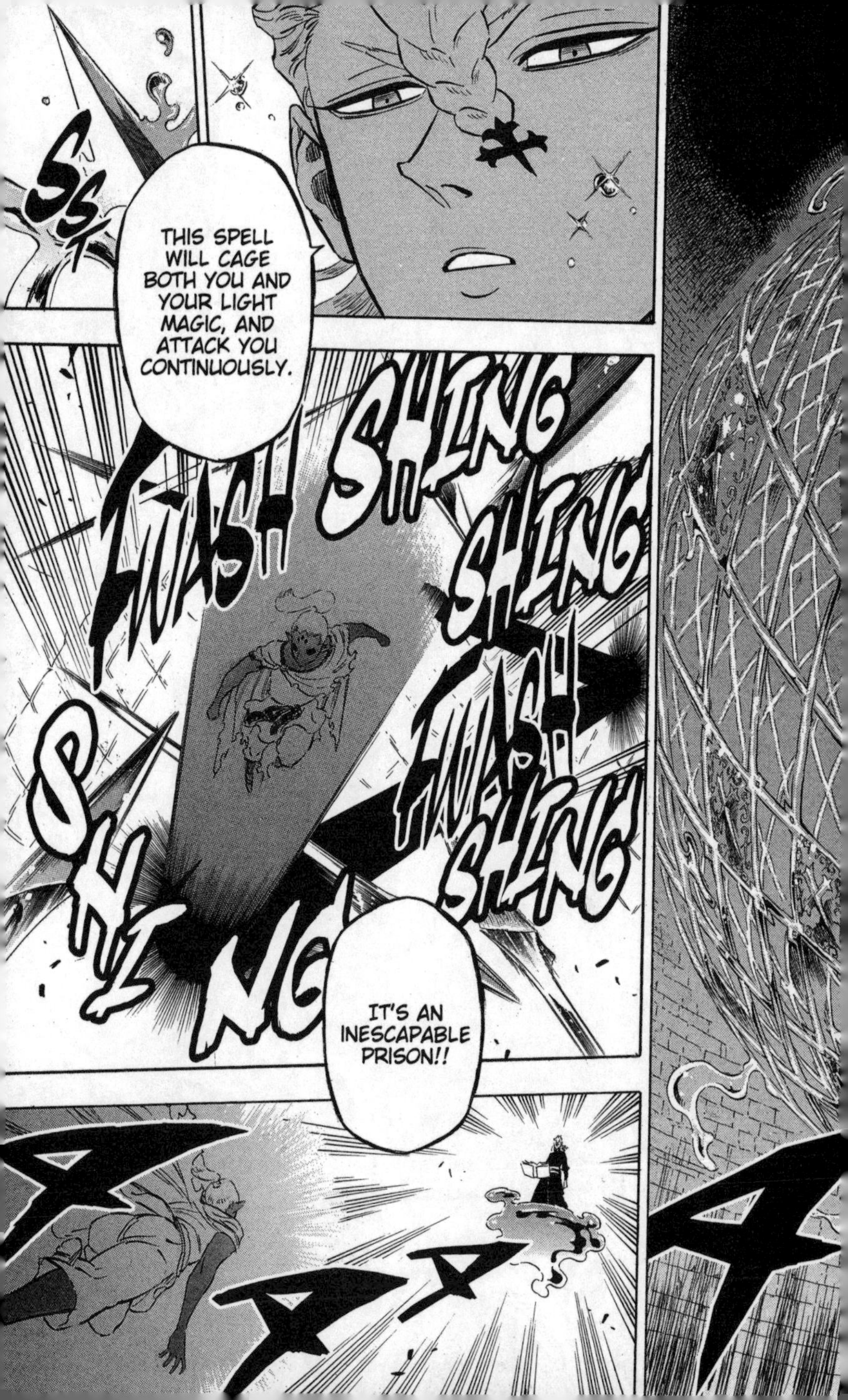
THIS SPELL WILL CAGE BOTH YOU AND YOUR LIGHT MAGIC, AND ATTACK YOU CONTINUOUSLY.
SHING
SHING
FWASH
SHING
FWASH
SHING
IT'S AN INESCAPABLE PRISON!!

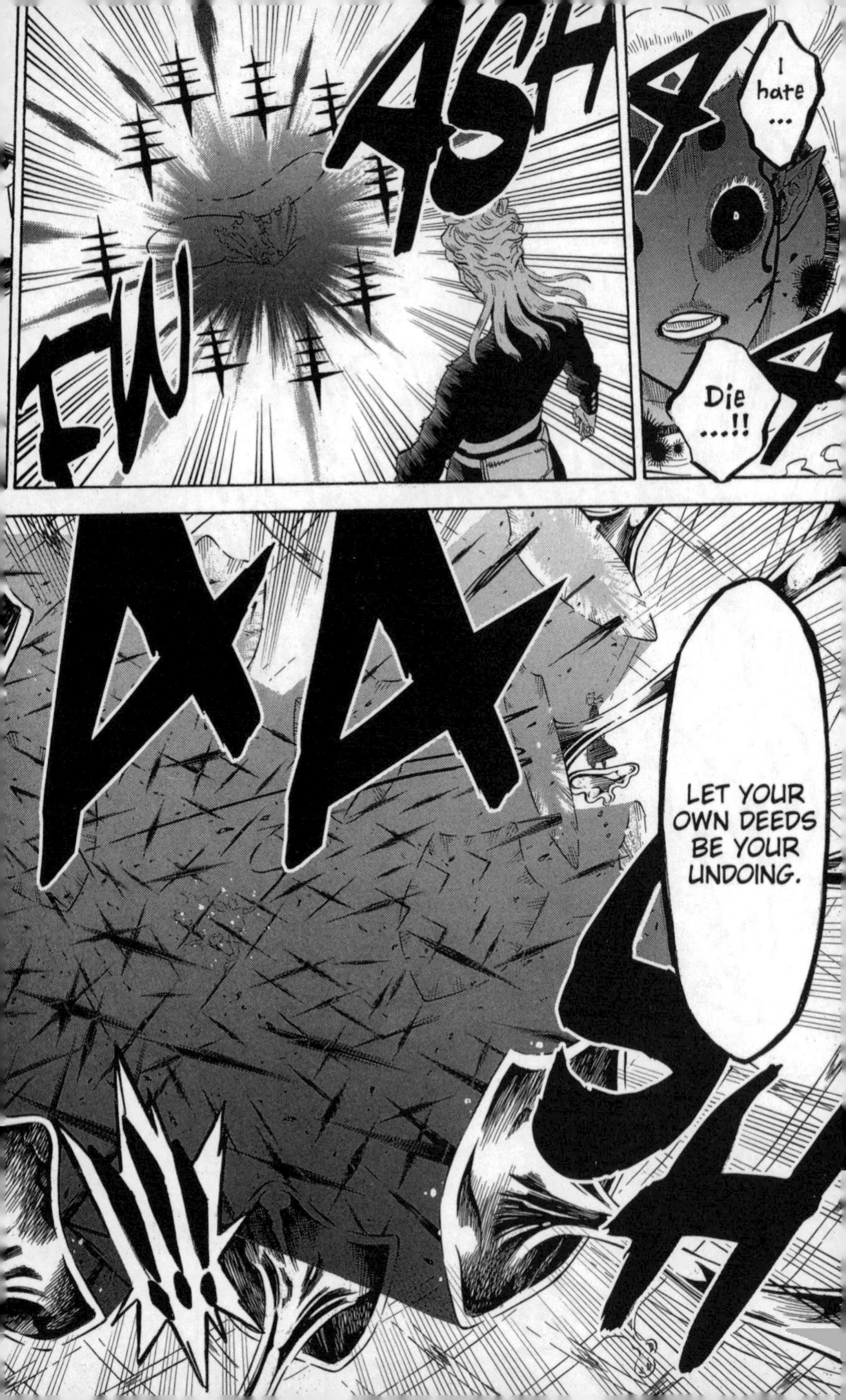
I hate ...
Die ...!!
LET YOUR OWN DEEDS BE YOUR UNDOING.

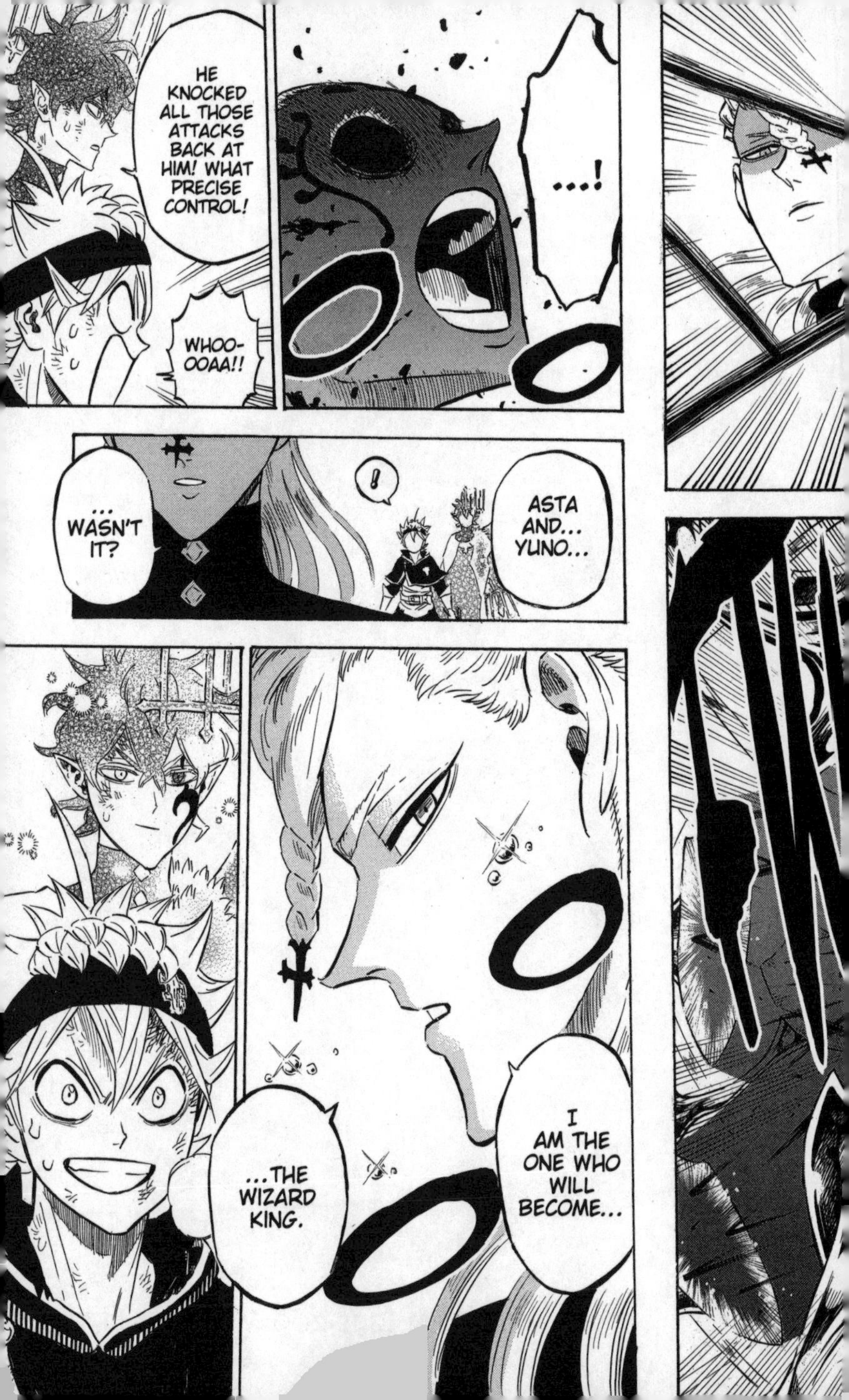
...!
HE KNOCKED ALL THOSE ATTACKS BACK AT HIM! WHAT PRECISE CONTROL!
WHOO-OOAA!!
ASTA AND... YUNO...
!
... WASN'T IT?
I AM THE ONE WHO WILL BECOME...
...THE WIZARD KING.

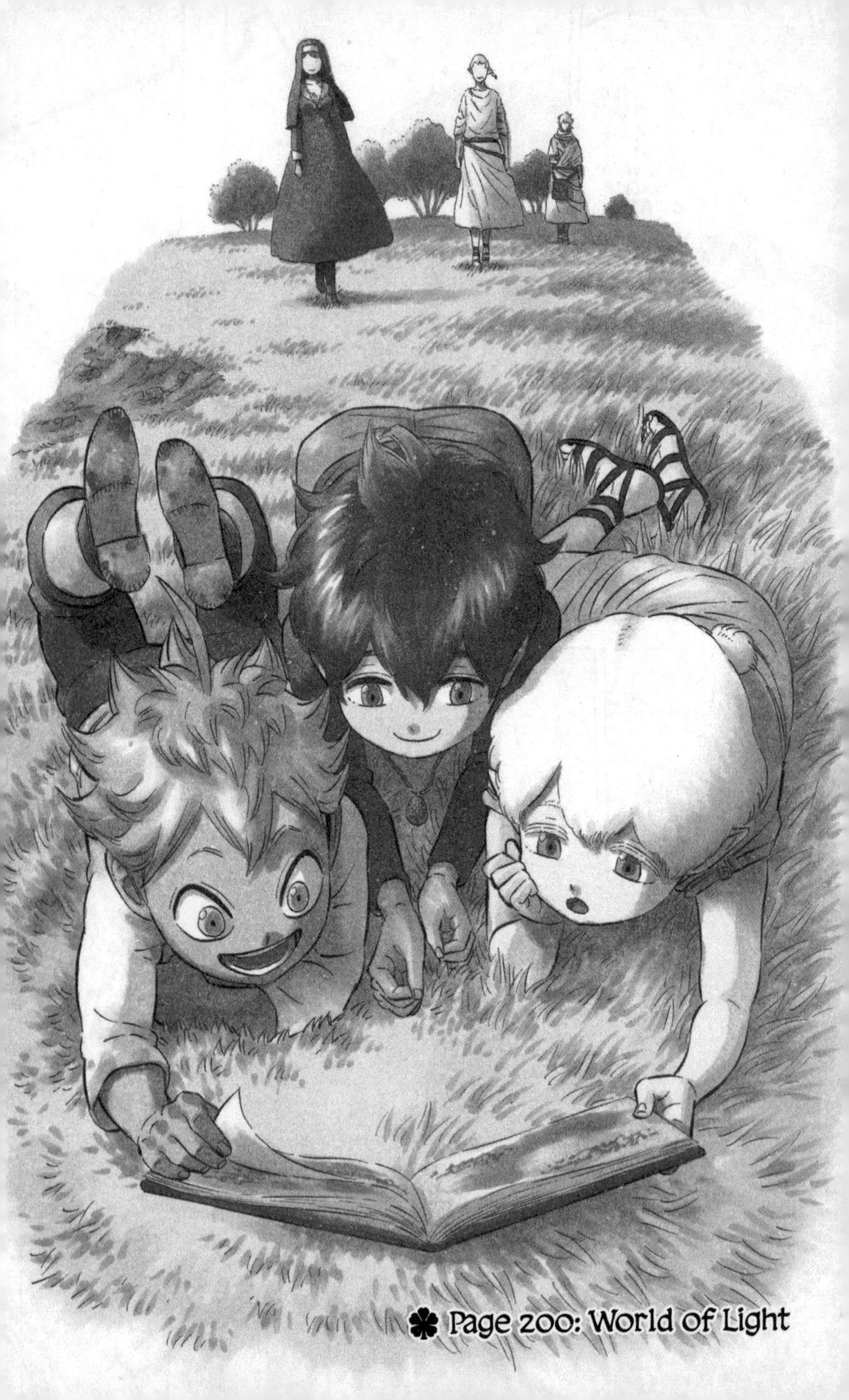
Page 200: World of Light

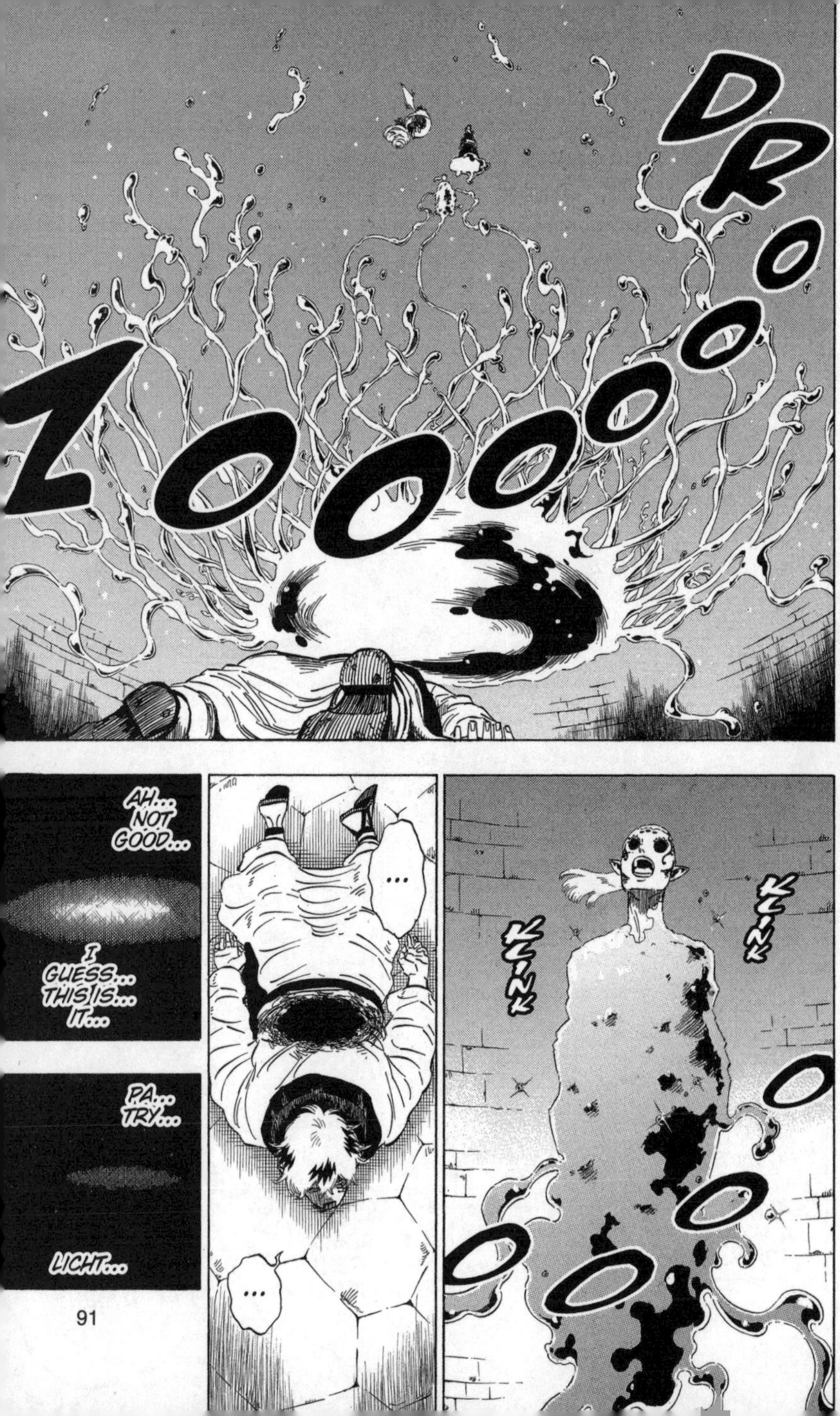
DROOOO
ZOOOOO
KLINK
KLINK
OOOOO
...
...
AH... NOT GOOD...
I GUESS... THIS IS... IT...
PA... TRY...
LICHT...

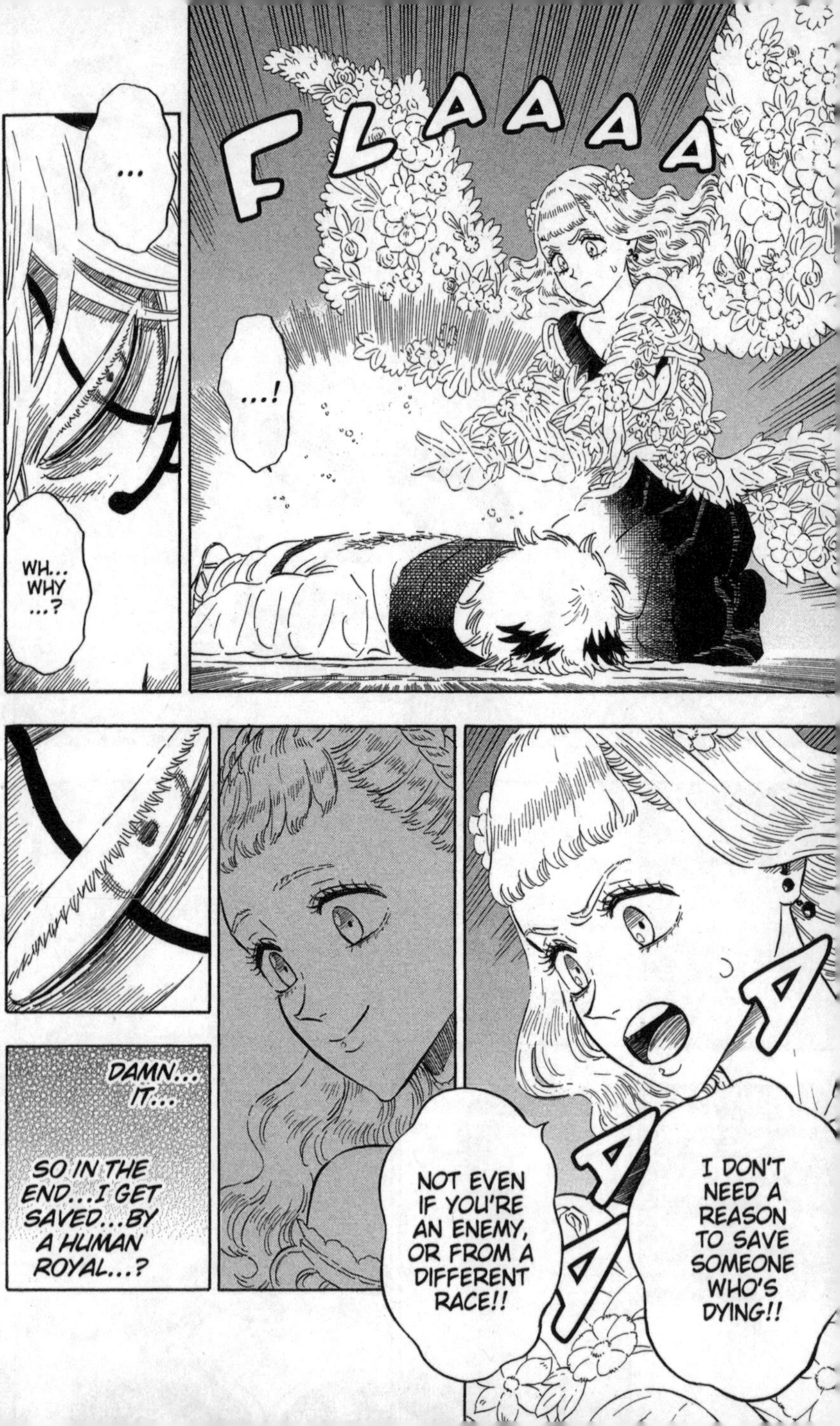
FLAAAA
...!
...
WH... WHY ...?
I DON'T NEED A REASON TO SAVE SOMEONE WHO'S DYING!!
NOT EVEN IF YOU'RE AN ENEMY, OR FROM A DIFFERENT RACE!!
DAMN... IT...
SO IN THE END...I GET SAVED...BY A HUMAN ROYAL...?

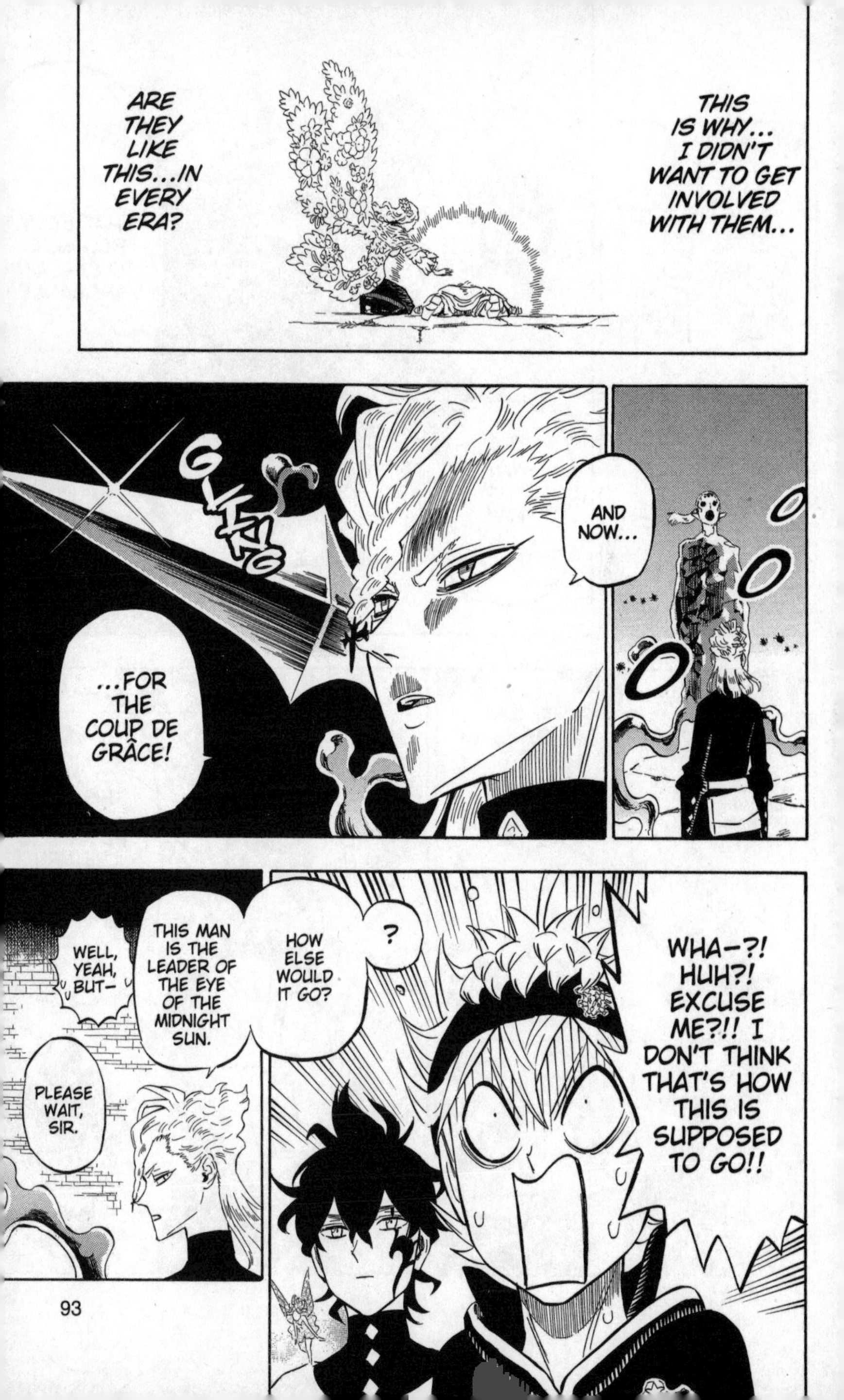
THIS IS WHY... I DIDN'T WANT TO GET INVOLVED WITH THEM...
ARE THEY LIKE THIS...IN EVERY ERA?
AND NOW...
GLING
...FOR THE COUP DE GRÂCE!
WHA-?! HUH?! EXCUSE ME?!! I DON'T THINK THAT'S HOW THIS IS SUPPOSED TO GO!!
?
HOW ELSE WOULD IT GO?
THIS MAN IS THE LEADER OF THE EYE OF THE MIDNIGHT SUN.
WELL, YEAH, BUT-
PLEASE WAIT, SIR.

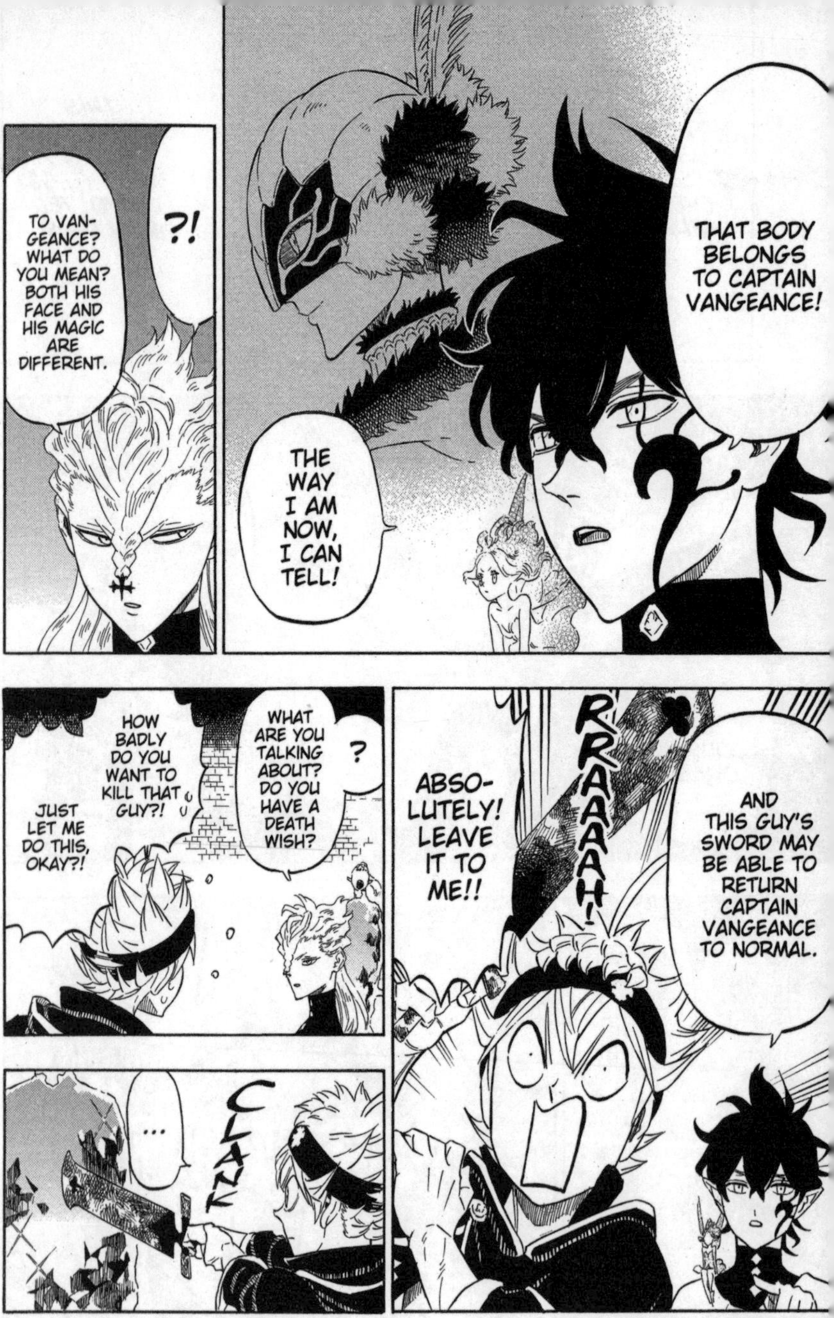
THAT BODY BELONGS TO CAPTAIN VANGEANCE!
THE WAY I AM NOW, I CAN TELL!
?!
TO VAN- GEANCE? WHAT DO YOU MEAN? BOTH HIS FACE AND HIS MAGIC ARE DIFFERENT.
AND THIS GUY'S SWORD MAY BE ABLE TO RETURN CAPTAIN VANGEANCE TO NORMAL.
RRAAAAH!
ABSO- LUTELY! LEAVE IT TO ME!!
?
WHAT ARE YOU TALKING ABOUT? DO YOU HAVE A DEATH WISH?
HOW BADLY DO YOU WANT TO KILL THAT GUY?!
JUST LET ME DO THIS, OKAY?!
CLANK
...

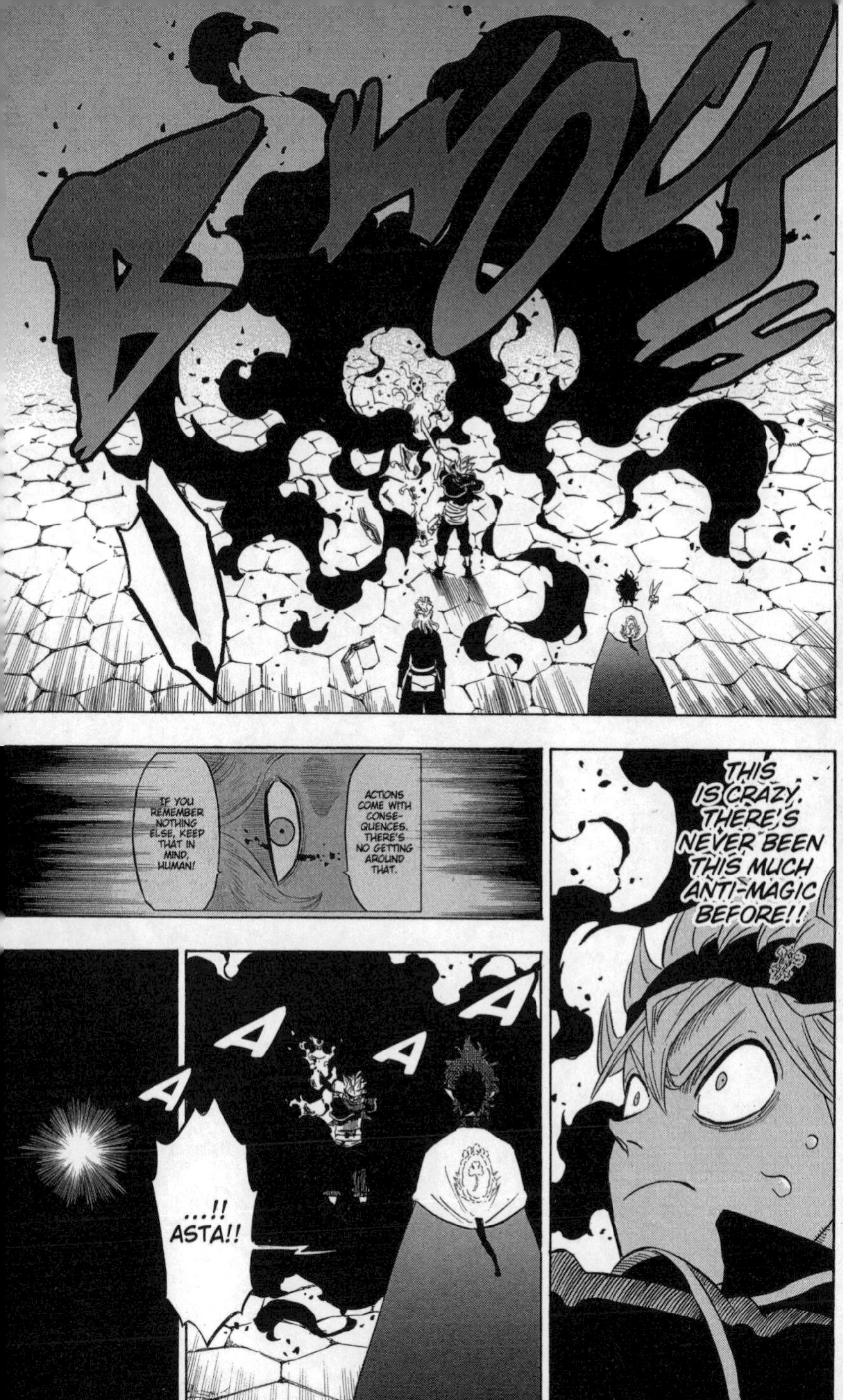

THIS IS CRAZY. THERE'S NEVER BEEN THIS MUCH ANTI-MAGIC BEFORE!!
ACTIONS COME WITH CONSE-QUENCES. THERE'S NO GETTING AROUND THAT.
IF YOU REMEMBER NOTHING ELSE, KEEP THAT IN MIND, HUMAN!
AAAAA
...!! ASTA!!

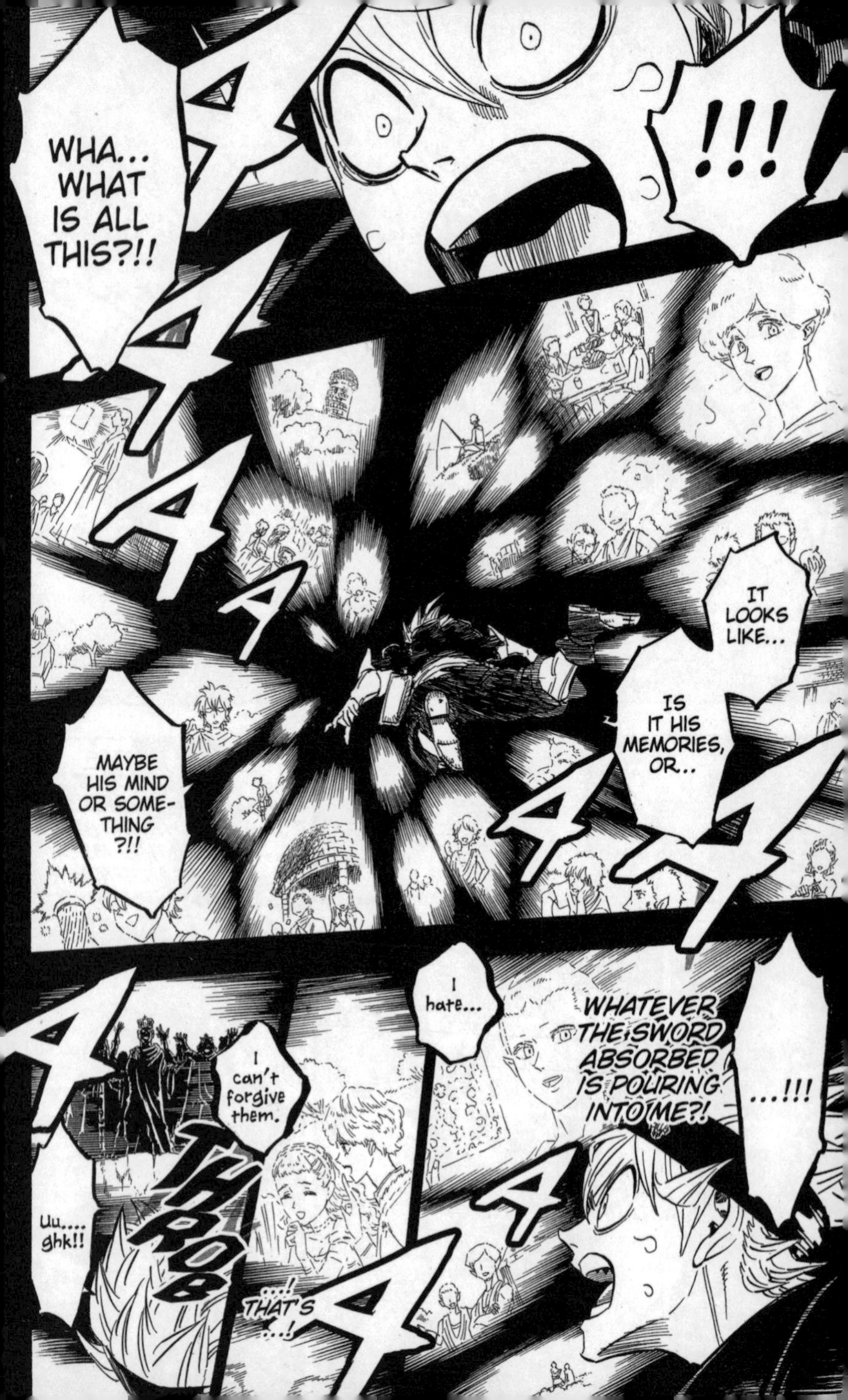
!!!
WHA... WHAT IS ALL THIS?!!
IT LOOKS LIKE...
IS IT HIS MEMORIES, OR..
MAYBE HIS MIND OR SOME-THING ?!!
...!!!
WHATEVER THE SWORD ABSORBED IS POURING INTO ME?!
I hate...
I can't forgive them.
...! THAT'S ...!
THROB
Uu.... ghk!!

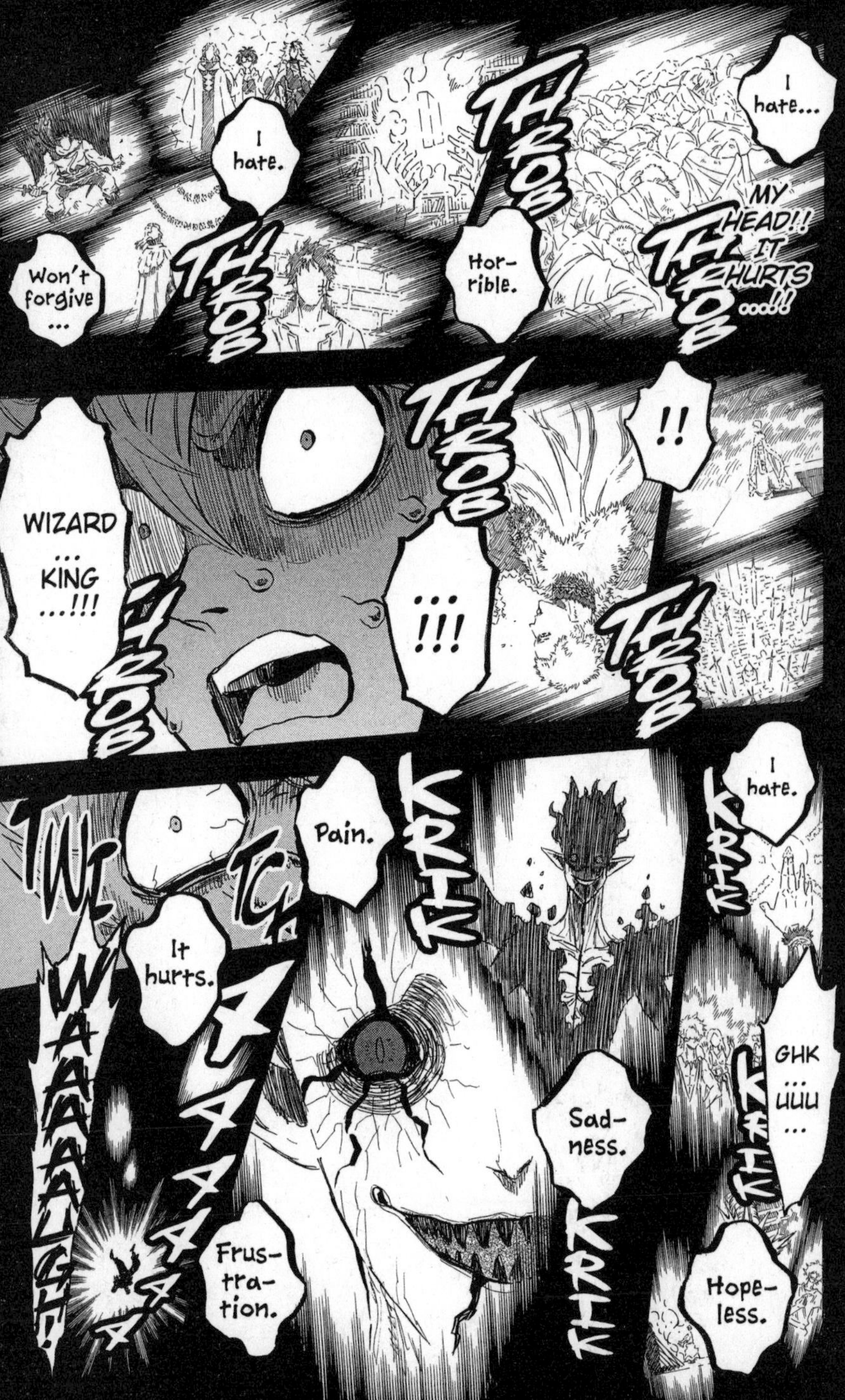
I hate...
MY HEAD!! IT HURTS...!!
THROB
THROB
Hor-rible.
I hate.
THROB
Won't forgive...
!!
THROB
THROB
...!!!
WIZARD... KING...!!!
THROB
I hate.
KRIK
GHK... uuu...
KRIK
Hope-less.
KRIK
Pain.
Sad-ness.
KRIK
Frus-tra-tion.
TWI
TCH
It hurts.
WAAAAAAAGH!
AAAAAA

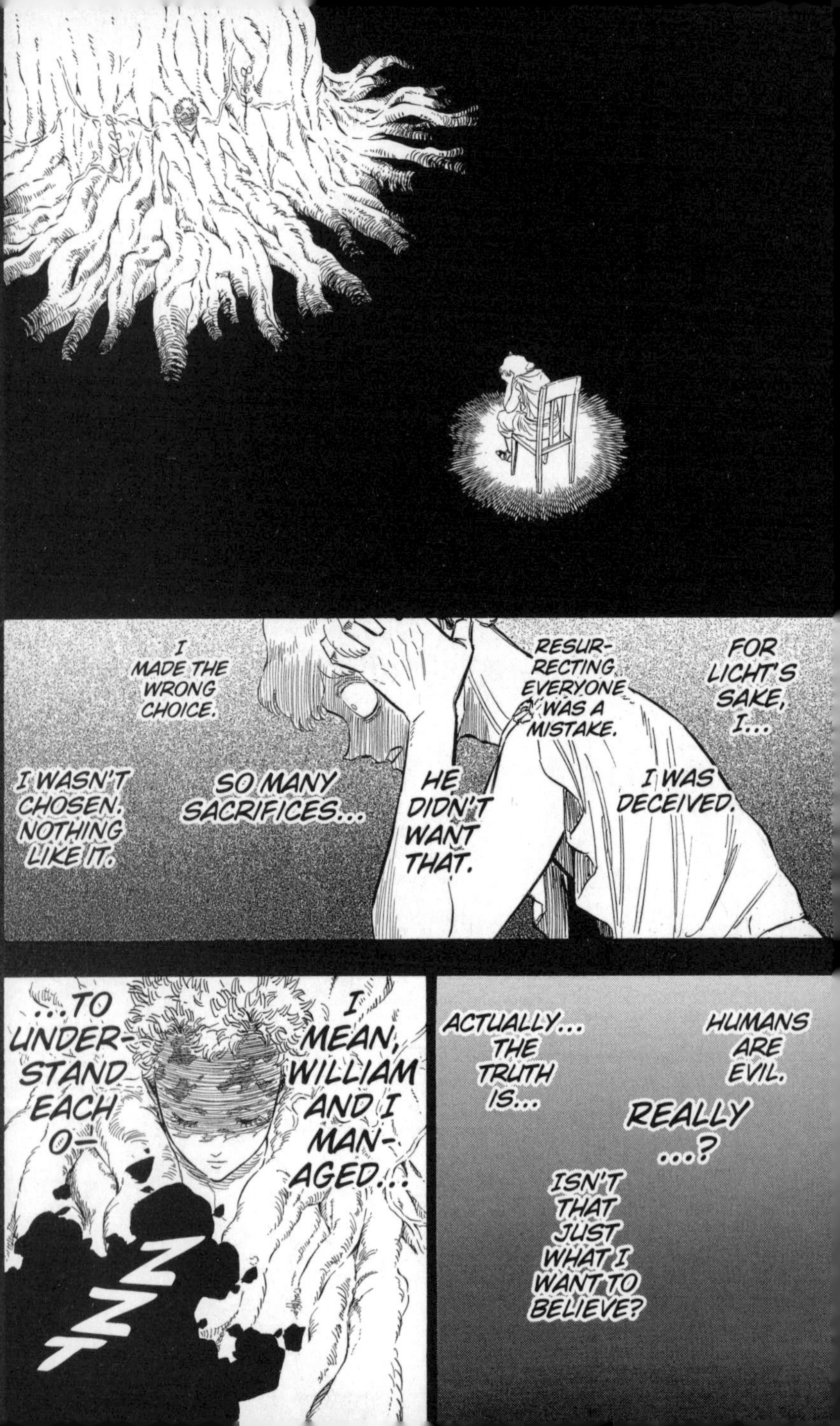
FOR LICHT'S SAKE, I...
RESURRECTING EVERYONE WAS A MISTAKE.
I MADE THE WRONG CHOICE.
I WAS DECEIVED.
HE DIDN'T WANT THAT.
SO MANY SACRIFICES...
I WASN'T CHOSEN. NOTHING LIKE IT.
HUMANS ARE EVIL.
ACTUALLY... THE TRUTH IS...
REALLY ...?
ISN'T THAT JUST WHAT I WANT TO BELIEVE?
I MEAN, WILLIAM AND I MANAGED...
...TO UNDERSTAND EACH O—
ZNN

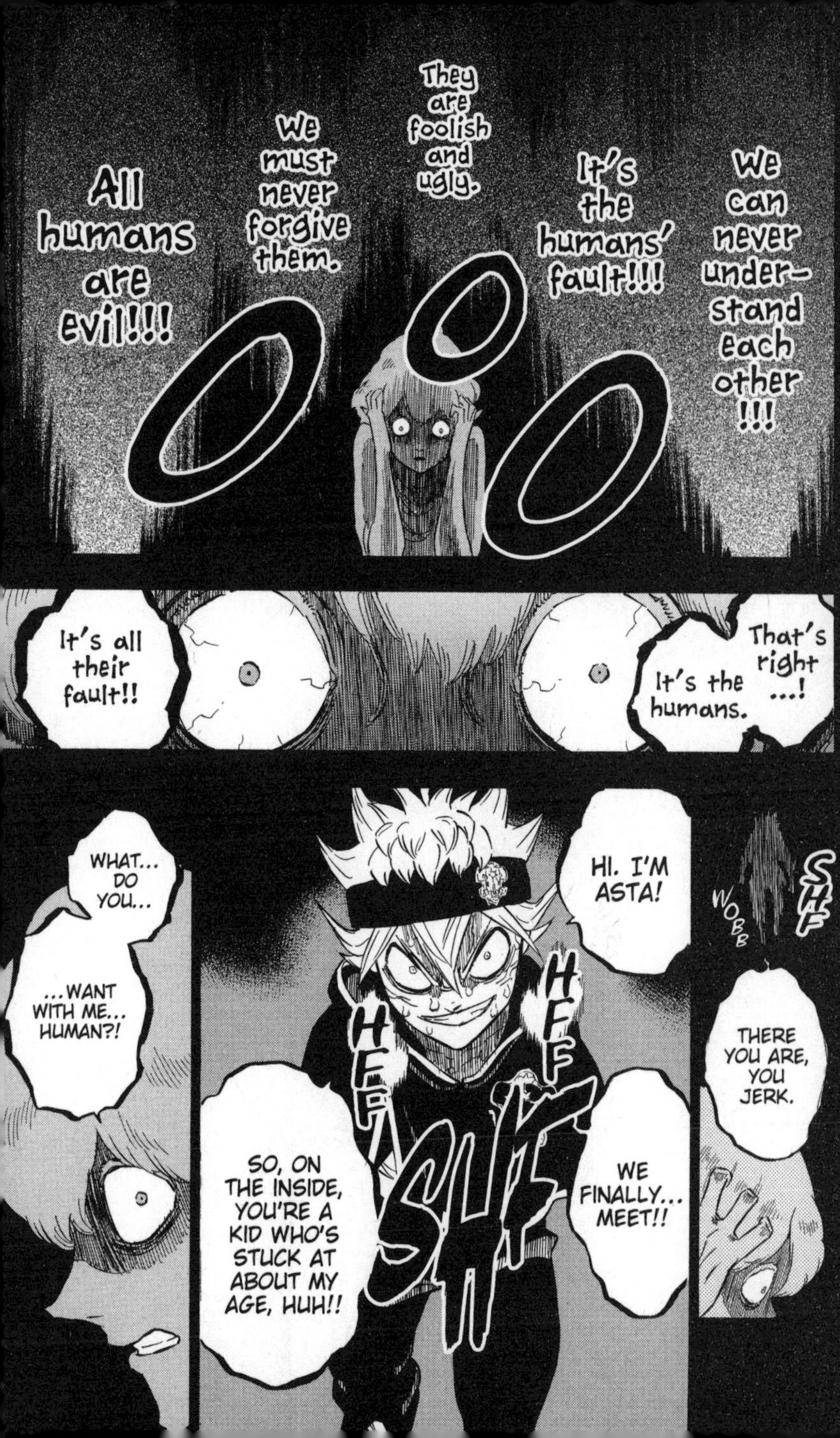
We can never under-stand each other!!!
It's the humans' fault!!!
They are foolish and ugly.
We must never forgive them.
All humans are evil!!!
That's right...!
It's the humans.
It's all their fault!!
SHF
WOBB
THERE YOU ARE, YOU JERK.
HI. I'M ASTA!
HEF
HEF
WE FINALLY... MEET!!
SHF
SO, ON THE INSIDE, YOU'RE A KID WHO'S STUCK AT ABOUT MY AGE, HUH!!
WHAT... DO YOU...
...WANT WITH ME... HUMAN?!

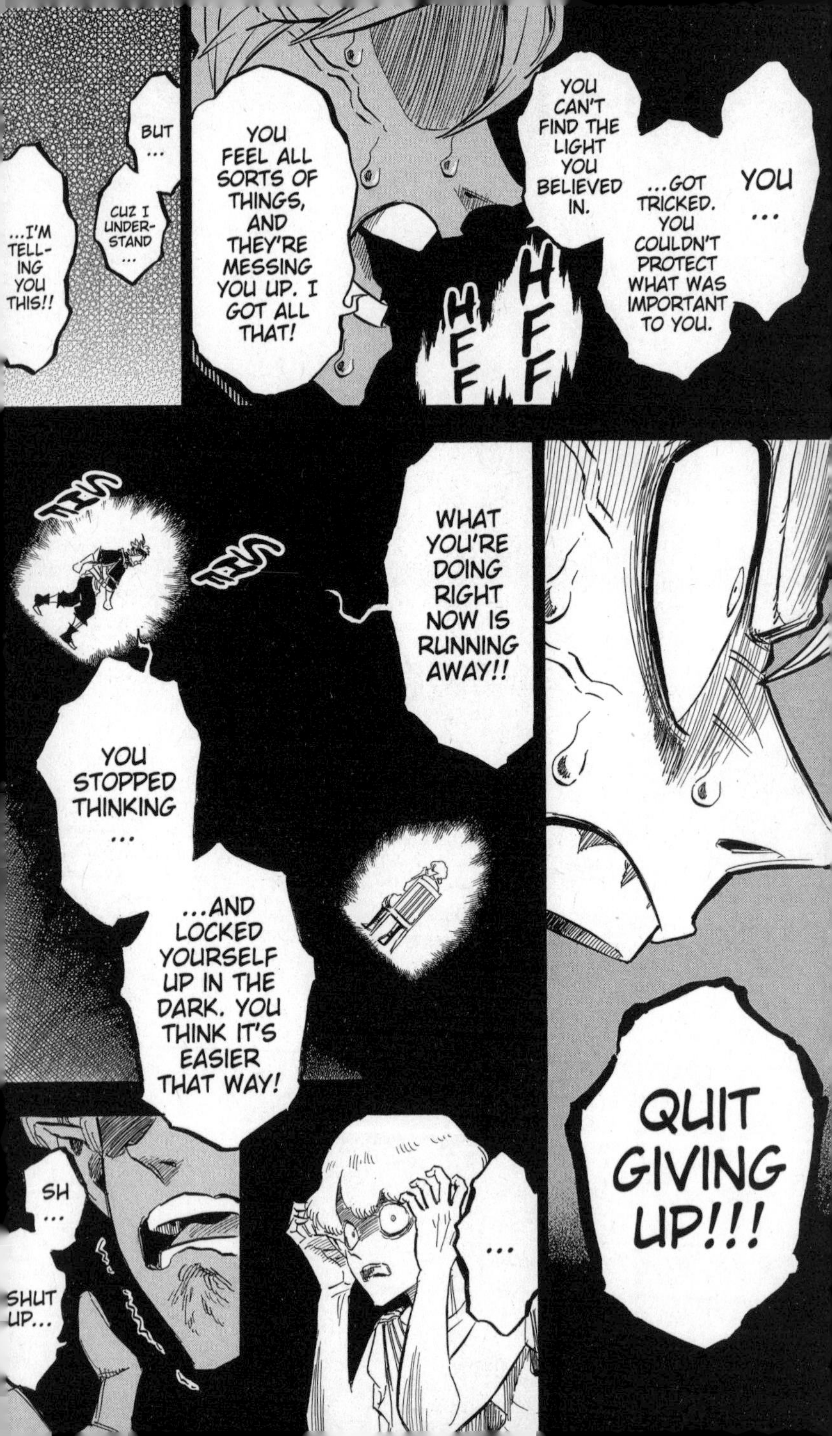
YOU ...
...GOT TRICKED. YOU COULDN'T PROTECT WHAT WAS IMPORTANT TO YOU.
YOU CAN'T FIND THE LIGHT YOU BELIEVED IN.
HFF HFF
YOU FEEL ALL SORTS OF THINGS, AND THEY'RE MESSING YOU UP. I GOT ALL THAT!
BUT ...
CUZ I UNDER-STAND ...
...I'M TELL-ING YOU THIS!!
WHAT YOU'RE DOING RIGHT NOW IS RUNNING AWAY!!
YOU STOPPED THINKING ...
...AND LOCKED YOURSELF UP IN THE DARK. YOU THINK IT'S EASIER THAT WAY!
QUIT GIVING UP!!!
...
SH ...
SHUT UP...

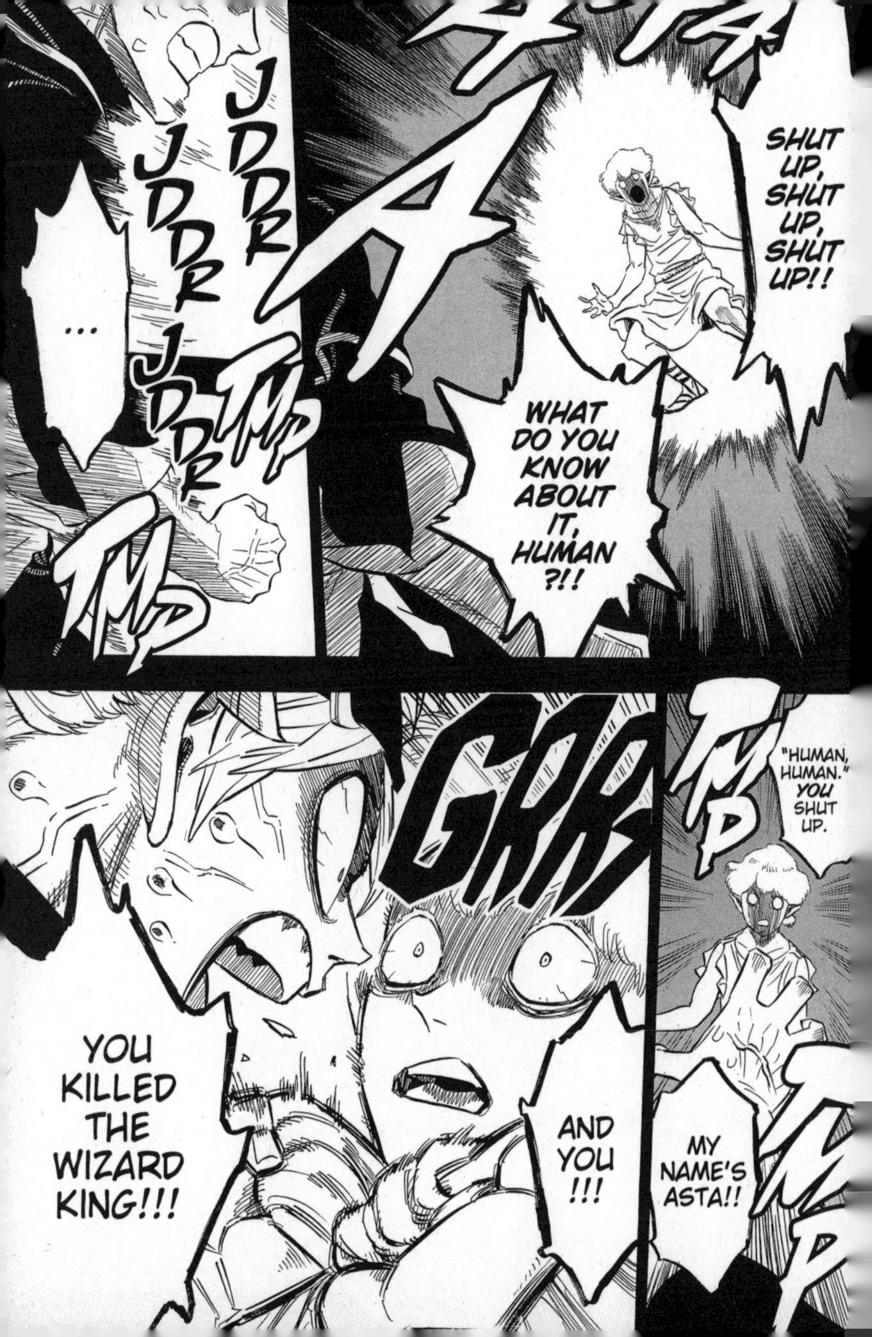
SHUT UP, SHUT UP, SHUT UP!!
WHAT DO YOU KNOW ABOUT IT, HUMAN?!!
JDDR JDDR
JDDR
...
TMP
TMP
TMP
"HUMAN, HUMAN." YOU SHUT UP.
MY NAME'S ASTA!!
TMP
GRR
AND YOU!!!
YOU KILLED THE WIZARD KING!!!

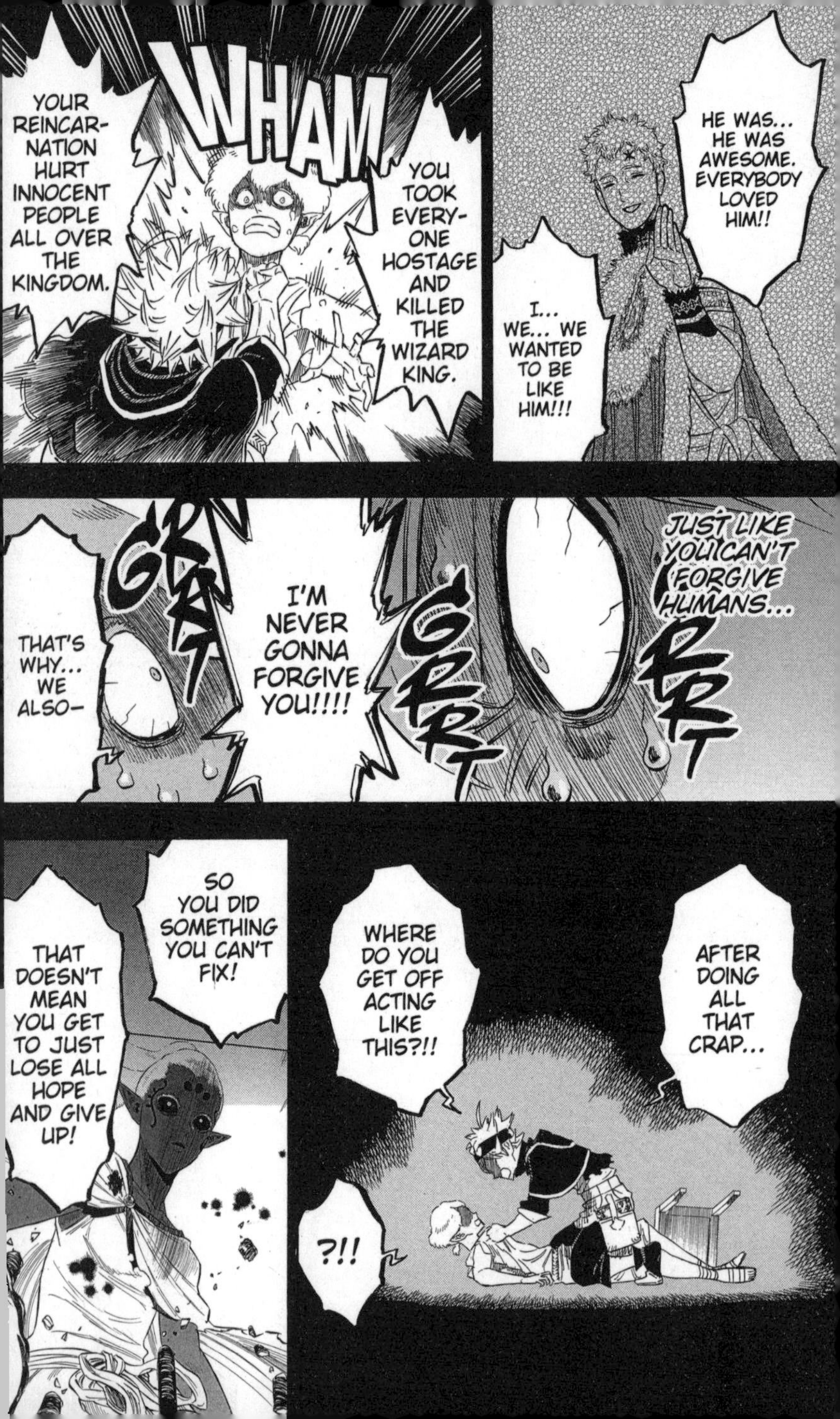
HE WAS... HE WAS AWESOME. EVERYBODY LOVED HIM!!
I... WE... WE WANTED TO BE LIKE HIM!!!
WHAM
YOU TOOK EVERYONE HOSTAGE AND KILLED THE WIZARD KING.
YOUR REINCARNATION HURT INNOCENT PEOPLE ALL OVER THE KINGDOM.
JUST LIKE YOU CAN'T FORGIVE HUMANS...
GRRT
GRRT
I'M NEVER GONNA FORGIVE YOU!!!!!
GRRT
THAT'S WHY... WE ALSO—
AFTER DOING ALL THAT CRAP...
WHERE DO YOU GET OFF ACTING LIKE THIS?!!
?!!
SO YOU DID SOMETHING YOU CAN'T FIX!
THAT DOESN'T MEAN YOU GET TO JUST LOSE ALL HOPE AND GIVE UP!

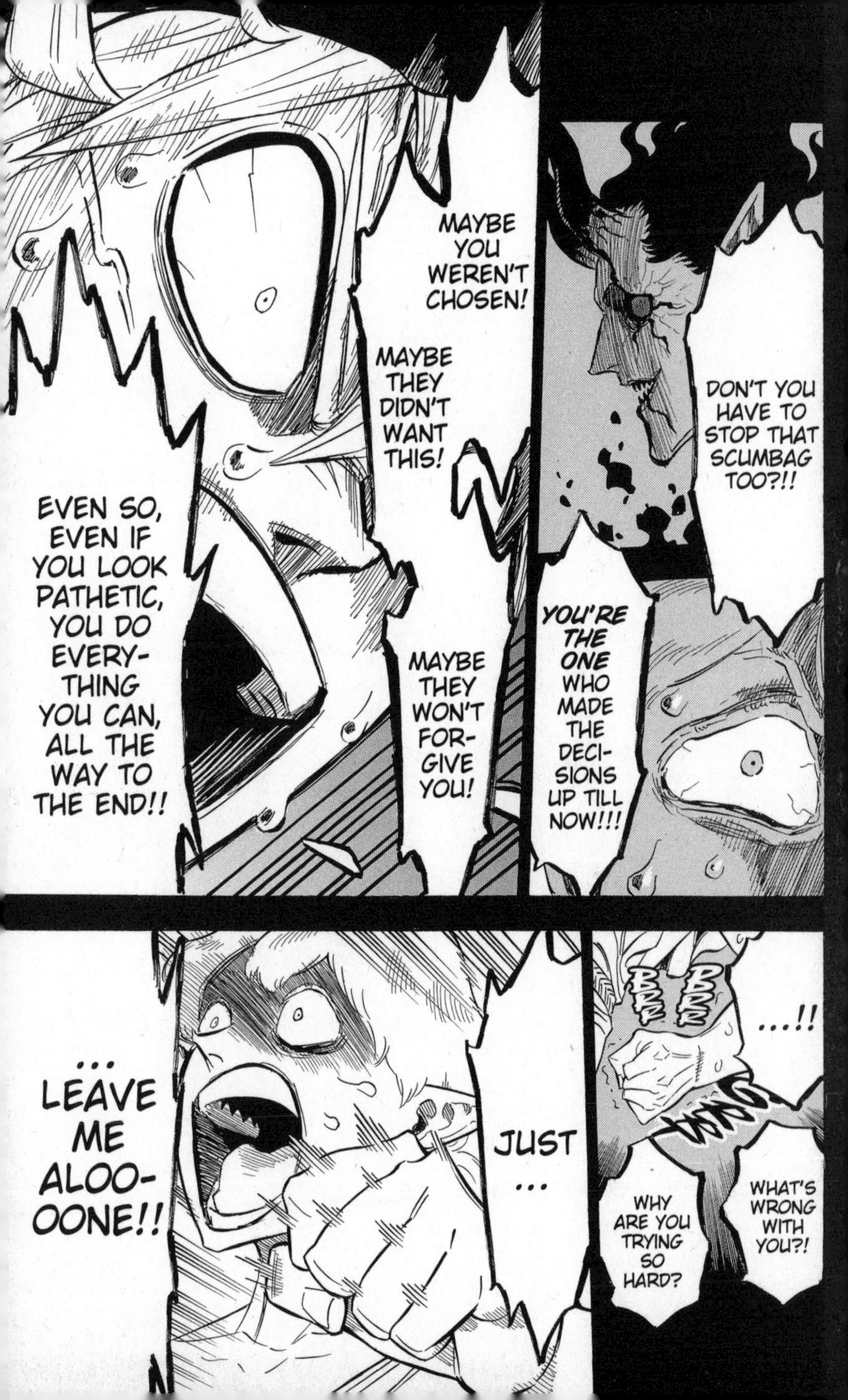
DON'T YOU HAVE TO STOP THAT SCUMBAG TOO?!!
YOU'RE THE ONE WHO MADE THE DECISIONS UP TILL NOW!!!
MAYBE YOU WEREN'T CHOSEN!
MAYBE THEY DIDN'T WANT THIS!
MAYBE THEY WON'T FORGIVE YOU!
EVEN SO, EVEN IF YOU LOOK PATHETIC, YOU DO EVERYTHING YOU CAN, ALL THE WAY TO THE END!!
...!!
WHAT'S WRONG WITH YOU?!
WHY ARE YOU TRYING SO HARD?
JUST ...
... LEAVE ME ALOOO-OONE!!

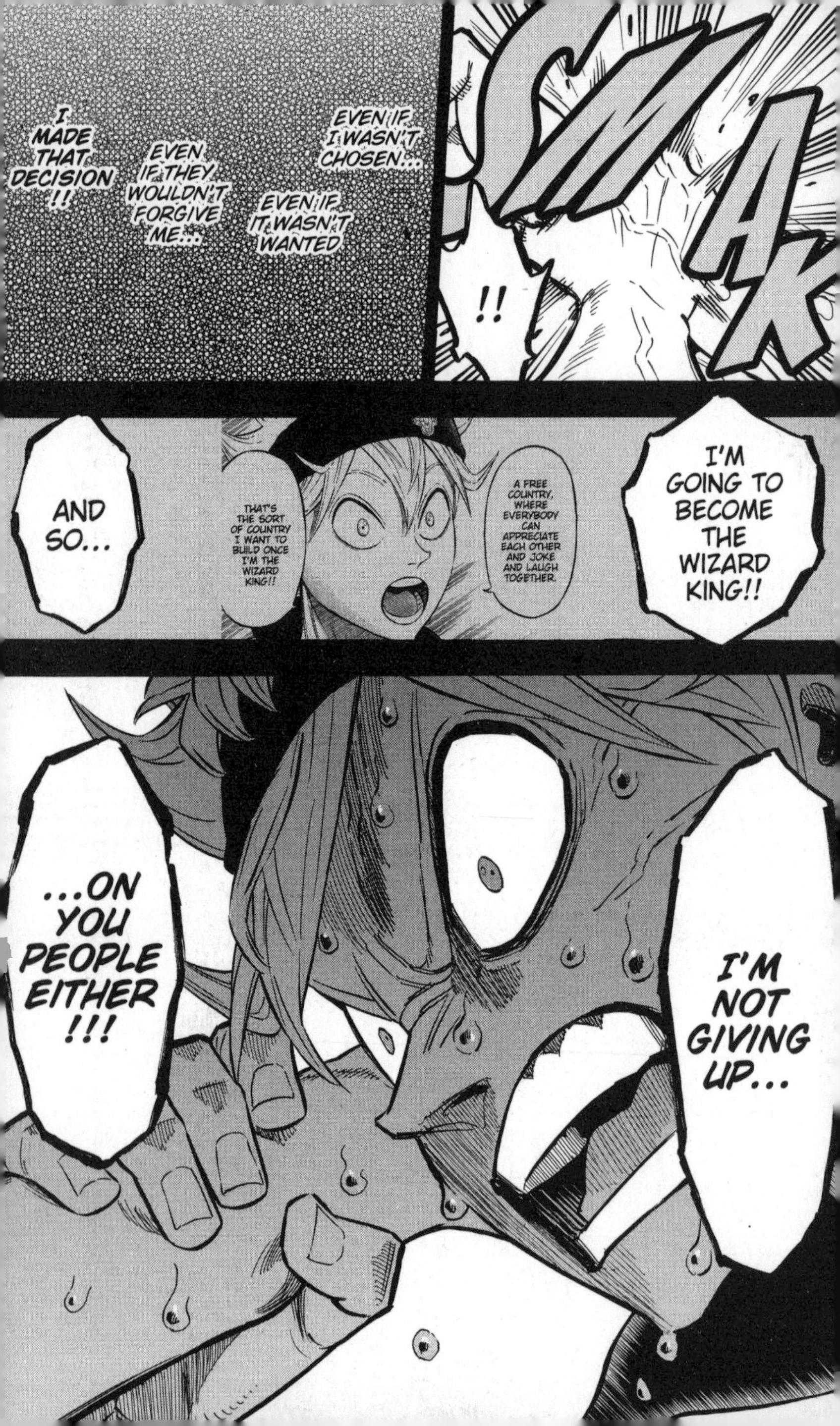
!!
EVEN IF I WASN'T CHOSEN...
EVEN IF IT WASN'T WANTED
EVEN IF THEY WOULDN'T FORGIVE ME...
I MADE THAT DECISION!!
I'M GOING TO BECOME THE WIZARD KING!!
A FREE COUNTRY, WHERE EVERYBODY CAN APPRECIATE EACH OTHER AND JOKE AND LAUGH TOGETHER.
THAT'S THE SORT OF COUNTRY I WANT TO BUILD ONCE I'M THE WIZARD KING!!
AND SO...
I'M NOT GIVING UP...
...ON YOU PEOPLE EITHER!!!

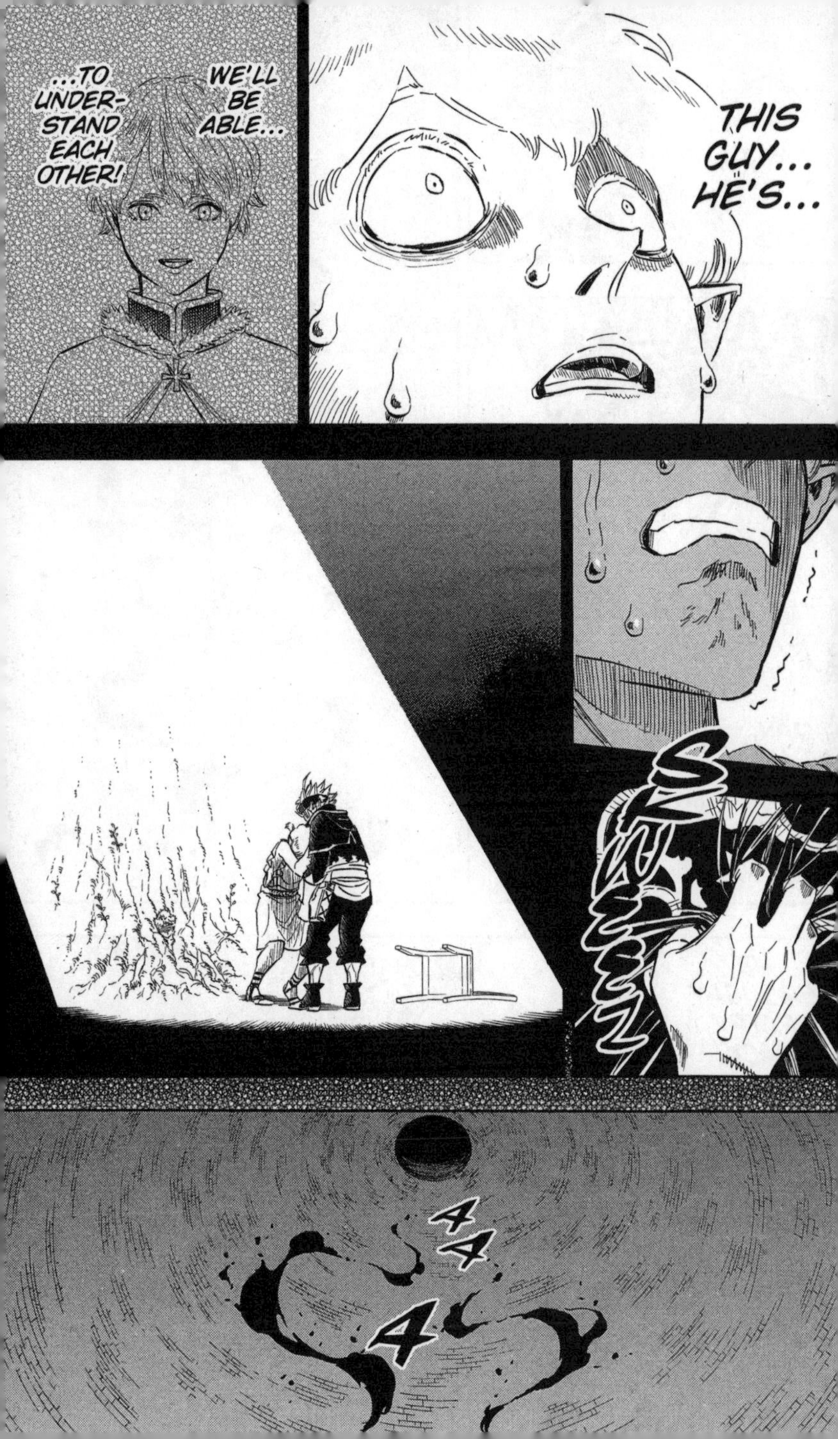
THIS GUY... HE'S...
WE'LL BE ABLE...
...TO UNDER-STAND EACH OTHER!

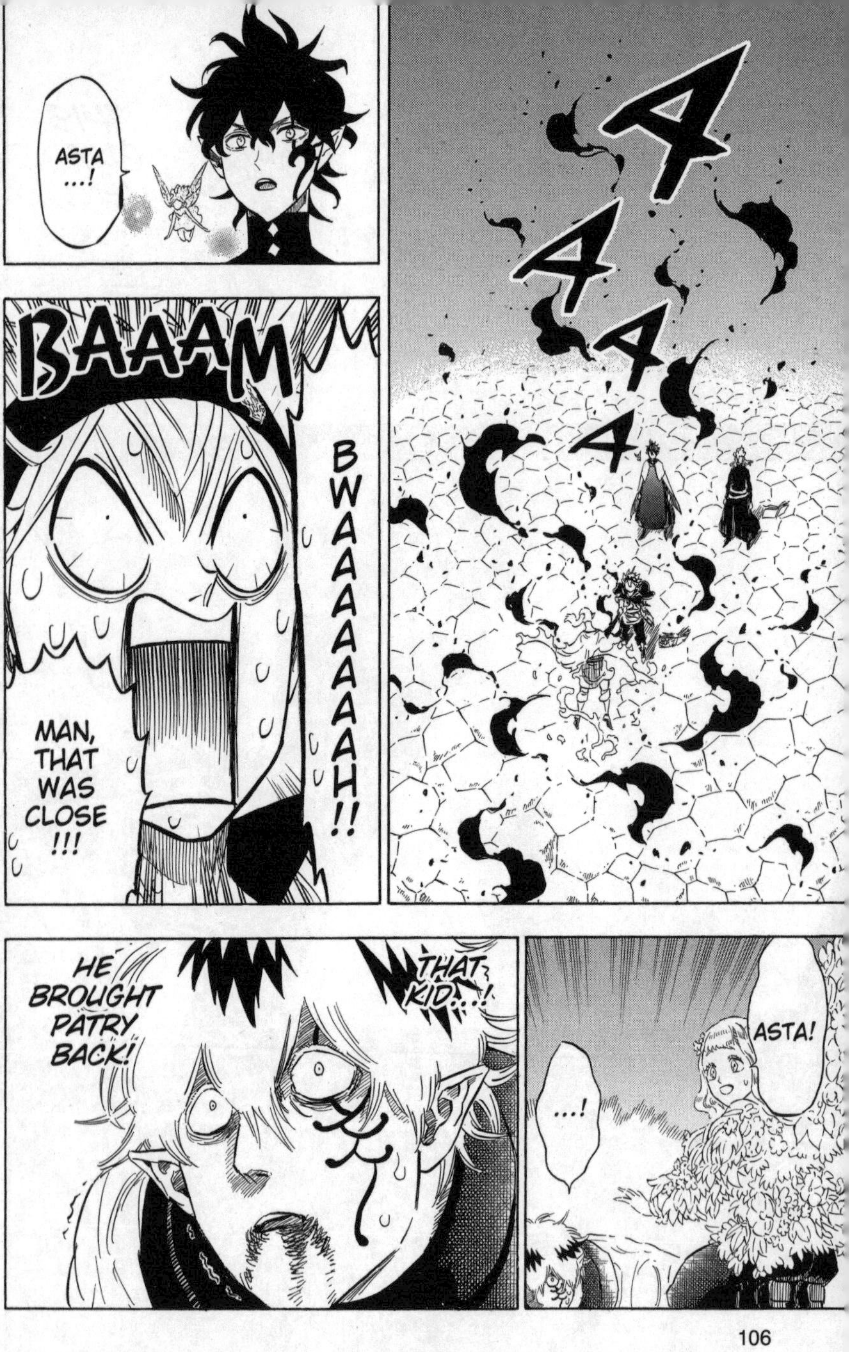
ASTA ...!
BAAAM
BWAAAAAAAH!!
MAN, THAT WAS CLOSE!!!
ASTA!
...!
THAT KID...!
HE BROUGHT PATRY BACK!

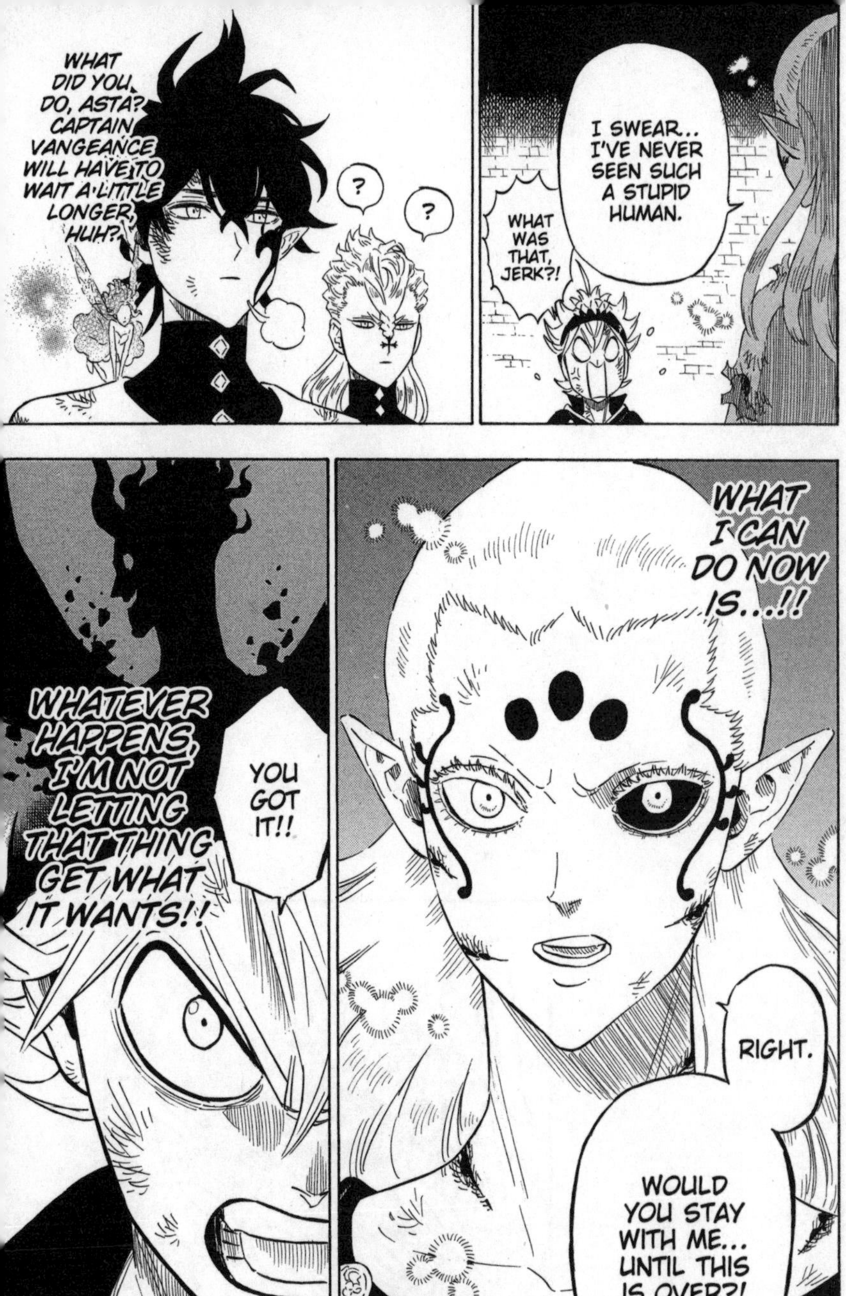
I SWEAR... I'VE NEVER SEEN SUCH A STUPID HUMAN.
WHAT WAS THAT, JERK?!
WHAT DID YOU DO, ASTA? CAPTAIN VANGEANCE WILL HAVE TO WAIT A LITTLE LONGER, HUH?
?
?
WHAT I CAN DO NOW IS...!!
RIGHT.
WOULD YOU STAY WITH ME... UNTIL THIS IS OVER?!
YOU GOT IT!!
WHATEVER HAPPENS, I'M NOT LETTING THAT THING GET WHAT IT WANTS!!

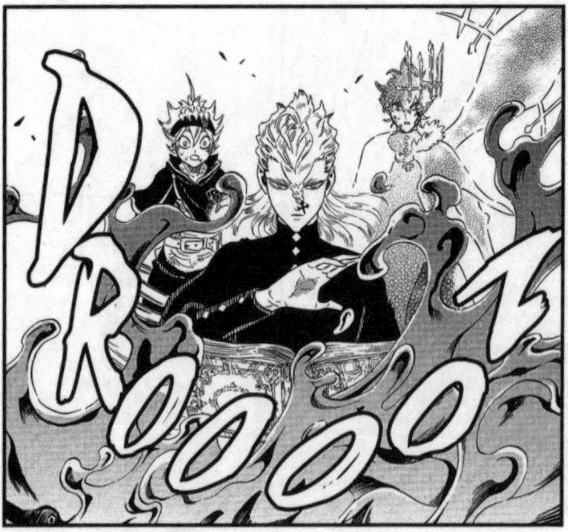
DROOOOOM

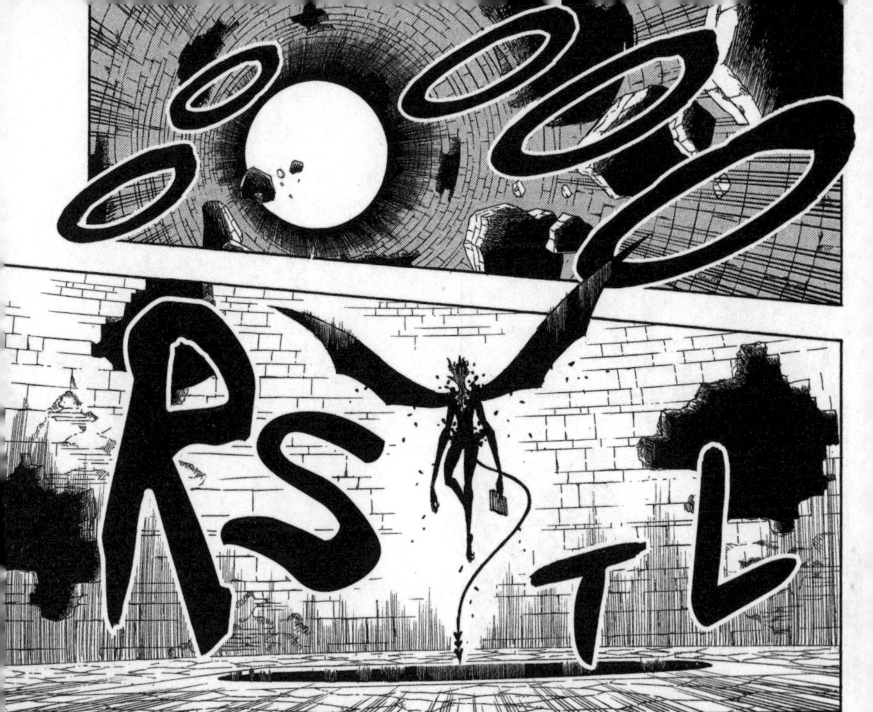
RSTL

Page 201: The Top Level of the Shadow Palace

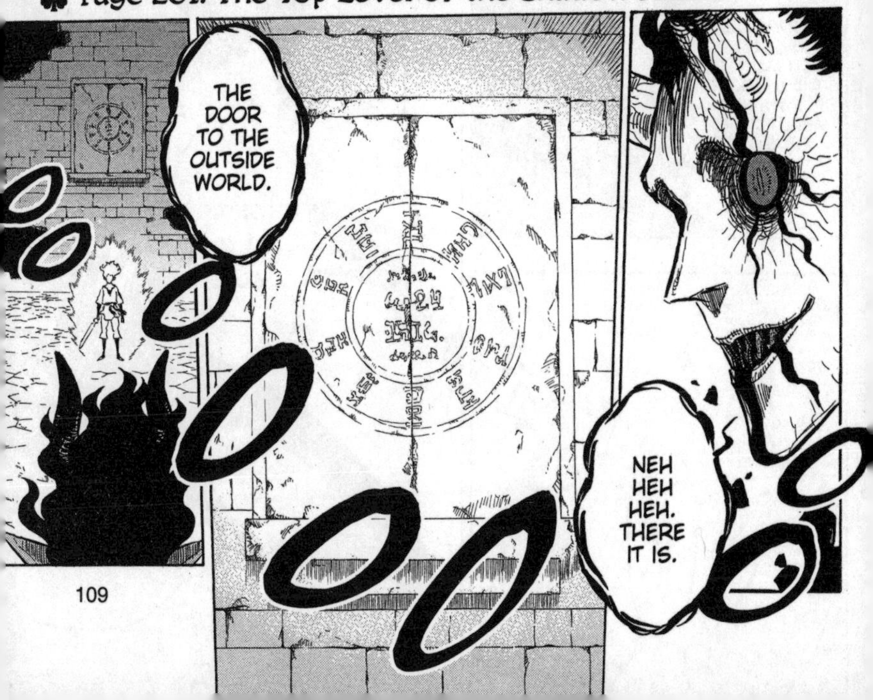
NEH HEH HEH. THERE IT IS.
THE DOOR TO THE OUTSIDE WORLD.

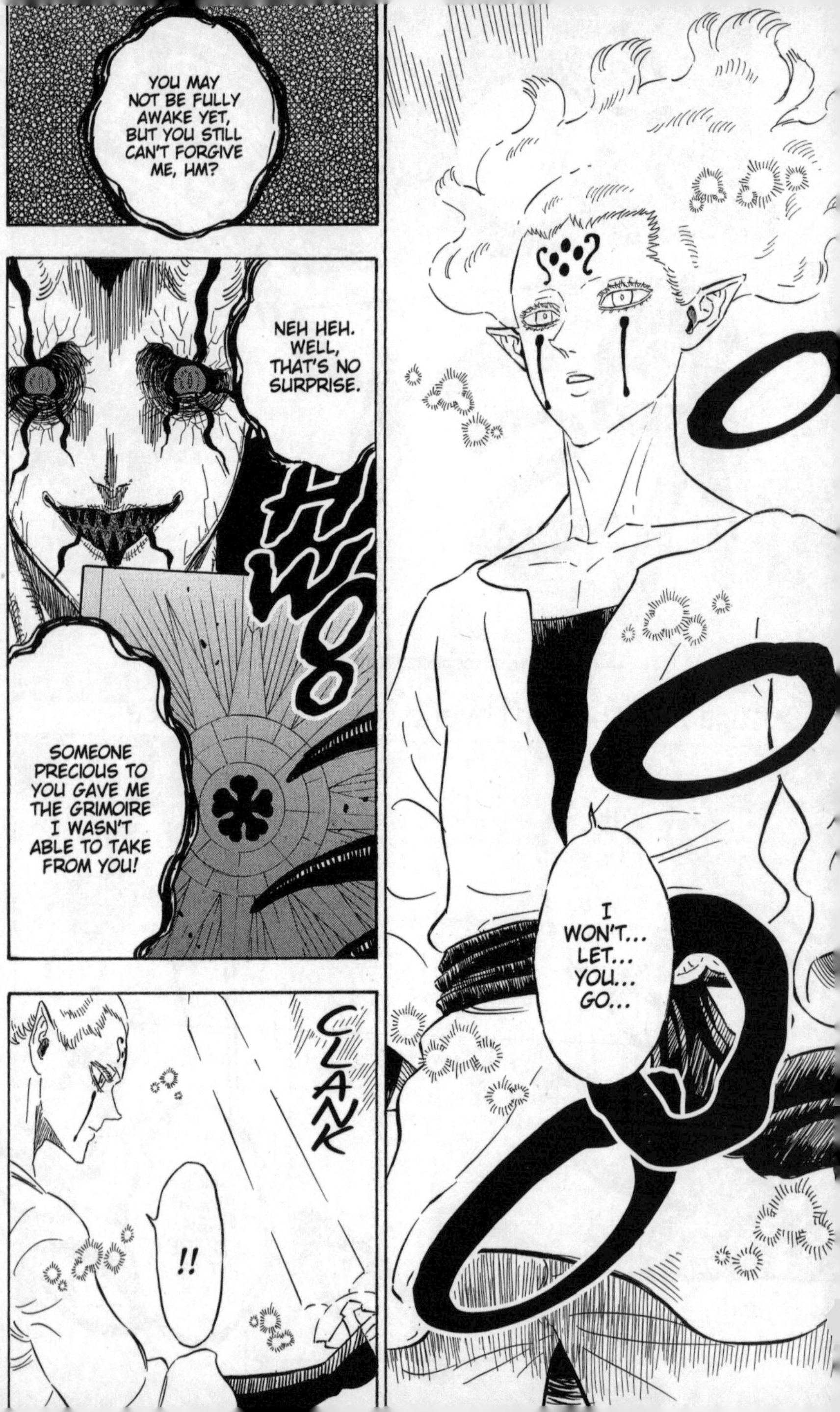
I WON'T... LET... YOU... GO...
YOU MAY NOT BE FULLY AWAKE YET, BUT YOU STILL CAN'T FORGIVE ME, HM?
NEH HEH. WELL, THAT'S NO SURPRISE.
FWOOSH
SOMEONE PRECIOUS TO YOU GAVE ME THE GRIMOIRE I WASN'T ABLE TO TAKE FROM YOU!
CLANK
!!

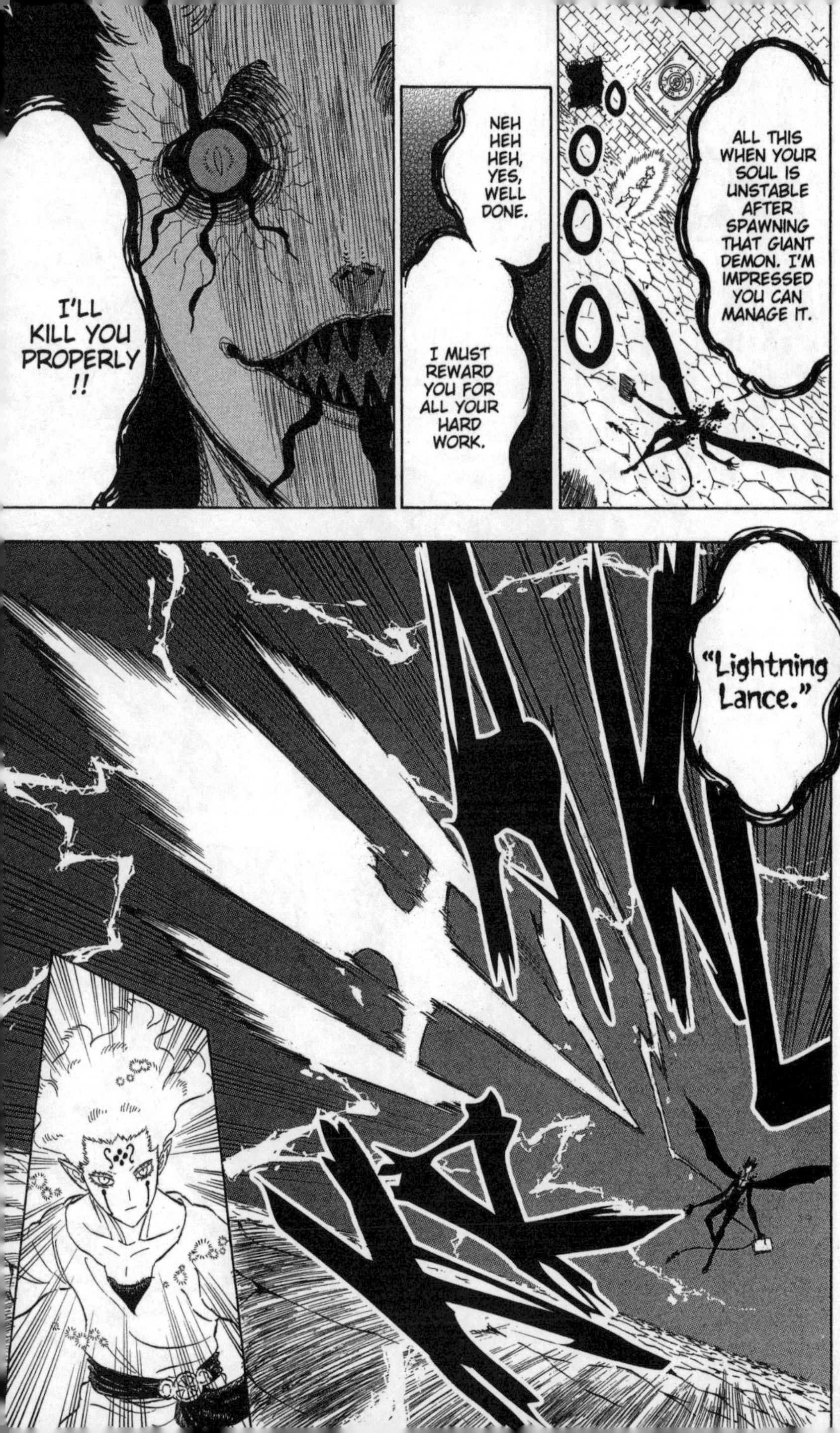
ALL THIS WHEN YOUR SOUL IS UNSTABLE AFTER SPAWNING THAT GIANT DEMON. I'M IMPRESSED YOU CAN MANAGE IT.
NEH HEH HEH, YES, WELL DONE.
I MUST REWARD YOU FOR ALL YOUR HARD WORK.
I'LL KILL YOU PROPERLY!!
"Lightning Lance."

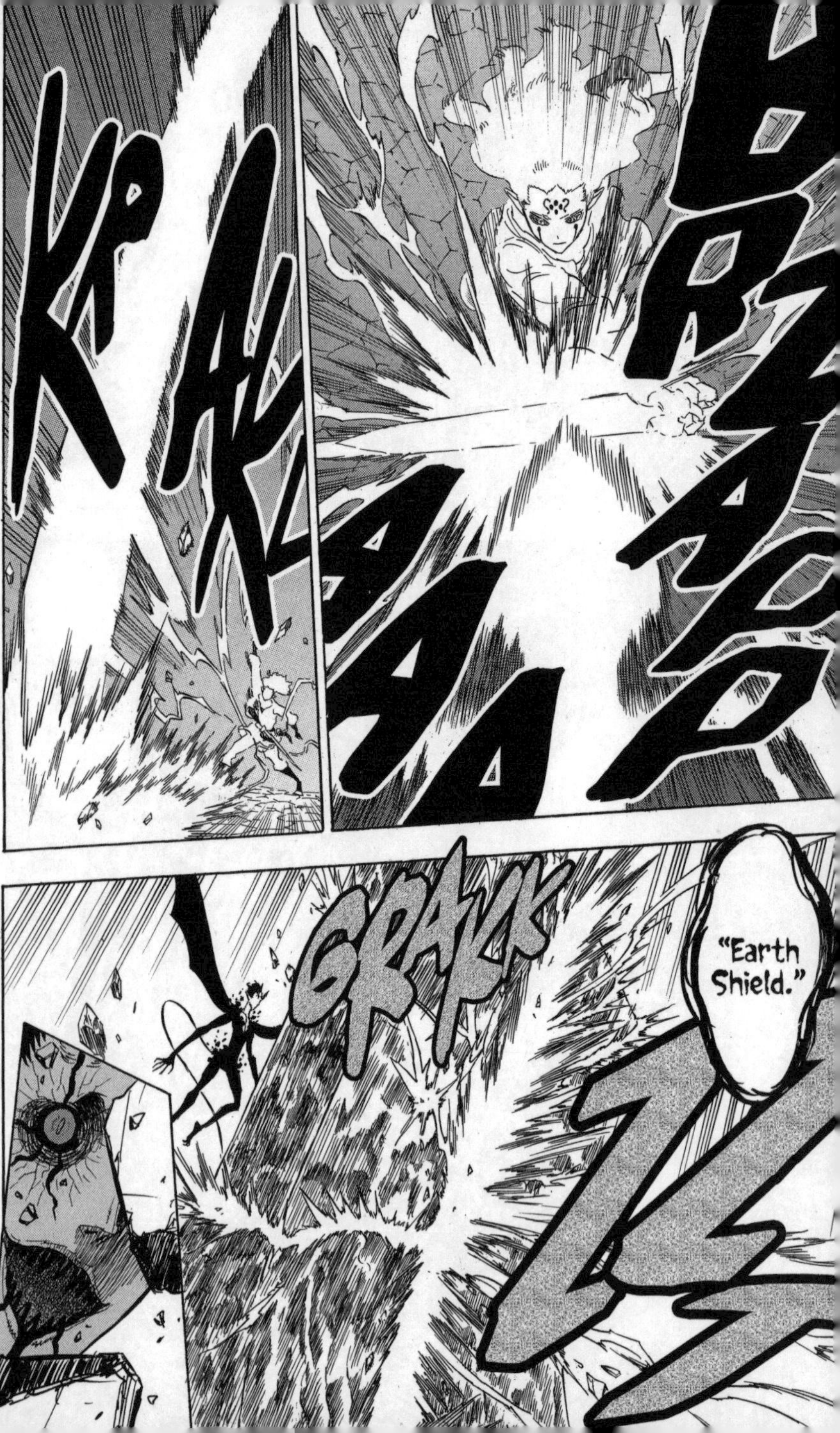
"Earth Shield."
CRACK

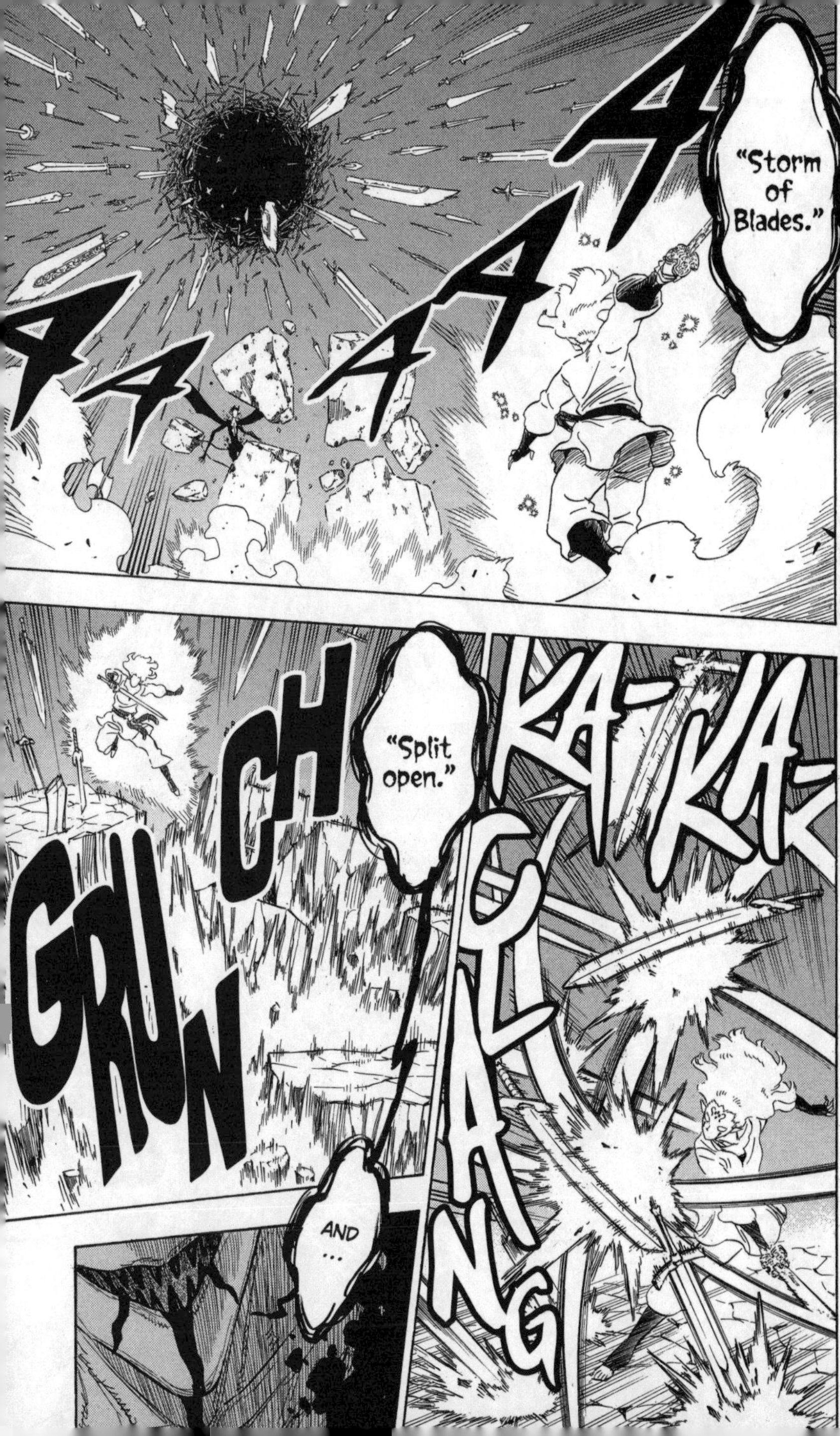
"Storm of Blades."
AAAAAAA
KA-KA-KA-
"Split open."
CLANG!
CRUNCH
AND ...

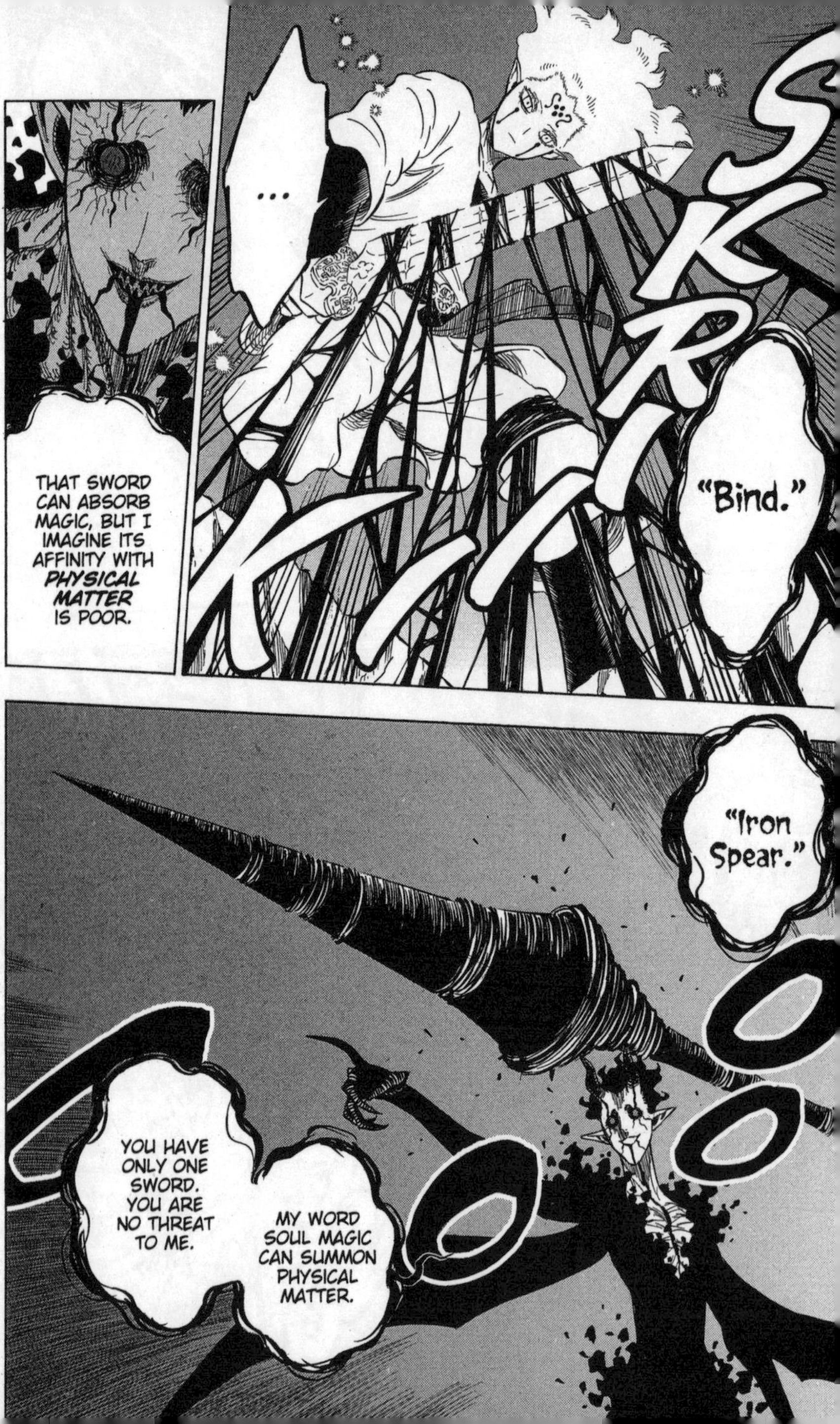
SKRIIK
...
"Bind."
THAT SWORD CAN ABSORB MAGIC, BUT I IMAGINE ITS AFFINITY WITH PHYSICAL MATTER IS POOR.
"Iron Spear."
OOOO
MY WORD SOUL MAGIC CAN SUMMON PHYSICAL MATTER.
YOU HAVE ONLY ONE SWORD. YOU ARE NO THREAT TO ME.

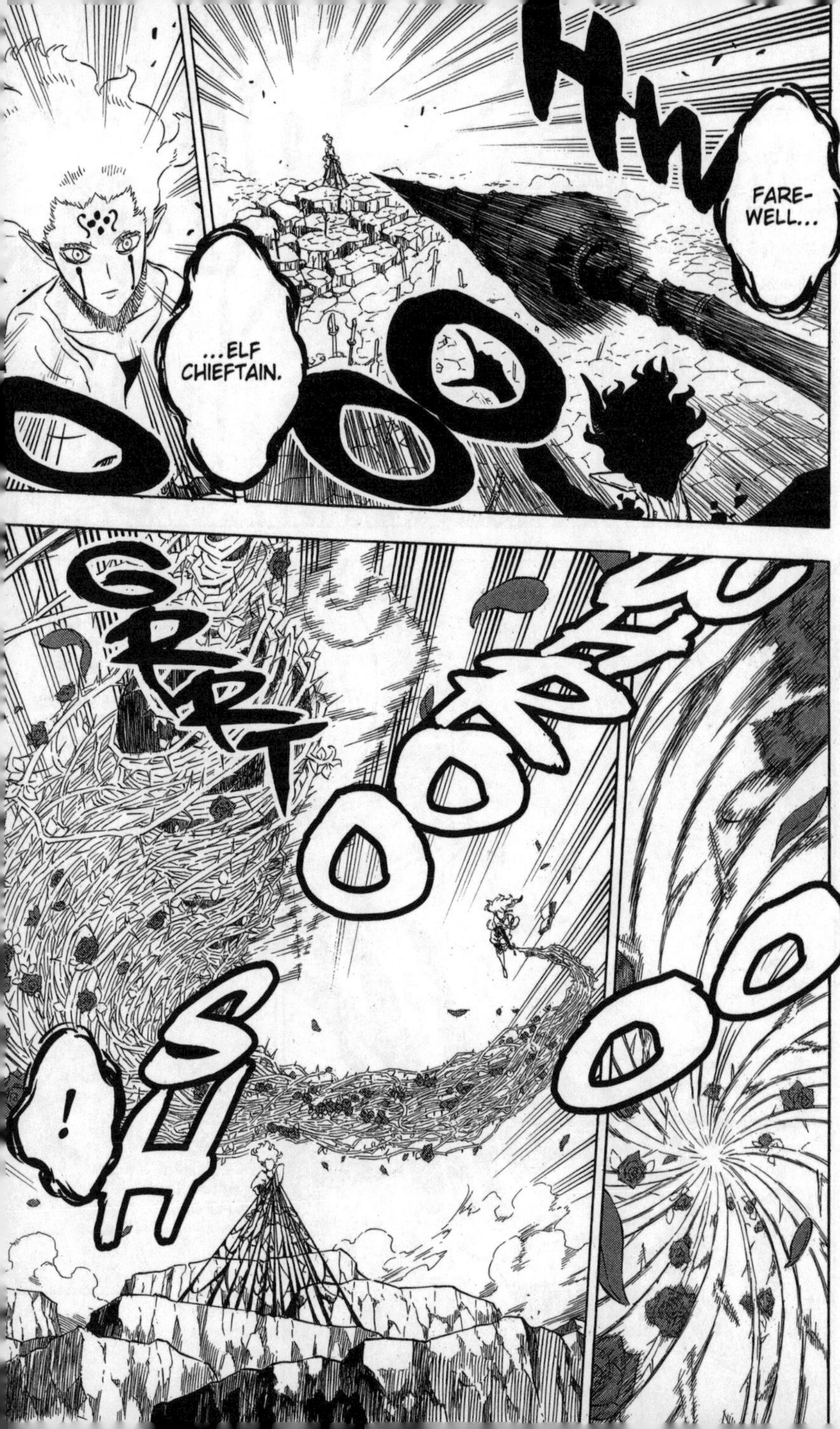
HWOOOO
FARE-WELL...
...ELF CHIEFTAIN.
GRRT
!

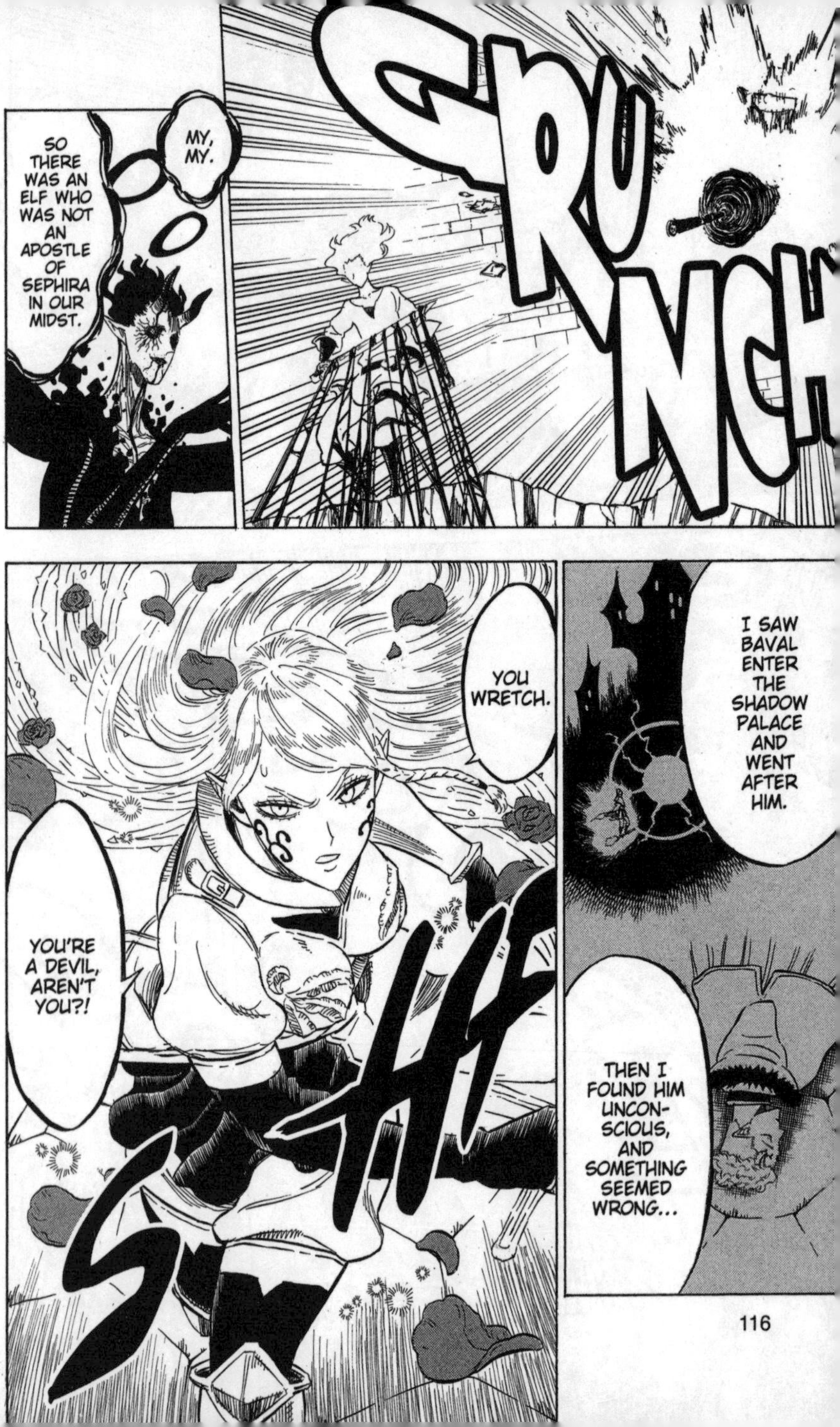
CRUNCH
MY, MY.
SO THERE WAS AN ELF WHO WAS NOT AN APOSTLE OF SEPHIRA IN OUR MIDST.
I SAW BAVAL ENTER THE SHADOW PALACE AND WENT AFTER HIM.
THEN I FOUND HIM UNCON-SCIOUS, AND SOMETHING SEEMED WRONG...
YOU WRETCH.
YOU'RE A DEVIL, AREN'T YOU?!

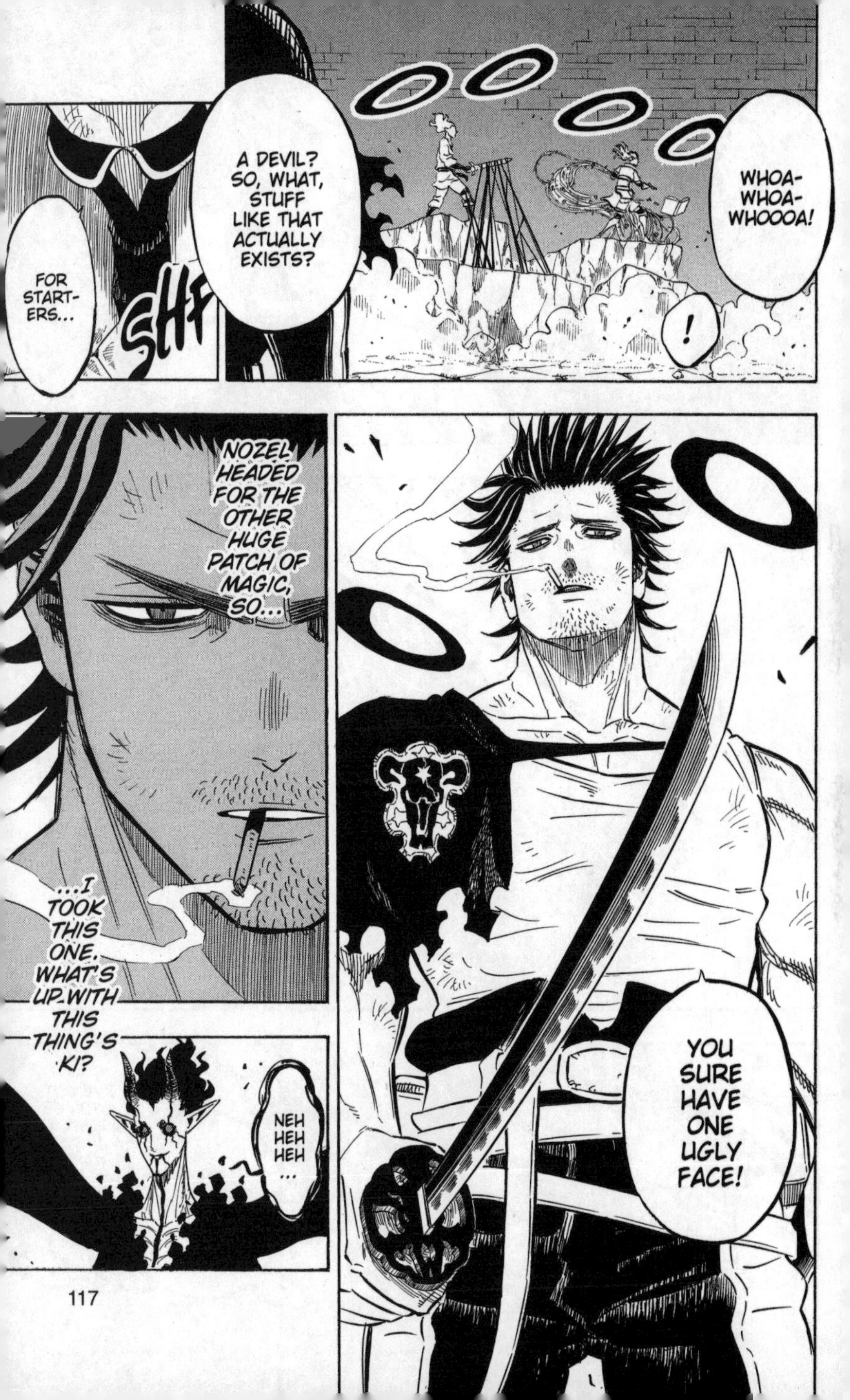
WHOA-WHOA-WHOOOA!
!
A DEVIL? SO, WHAT, STUFF LIKE THAT ACTUALLY EXISTS?
SHF
FOR STARTERS...
YOU SURE HAVE ONE UGLY FACE!
NOZEL HEADED FOR THE OTHER HUGE PATCH OF MAGIC, SO...
...I TOOK THIS ONE. WHAT'S UP WITH THIS THING'S KI?
NEH HEH HEH...

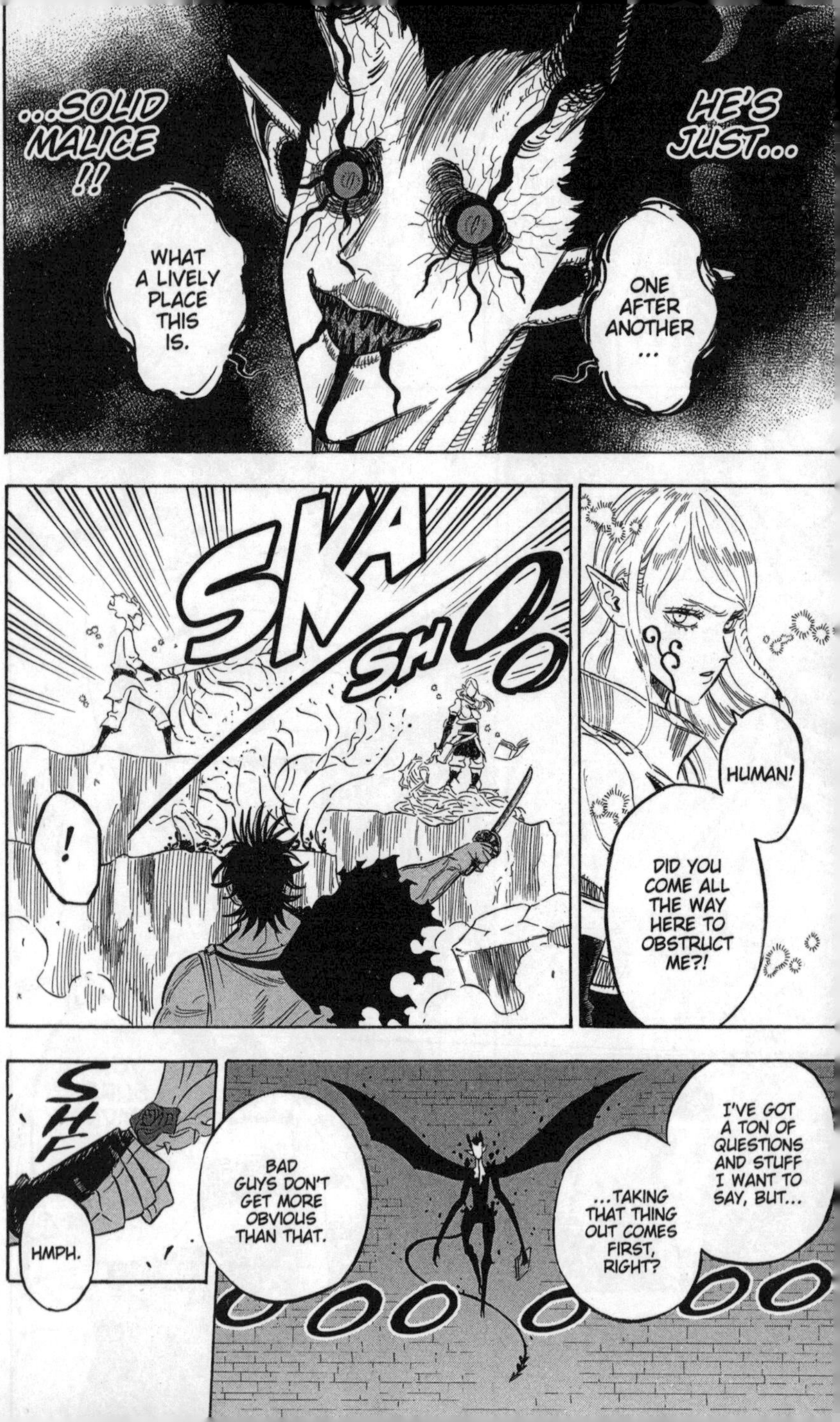
HE'S JUST...
ONE AFTER ANOTHER ...
...SOLID MALICE !!
WHAT A LIVELY PLACE THIS IS.
HUMAN!
DID YOU COME ALL THE WAY HERE TO OBSTRUCT ME?!
SKA
SHOOO
!
I'VE GOT A TON OF QUESTIONS AND STUFF I WANT TO SAY, BUT...
...TAKING THAT THING OUT COMES FIRST, RIGHT?
BAD GUYS DON'T GET MORE OBVIOUS THAN THAT.
SHF
HMPH.

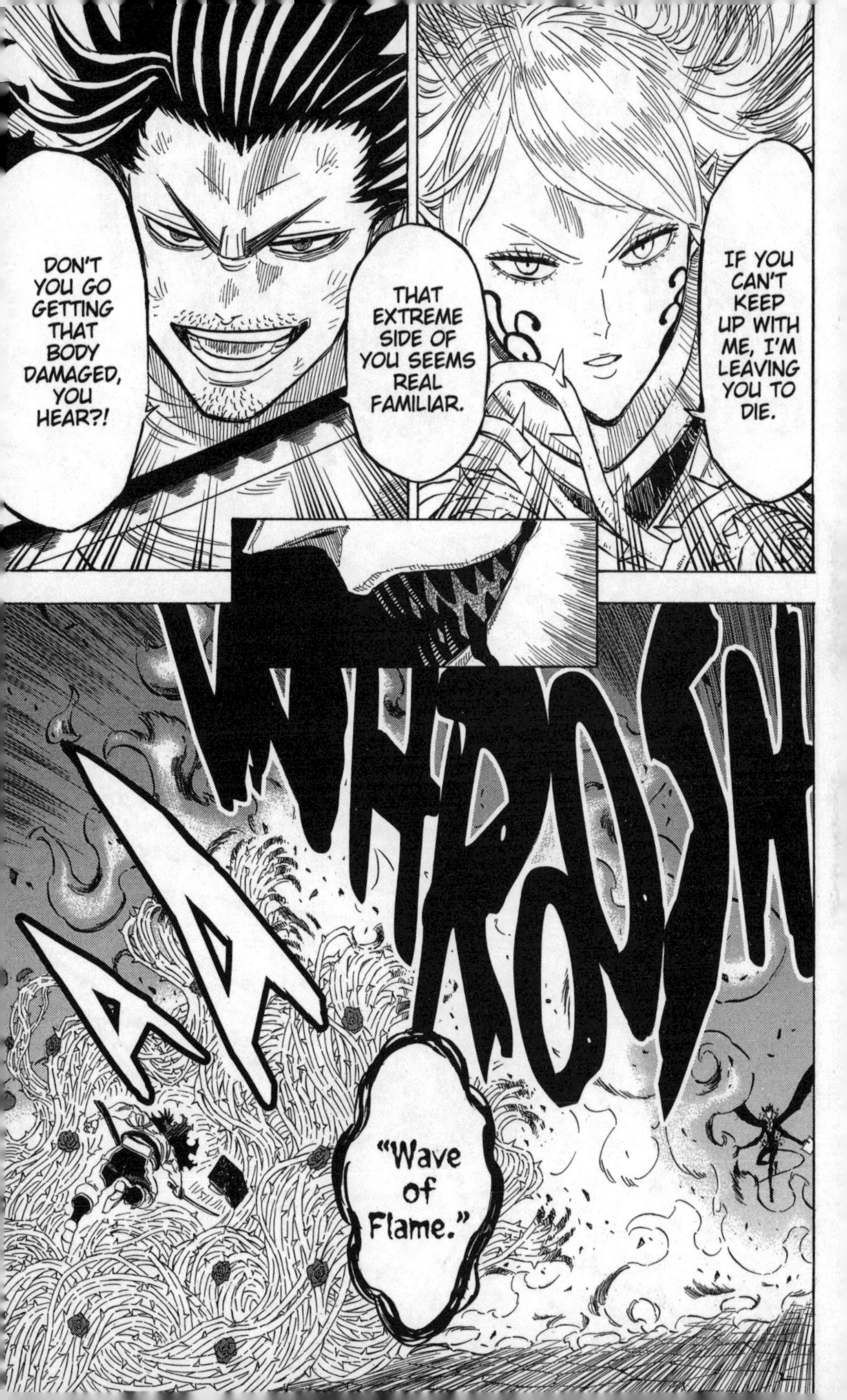
IF YOU CAN'T KEEP UP WITH ME, I'M LEAVING YOU TO DIE.
THAT EXTREME SIDE OF YOU SEEMS REAL FAMILIAR.
DON'T YOU GO GETTING THAT BODY DAMAGED, YOU HEAR?!
WHOOOSH
"Wave of Flame."

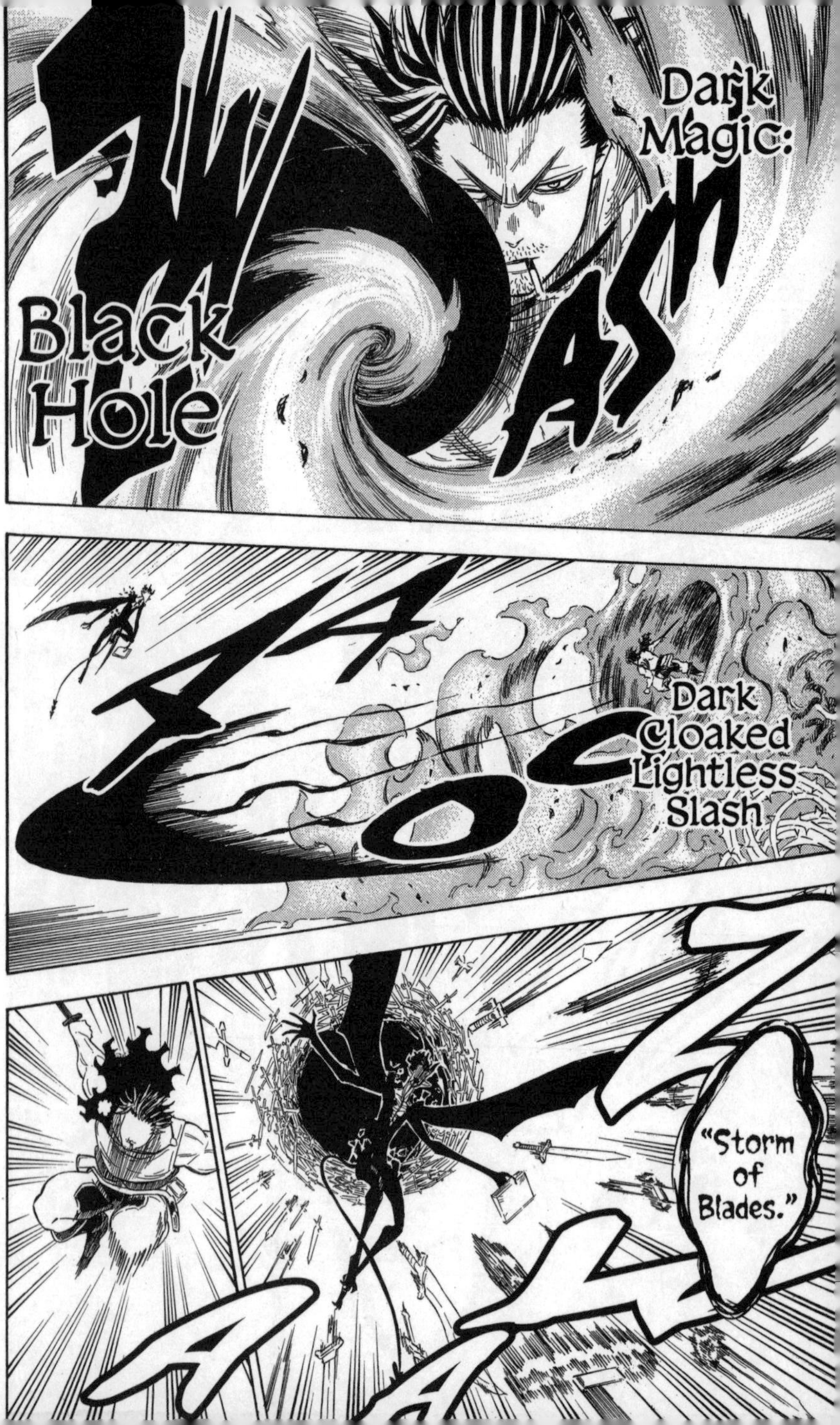
Dark Magic:
Black Hole
Dark Cloaked Lightless Slash
"Storm of Blades."

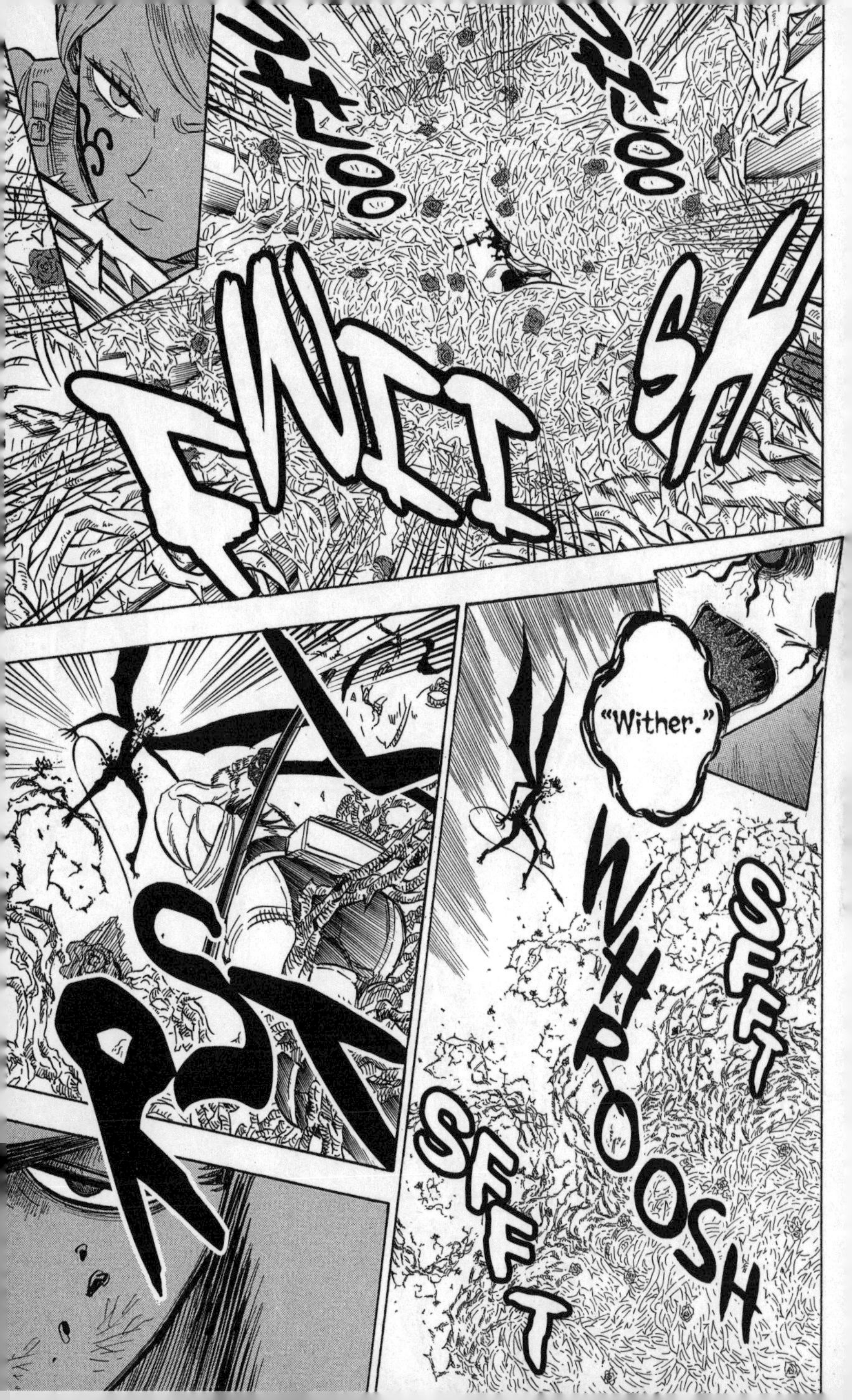
"Wither."
WHROOSH
SFFT
SFFT

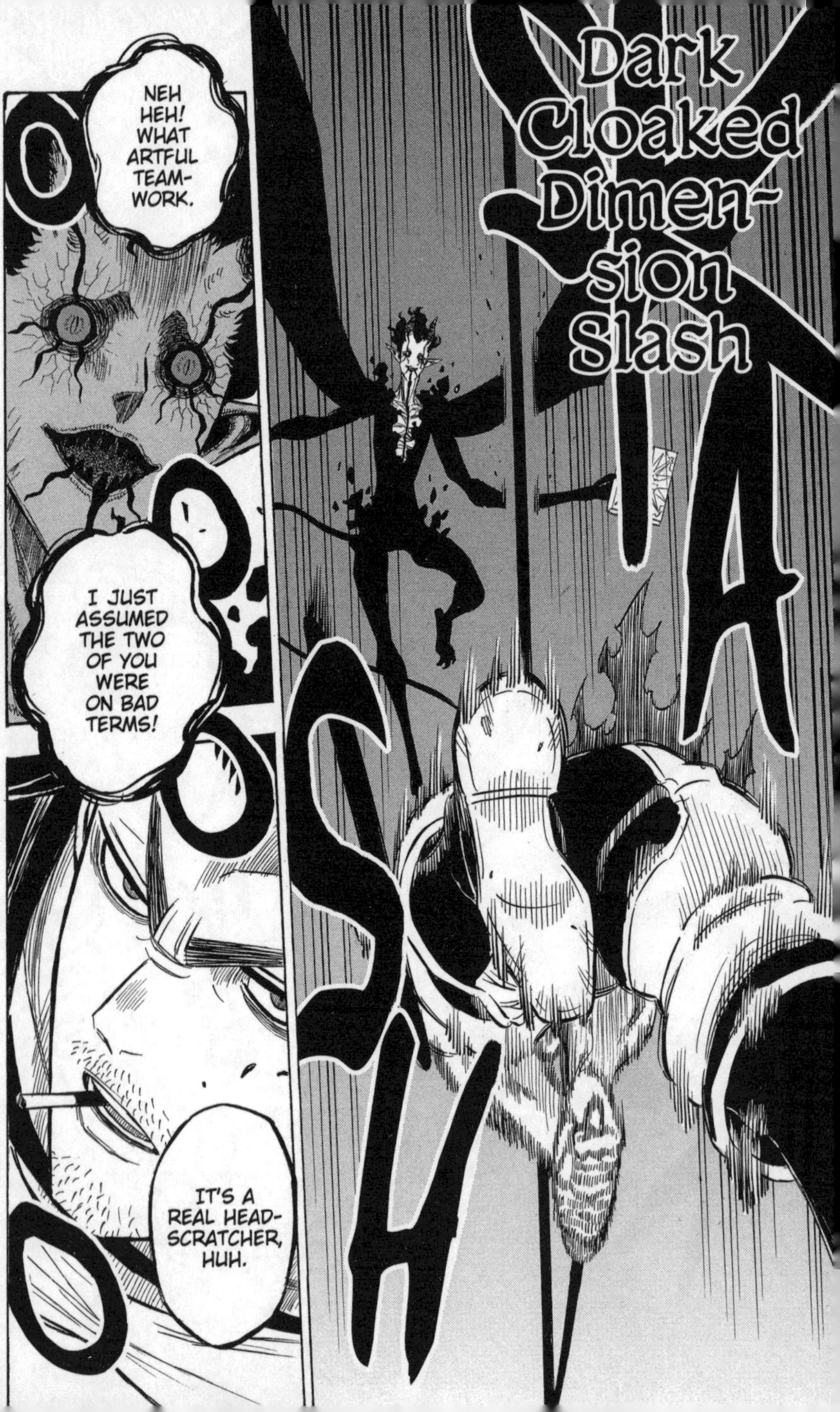
Dark Cloaked Dimension-Slash
NEH HEH! WHAT ARTFUL TEAMWORK.
I JUST ASSUMED THE TWO OF YOU WERE ON BAD TERMS!
IT'S A REAL HEAD-SCRATCHER, HUH.

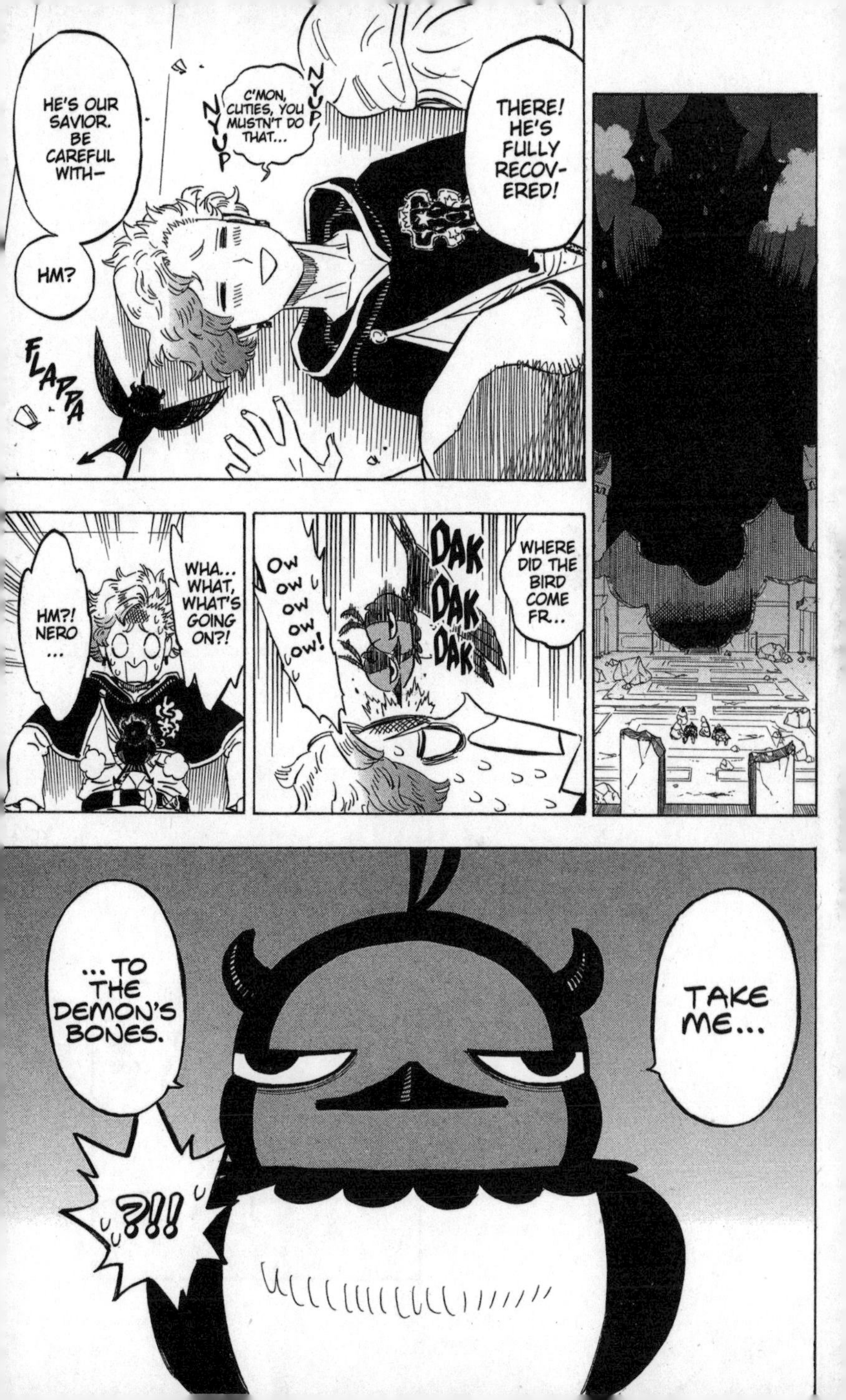
THERE! HE'S FULLY RECOVERED!
NYUP NYUP
C'MON, CUTIES, YOU MUSTN'T DO THAT...
HE'S OUR SAVIOR. BE CAREFUL WITH–
HM?
FLAPPA
WHERE DID THE BIRD COME FR...
DAK DAK DAK
OW OW OW OW OW!
WHA... WHAT, WHAT'S GOING ON?!
HM?! NERO...
TAKE ME...
... TO THE DEMON'S BONES.
?!!

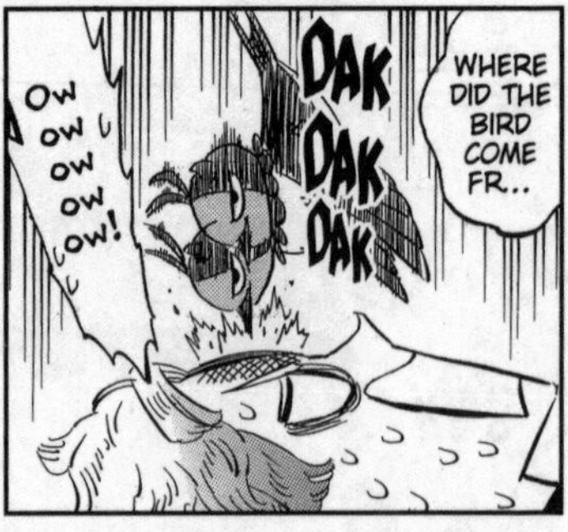
WHERE DID THE BIRD COME FR...
DAK DAK DAK
Ow ow ow ow ow!

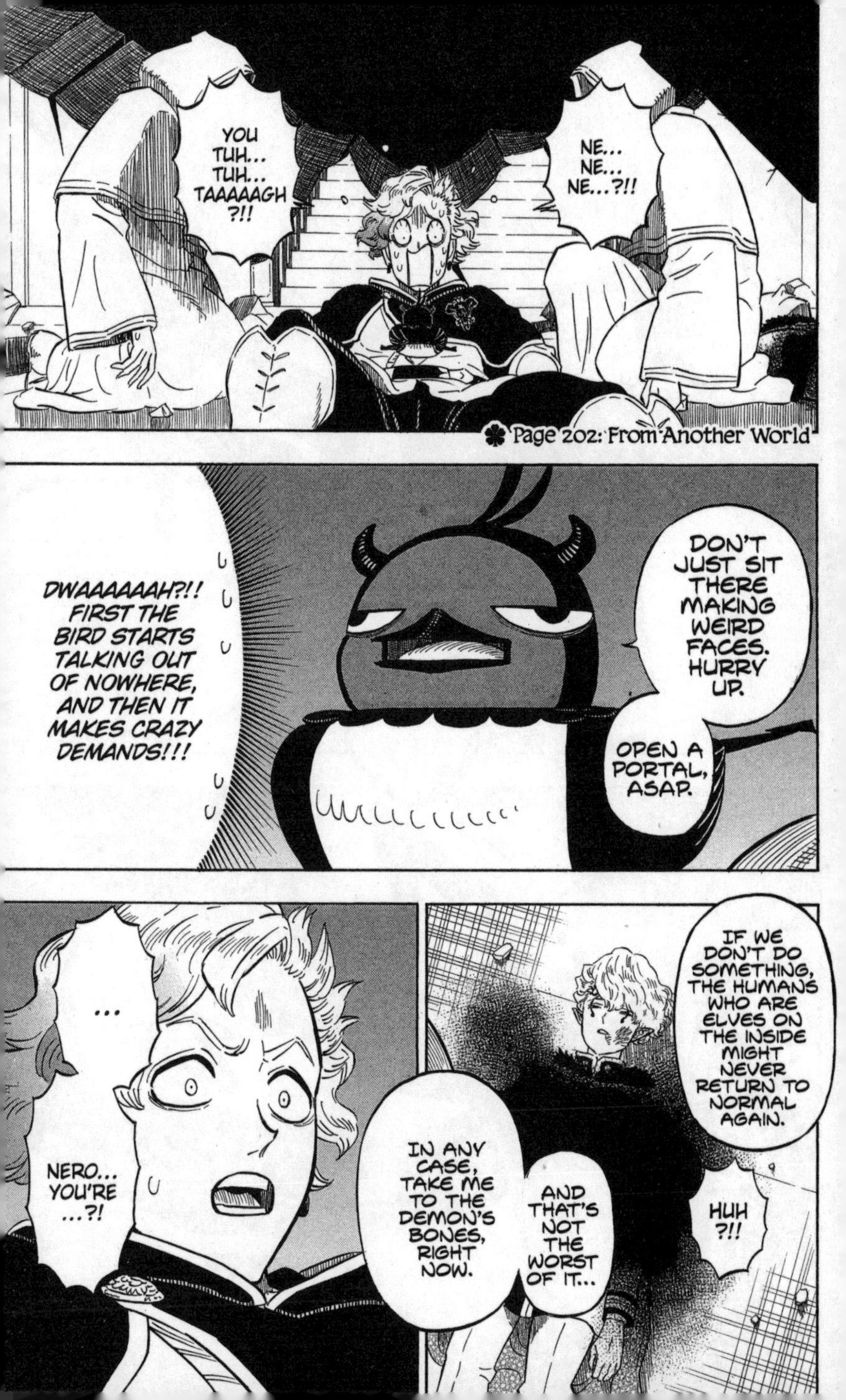
NE... NE... NE...?!!
YOU TUH... TUH... TAAAAAGH?!!
Page 202: From Another World
DON'T JUST SIT THERE MAKING WEIRD FACES. HURRY UP.
OPEN A PORTAL, ASAP.
DWAAAAAAH?!! FIRST THE BIRD STARTS TALKING OUT OF NOWHERE, AND THEN IT MAKES CRAZY DEMANDS!!!
...
NERO... YOU'RE ...?!
IN ANY CASE, TAKE ME TO THE DEMON'S BONES, RIGHT NOW.
AND THAT'S NOT THE WORST OF IT...
IF WE DON'T DO SOMETHING, THE HUMANS WHO ARE ELVES ON THE INSIDE MIGHT NEVER RETURN TO NORMAL AGAIN.
HUH ?!!

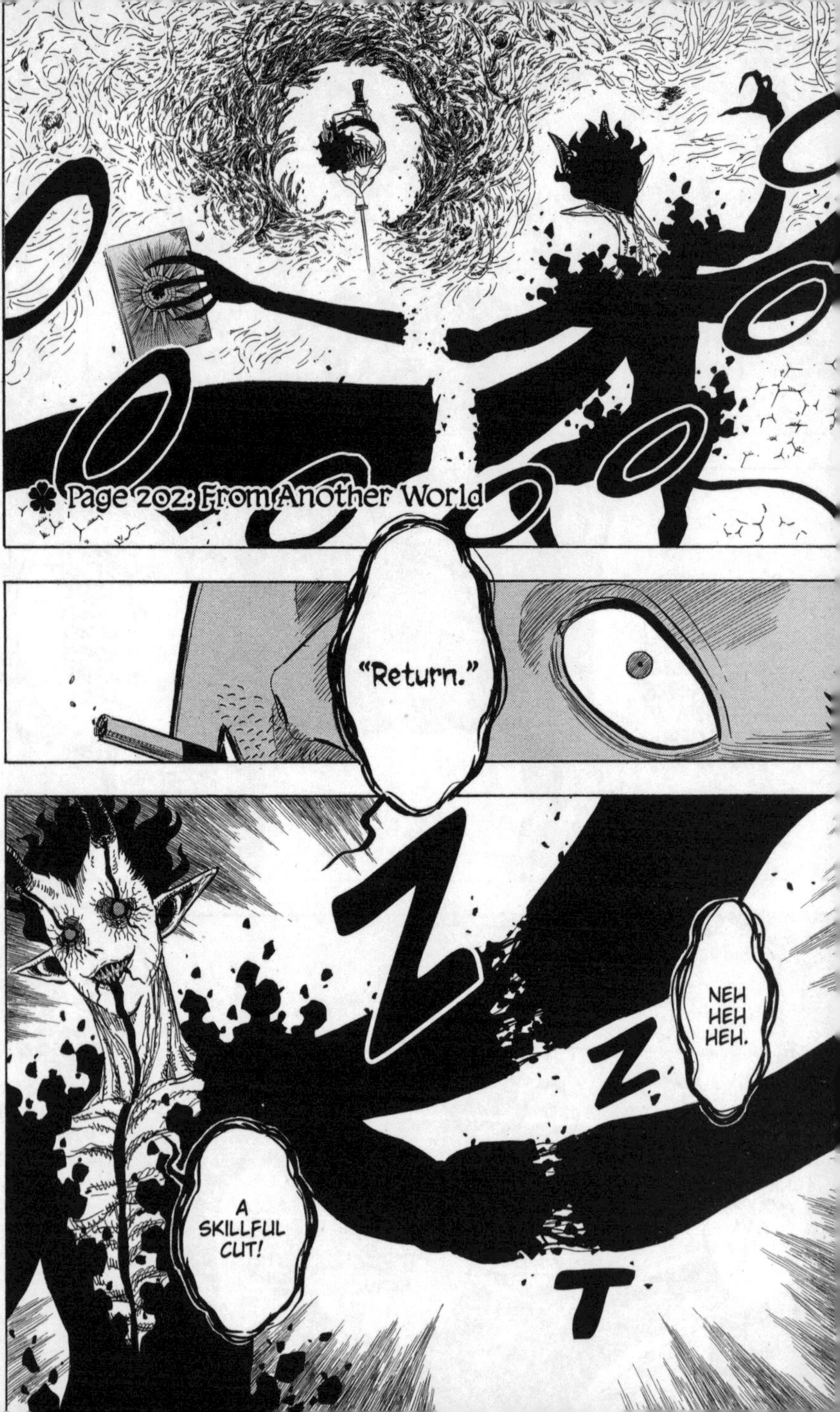
Page 202: From Another World
"Return."
NEH HEH HEH.
A SKILLFUL CUT!
ZZT

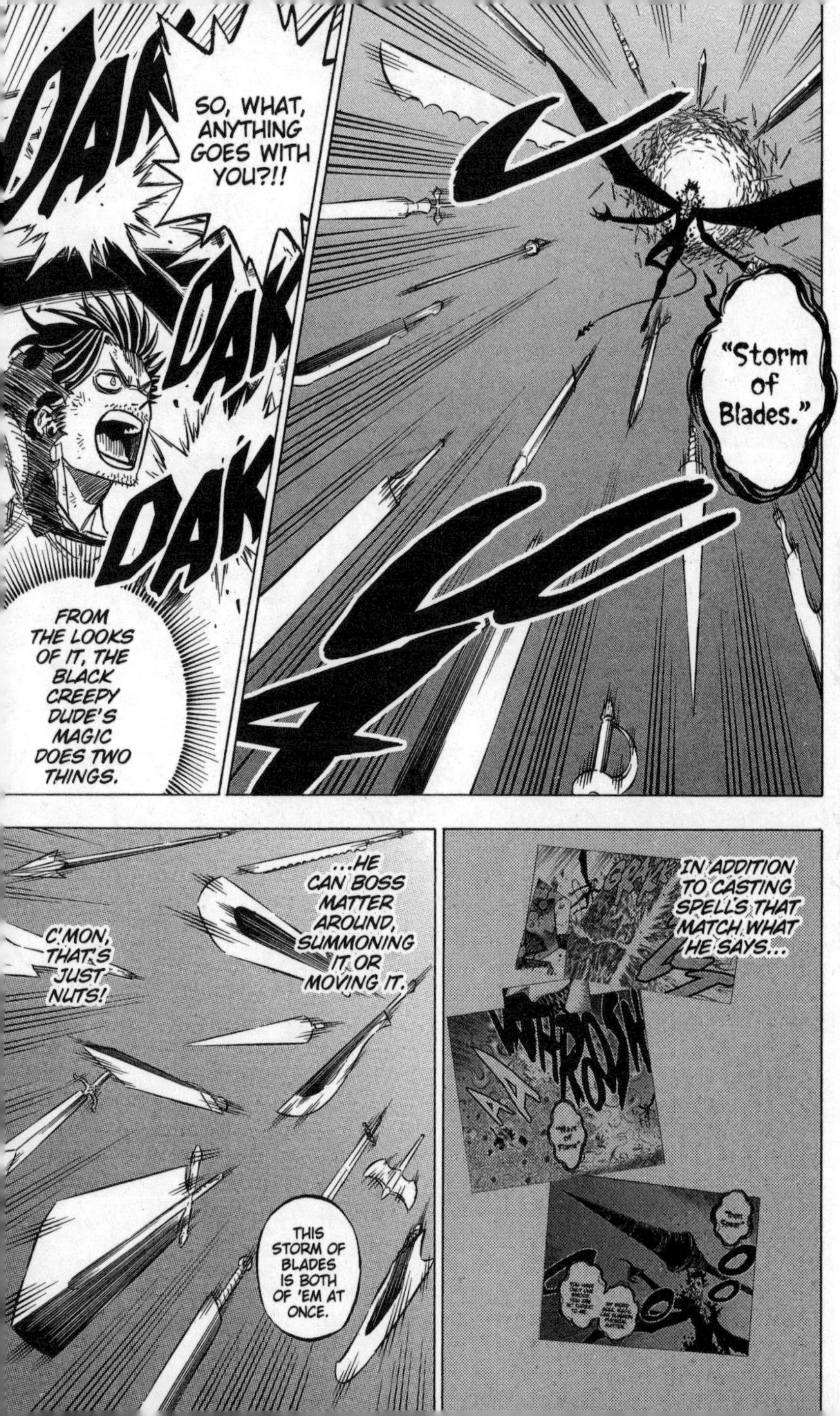
"Storm of Blades."
SO, WHAT, ANYTHING GOES WITH YOU?!!
DAK
DAK
DAK
FROM THE LOOKS OF IT, THE BLACK CREEPY DUDE'S MAGIC DOES TWO THINGS.
IN ADDITION TO CASTING SPELLS THAT MATCH WHAT HE SAYS...
...HE CAN BOSS MATTER AROUND, SUMMONING IT OR MOVING IT.
C'MON, THAT'S JUST NUTS!
THIS STORM OF BLADES IS BOTH OF 'EM AT ONCE.

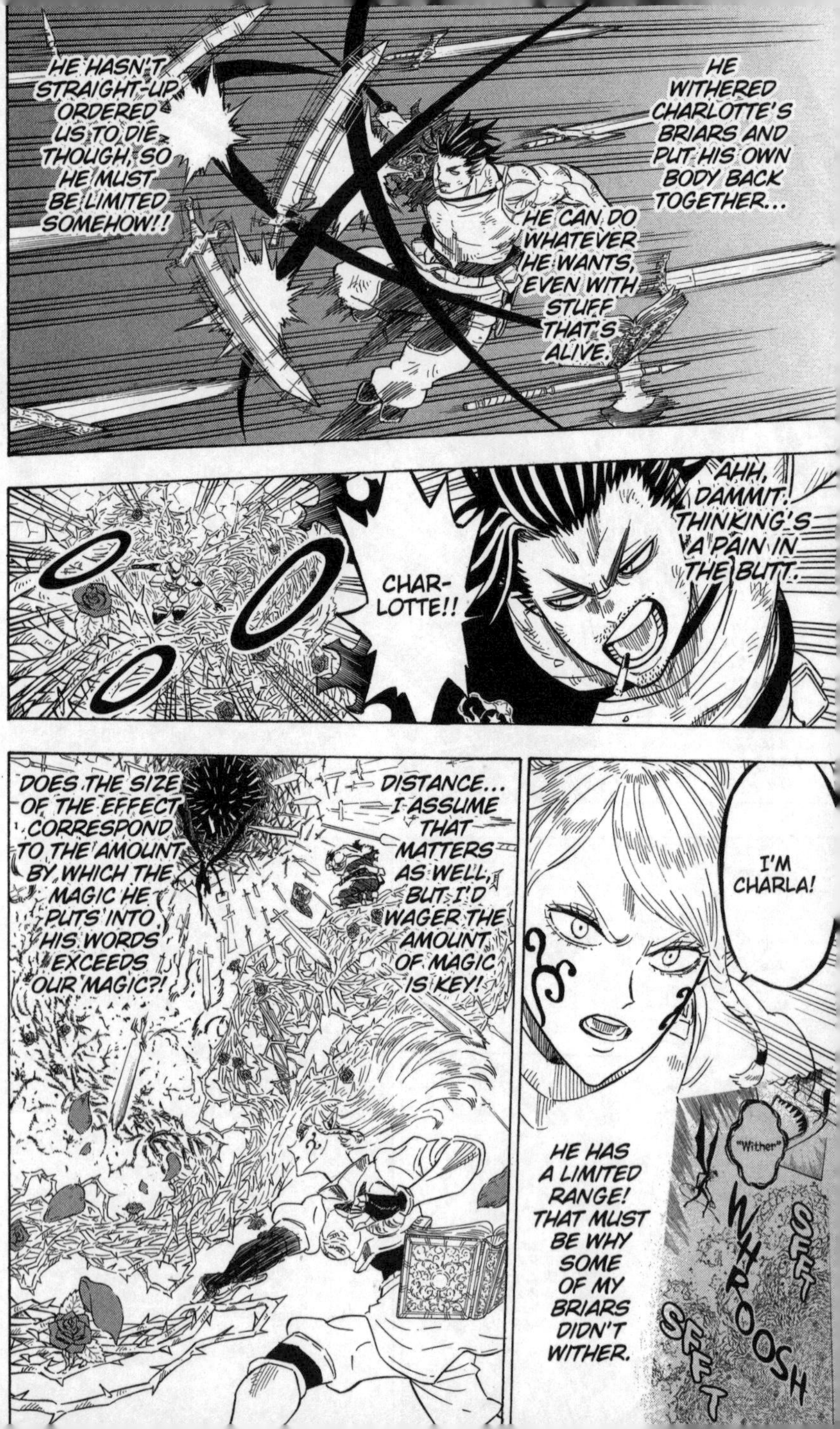
HE WITHERED CHARLOTTE'S BRIARS AND PUT HIS OWN BODY BACK TOGETHER...
HE CAN DO WHATEVER HE WANTS, EVEN WITH STUFF THAT'S ALIVE.
HE HASN'T STRAIGHT-UP ORDERED US TO DIE THOUGH, SO HE MUST BE LIMITED SOMEHOW!!
AHH, DAMMIT. THINKING'S A PAIN IN THE BUTT.
CHAR-LOTTE!!
I'M CHARLA!
"Wither"
WHROOSH
SEFT
SEFT
HE HAS A LIMITED RANGE! THAT MUST BE WHY SOME OF MY BRIARS DIDN'T WITHER.
DISTANCE... I ASSUME THAT MATTERS AS WELL, BUT I'D WAGER THE AMOUNT OF MAGIC IS KEY!
DOES THE SIZE OF THE EFFECT CORRESPOND TO THE AMOUNT BY WHICH THE MAGIC HE PUTS INTO HIS WORDS EXCEEDS OUR MAGIC?!

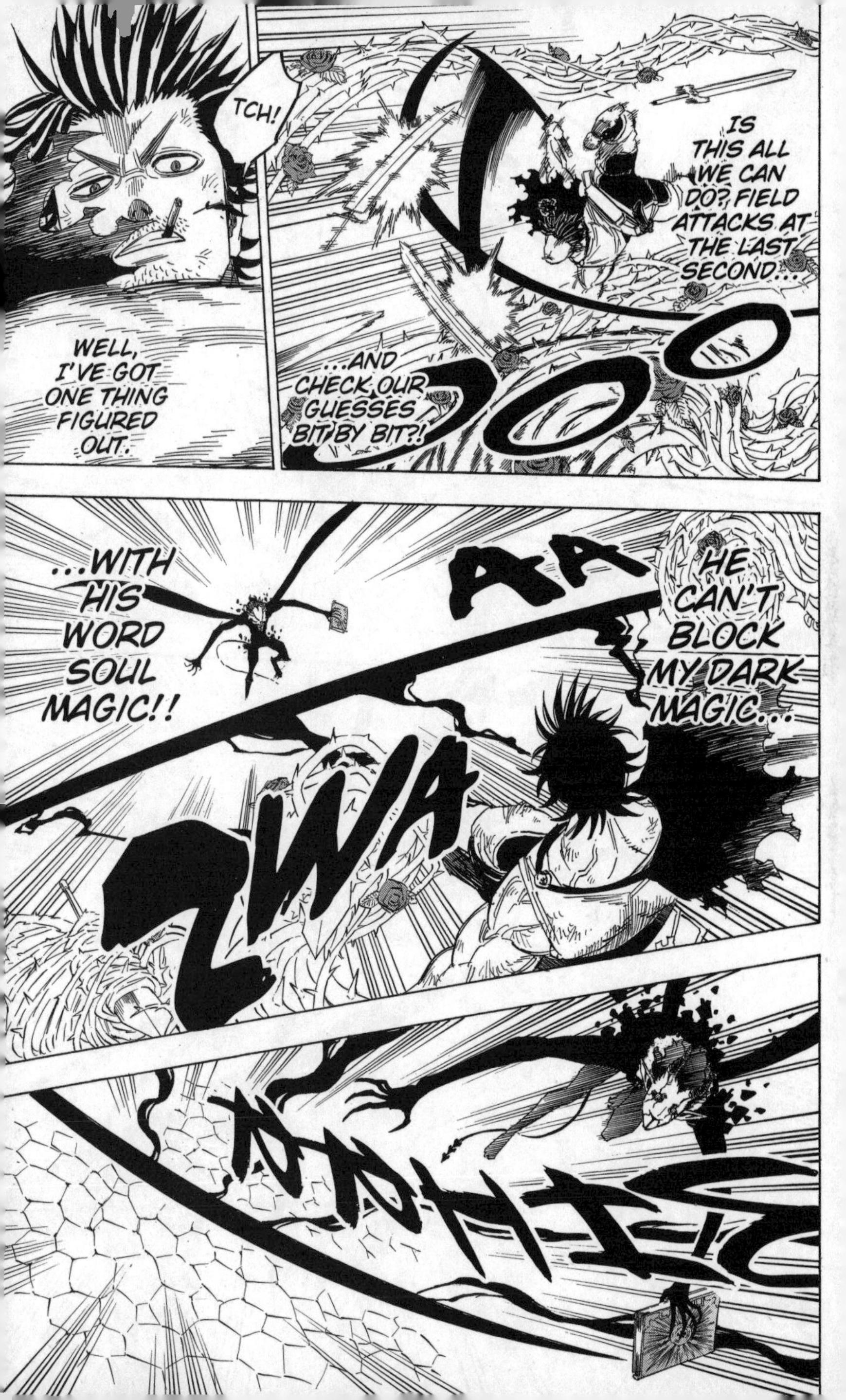
IS THIS ALL WE CAN DO? FIELD ATTACKS AT THE LAST SECOND...
...AND CHECK OUR GUESSES BIT BY BIT?!
DOOO
TCH!
WELL, I'VE GOT ONE THING FIGURED OUT.
HE CAN'T BLOCK MY DARK MAGIC...
...WITH HIS WORD SOUL MAGIC!!
ZWAA

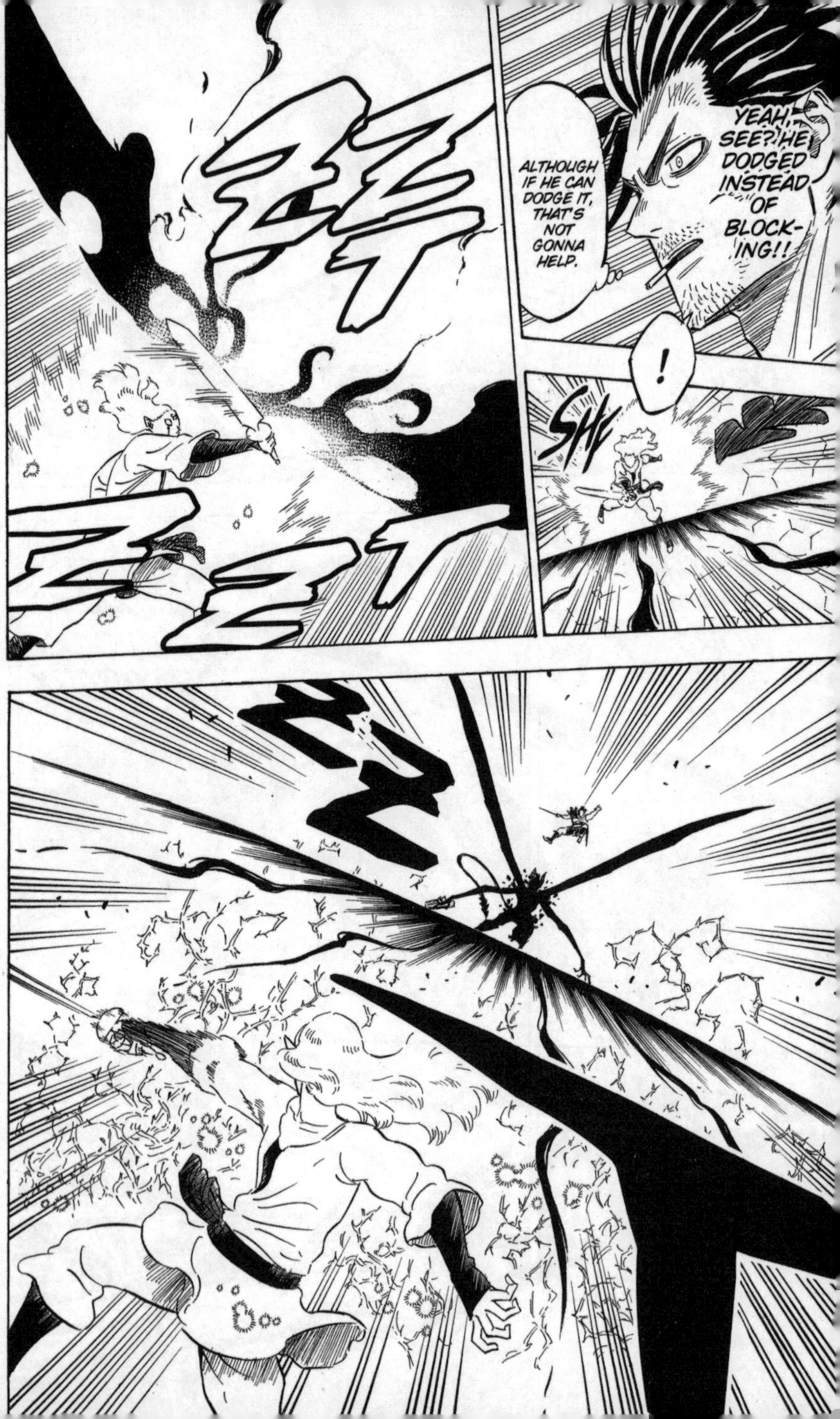
YEAH, SEE? HE DODGED INSTEAD OF BLOCK-ING!!
ALTHOUGH IF HE CAN DODGE IT, THAT'S NOT GONNA HELP.
!
SHF

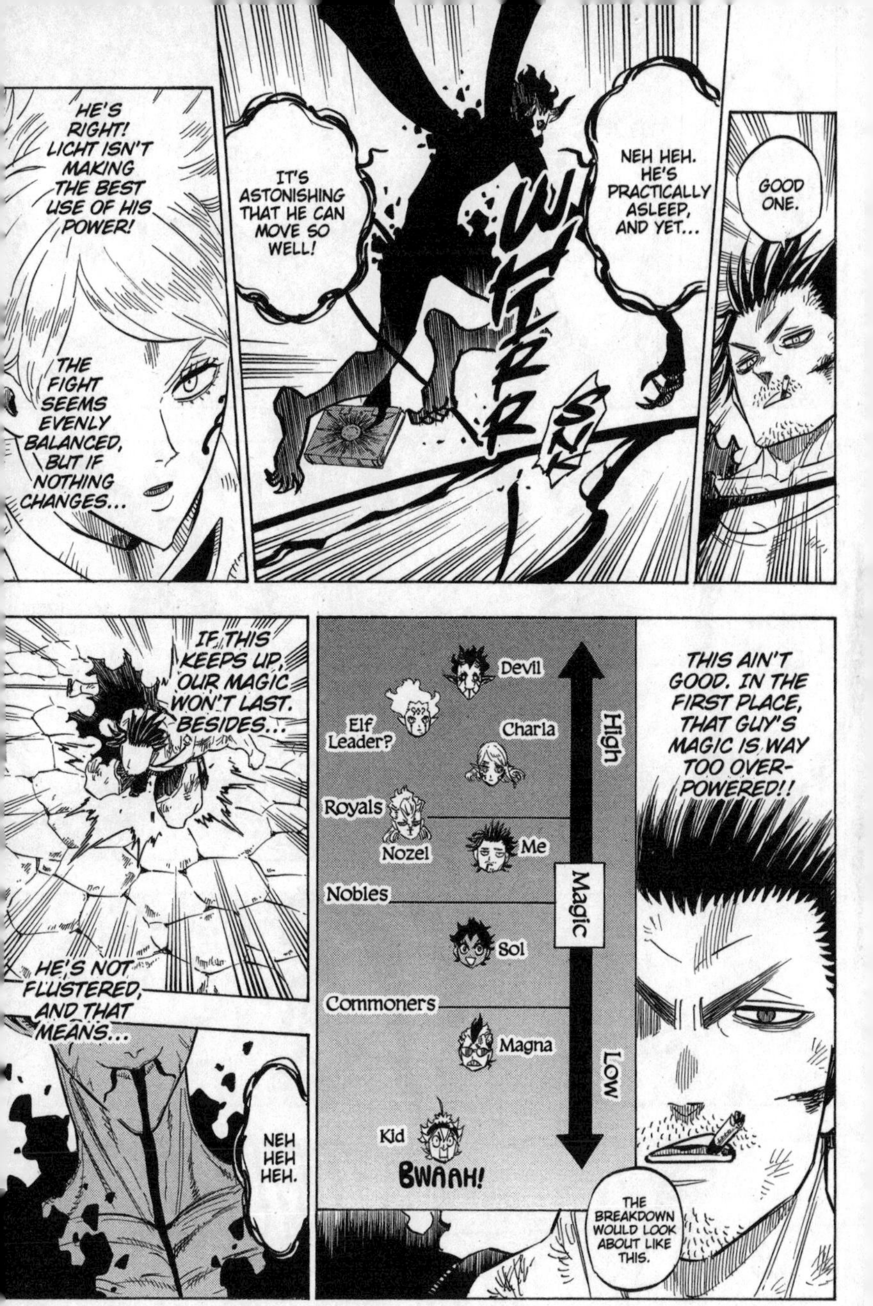
GOOD ONE.
NEH HEH. HE'S PRACTICALLY ASLEEP, AND YET...
IT'S ASTONISHING THAT HE CAN MOVE SO WELL!
WHIRR
SNK
HE'S RIGHT! LICHT ISN'T MAKING THE BEST USE OF HIS POWER!
THE FIGHT SEEMS EVENLY BALANCED, BUT IF NOTHING CHANGES...
THIS AIN'T GOOD. IN THE FIRST PLACE, THAT GUY'S MAGIC IS WAY TOO OVER-POWERED!!
THE BREAKDOWN WOULD LOOK ABOUT LIKE THIS.
Magic
High
Low
Devil
Elf Leader?
Charla
Royals
Nozel
Me
Nobles
Sol
Commoners
Magna
Kid
BWAAH!
IF THIS KEEPS UP, OUR MAGIC WON'T LAST. BESIDES...
HE'S NOT FLUSTERED, AND THAT MEANS...
NEH HEH HEH.

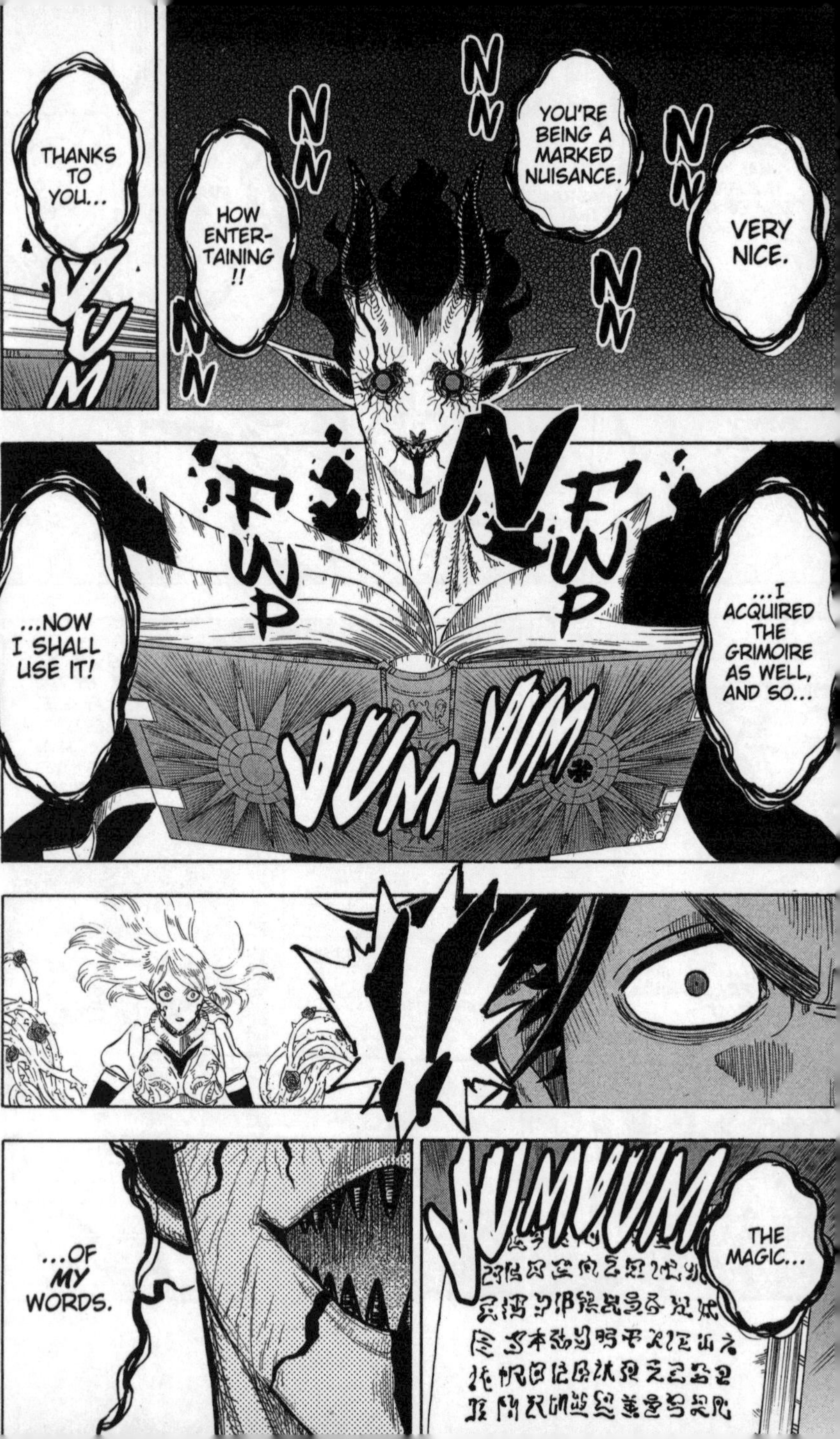
NNNNNNNN
VERY NICE.
YOU'RE BEING A MARKED NUISANCE.
HOW ENTERTAINING!!
THANKS TO YOU...
VUM
...I ACQUIRED THE GRIMOIRE AS WELL, AND SO...
...NOW I SHALL USE IT!
FWP FWP
VUM VUM
THE MAGIC...
VUMVUM
...OF MY WORDS.

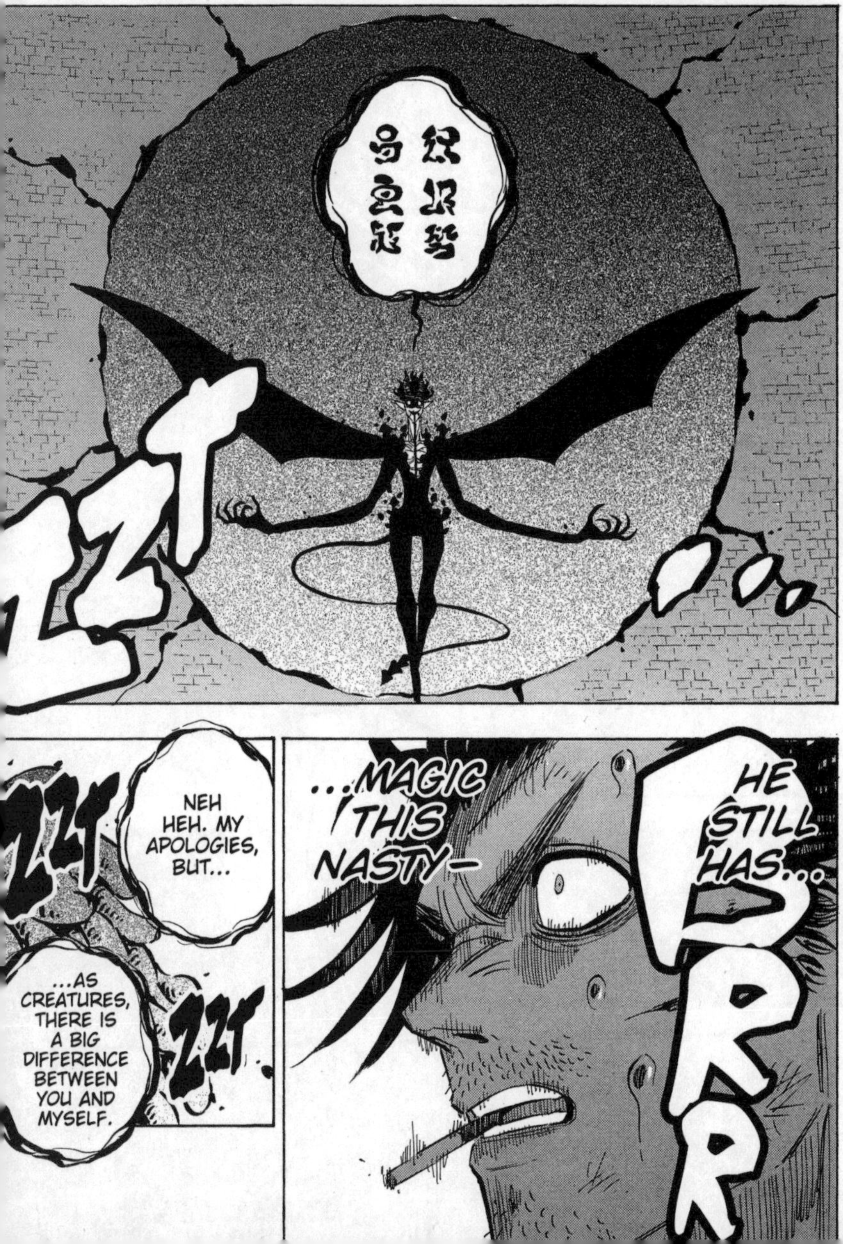
ZZT
NEH HEH. MY APOLOGIES, BUT...
...AS CREATURES, THERE IS A BIG DIFFERENCE BETWEEN YOU AND MYSELF.
ZZT
ZZT
...MAGIC THIS NASTY—
HE STILL HAS...
DRRR

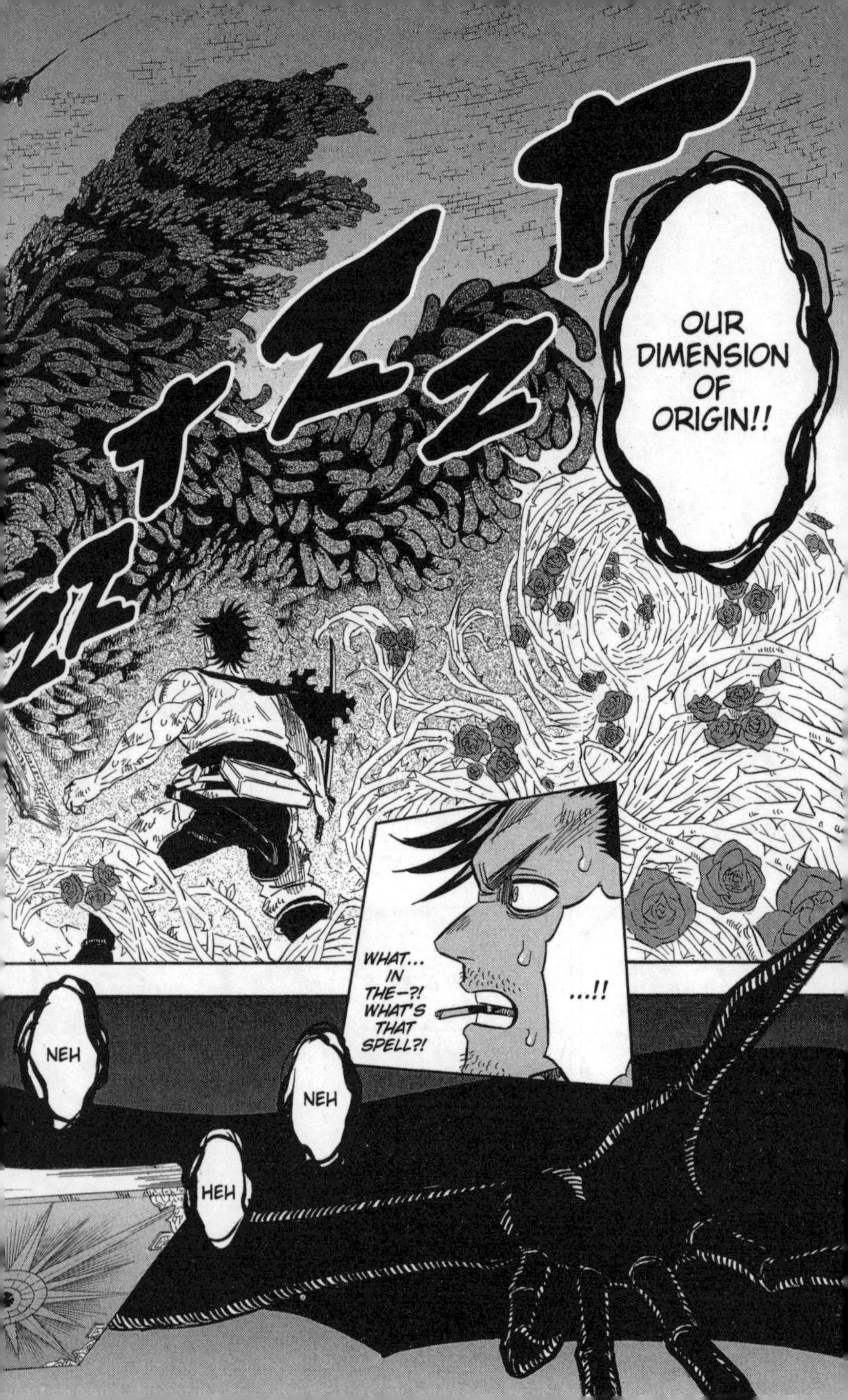
OUR DIMENSION OF ORIGIN!!
...!!
WHAT... IN THE-?! WHAT'S THAT SPELL?!
NEH
NEH
HEH

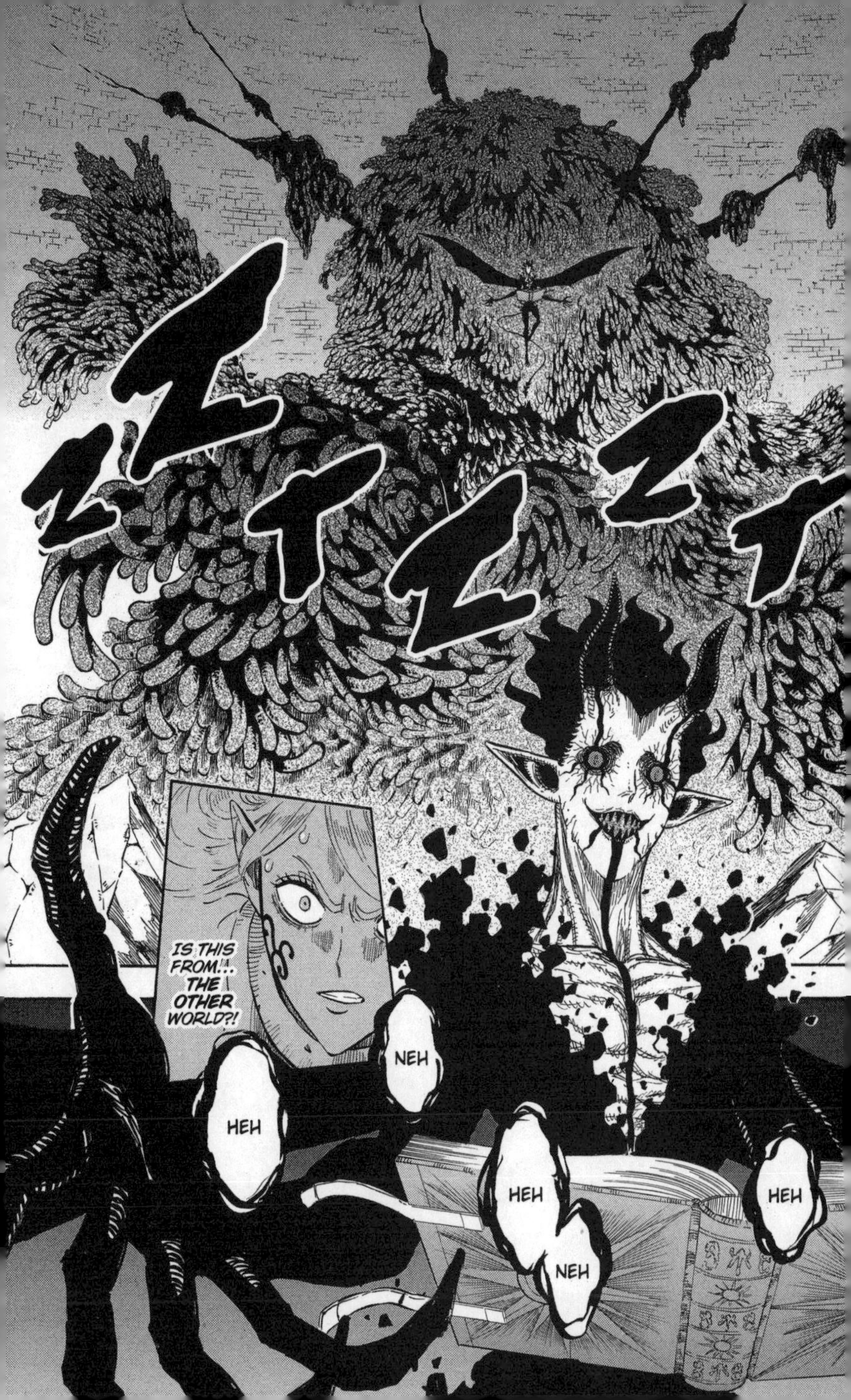
IS THIS FROM... THE OTHER WORLD?!
NEH
HEH
HEH
HEH
NEH

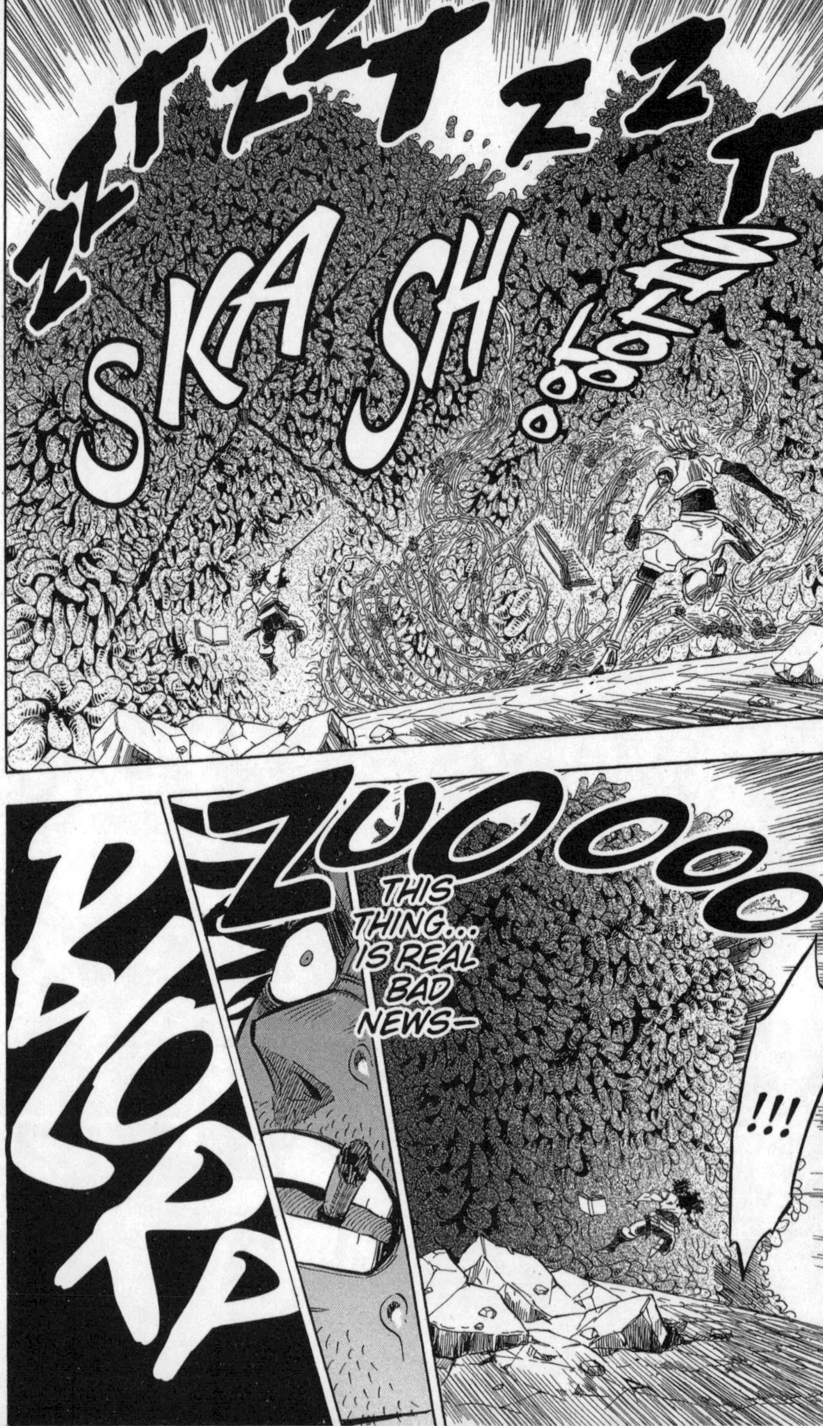
ZZZZZZZT
SKASH
SHLOOOOO
ZUOOOO
THIS THING... IS REAL BAD NEWS—
!!!
DADORA

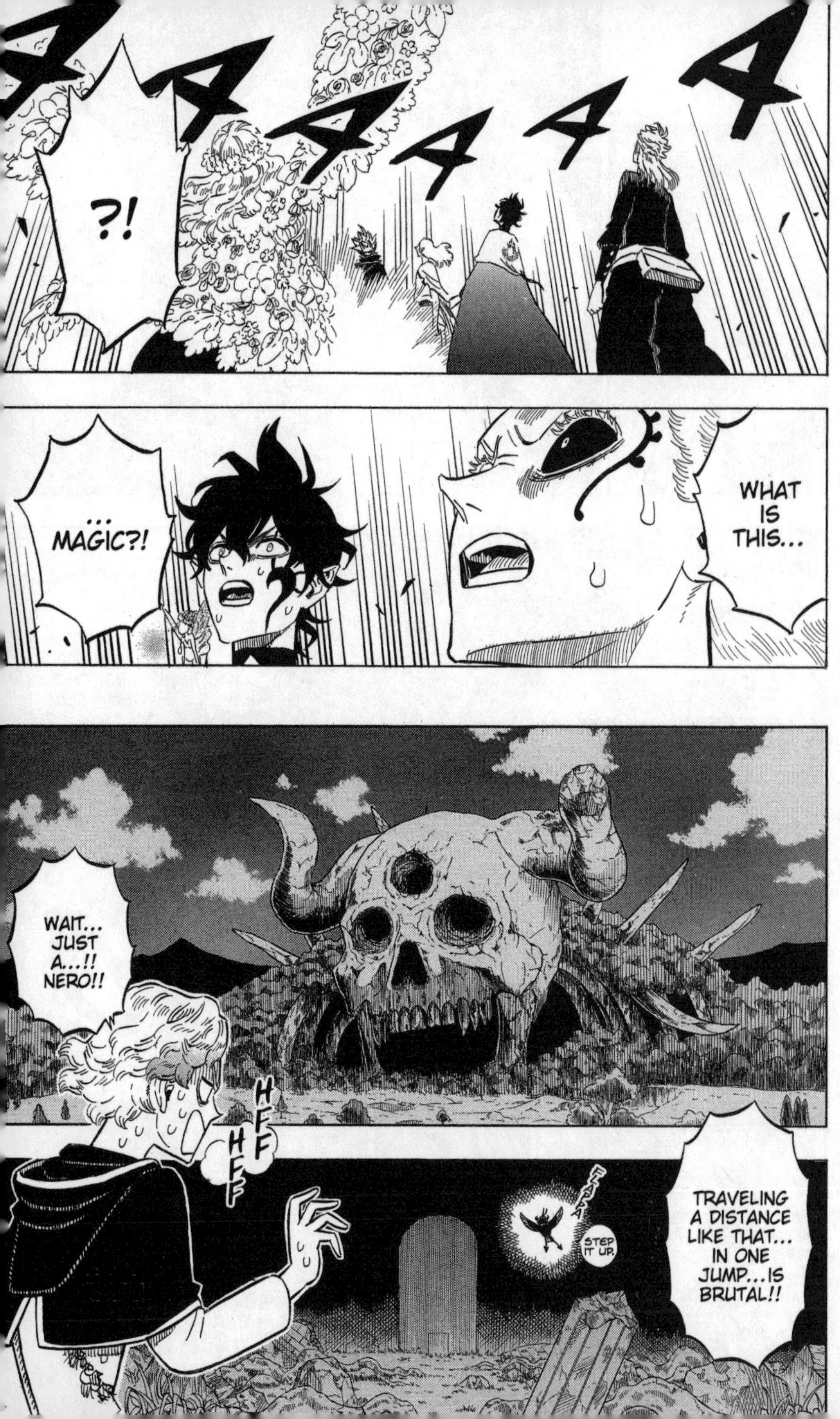
AAAAAAA
?!
WHAT IS THIS...
...MAGIC?!
WAIT... JUST A...!! NERO!!
TRAVELING A DISTANCE LIKE THAT... IN ONE JUMP... IS BRUTAL!!
FLAPA
STEP IT UP.
HFF HFF

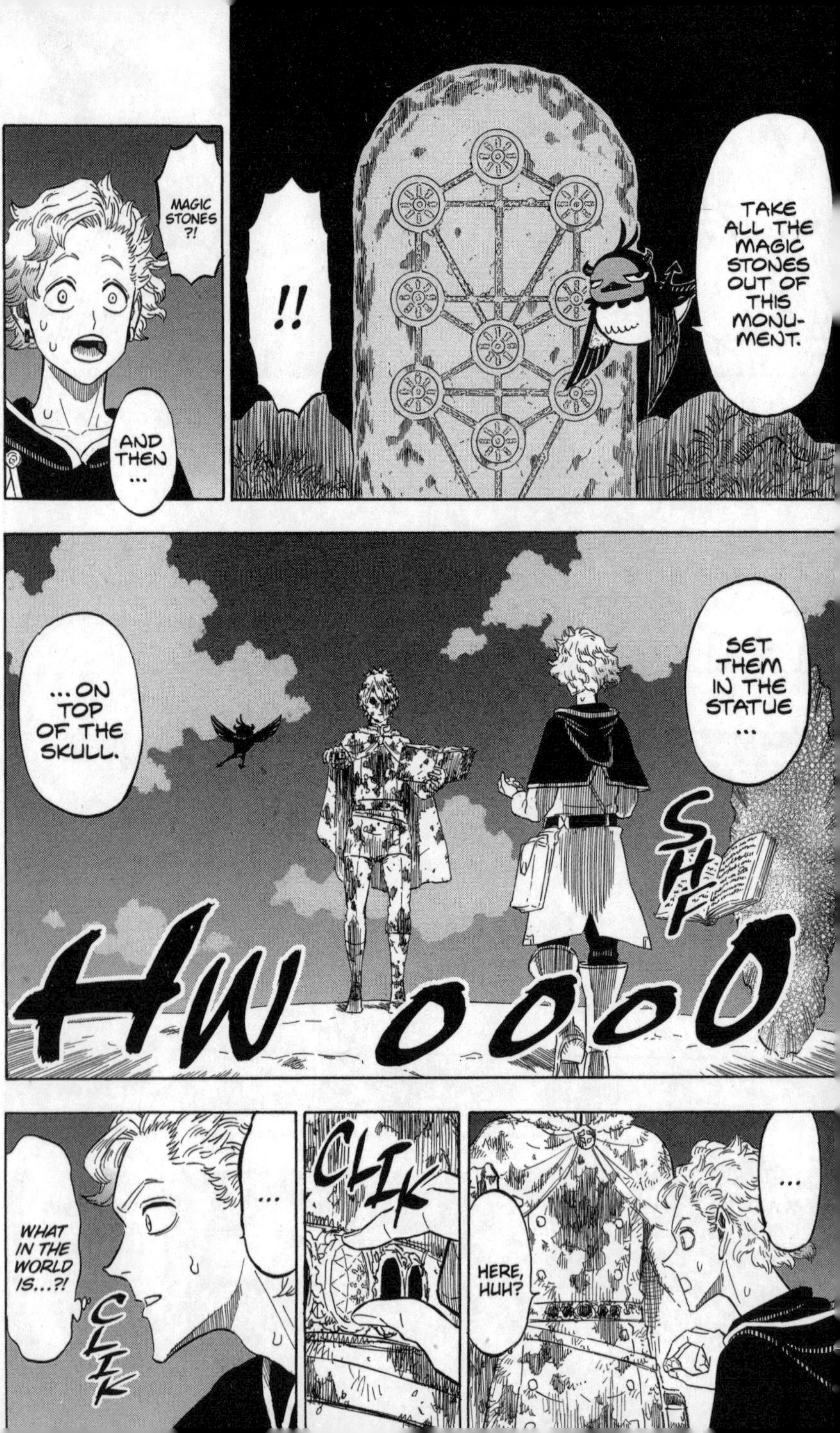
TAKE ALL THE MAGIC STONES OUT OF THIS MONUMENT.
!!
MAGIC STONES ?!
AND THEN ...
SET THEM IN THE STATUE ...
SHF
...ON TOP OF THE SKULL.
HWOOOO
...
HERE, HUH?
CLIK
...
WHAT IN THE WORLD IS...?!
CLIK

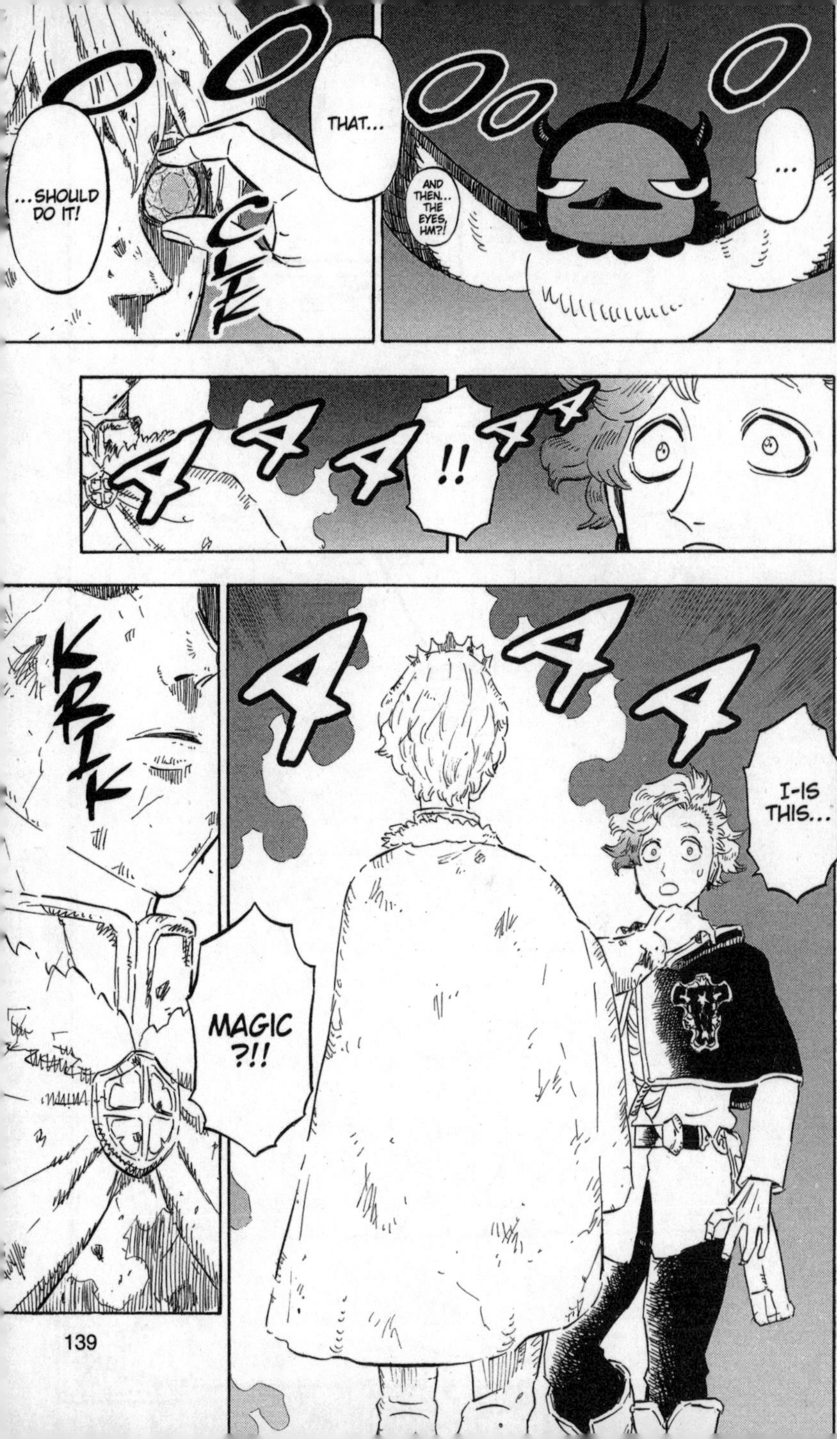
OOOO
...
AND THEN... THE EYES, HM?!
THAT...
...SHOULD DO IT!
CLIK
AA
!!
AAAA
AAAA
I-IS THIS...
MAGIC ?!!
KRIK

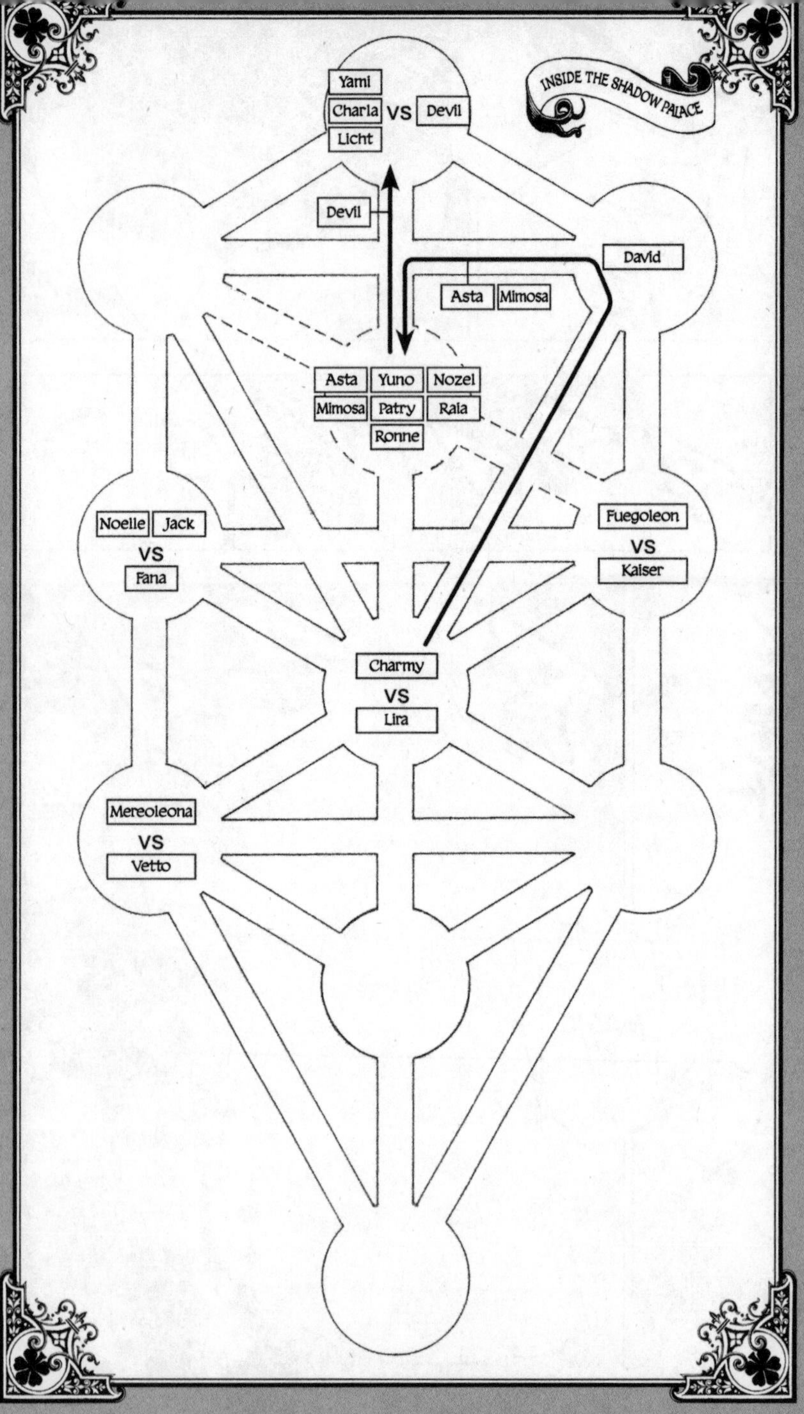
INSIDE THE SHADOW PALACE
Yami
Charla
Licht
VS
Devil
Devil
David
Asta
Mimosa
Asta
Yuno
Nozel
Mimosa
Patry
Raia
Ronne
Noelle
Jack
VS
Fana
Fuegoleon
VS
Kaiser
Charmy
VS
Lira
Mereoleona
VS
Vetto

Page 203: Breaking the Seal

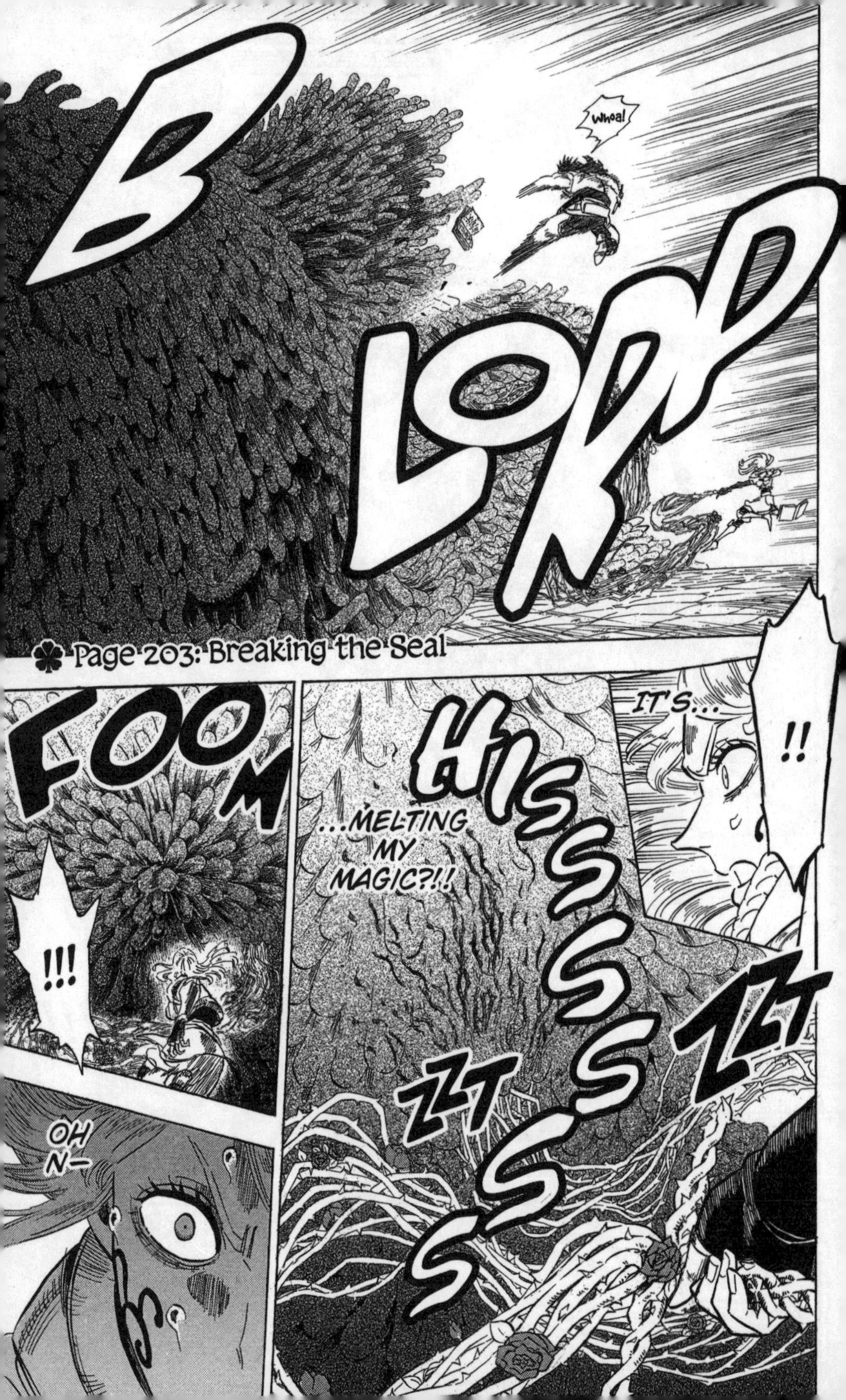
BLOOOM
Whoa!
IT'S...
!!
HISSSSSS
...MELTING MY MAGIC?!!
ZZT
ZZT
FOOM
!!!
OH N—

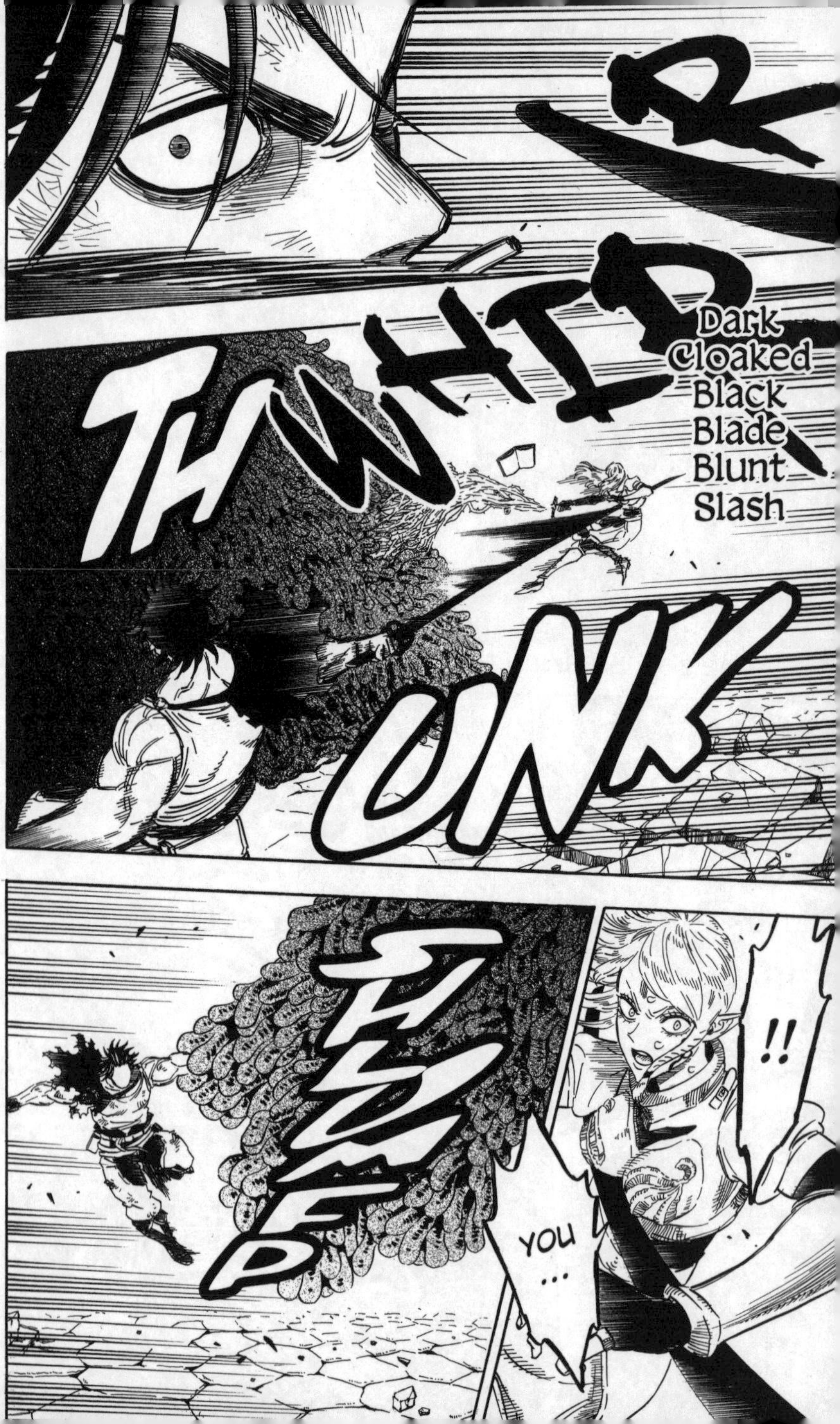
THWHIP
Dark Cloaked Black Blade Blunt Slash
!!
YOU ...

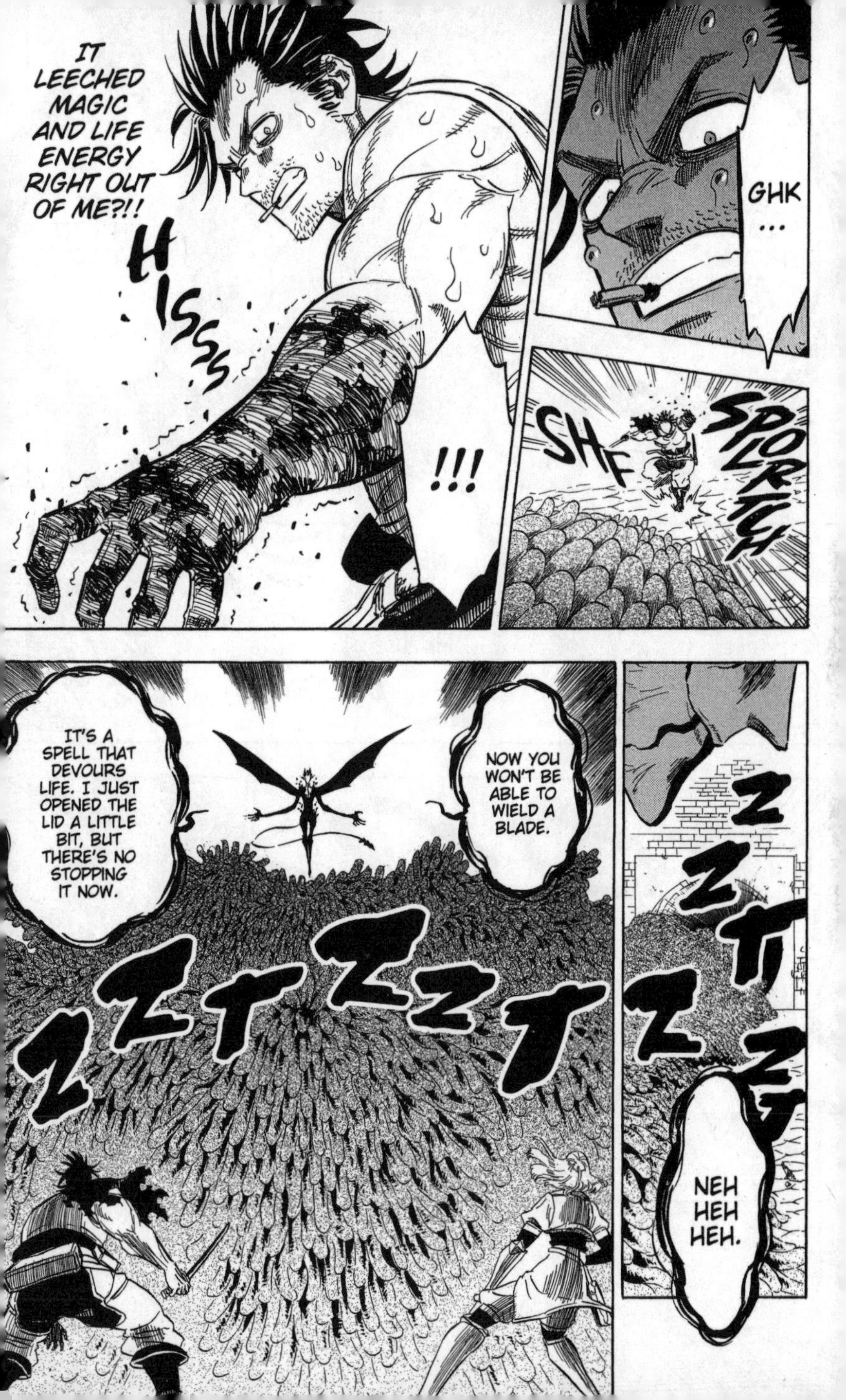

GHK ...
SHF
SPLORTCH
IT LEECHED MAGIC AND LIFE ENERGY RIGHT OUT OF ME?!!
HISSS
!!!
ZZT
NEH HEH HEH.
NOW YOU WON'T BE ABLE TO WIELD A BLADE.
IT'S A SPELL THAT DEVOURS LIFE. I JUST OPENED THE LID A LITTLE BIT, BUT THERE'S NO STOPPING IT NOW.
ZZZT

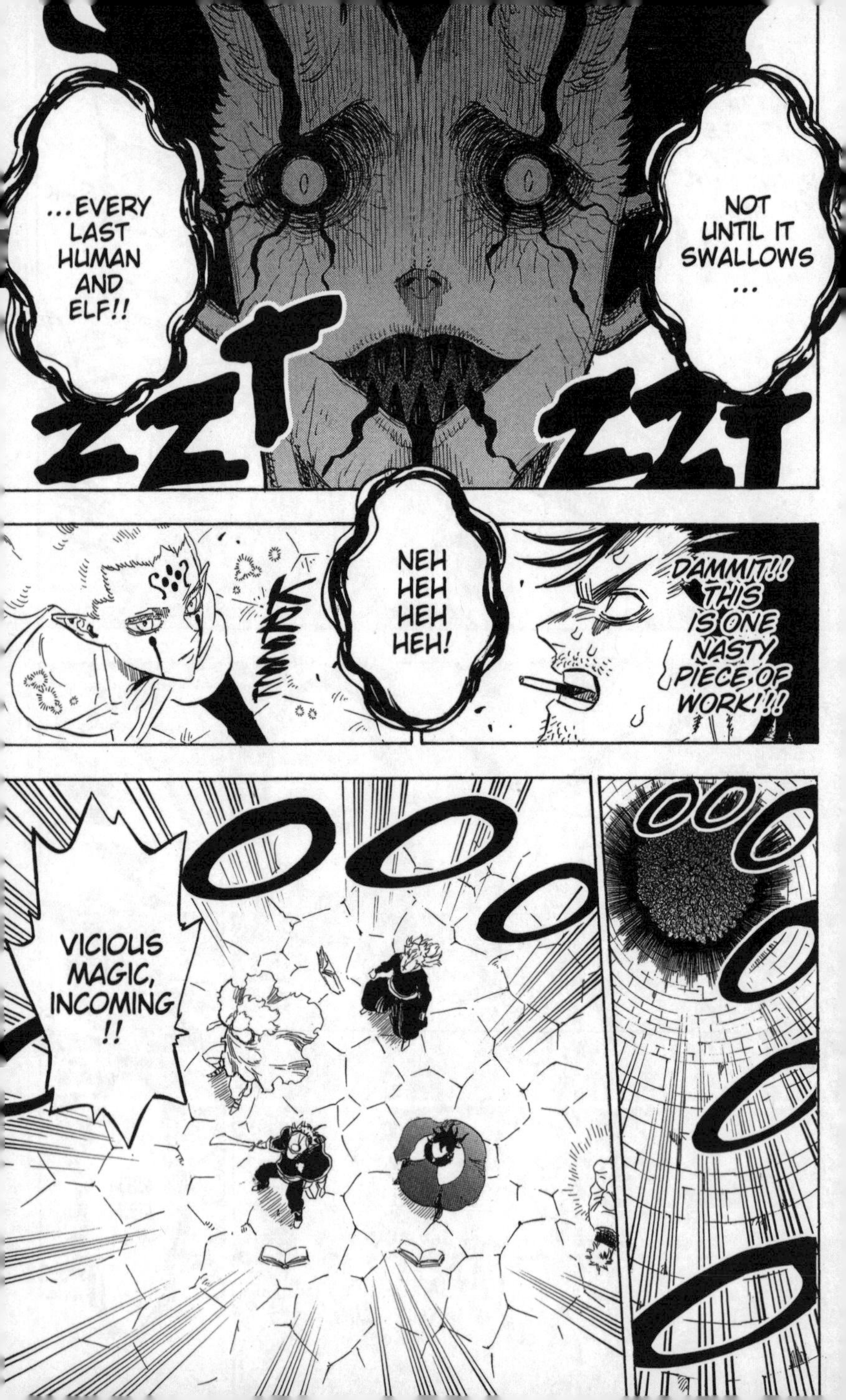
NOT UNTIL IT SWALLOWS...
...EVERY LAST HUMAN AND ELF!!
ZZT
ZZT
DAMMIT!! THIS IS ONE NASTY PIECE OF WORK!!!
NEH HEH HEH HEH!
OOOOOO
VICIOUS MAGIC, INCOMING!!
OOOO

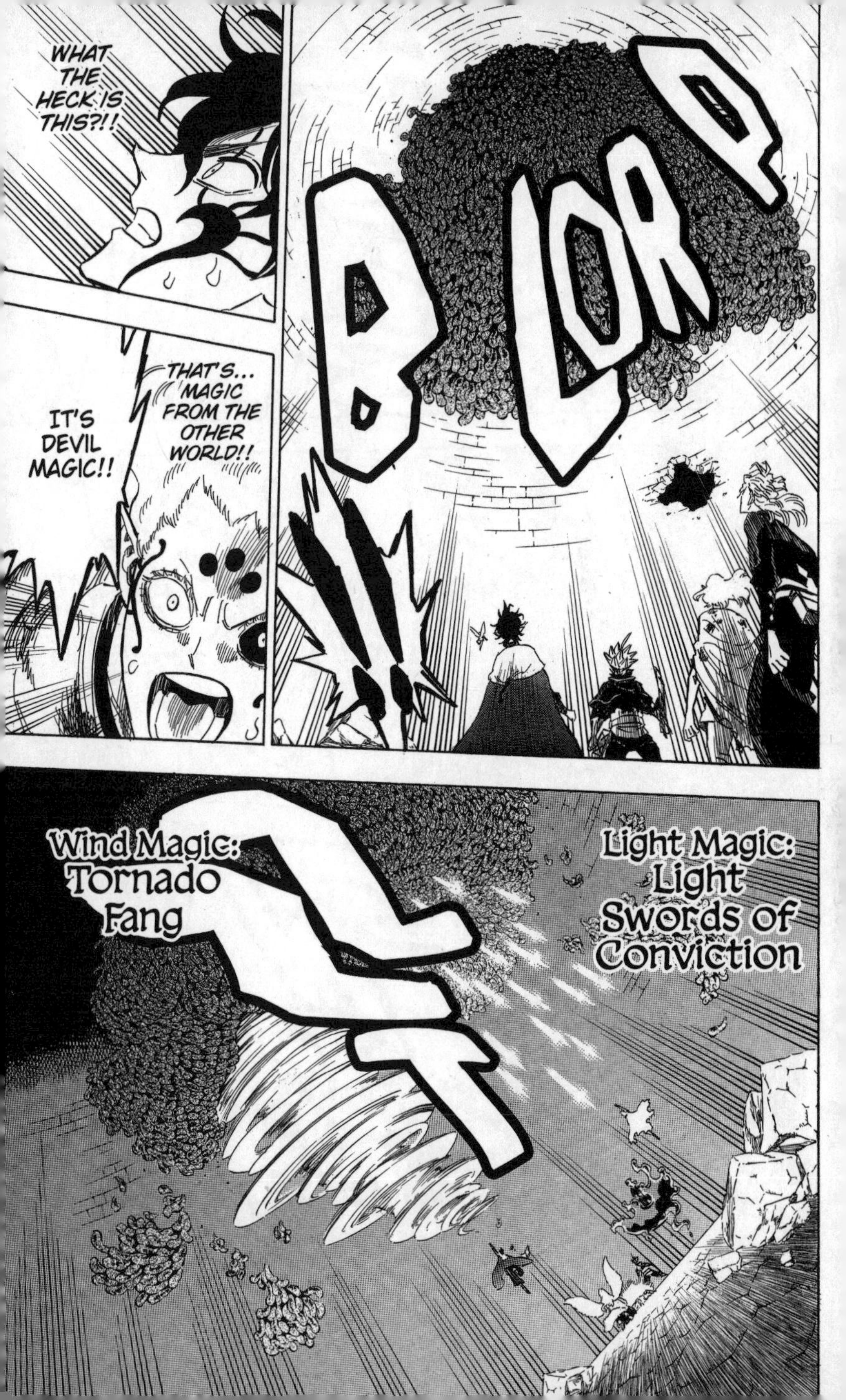
BLORP
WHAT THE HECK IS THIS?!!
!!
THAT'S... MAGIC FROM THE OTHER WORLD!!
IT'S DEVIL MAGIC!!
Light Magic: Light Swords of Conviction
Wind Magic: Tornado Fang

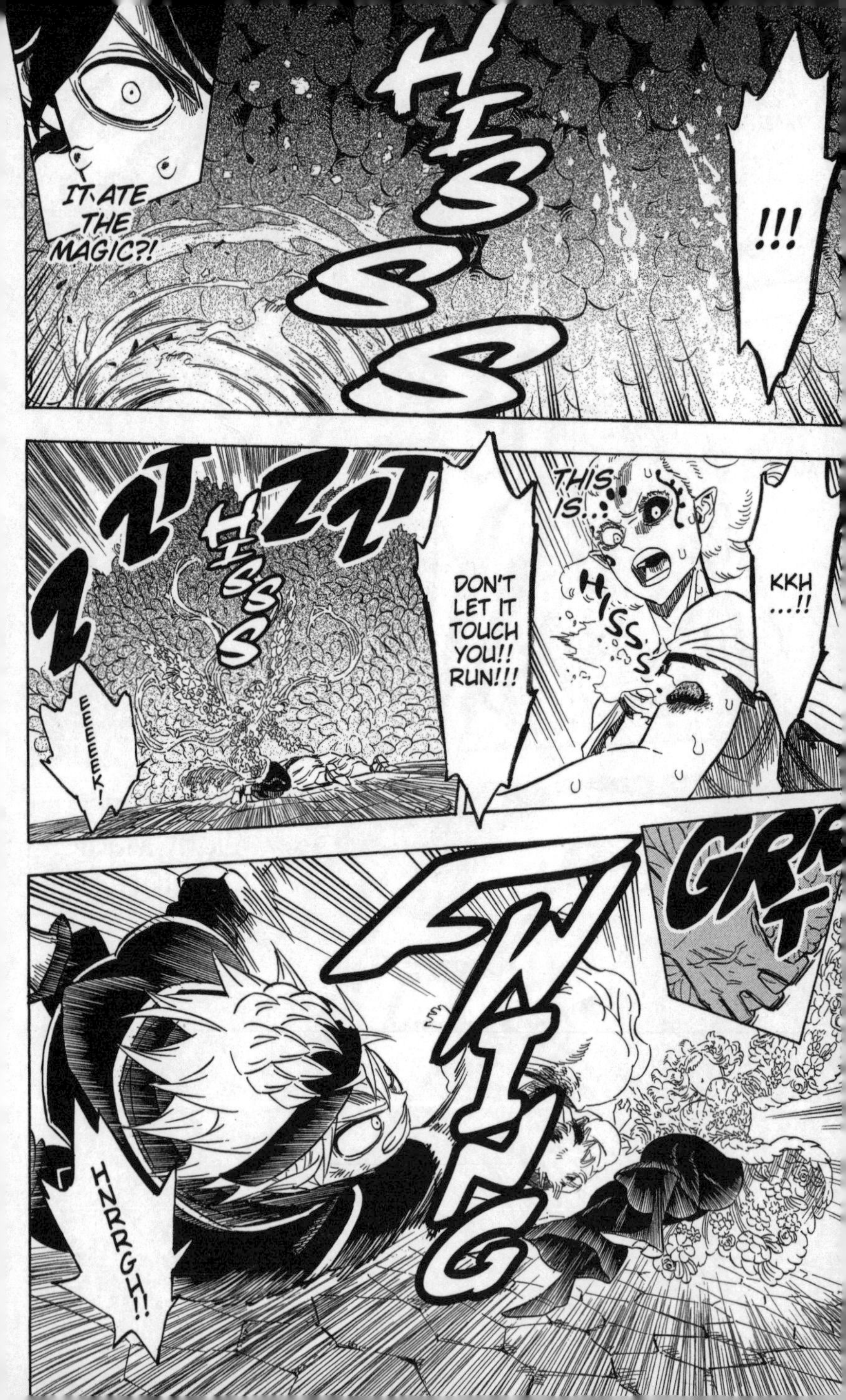
!!!
HISSSS
IT ATE THE MAGIC?!
KKH...!!
THIS IS...
HISSS
DON'T LET IT TOUCH YOU!! RUN!!!
HISSSS
EEEEEK!
HNRRGH!!

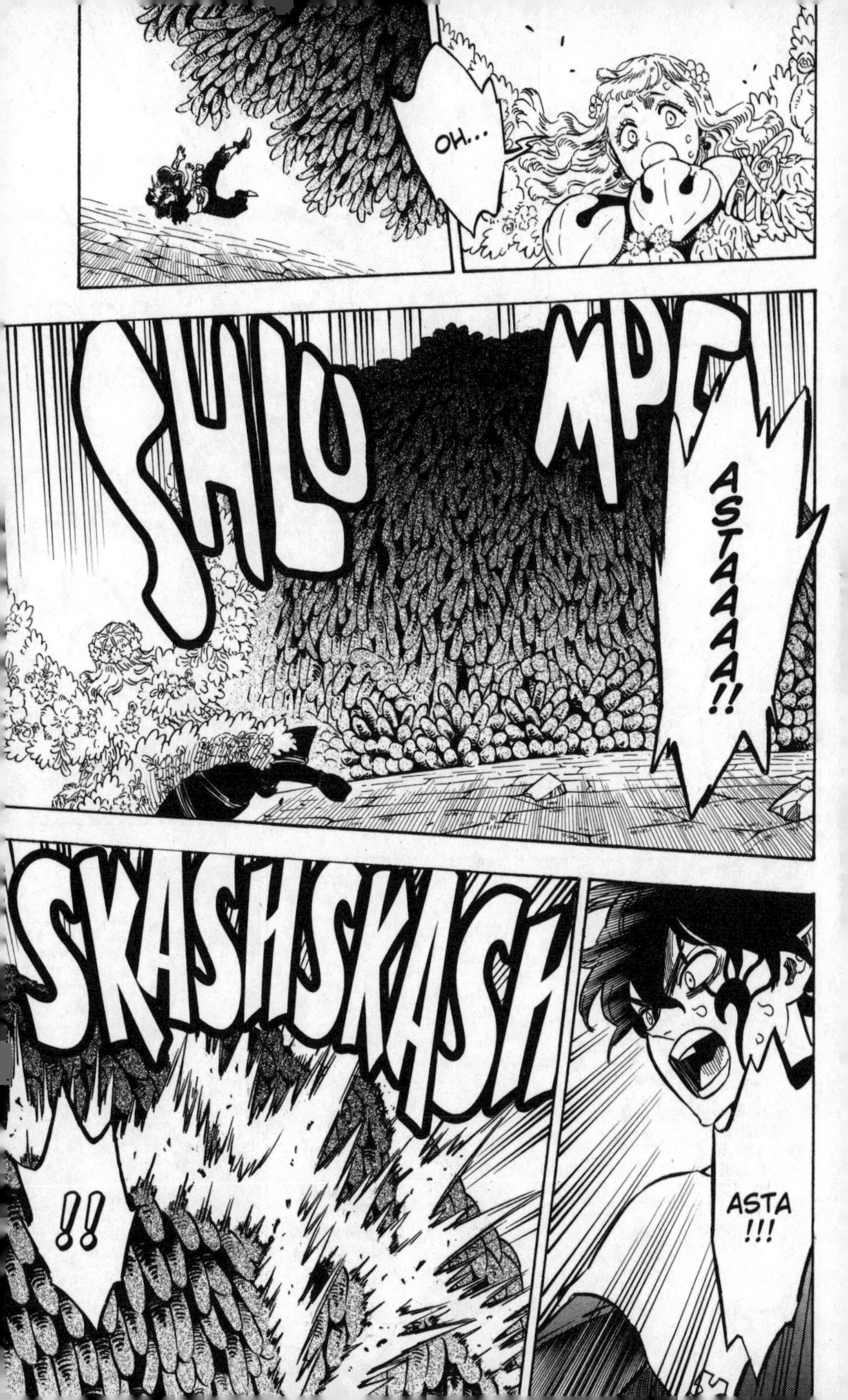
OH...
SHLUMPF
ASTAAAAA!!
ASTA !!!
SKASHSKASH
!!

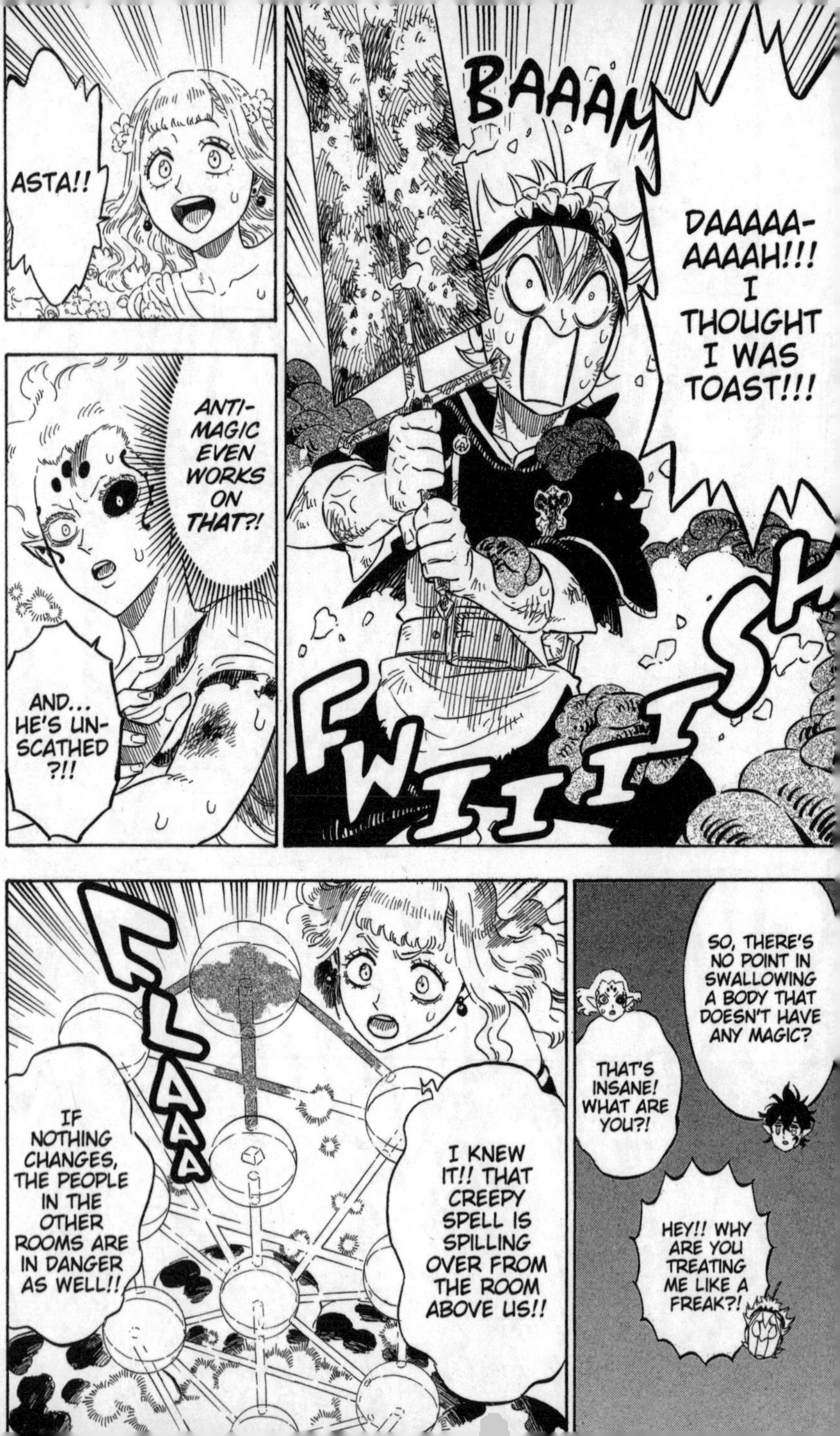

BAAAM
DAAAAA-AAAAH!!! I THOUGHT I WAS TOAST!!!
FWIIIISH
ASTA!!
ANTI-MAGIC EVEN WORKS ON THAT?!
AND... HE'S UN-SCATHED?!!
SO, THERE'S NO POINT IN SWALLOWING A BODY THAT DOESN'T HAVE ANY MAGIC?
THAT'S INSANE! WHAT ARE YOU?!
HEY!! WHY ARE YOU TREATING ME LIKE A FREAK?!
FLAAAA
I KNEW IT!! THAT CREEPY SPELL IS SPILLING OVER FROM THE ROOM ABOVE US!!
IF NOTHING CHANGES, THE PEOPLE IN THE OTHER ROOMS ARE IN DANGER AS WELL!!

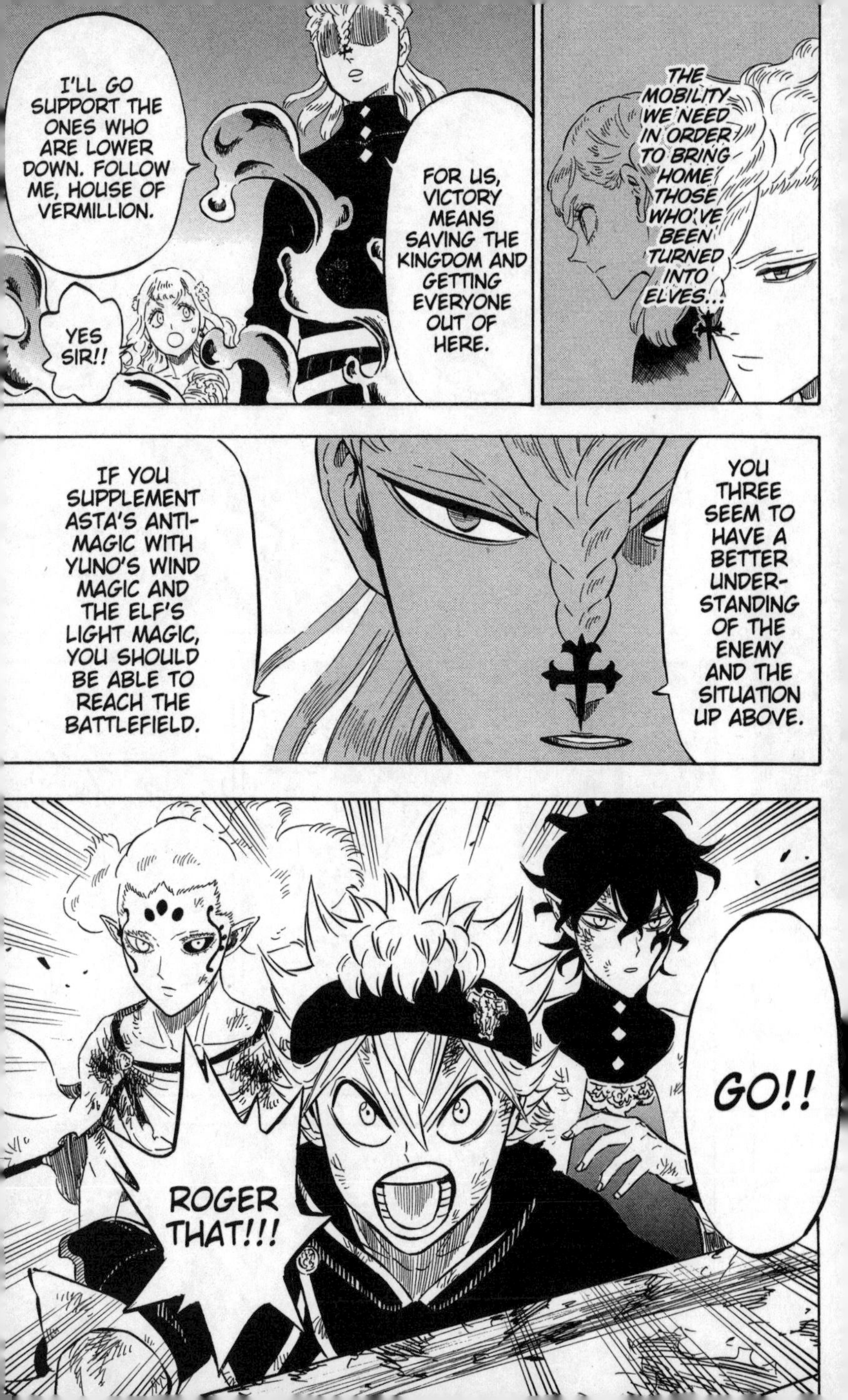
THE MOBILITY WE NEED IN ORDER TO BRING HOME THOSE WHO'VE BEEN TURNED INTO ELVES...
FOR US, VICTORY MEANS SAVING THE KINGDOM AND GETTING EVERYONE OUT OF HERE.
I'LL GO SUPPORT THE ONES WHO ARE LOWER DOWN. FOLLOW ME, HOUSE OF VERMILLION.
YES SIR!!
YOU THREE SEEM TO HAVE A BETTER UNDER-STANDING OF THE ENEMY AND THE SITUATION UP ABOVE.
IF YOU SUPPLEMENT ASTA'S ANTI-MAGIC WITH YUNO'S WIND MAGIC AND THE ELF'S LIGHT MAGIC, YOU SHOULD BE ABLE TO REACH THE BATTLEFIELD.
GO!!
ROGER THAT!!!

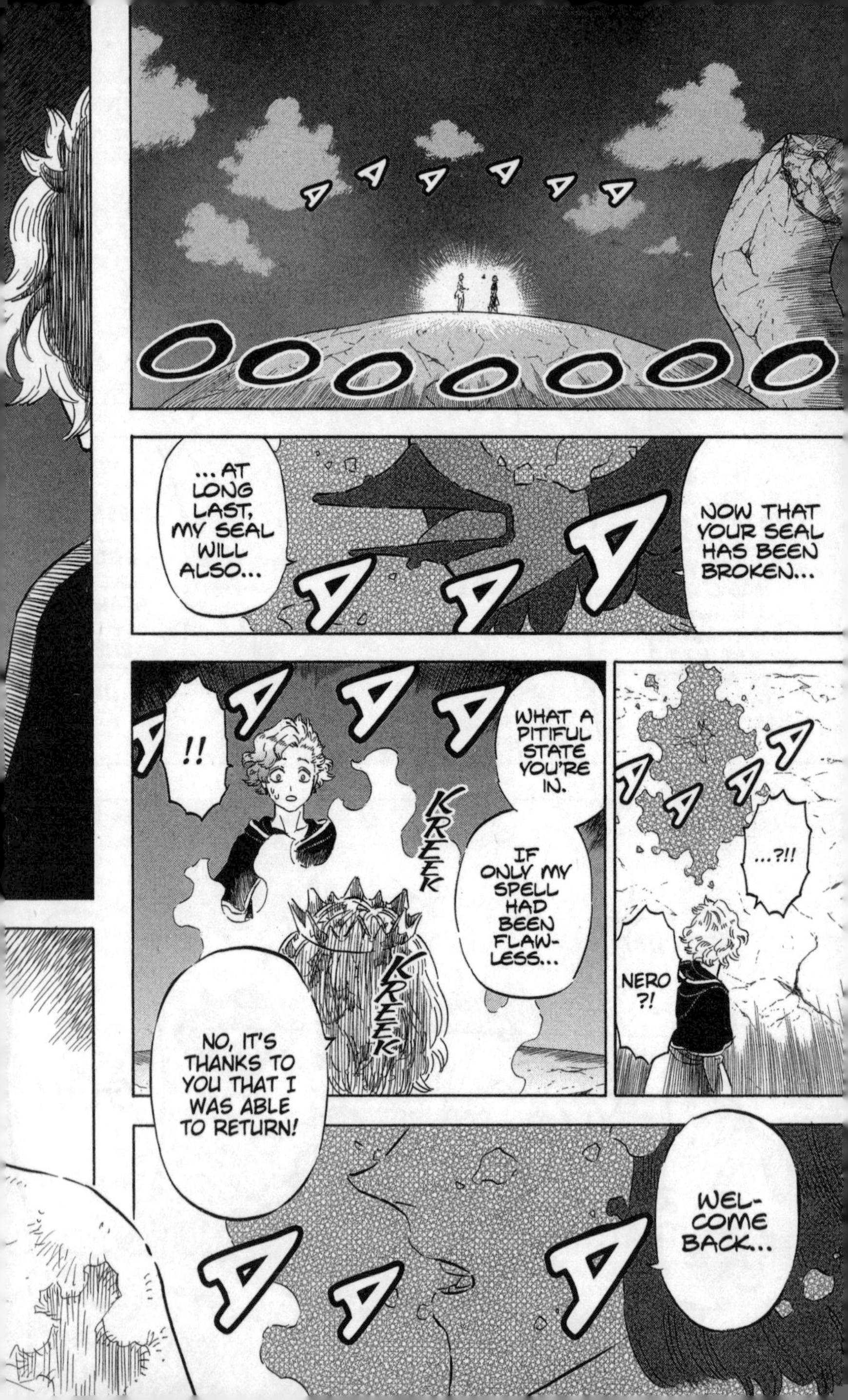
AAAAAA
OOOOOOO
NOW THAT YOUR SEAL HAS BEEN BROKEN...
AAA
...AT LONG LAST, MY SEAL WILL ALSO...
AAAAA
...?!!
NERO ?!
AAAA
WHAT A PITIFUL STATE YOU'RE IN.
IF ONLY MY SPELL HAD BEEN FLAWLESS...
KREEK
KREEK
!!
NO, IT'S THANKS TO YOU THAT I WAS ABLE TO RETURN!
WELCOME BACK...
AAA

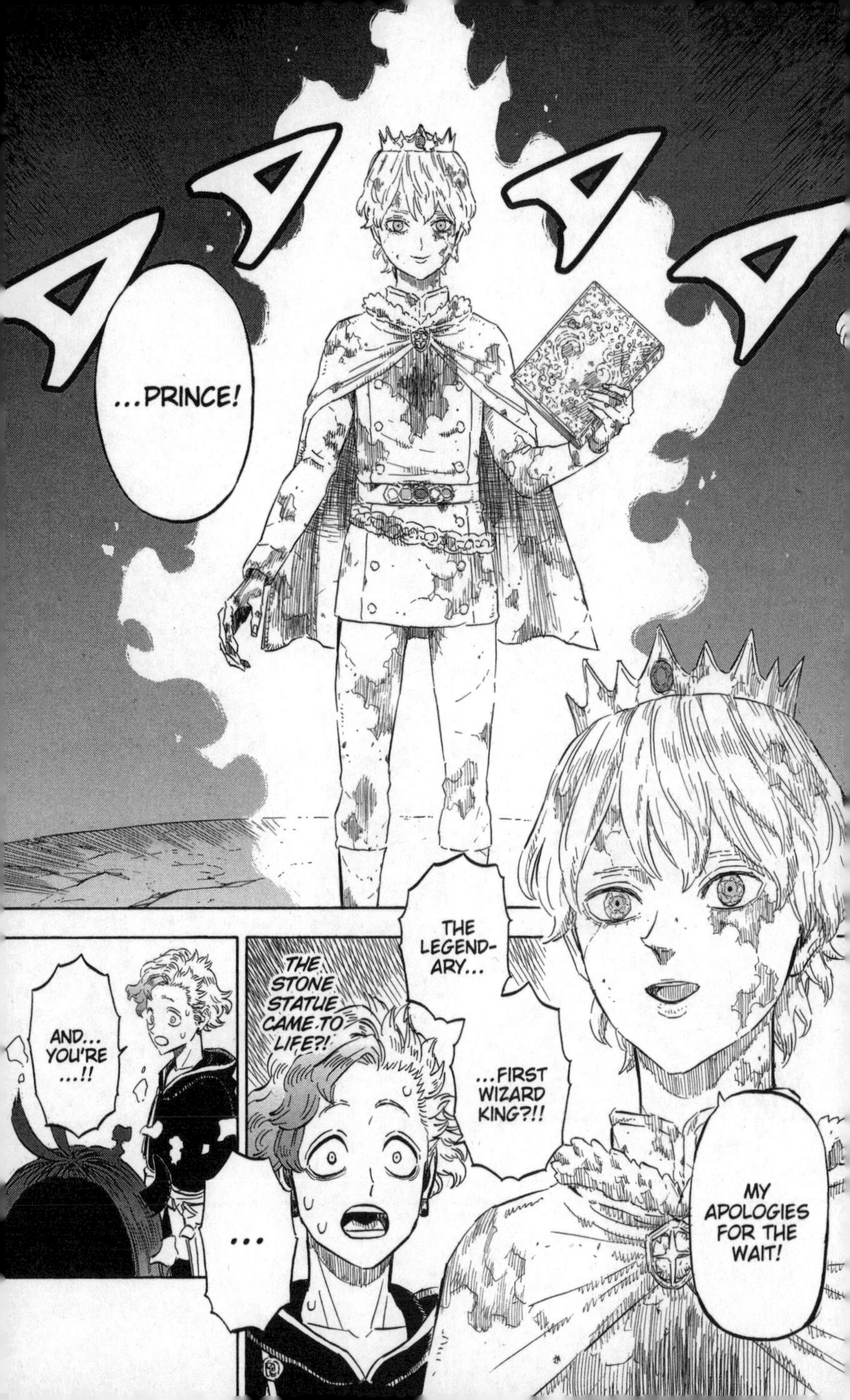
AAAA
...PRINCE!
MY APOLOGIES FOR THE WAIT!
THE LEGEND-ARY...
...FIRST WIZARD KING?!!
THE STONE STATUE CAME TO LIFE?!
...
AND... YOU'RE ...!!

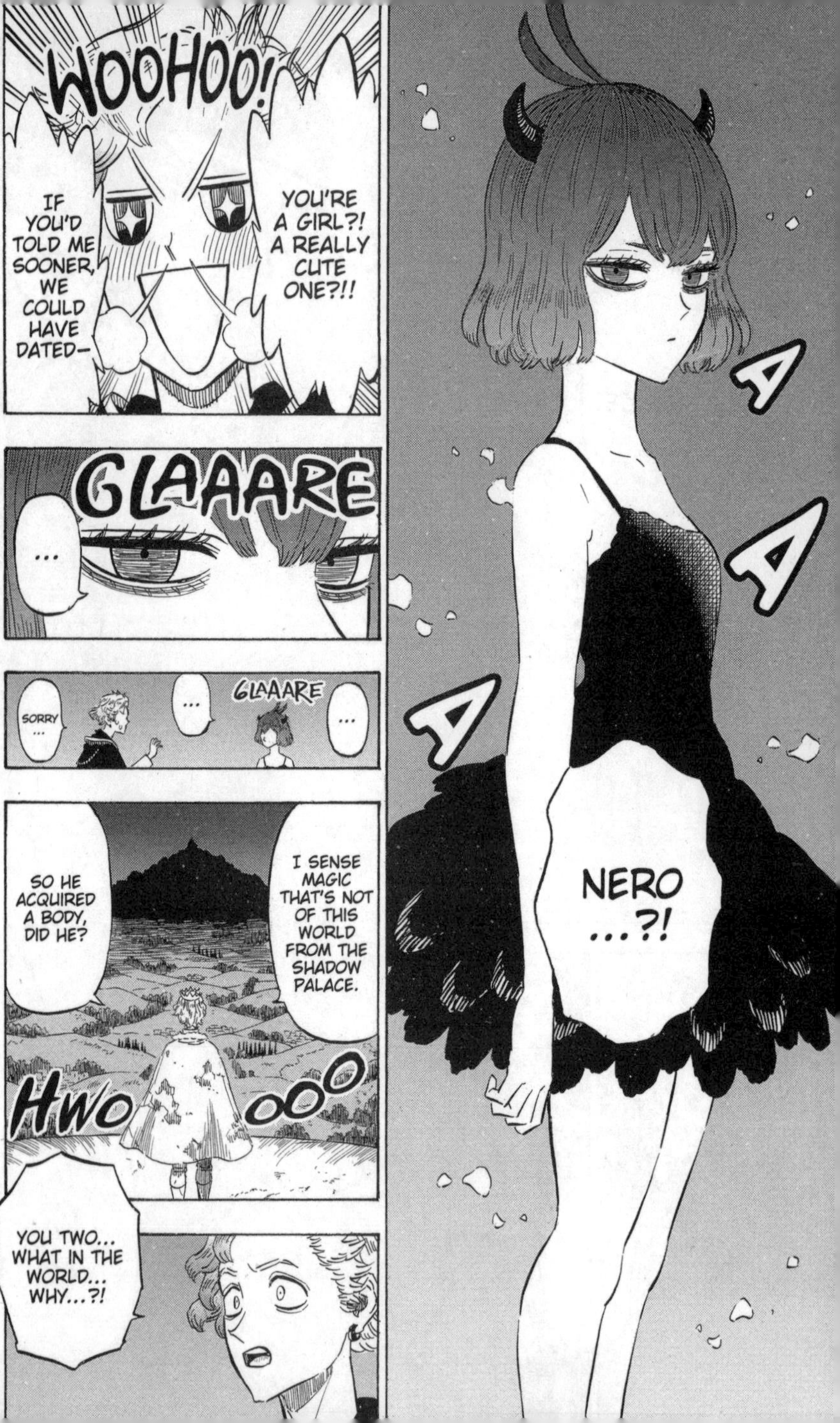
AAA
NERO ...?!
WOOHOO!
YOU'RE A GIRL?! A REALLY CUTE ONE?!!
IF YOU'D TOLD ME SOONER, WE COULD HAVE DATED—
GLAAARE
...
...
GLAAARE
...
SORRY...
I SENSE MAGIC THAT'S NOT OF THIS WORLD FROM THE SHADOW PALACE.
SO HE ACQUIRED A BODY, DID HE?
HWOOOOO
YOU TWO... WHAT IN THE WORLD... WHY...?!

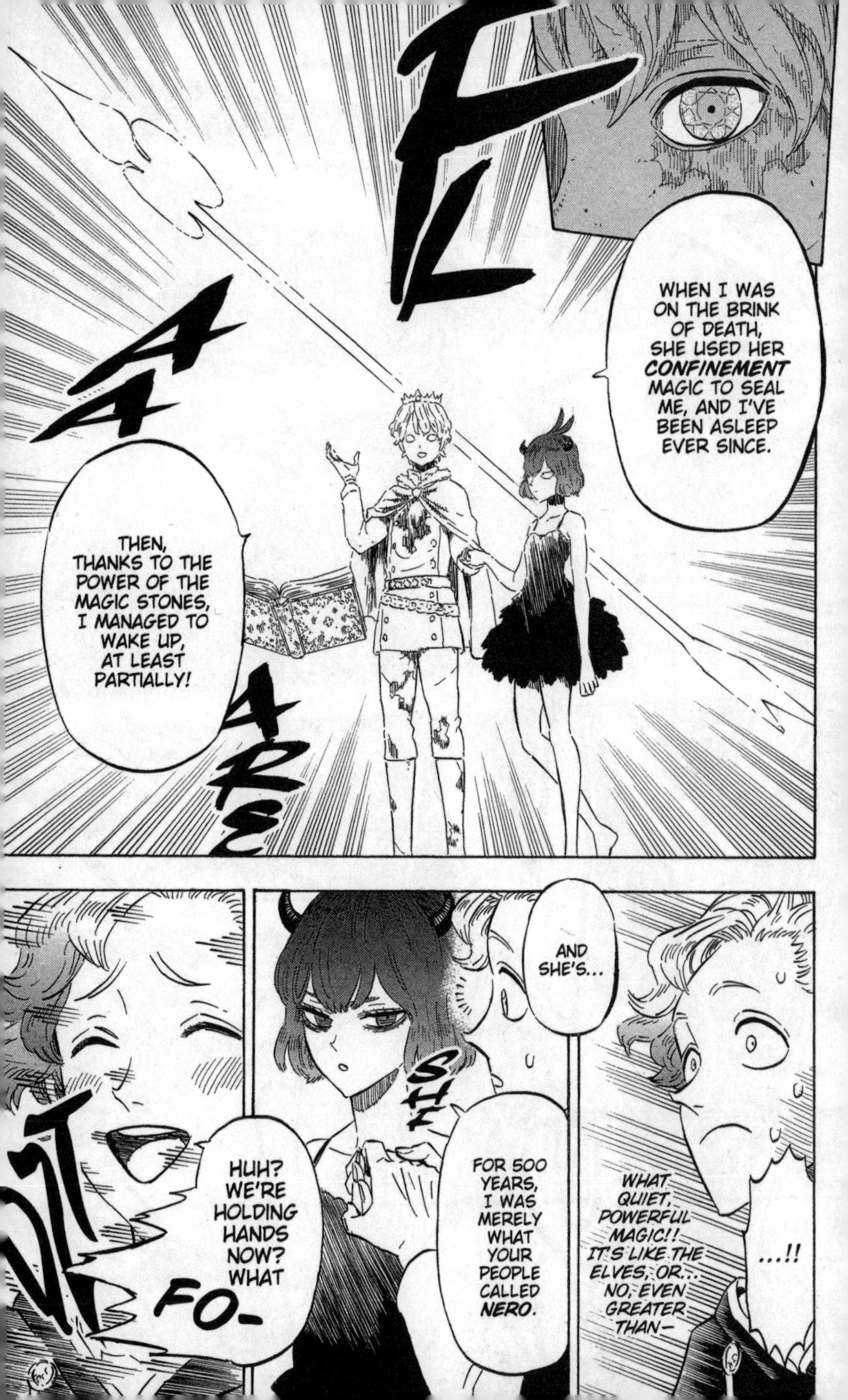
WHEN I WAS ON THE BRINK OF DEATH, SHE USED HER ***CONFINEMENT*** MAGIC TO SEAL ME, AND I'VE BEEN ASLEEP EVER SINCE.
THEN, THANKS TO THE POWER OF THE MAGIC STONES, I MANAGED TO WAKE UP, AT LEAST PARTIALLY!
...!!
WHAT QUIET, POWERFUL MAGIC!! IT'S LIKE THE ELVES, OR... NO, EVEN GREATER THAN—
AND SHE'S...
FOR 500 YEARS, I WAS MERELY WHAT YOUR PEOPLE CALLED ***NERO***.
HUH? WE'RE HOLDING HANDS NOW? WHAT FO-

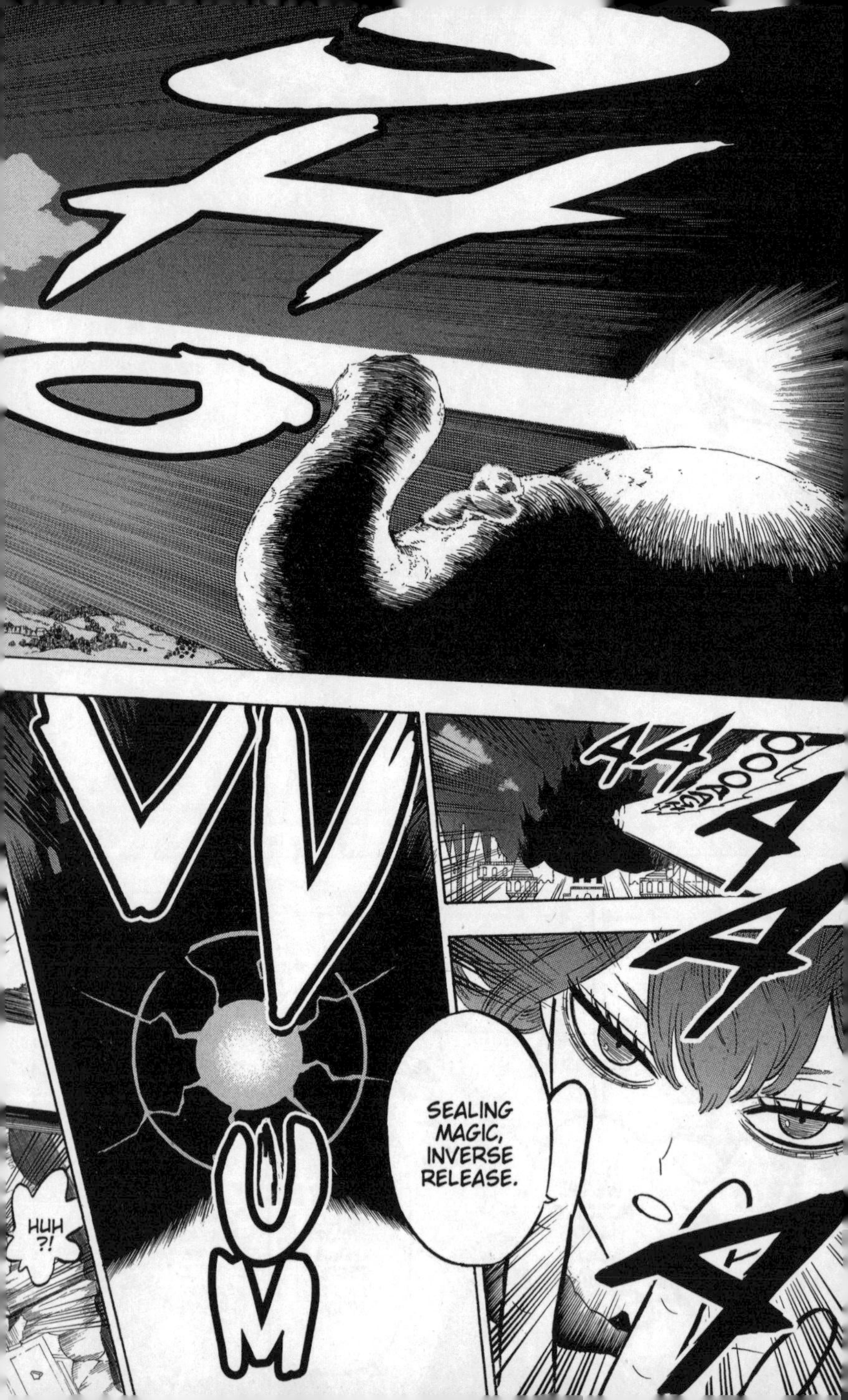
OOOAGH
SEALING MAGIC, INVERSE RELEASE.
VVVUUM
HUH ?!

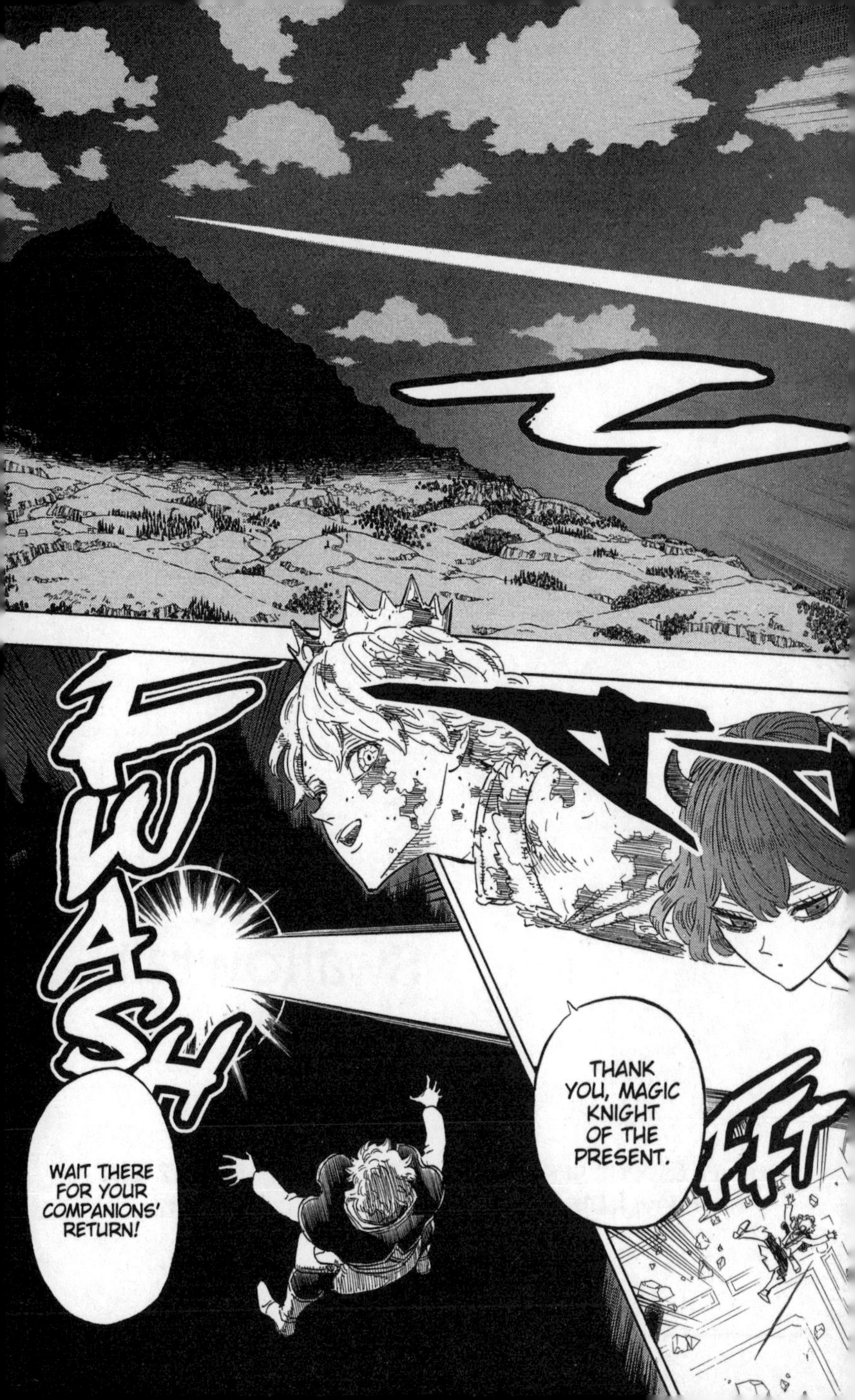
THANK YOU, MAGIC KNIGHT OF THE PRESENT.
FFT
FWASH
WAIT THERE FOR YOUR COMPANIONS' RETURN!

Secre
Swallowtail
(Nero)

Age: 17 (Spent 500 years as a bird)   Height: 152 cm
Birthday: June 18   Sign: Gemini   Blood Type: A
Likes: Fluffy, soft things

C h a r a c t e r   P r o f i l e

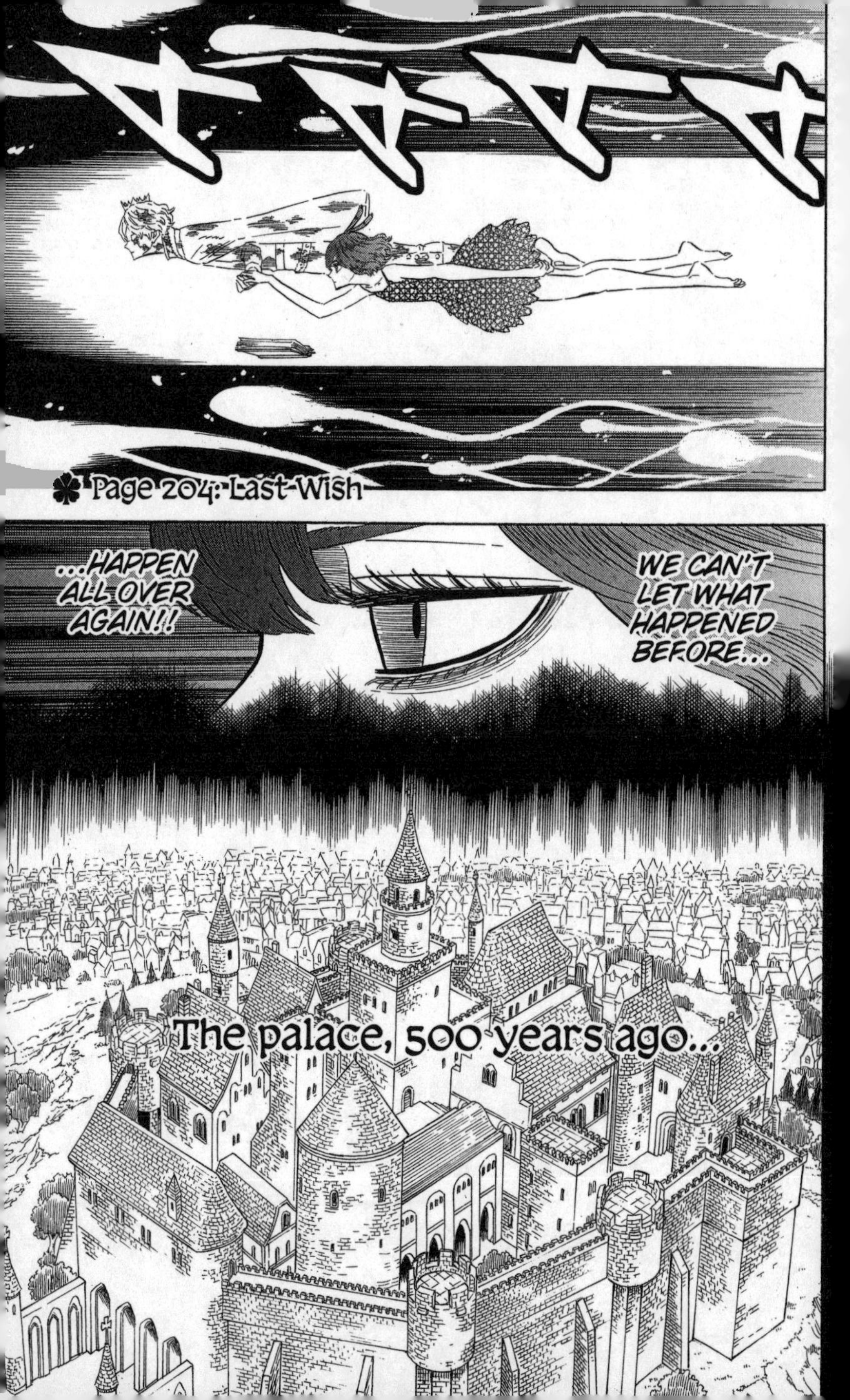
Page 204: Last Wish
WE CAN'T LET WHAT HAPPENED BEFORE...
...HAPPEN ALL OVER AGAIN!!
The palace, 500 years ago...

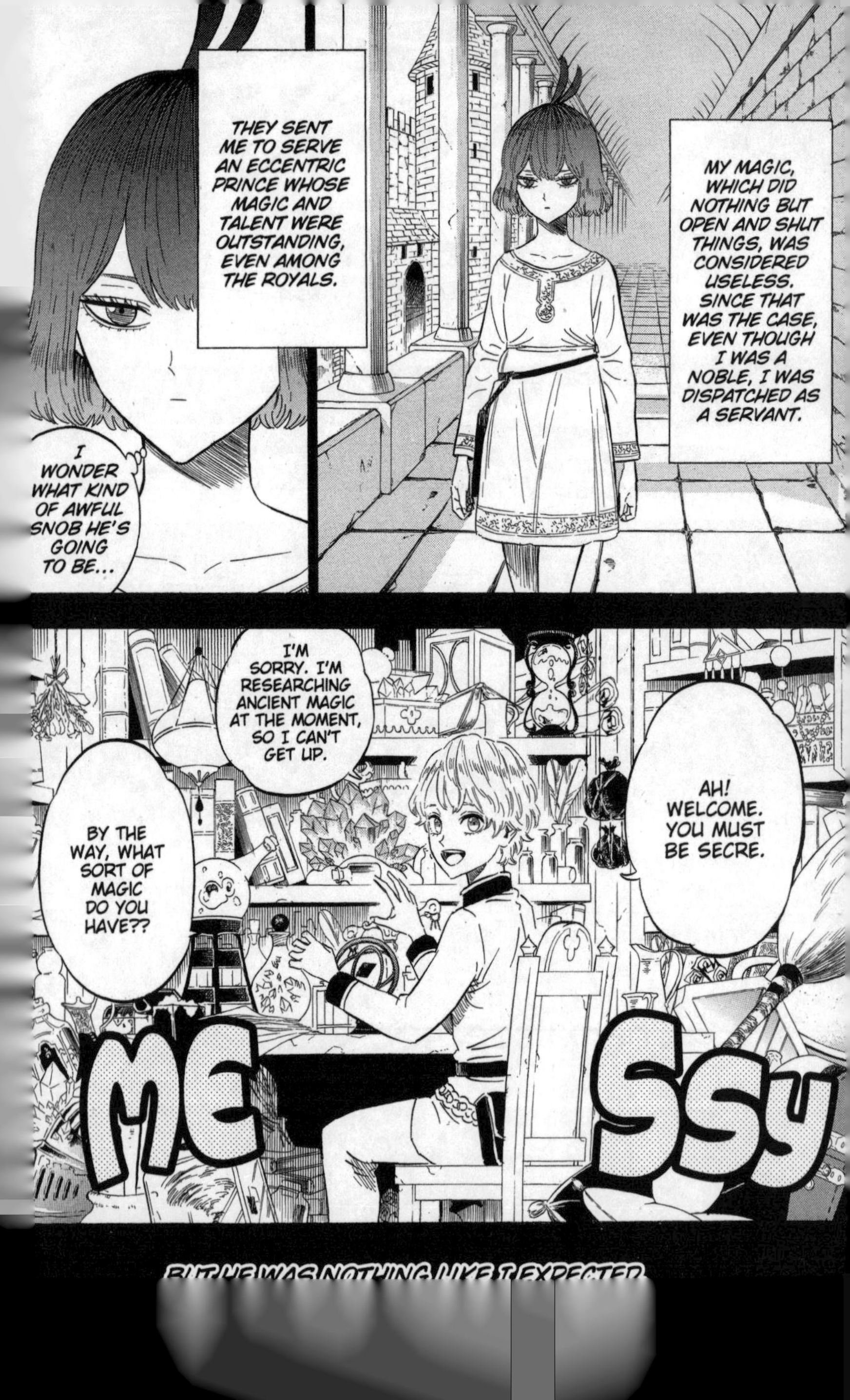
MY MAGIC, WHICH DID NOTHING BUT OPEN AND SHUT THINGS, WAS CONSIDERED USELESS. SINCE THAT WAS THE CASE, EVEN THOUGH I WAS A NOBLE, I WAS DISPATCHED AS A SERVANT.
THEY SENT ME TO SERVE AN ECCENTRIC PRINCE WHOSE MAGIC AND TALENT WERE OUTSTANDING, EVEN AMONG THE ROYALS.
I WONDER WHAT KIND OF AWFUL SNOB HE'S GOING TO BE...
AH! WELCOME. YOU MUST BE SECRE.
I'M SORRY. I'M RESEARCHING ANCIENT MAGIC AT THE MOMENT, SO I CAN'T GET UP.
BY THE WAY, WHAT SORT OF MAGIC DO YOU HAVE??
MESSY

BUT HE WAS NOTHING LIKE I EXPECTED

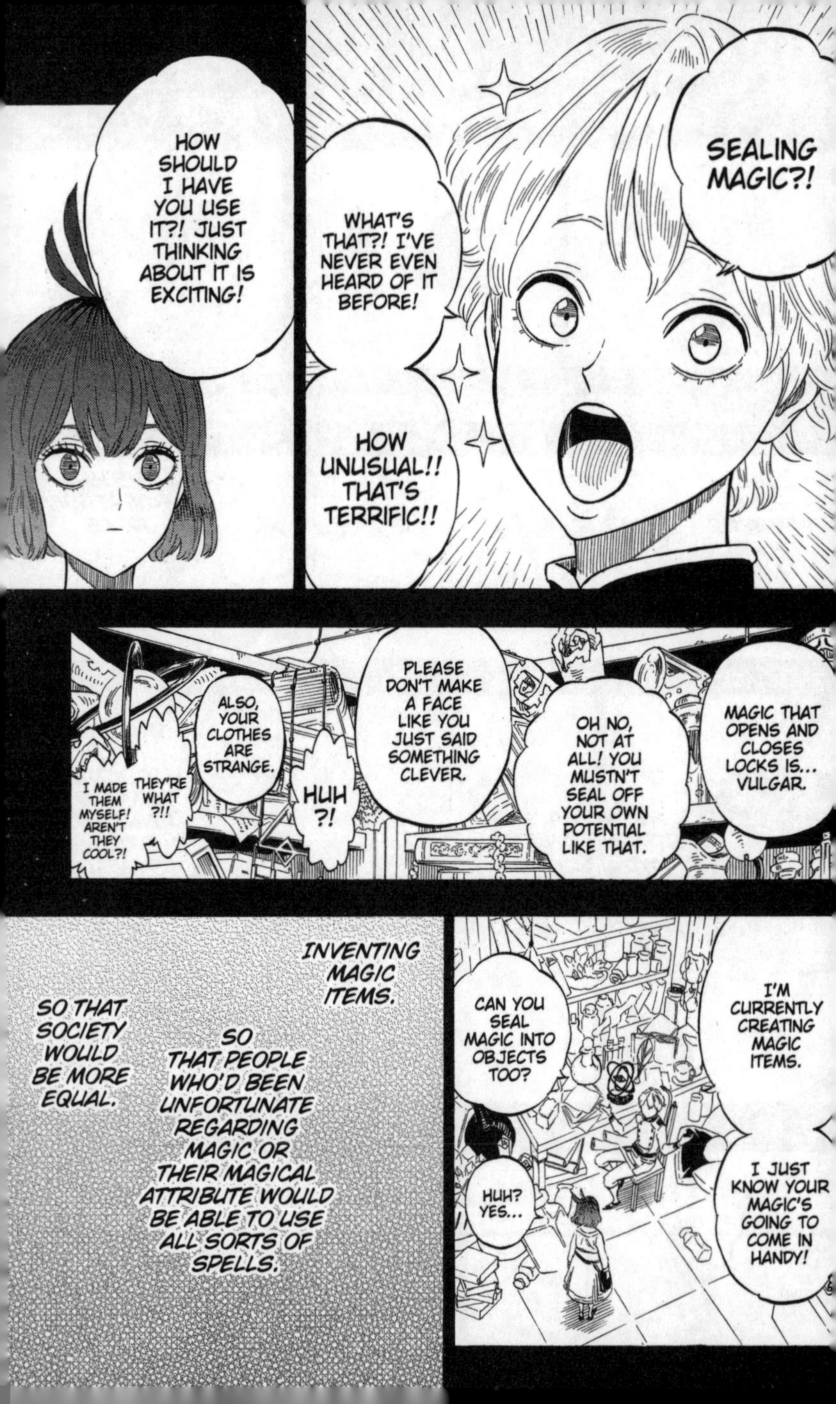
SEALING MAGIC?!
WHAT'S THAT?! I'VE NEVER EVEN HEARD OF IT BEFORE!
HOW UNUSUAL!! THAT'S TERRIFIC!!
HOW SHOULD I HAVE YOU USE IT?! JUST THINKING ABOUT IT IS EXCITING!
MAGIC THAT OPENS AND CLOSES LOCKS IS... VULGAR.
OH NO, NOT AT ALL! YOU MUSTN'T SEAL OFF YOUR OWN POTENTIAL LIKE THAT.
PLEASE DON'T MAKE A FACE LIKE YOU JUST SAID SOMETHING CLEVER.
HUH ?!
ALSO, YOUR CLOTHES ARE STRANGE.
THEY'RE WHAT ?!!
I MADE THEM MYSELF! AREN'T THEY COOL?!
I'M CURRENTLY CREATING MAGIC ITEMS.
CAN YOU SEAL MAGIC INTO OBJECTS TOO?
I JUST KNOW YOUR MAGIC'S GOING TO COME IN HANDY!
HUH? YES...
INVENTING MAGIC ITEMS.
SO THAT PEOPLE WHO'D BEEN UNFORTUNATE REGARDING MAGIC OR THEIR MAGICAL ATTRIBUTE WOULD BE ABLE TO USE ALL SORTS OF SPELLS.
SO THAT SOCIETY WOULD BE MORE EQUAL.

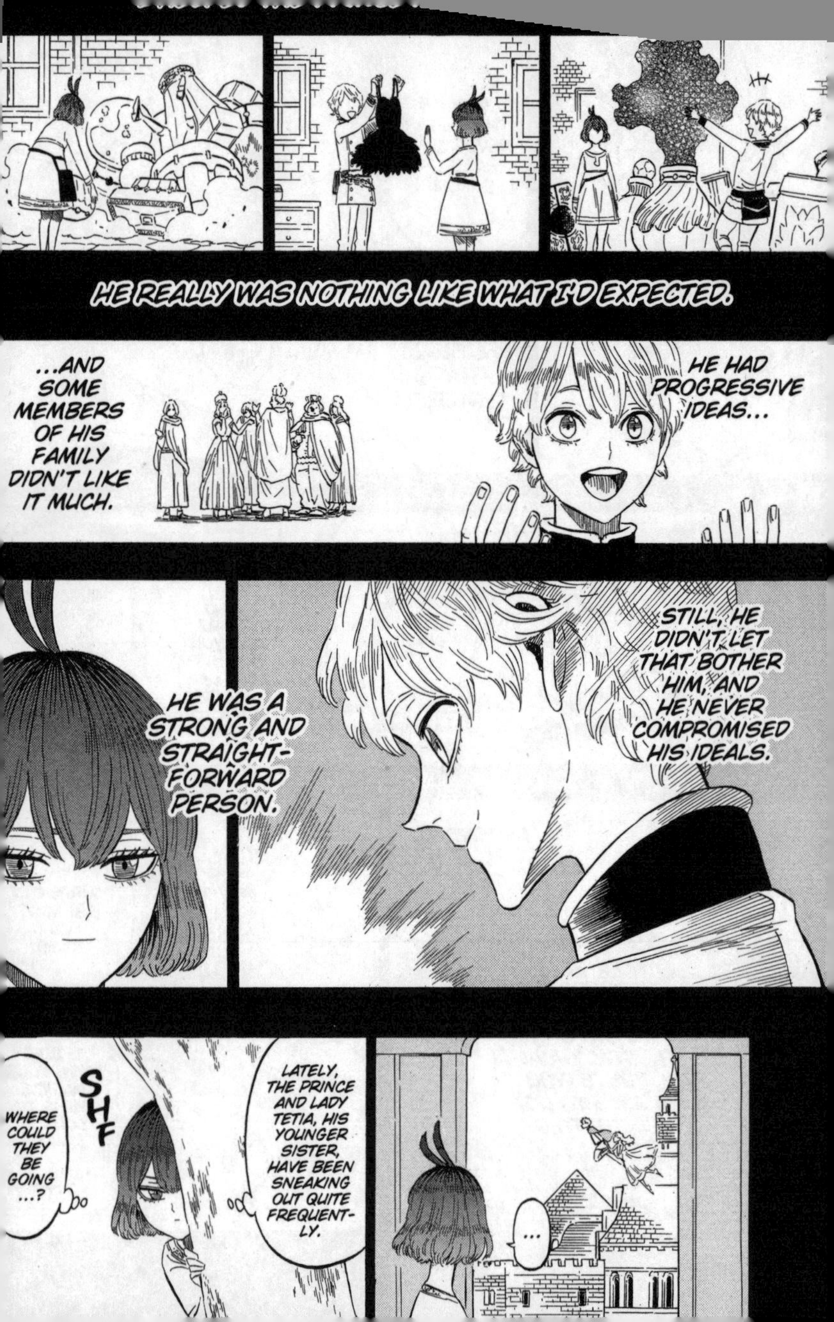
HE REALLY WAS NOTHING LIKE WHAT I'D EXPECTED.
HE HAD PROGRESSIVE IDEAS...
...AND SOME MEMBERS OF HIS FAMILY DIDN'T LIKE IT MUCH.
STILL, HE DIDN'T LET THAT BOTHER HIM, AND HE NEVER COMPROMISED HIS IDEALS.
HE WAS A STRONG AND STRAIGHT-FORWARD PERSON.
...
LATELY, THE PRINCE AND LADY TETIA, HIS YOUNGER SISTER, HAVE BEEN SNEAKING OUT QUITE FREQUENT-LY.
SHF
WHERE COULD THEY BE GOING ...?

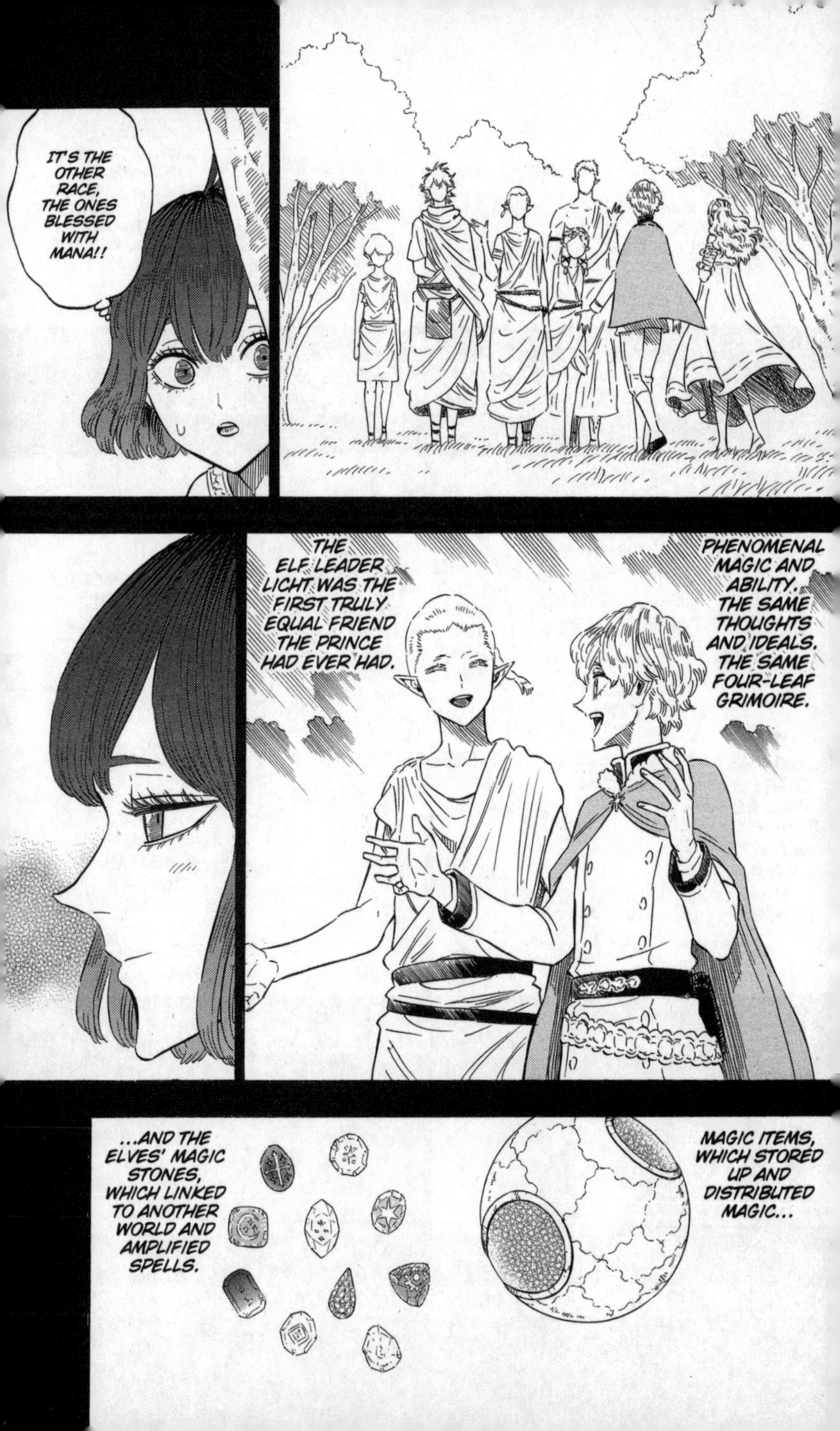
IT'S THE OTHER RACE, THE ONES BLESSED WITH MANA!!
PHENOMENAL MAGIC AND ABILITY. THE SAME THOUGHTS AND IDEALS. THE SAME FOUR-LEAF GRIMOIRE.
THE ELF LEADER LICHT WAS THE FIRST TRULY EQUAL FRIEND THE PRINCE HAD EVER HAD.
MAGIC ITEMS, WHICH STORED UP AND DISTRIBUTED MAGIC...
...AND THE ELVES' MAGIC STONES, WHICH LINKED TO ANOTHER WORLD AND AMPLIFIED SPELLS.

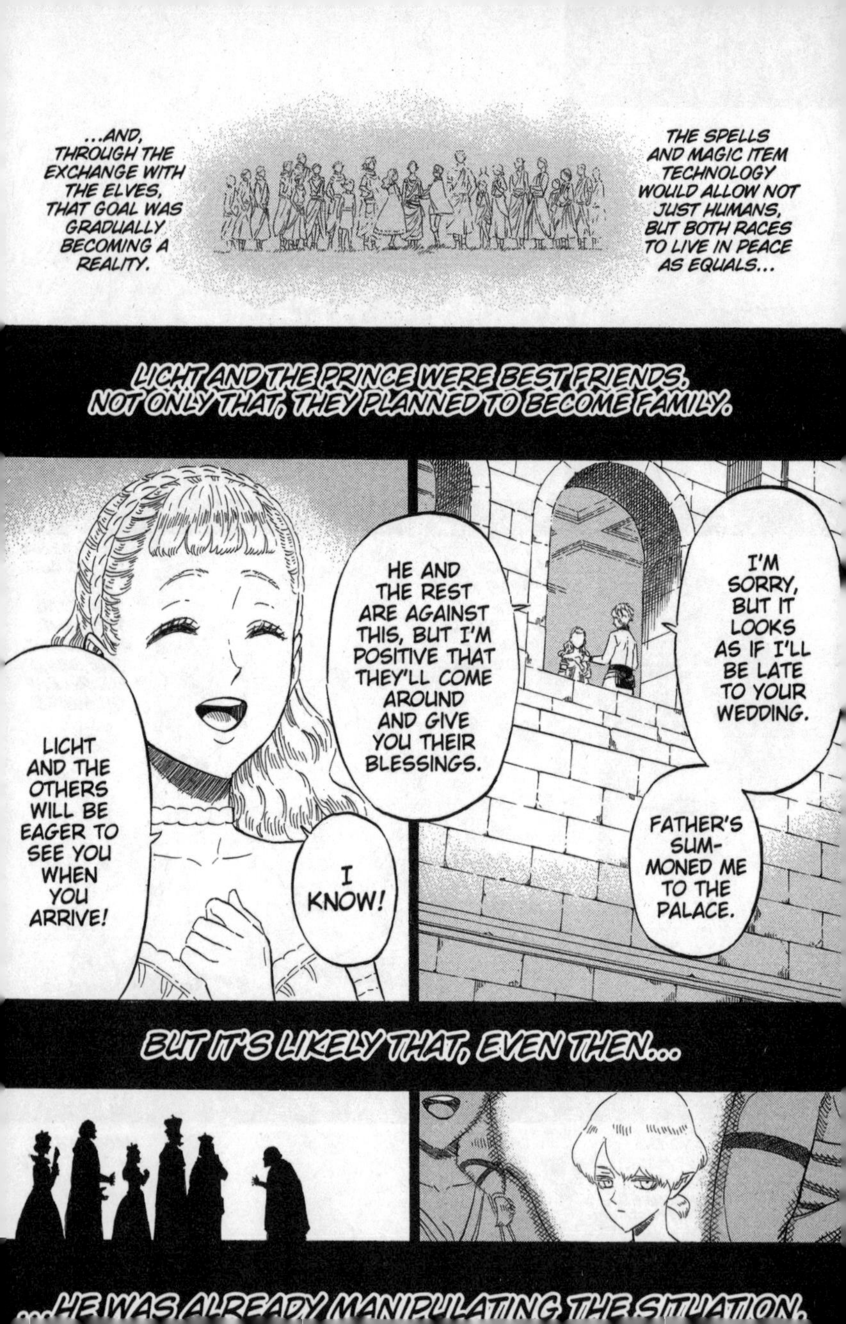
THE SPELLS AND MAGIC ITEM TECHNOLOGY WOULD ALLOW NOT JUST HUMANS, BUT BOTH RACES TO LIVE IN PEACE AS EQUALS...
...AND, THROUGH THE EXCHANGE WITH THE ELVES, THAT GOAL WAS GRADUALLY BECOMING A REALITY.
LICHT AND THE PRINCE WERE BEST FRIENDS. NOT ONLY THAT, THEY PLANNED TO BECOME FAMILY.
I'M SORRY, BUT IT LOOKS AS IF I'LL BE LATE TO YOUR WEDDING.
FATHER'S SUMMONED ME TO THE PALACE.
HE AND THE REST ARE AGAINST THIS, BUT I'M POSITIVE THAT THEY'LL COME AROUND AND GIVE YOU THEIR BLESSINGS.
LICHT AND THE OTHERS WILL BE EAGER TO SEE YOU WHEN YOU ARRIVE!
I KNOW!
BUT IT'S LIKELY THAT, EVEN THEN...
...HE WAS ALREADY MANIPULATING THE SITUATION.

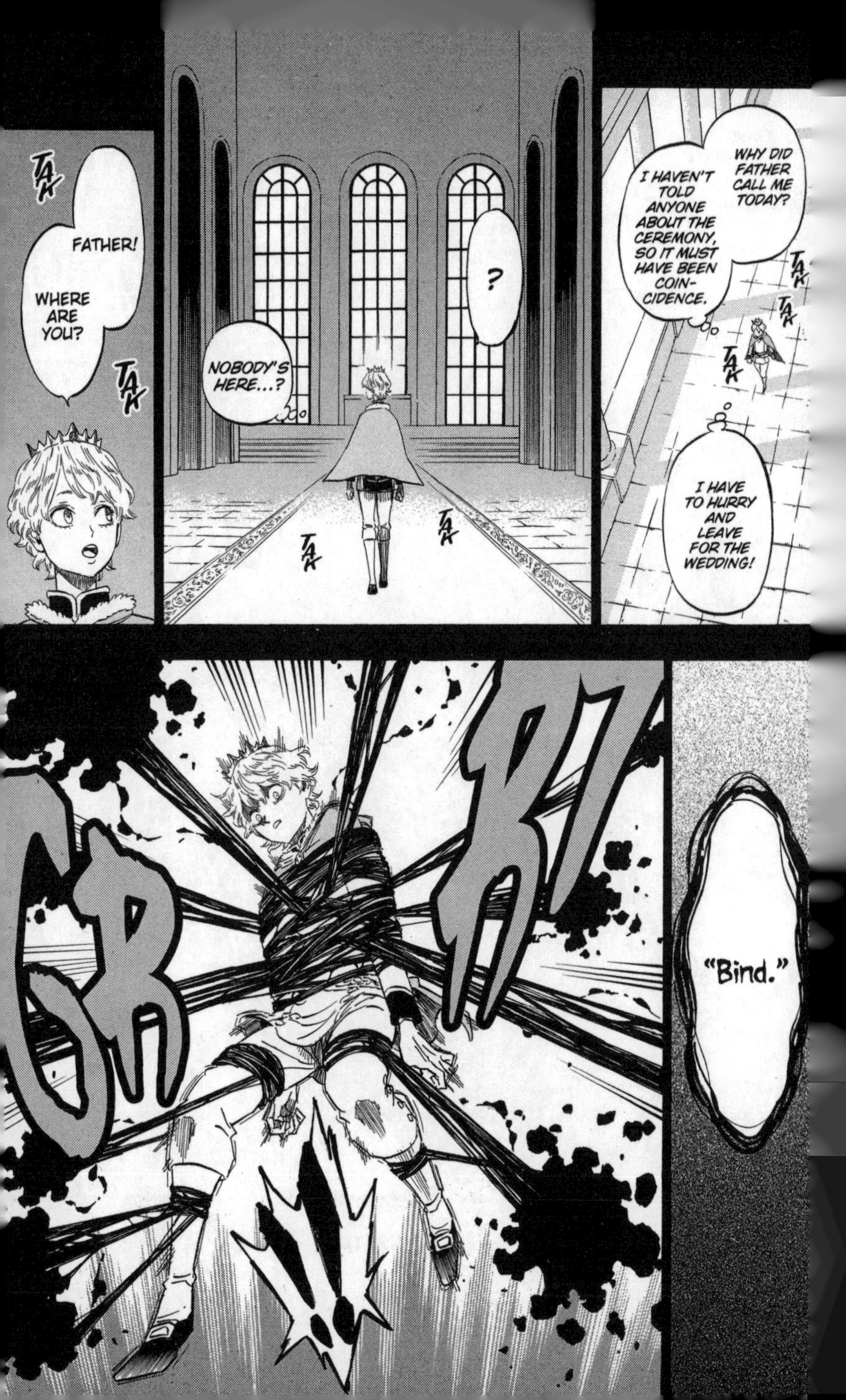
WHY DID FATHER CALL ME TODAY?
I HAVEN'T TOLD ANYONE ABOUT THE CEREMONY, SO IT MUST HAVE BEEN COIN-CIDENCE.
TAK
TAK
TAK
I HAVE TO HURRY AND LEAVE FOR THE WEDDING!
?
NOBODY'S HERE...?
TAK
TAK
TAK
FATHER!
WHERE ARE YOU?
TAK
"Bind."
!!

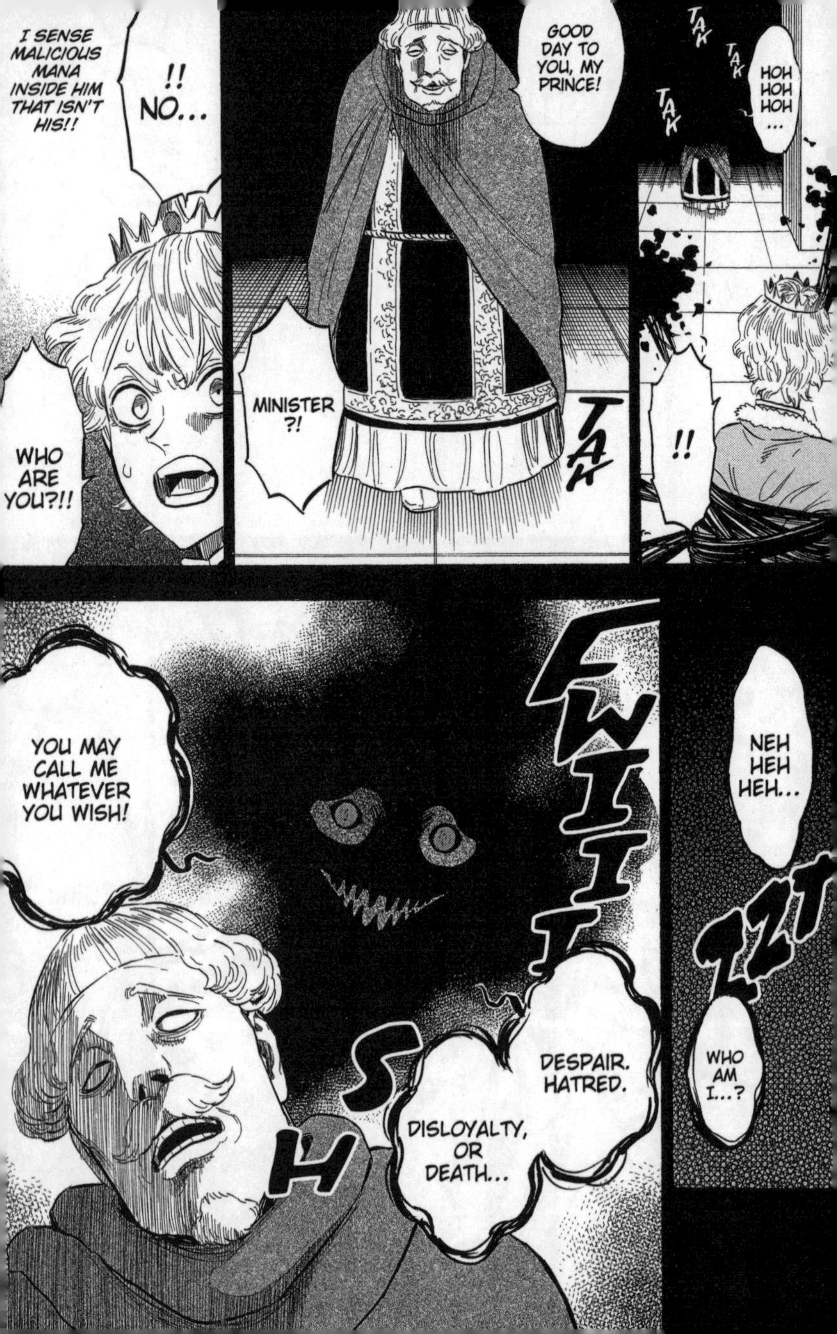
TAK
TAK
TAK
HOH HOH HOH...
!!
GOOD DAY TO YOU, MY PRINCE!
MINISTER?!
TAK
!! NO...
I SENSE MALICIOUS MANA INSIDE HIM THAT ISN'T HIS!!
WHO ARE YOU?!!
NEH HEH HEH...
ZZT
WHO AM I...?
FWISH
YOU MAY CALL ME WHATEVER YOU WISH!
DESPAIR. HATRED.
DISLOYALTY, OR DEATH...

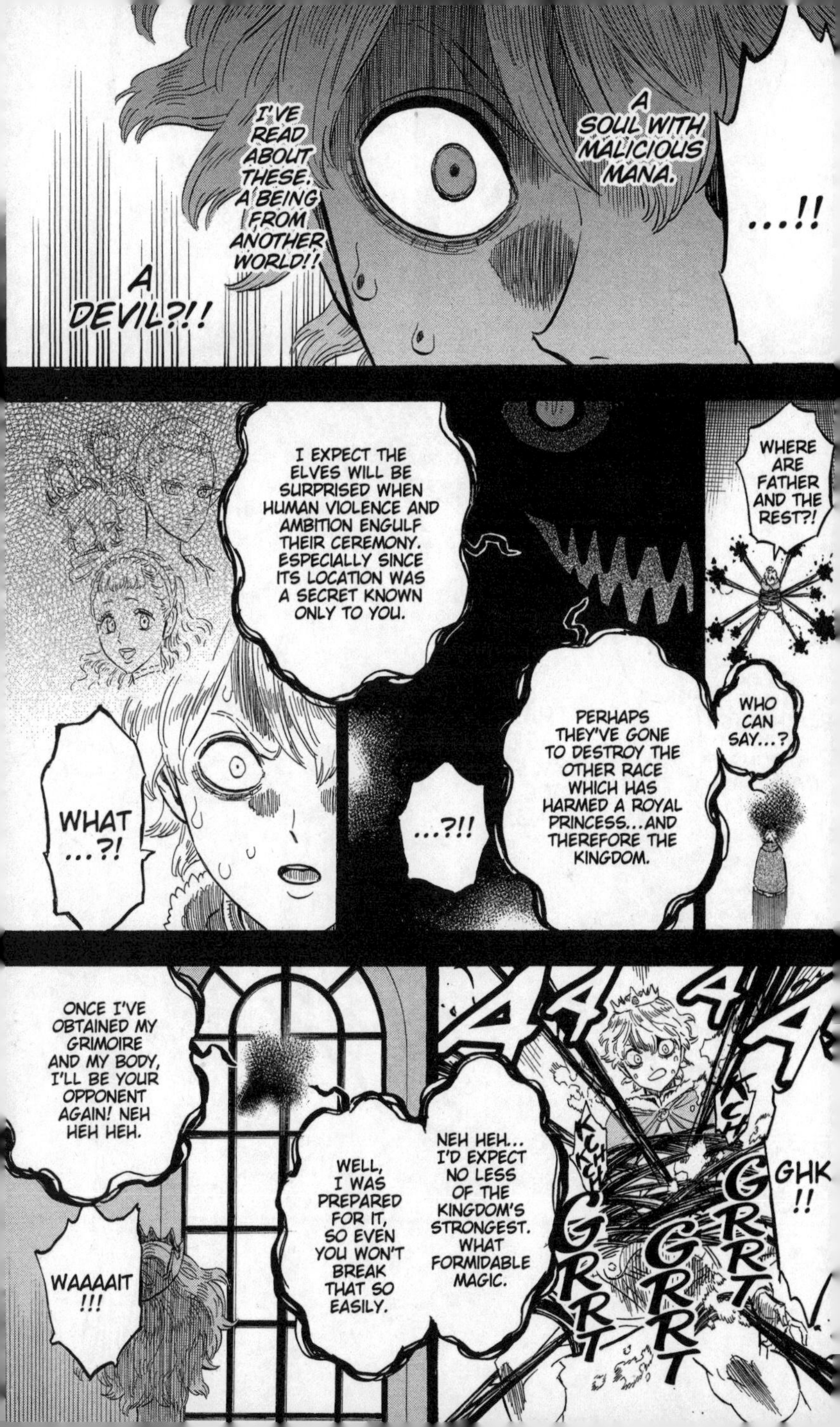
A SOUL WITH MALICIOUS MANA.
...!!
I'VE READ ABOUT THESE. A BEING FROM ANOTHER WORLD!!
A DEVIL?!!
WHERE ARE FATHER AND THE REST?!
WHO CAN SAY...?
PERHAPS THEY'VE GONE TO DESTROY THE OTHER RACE WHICH HAS HARMED A ROYAL PRINCESS...AND THEREFORE THE KINGDOM.
...?!!
I EXPECT THE ELVES WILL BE SURPRISED WHEN HUMAN VIOLENCE AND AMBITION ENGULF THEIR CEREMONY. ESPECIALLY SINCE ITS LOCATION WAS A SECRET KNOWN ONLY TO YOU.
WHAT ...?!
AAAA
GHK !!
GRRT GRRT GRRT
NEH HEH... I'D EXPECT NO LESS OF THE KINGDOM'S STRONGEST. WHAT FORMIDABLE MAGIC.
WELL, I WAS PREPARED FOR IT, SO EVEN YOU WON'T BREAK THAT SO EASILY.
ONCE I'VE OBTAINED MY GRIMOIRE AND MY BODY, I'LL BE YOUR OPPONENT AGAIN! NEH HEH HEH.
WAAAAIT !!!

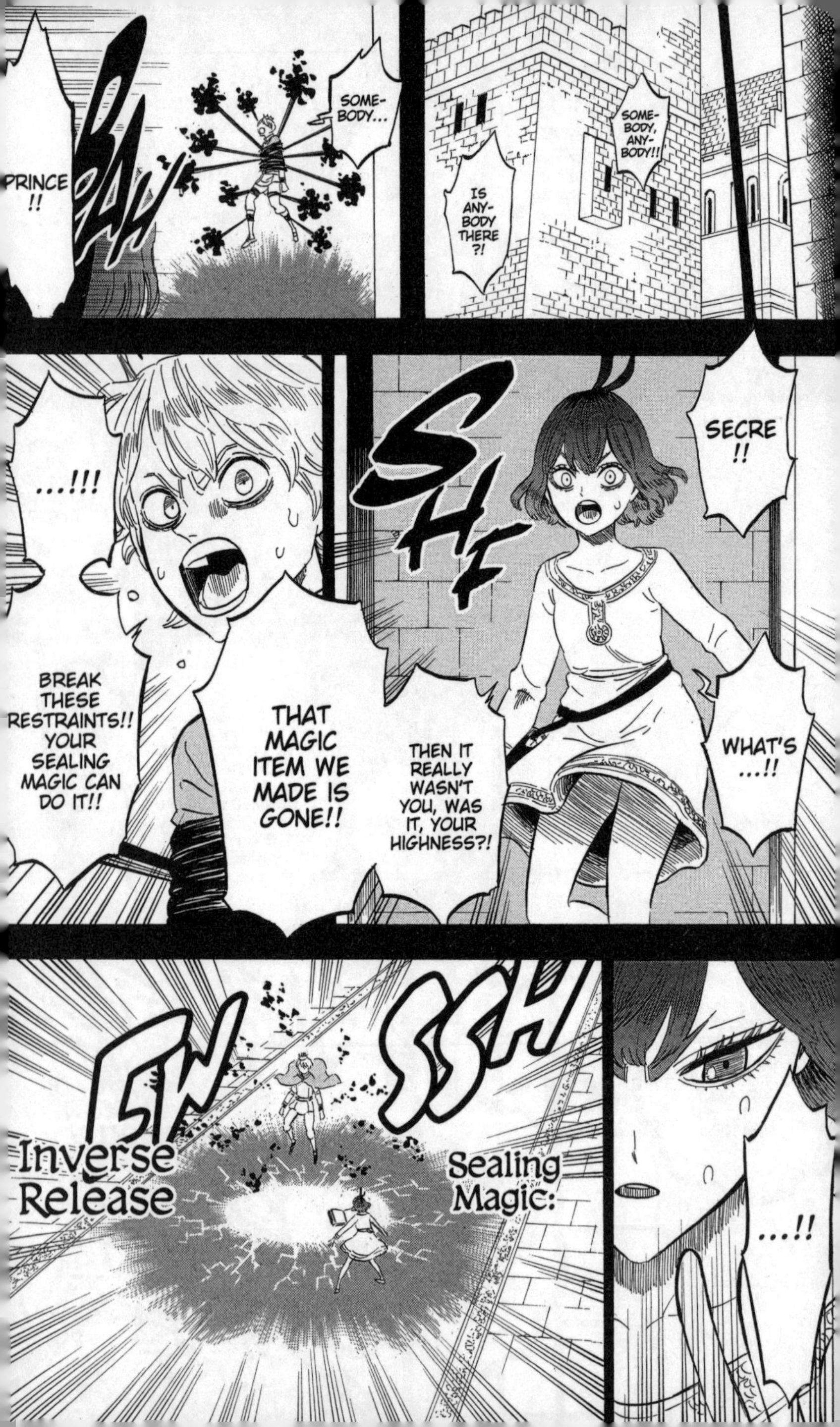
SOMEBODY, ANYBODY!!
IS ANYBODY THERE?!
SOME-BODY...
PRINCE!!
SECRE!!
WHAT'S...!!
THEN IT REALLY WASN'T YOU, WAS IT, YOUR HIGHNESS?!
...!!!
THAT MAGIC ITEM WE MADE IS GONE!!
BREAK THESE RESTRAINTS!! YOUR SEALING MAGIC CAN DO IT!!
...!!
SSH
Sealing Magic:
Inverse Release

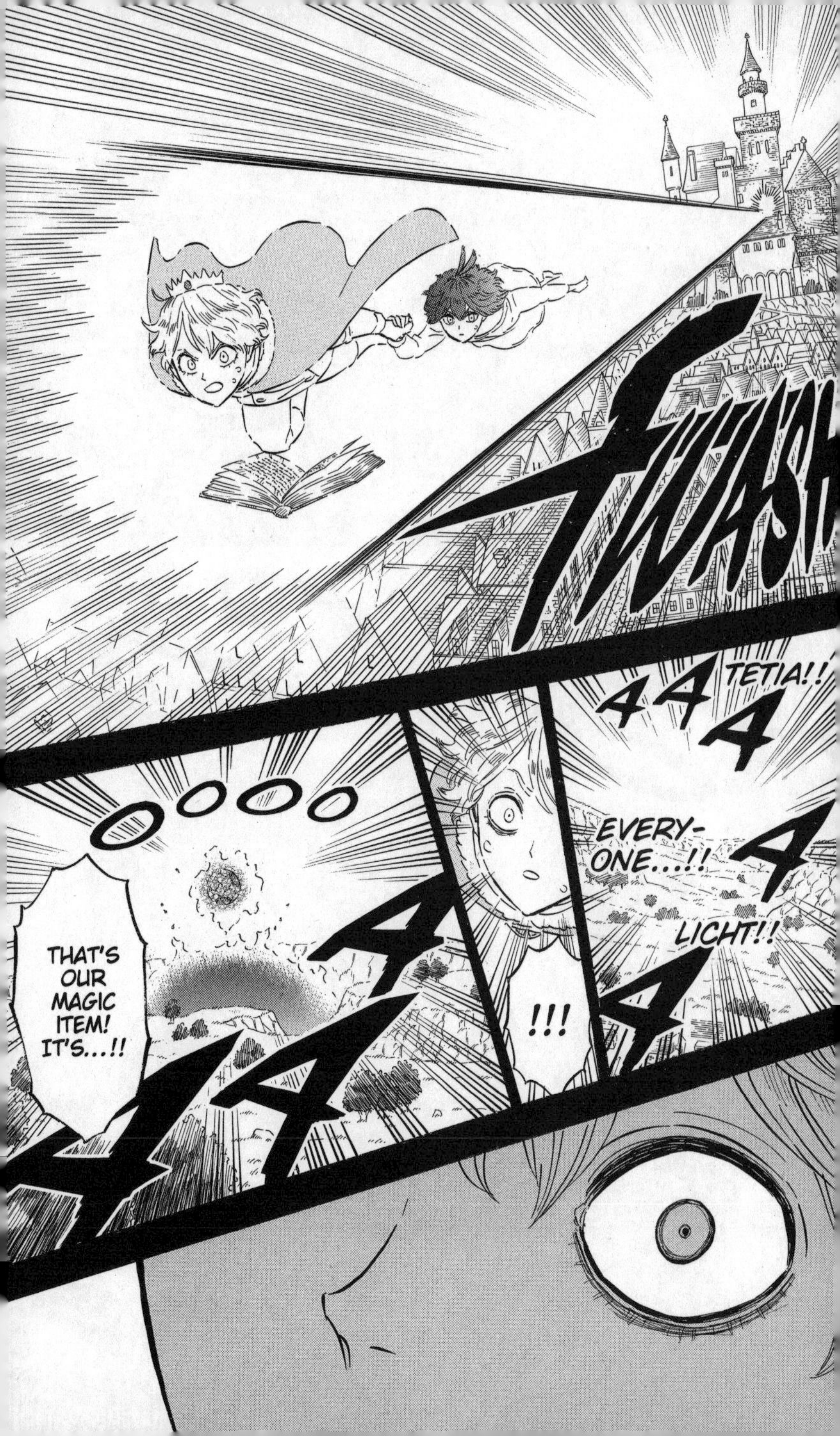
FLASH
TETIA!!
EVERY-ONE...!!
LICHT!!
!!!
THAT'S OUR MAGIC ITEM! IT'S...!!

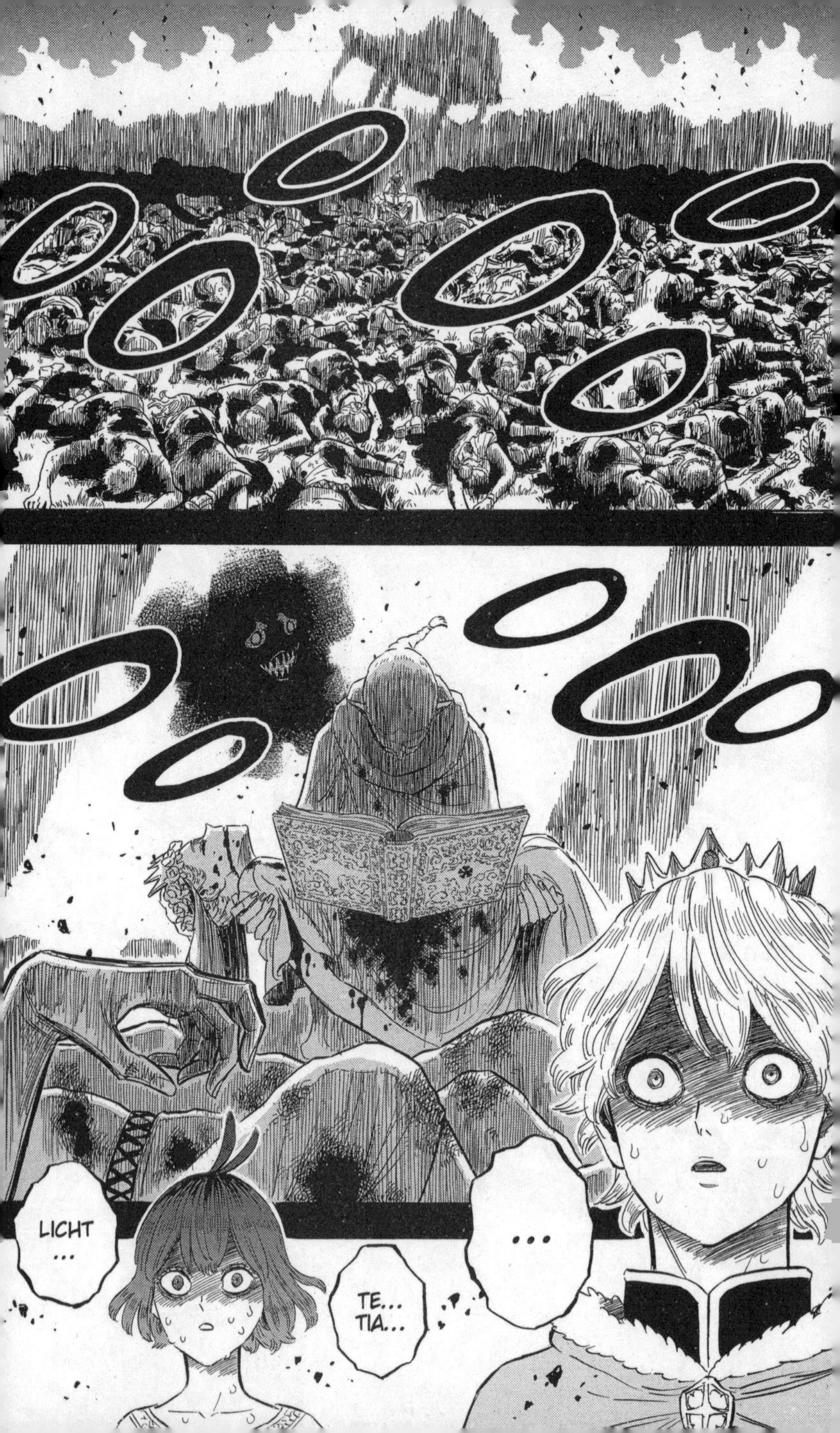
...
TE... TIA...
LICHT ...

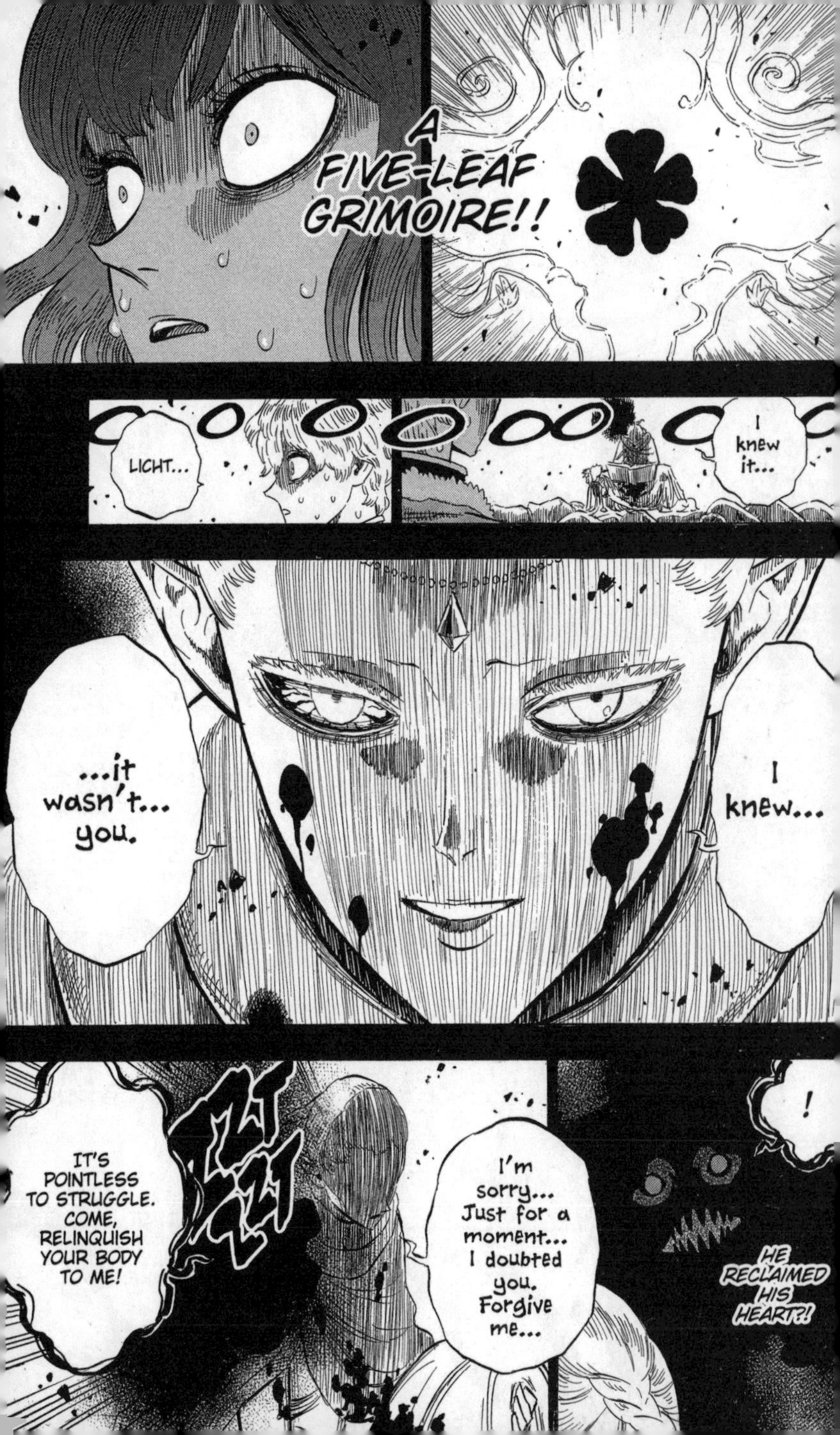
A FIVE-LEAF GRIMOIRE!!
I knew it...
LICHT...
I knew...
...it wasn't... you.
!
HE RECLAIMED HIS HEART?!
I'm sorry... Just for a moment... I doubted you. Forgive me...
IT'S POINTLESS TO STRUGGLE. COME, RELINQUISH YOUR BODY TO ME!

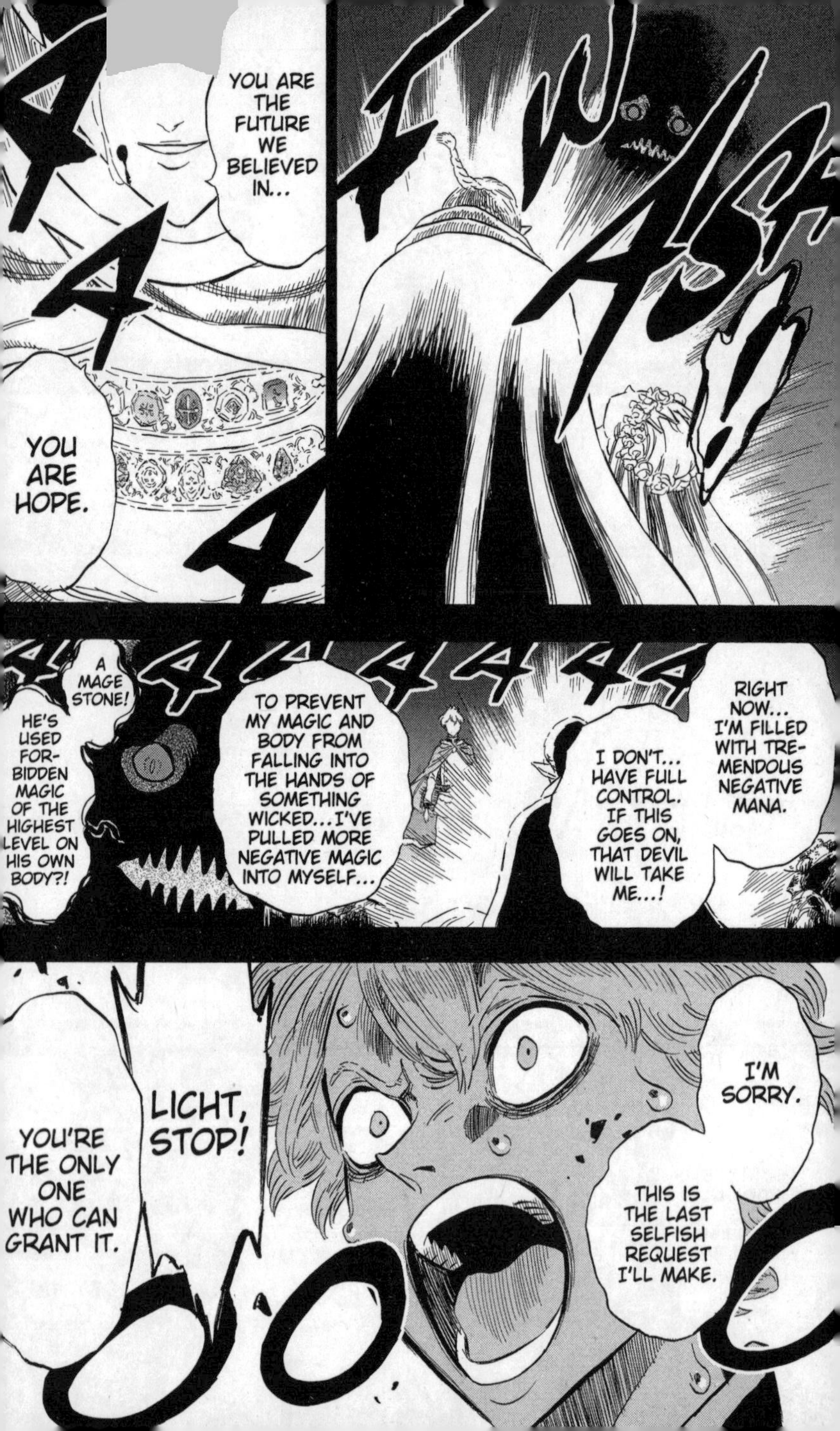
YOU ARE THE FUTURE WE BELIEVED IN...
YOU ARE HOPE.
RIGHT NOW... I'M FILLED WITH TRE-MENDOUS NEGATIVE MANA.
I DON'T... HAVE FULL CONTROL. IF THIS GOES ON, THAT DEVIL WILL TAKE ME...!
TO PREVENT MY MAGIC AND BODY FROM FALLING INTO THE HANDS OF SOMETHING WICKED...I'VE PULLED MORE NEGATIVE MAGIC INTO MYSELF...
A MAGE STONE!
HE'S USED FOR-BIDDEN MAGIC OF THE HIGHEST LEVEL ON HIS OWN BODY?!
I'M SORRY.
THIS IS THE LAST SELFISH REQUEST I'LL MAKE.
LICHT, STOP!
YOU'RE THE ONLY ONE WHO CAN GRANT IT.

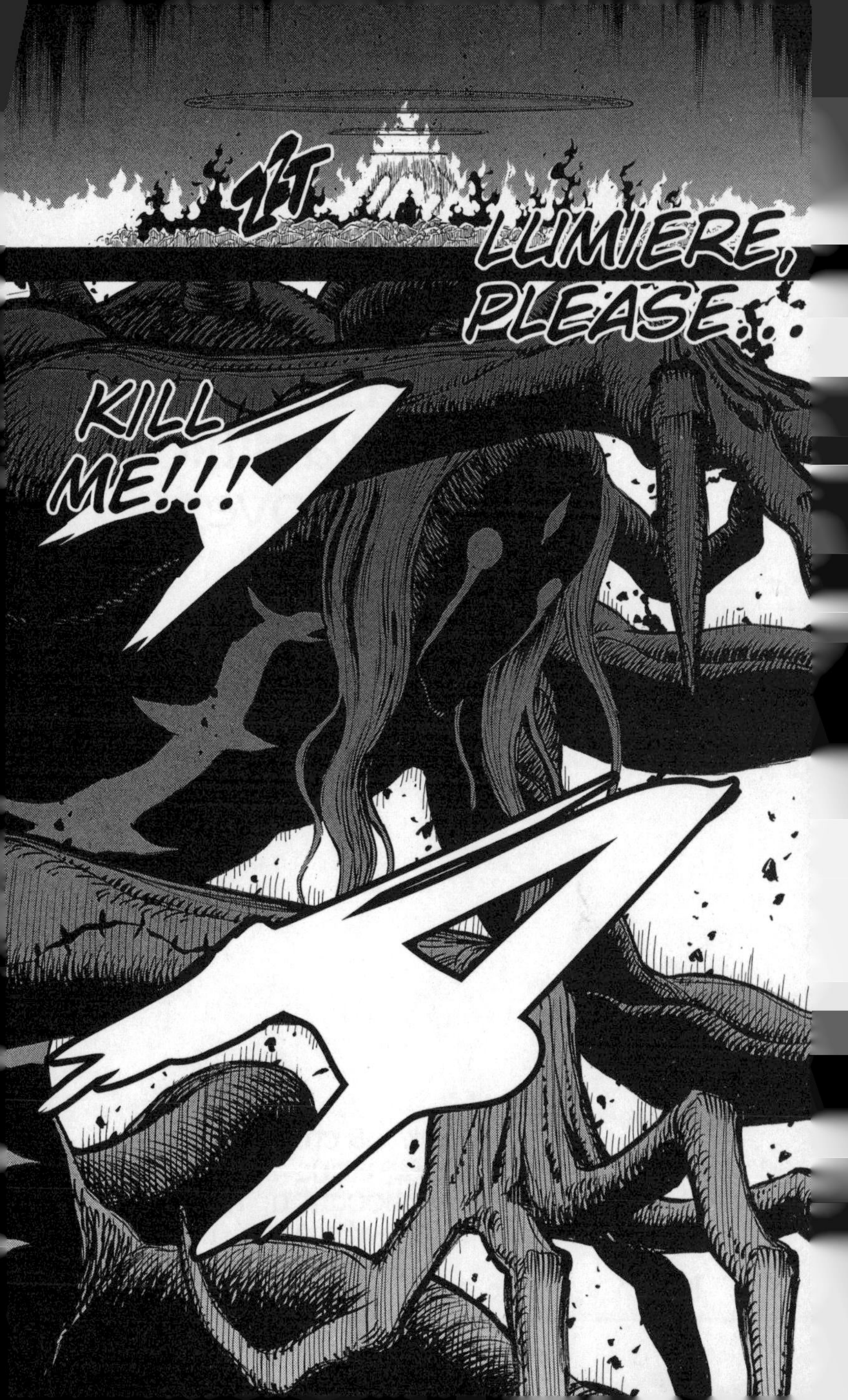
LUMIERE, PLEASE...
KILL ME!!!

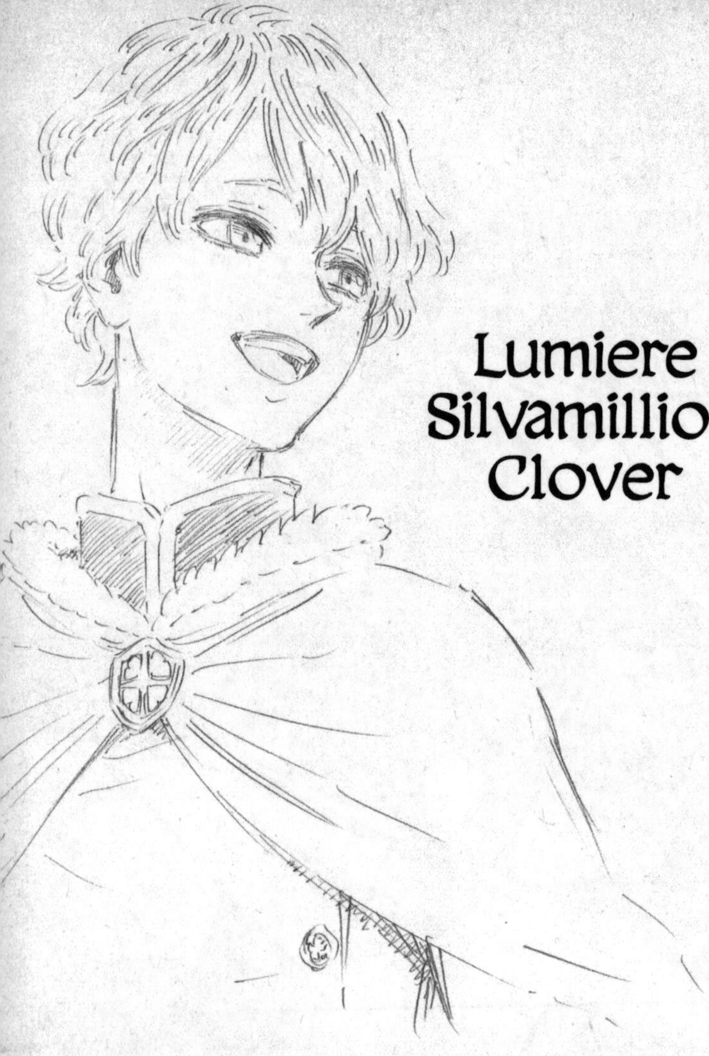

Lumiere Silvamillion Clover

Age: 25 Height: 168 cm
Birthday: February 12 Sign: Aquarius Blood Type: O
Likes: Making clothes he thought up himself, Everything that's filled with possibility

Character Profile

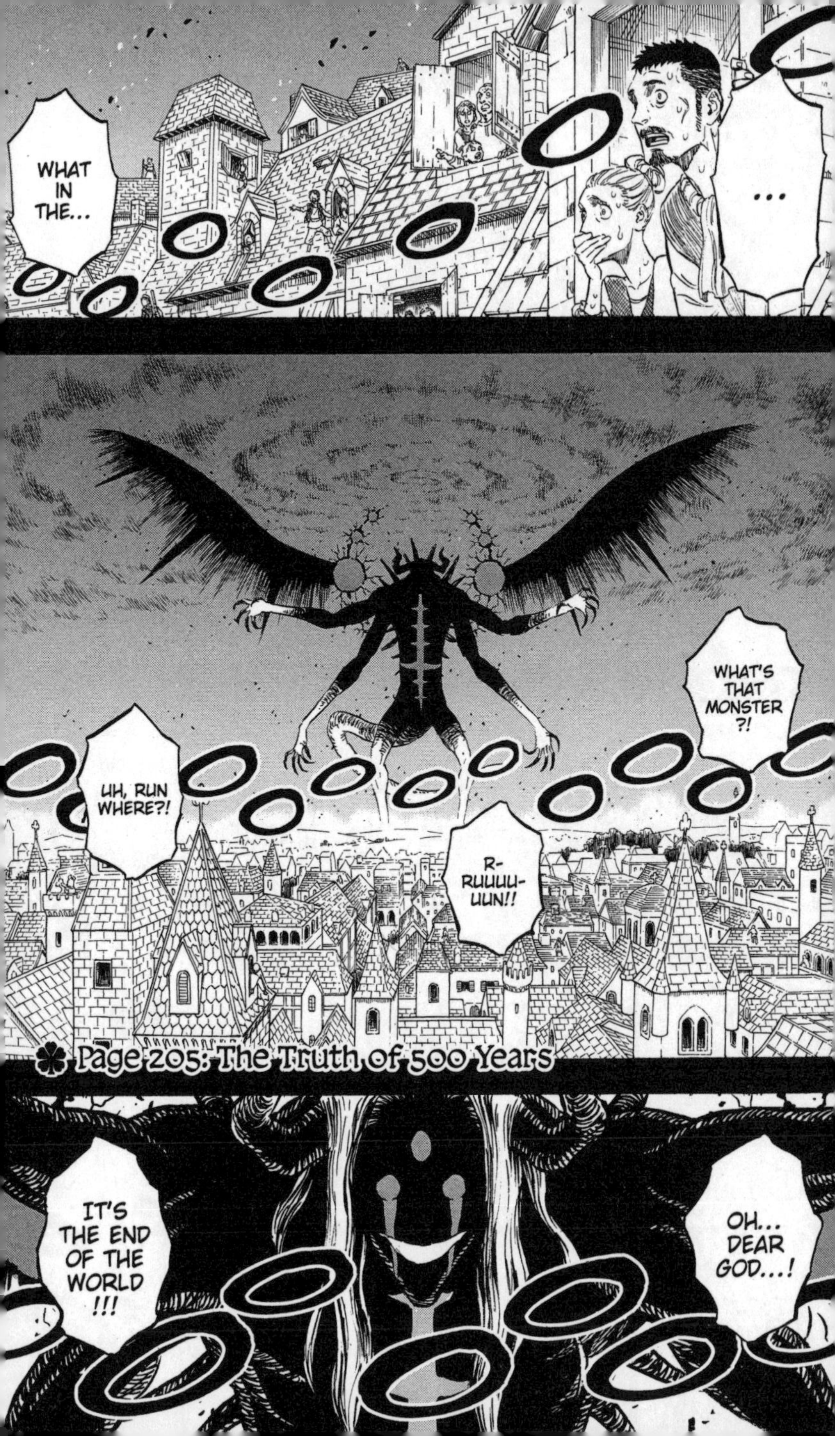
...
WHAT IN THE...
WHAT'S THAT MONSTER?!
R-RUUUU-UUN!!
UH, RUN WHERE?!
OH... DEAR GOD...!
IT'S THE END OF THE WORLD!!!

Page 205: The Truth of 500 Years

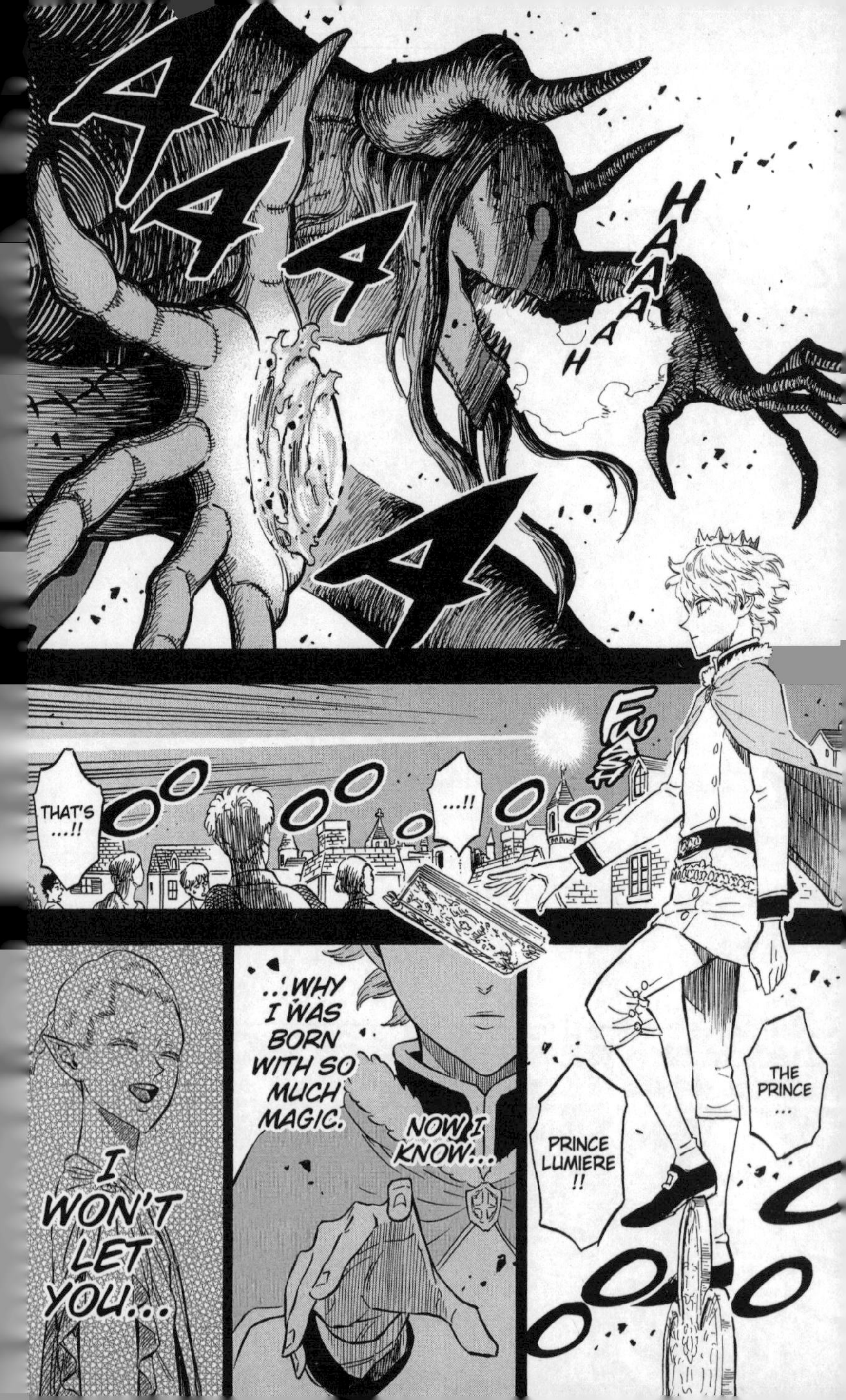
HAAAAAH
AAAAA
FWSH
OOOOOOOOO
...!!
THAT'S ...!!
THE PRINCE ...
PRINCE LUMIERE !!
OOOOO
...WHY I WAS BORN WITH SO MUCH MAGIC.
NOW I KNOW...
I WON'T LET YOU...

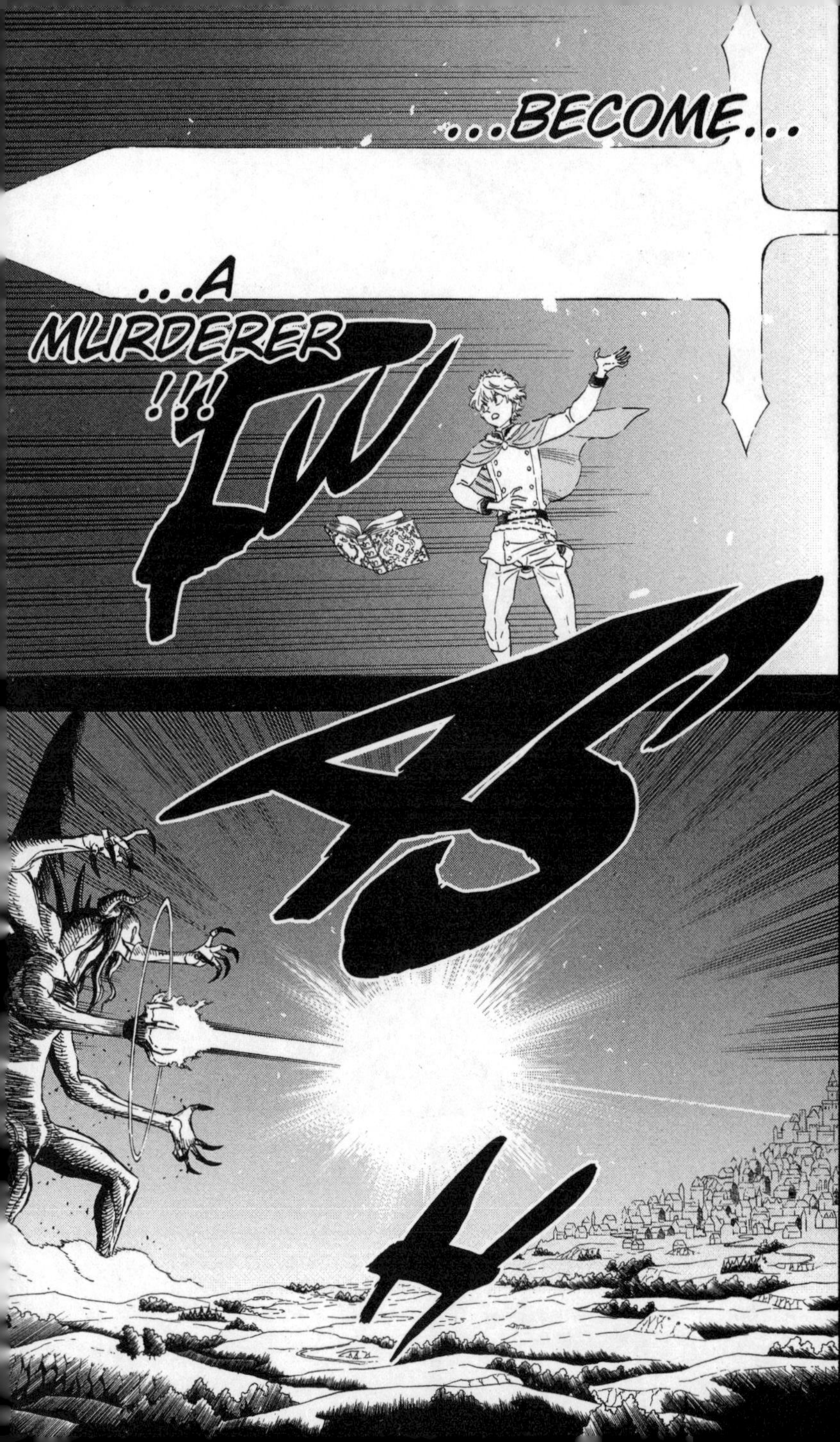
...BECOME...
...A MURDERER!!!

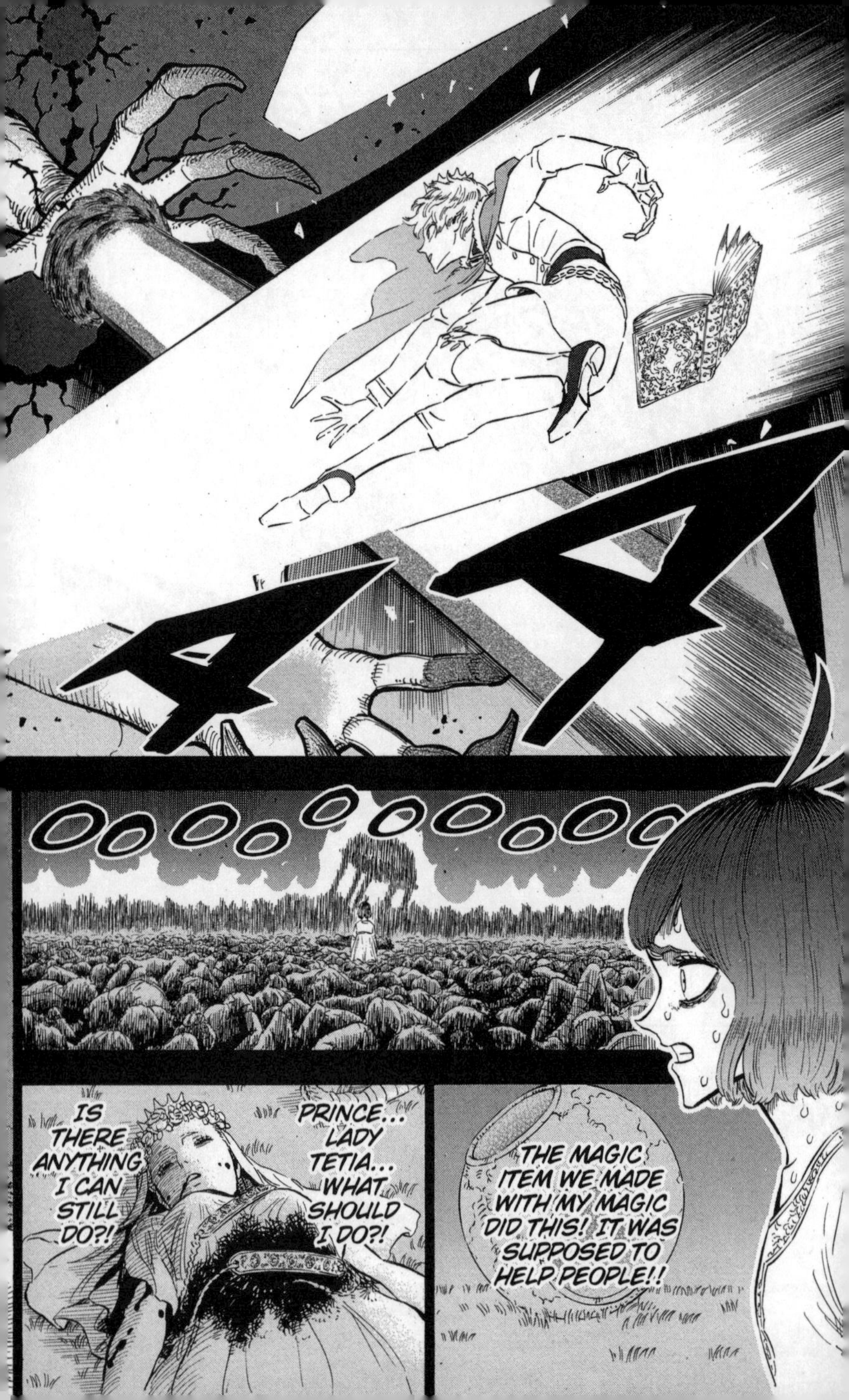
AAA
OOOOOOOOOOOOO
THE MAGIC ITEM WE MADE WITH MY MAGIC DID THIS! IT WAS SUPPOSED TO HELP PEOPLE!!
PRINCE... LADY TETIA... WHAT SHOULD I DO?!
IS THERE ANYTHING I CAN STILL DO?!

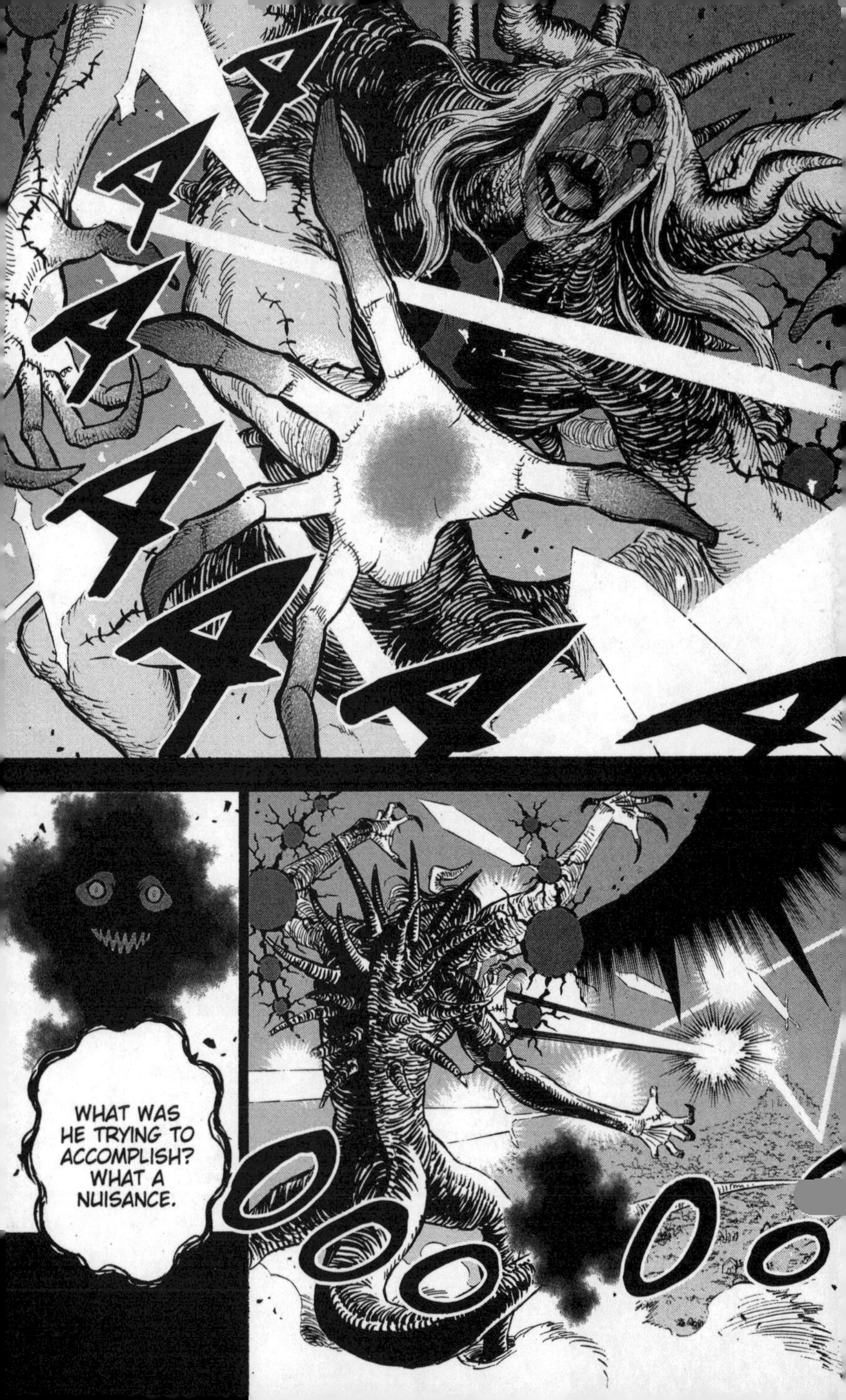
AAAAAAAAA
OOOOOOO
WHAT WAS HE TRYING TO ACCOMPLISH? WHAT A NUISANCE.

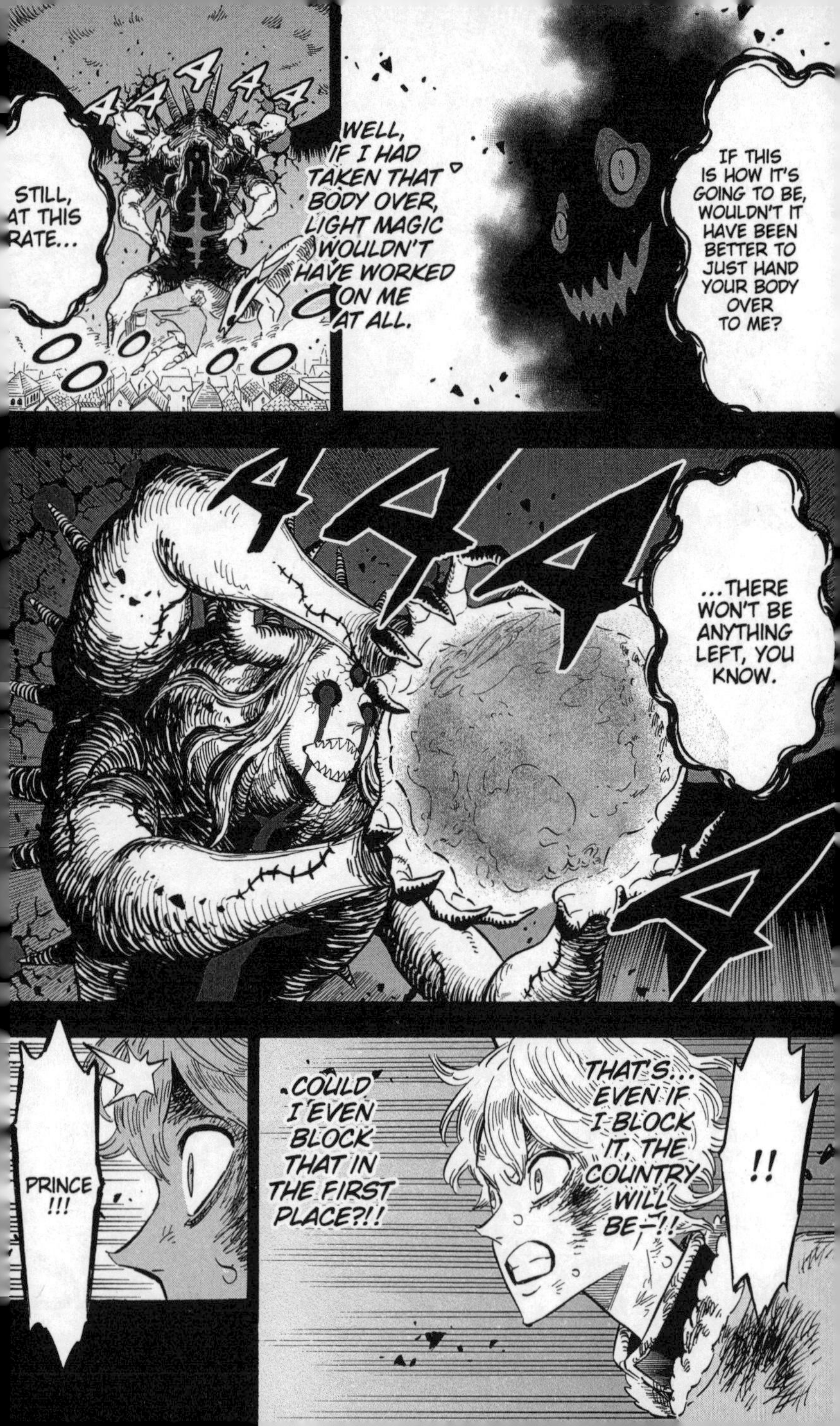
IF THIS IS HOW IT'S GOING TO BE, WOULDN'T IT HAVE BEEN BETTER TO JUST HAND YOUR BODY OVER TO ME?
WELL, IF I HAD TAKEN THAT BODY OVER, LIGHT MAGIC WOULDN'T HAVE WORKED ON ME AT ALL.
AAAAAA
STILL, AT THIS RATE...
OOOOOO
...THERE WON'T BE ANYTHING LEFT, YOU KNOW.
AAAAA
!!
THAT'S... EVEN IF I BLOCK IT, THE COUNTRY WILL BE—!!
COULD I EVEN BLOCK THAT IN THE FIRST PLACE?!!
PRINCE!!!

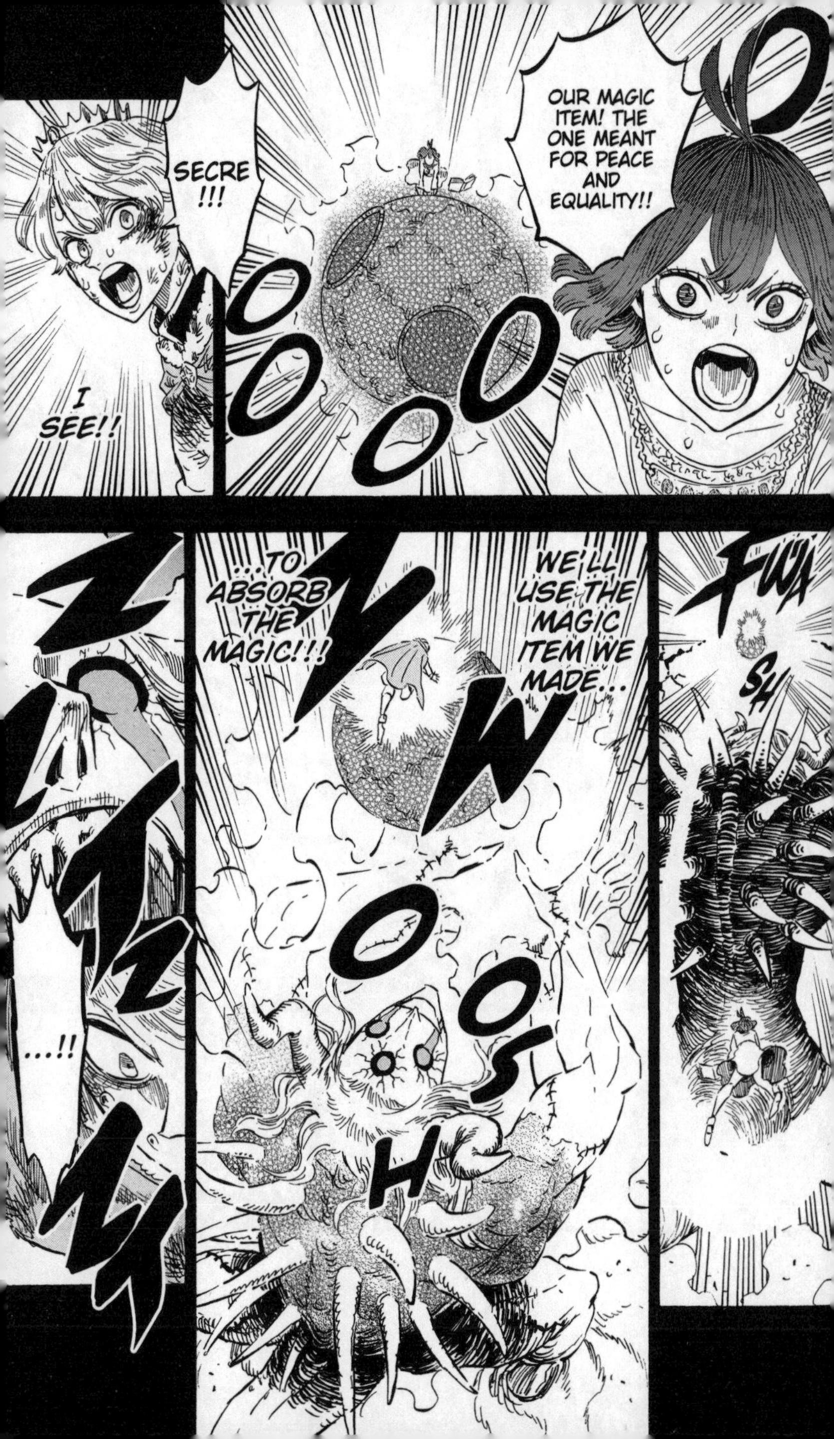
OUR MAGIC ITEM! THE ONE MEANT FOR PEACE AND EQUALITY!!
SECRE !!!
I SEE!!
WE'LL USE THE MAGIC ITEM WE MADE...
...TO ABSORB THE MAGIC!!!
...!!

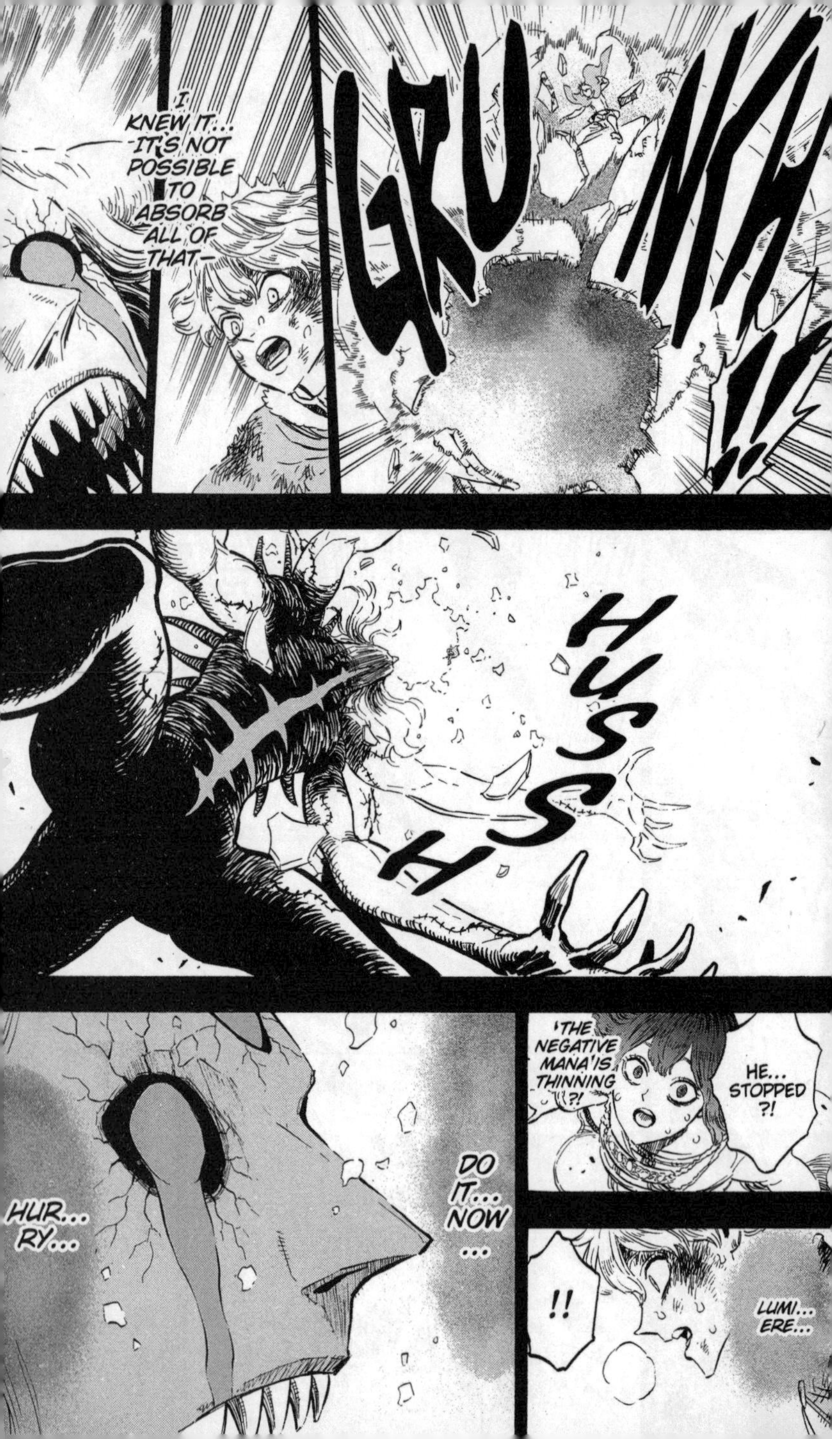
GRUNNH!!
I KNEW IT... IT'S NOT POSSIBLE TO ABSORB ALL OF THAT—
HUSSSH
HE... STOPPED?!
THE NEGATIVE MANA IS THINNING?!
LUMI... ERE...
!!
DO IT... NOW...
HUR... RY...

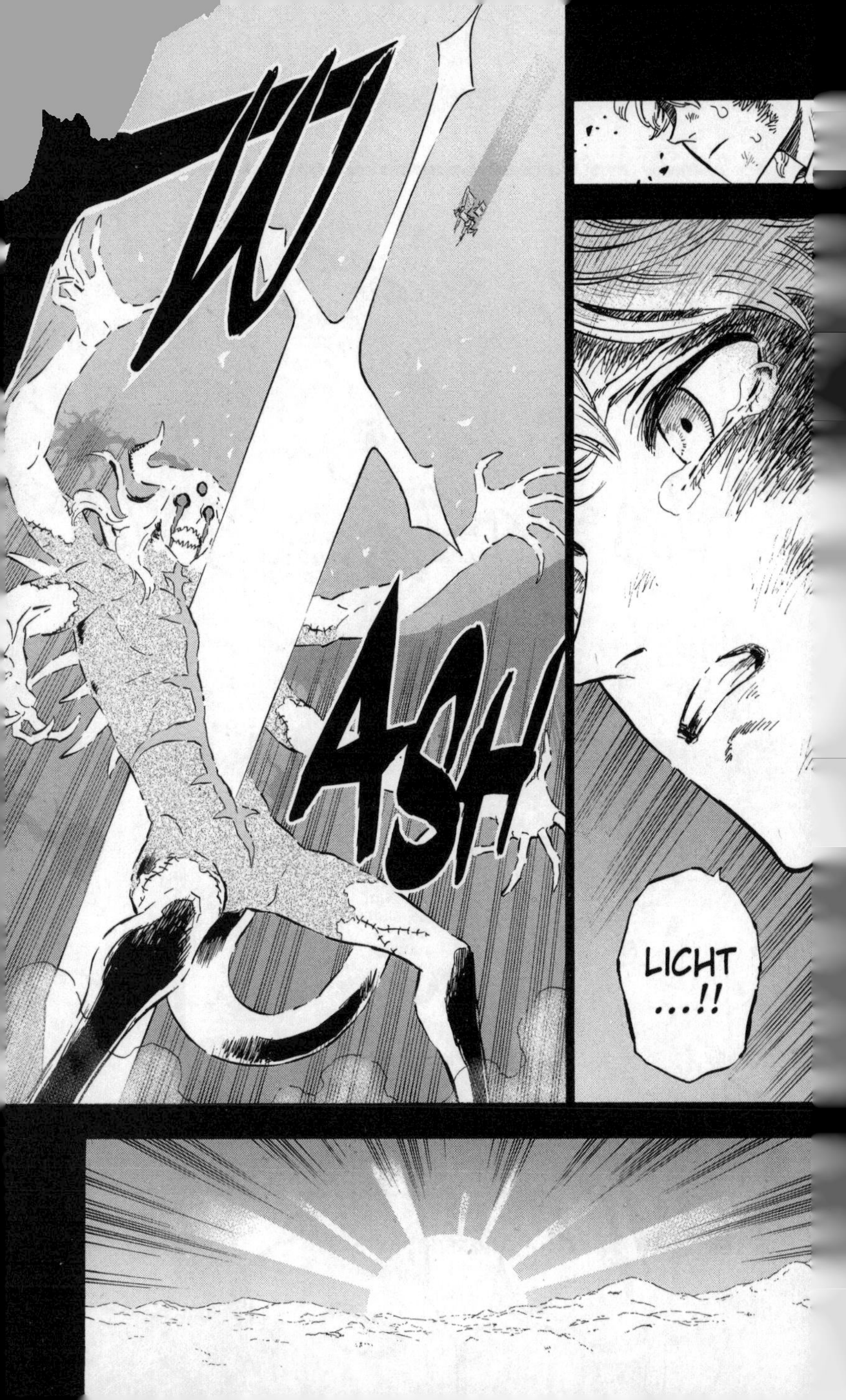
LICHT ...!!
WASH

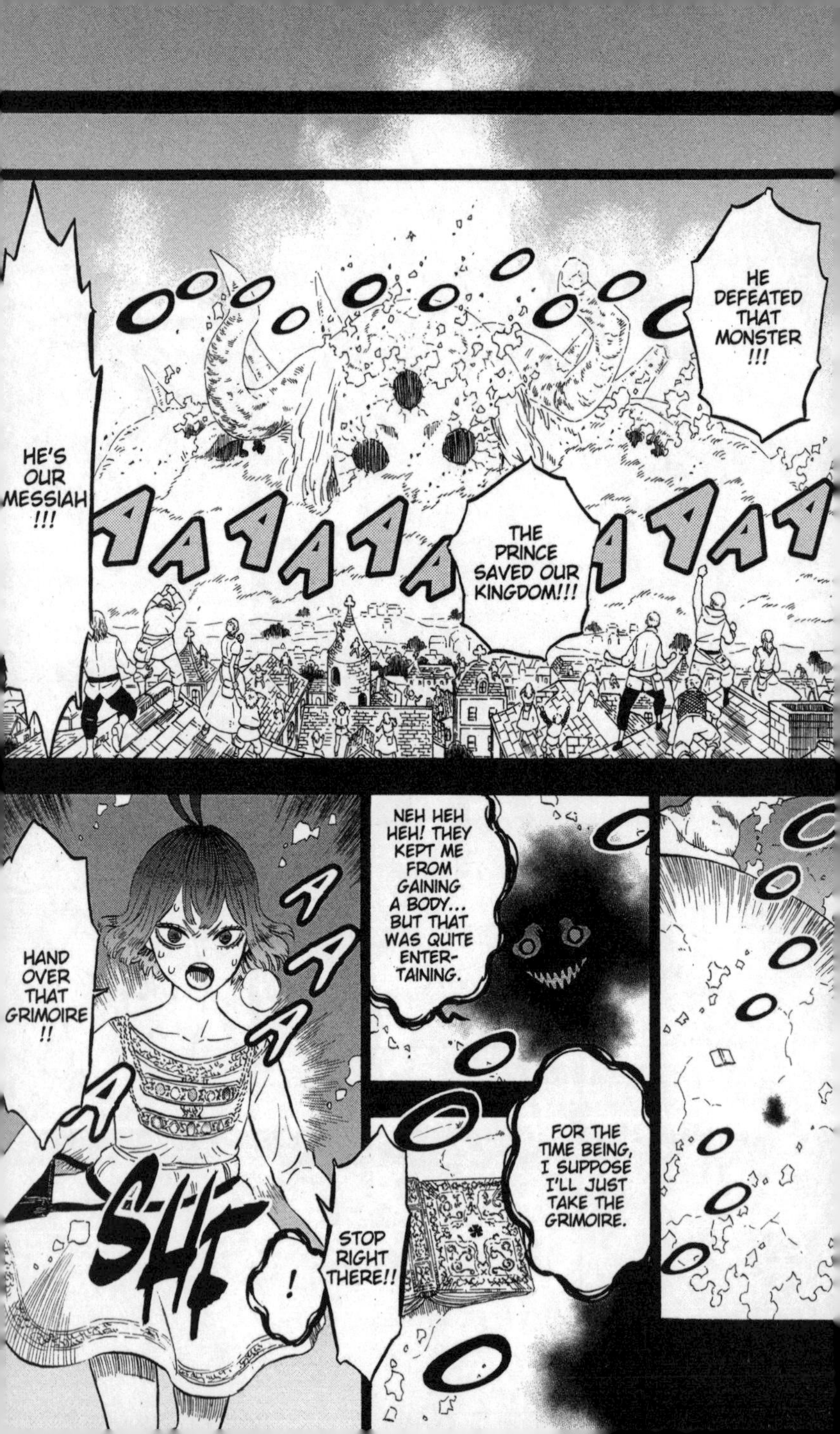
HE DEFEATED THAT MONSTER!!!
OOOOOOOOOO
THE PRINCE SAVED OUR KINGDOM!!!
HE'S OUR MESSIAH!!!
AAAAAAAAAA
NEH HEH HEH! THEY KEPT ME FROM GAINING A BODY... BUT THAT WAS QUITE ENTER-TAINING.
FOR THE TIME BEING, I SUPPOSE I'LL JUST TAKE THE GRIMOIRE.
STOP RIGHT THERE!!
!
HAND OVER THAT GRIMOIRE!!
SHF

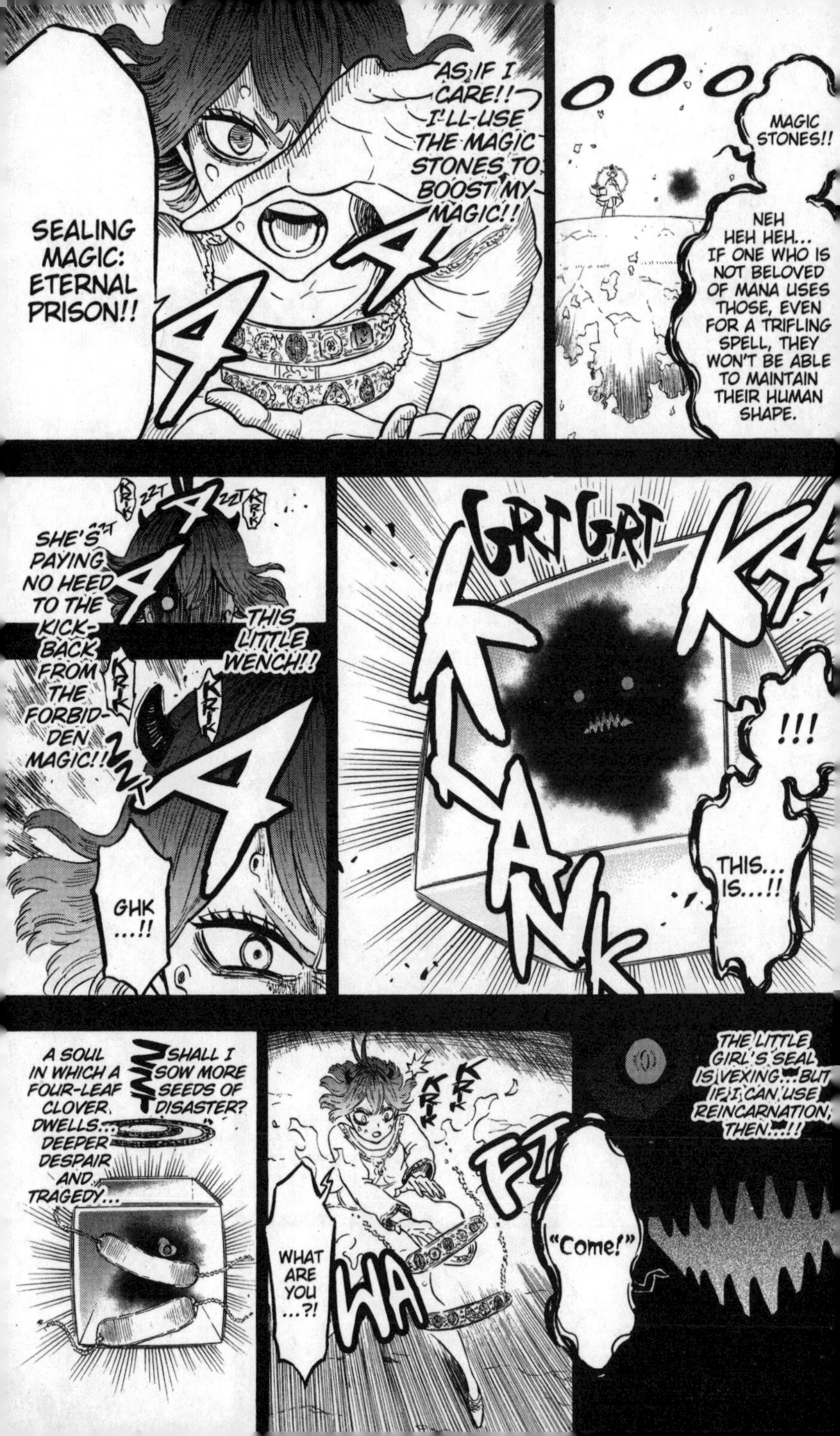
MAGIC STONES!!
NEH HEH HEH... IF ONE WHO IS NOT BELOVED OF MANA USES THOSE, EVEN FOR A TRIFLING SPELL, THEY WON'T BE ABLE TO MAINTAIN THEIR HUMAN SHAPE.
AS IF I CARE!! I'LL USE THE MAGIC STONES TO BOOST MY MAGIC!!
SEALING MAGIC: ETERNAL PRISON!!
GRT GRT
KLANK
!!!
THIS... IS...!!
THIS LITTLE WENCH!!
SHE'S PAYING NO HEED TO THE KICK-BACK FROM THE FORBIDDEN MAGIC!!
KRIK
ZZT
GHK ...!!
THE LITTLE GIRL'S SEAL IS VEXING... BUT IF I CAN USE REINCARNATION, THEN...!!
FT
"Come!"
KRIK KRIK
WHAT ARE YOU ...?!
WA
SHALL I SOW MORE SEEDS OF DISASTER?
A SOUL IN WHICH A FOUR-LEAF CLOVER DWELLS... DEEPER DESPAIR AND TRAGEDY...

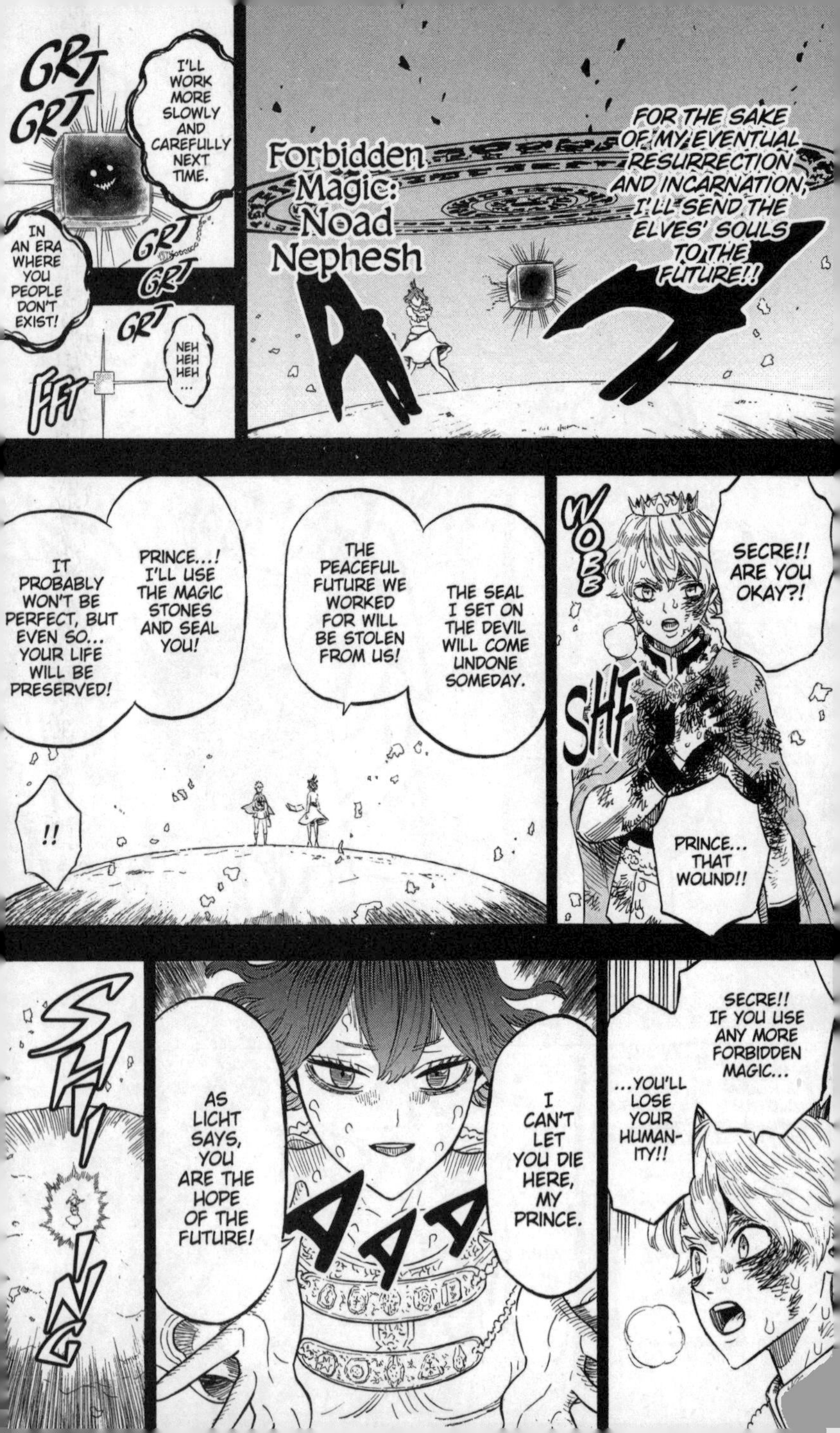
FOR THE SAKE OF MY EVENTUAL RESURRECTION AND INCARNATION, I'LL SEND THE ELVES' SOULS TO THE FUTURE!!
Forbidden Magic: Noad Nephesh
GRT GRT
I'LL WORK MORE SLOWLY AND CAREFULLY NEXT TIME.
IN AN ERA WHERE YOU PEOPLE DON'T EXIST!
GRT GRT GRT
NEH HEH HEH...
FFT
SECRE!! ARE YOU OKAY?!
WOBB
SHF
PRINCE... THAT WOUND!!
THE SEAL I SET ON THE DEVIL WILL COME UNDONE SOMEDAY.
THE PEACEFUL FUTURE WE WORKED FOR WILL BE STOLEN FROM US!
PRINCE...! I'LL USE THE MAGIC STONES AND SEAL YOU!
IT PROBABLY WON'T BE PERFECT, BUT EVEN SO... YOUR LIFE WILL BE PRESERVED!
!!
SECRE!! IF YOU USE ANY MORE FORBIDDEN MAGIC...
...YOU'LL LOSE YOUR HUMAN-ITY!!
I CAN'T LET YOU DIE HERE, MY PRINCE.
AS LICHT SAYS, YOU ARE THE HOPE OF THE FUTURE!
AAA
SHHIIING

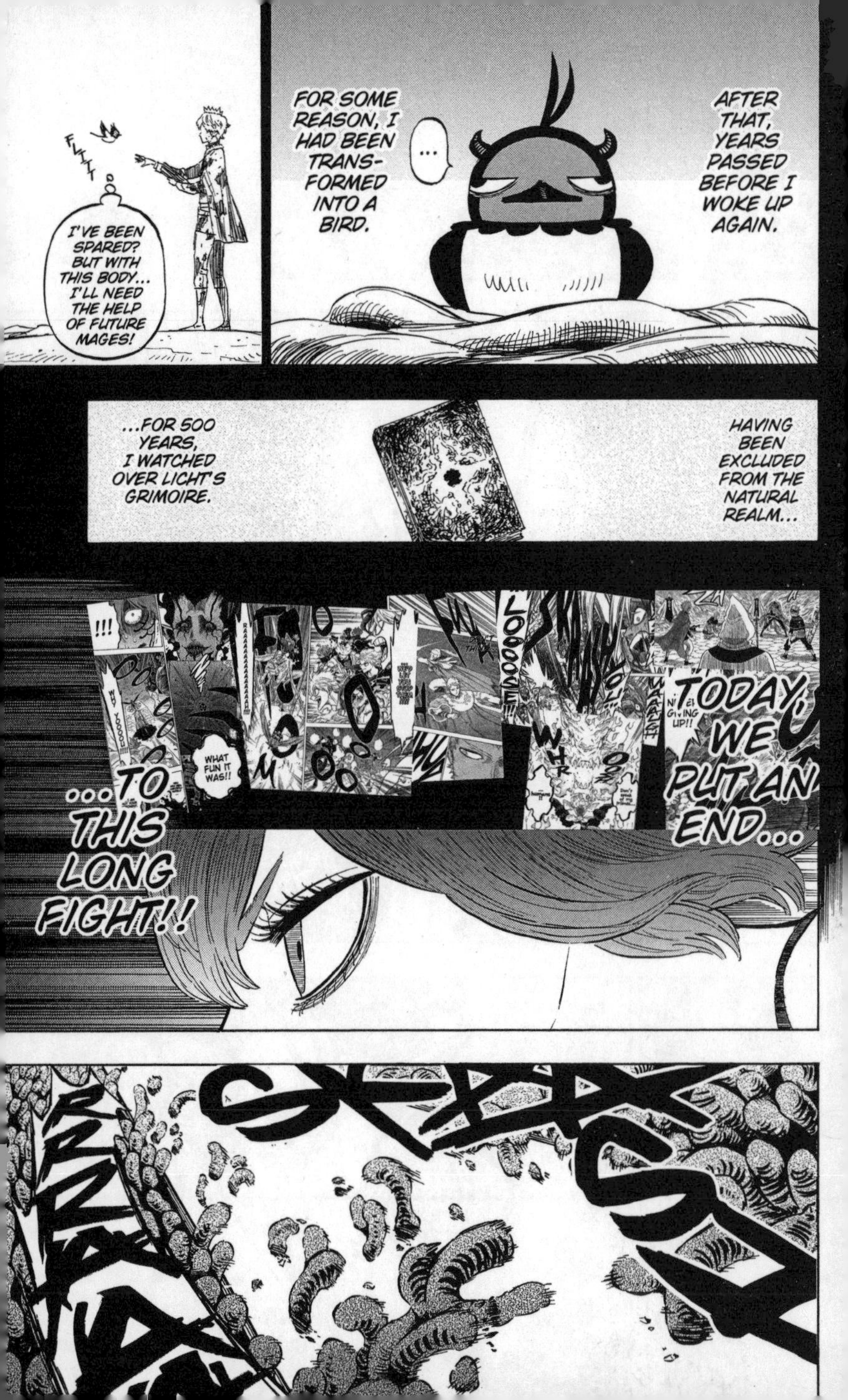
AFTER THAT, YEARS PASSED BEFORE I WOKE UP AGAIN.
FOR SOME REASON, I HAD BEEN TRANS-FORMED INTO A BIRD.
...
FLTTT
I'VE BEEN SPARED? BUT WITH THIS BODY... I'LL NEED THE HELP OF FUTURE MAGES!
HAVING BEEN EXCLUDED FROM THE NATURAL REALM...
...FOR 500 YEARS, I WATCHED OVER LICHT'S GRIMOIRE.
NOT GIVING UP!!
LOOOOOSE!!
WHAT FUN IT WAS!!
!!!
TODAY, WE PUT AN END...
...TO THIS LONG FIGHT!!

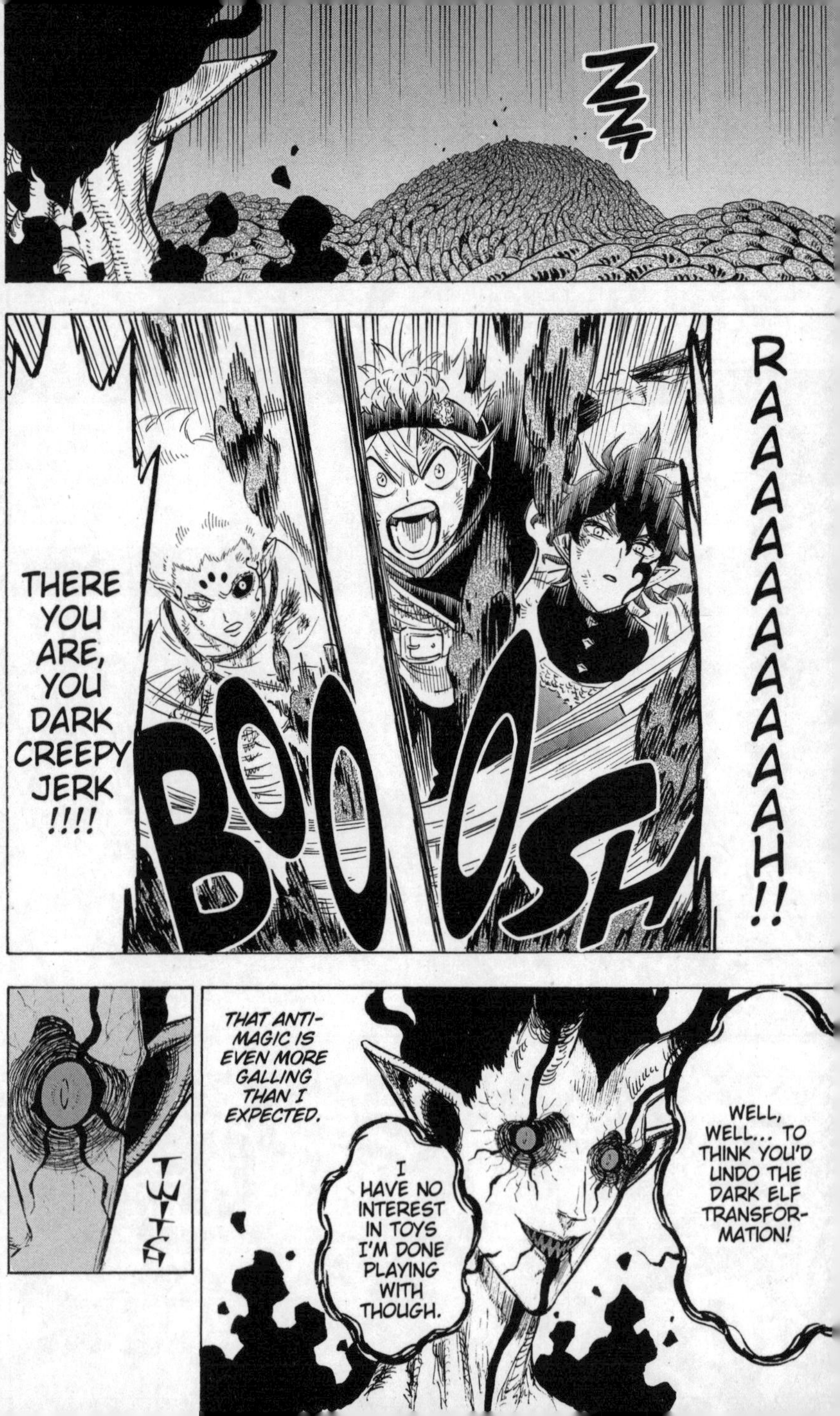
ZZZT
RAAAAAAAAAAH!!
THERE YOU ARE, YOU DARK CREEPY JERK!!!!
BOOOSH
WELL, WELL... TO THINK YOU'D UNDO THE DARK ELF TRANSFOR-MATION!
THAT ANTI-MAGIC IS EVEN MORE GALLING THAN I EXPECTED.
I HAVE NO INTEREST IN TOYS I'M DONE PLAYING WITH THOUGH.
TWITCH

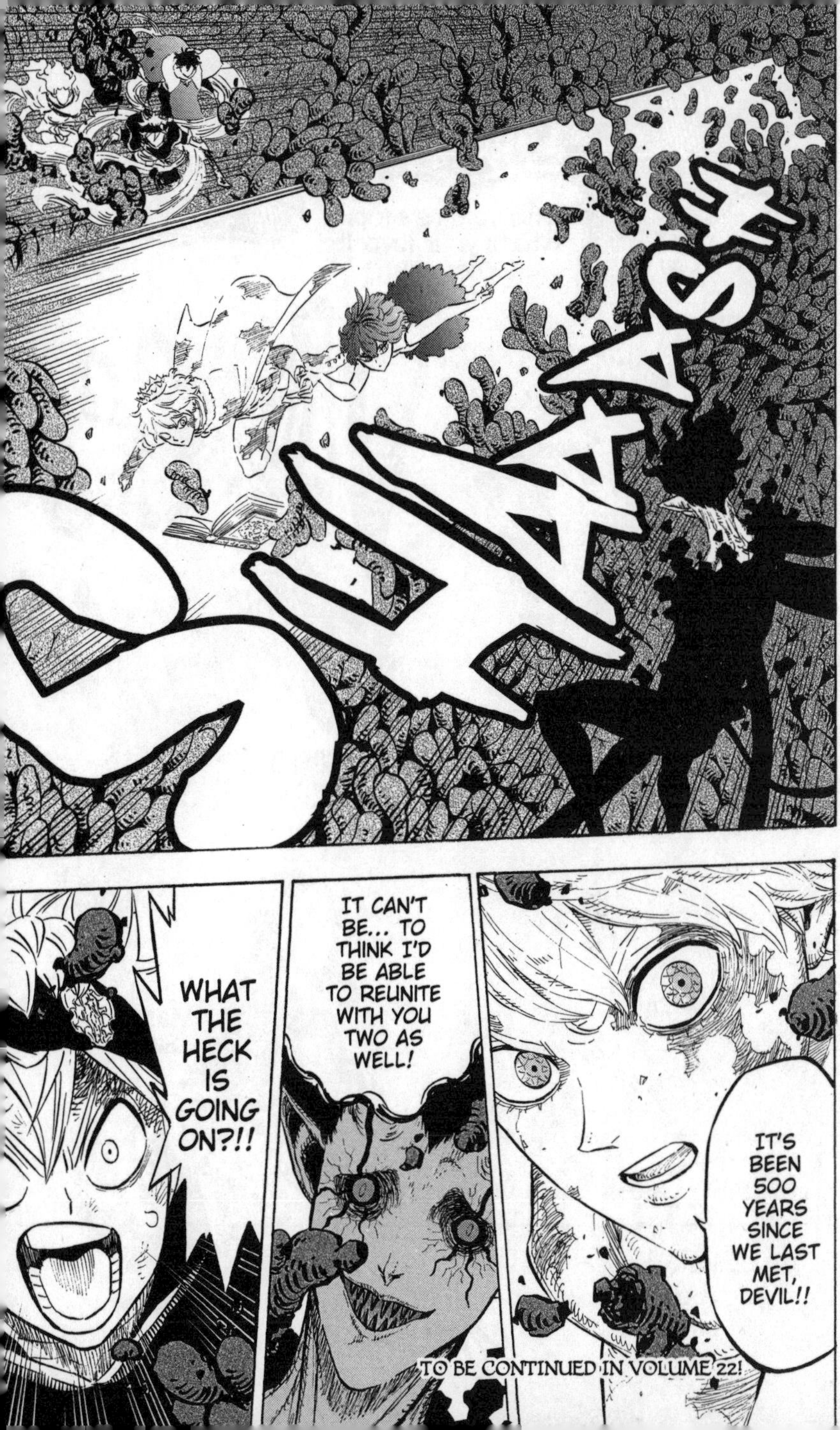
IT'S BEEN 500 YEARS SINCE WE LAST MET, DEVIL!!
IT CAN'T BE... TO THINK I'D BE ABLE TO REUNITE WITH YOU TWO AS WELL!
WHAT THE HECK IS GOING ON?!!
TO BE CONTINUED IN VOLUME 22!

The Blank Page Brigade

This volume's topic: What's your favorite Chinese dish?

Egg foo young with crab

Sōta Hishikawa

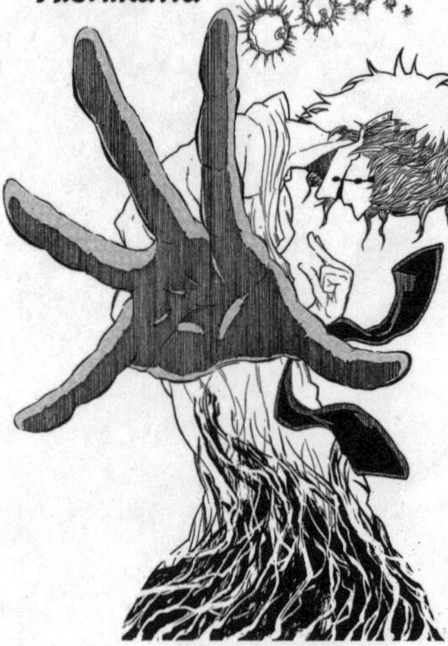

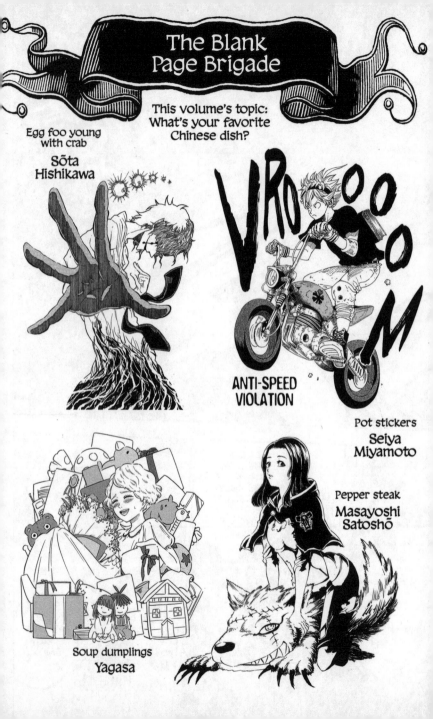

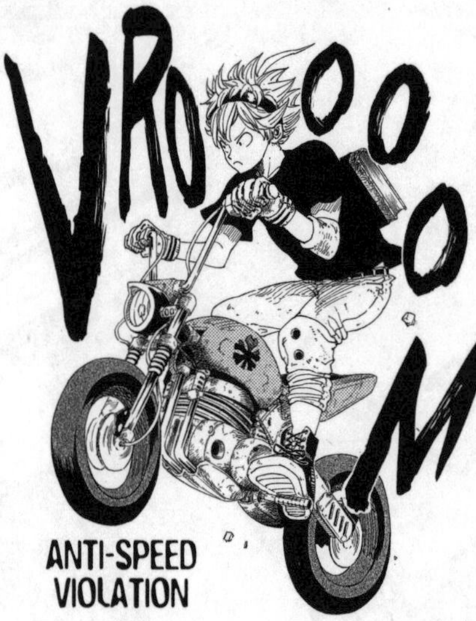
ANTI-SPEED
VIOLATION

Pot stickers

Seiya Miyamoto

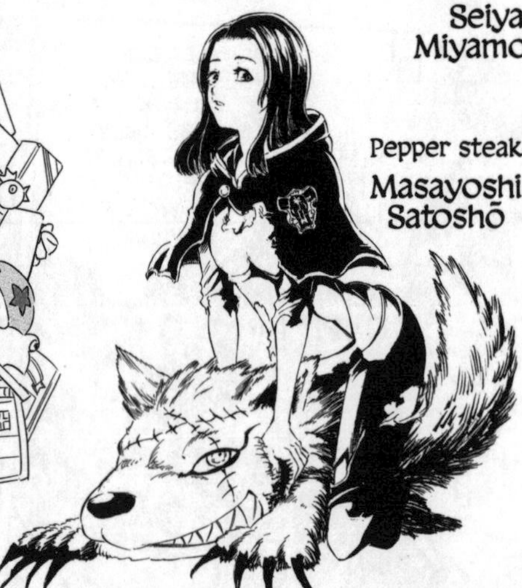

Pepper steak

Masayoshi Satoshō

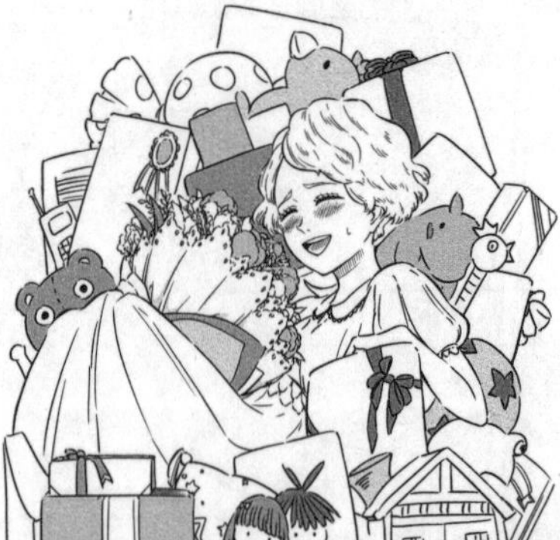

Soup dumplings

Yagasa

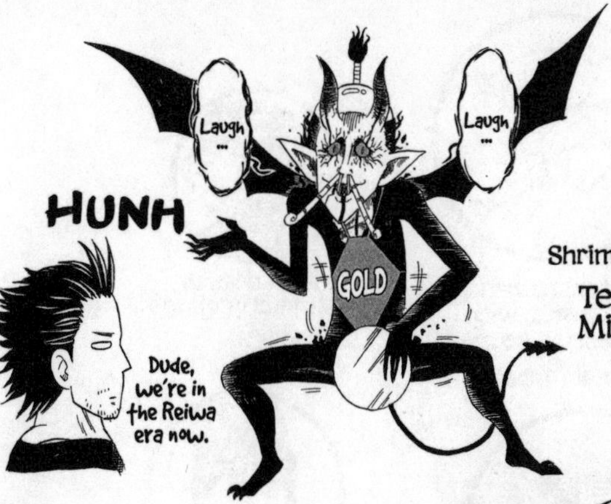
Laugh...
Laugh...
HUNH
GOLD
Dude, we're in the Reiwa era now.

Shrimp Shumai

Teruaki Mizuno

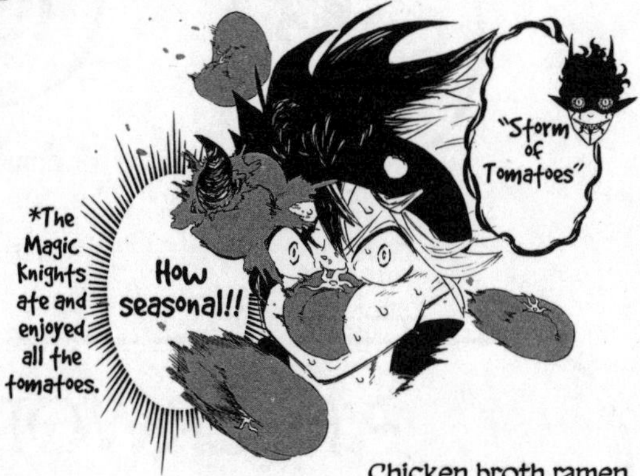
"Storm of Tomatoes"
How seasonal!!
*The Magic Knights ate and enjoyed all the tomatoes.

Twice-cooked pork

Yōtarō Hayakawa

Chicken broth ramen

Kazuhiro Wakao

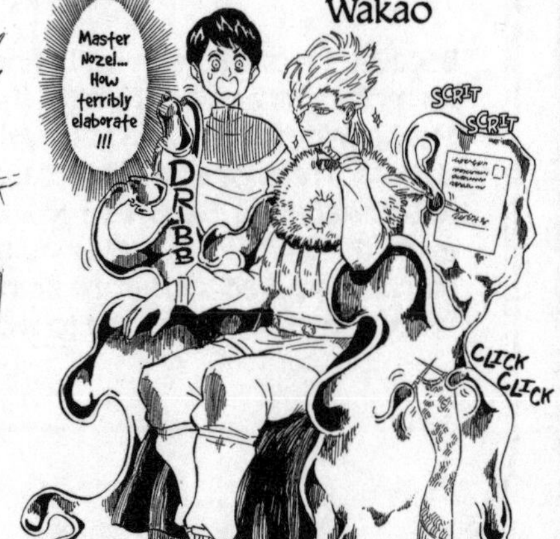
SCRIT
SCRIT
Master Nozel... How terribly elaborate!!!
DRIBB
CLICK CLICK

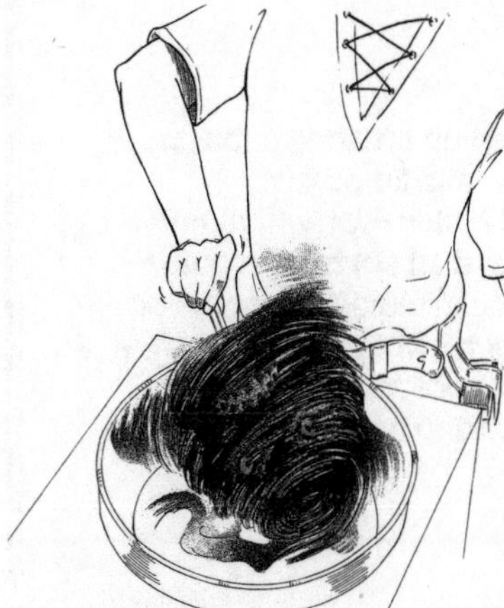

Chili shrimp

Hayato Gotō

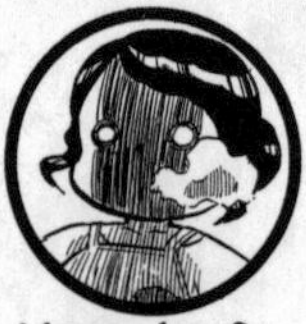

Mapo doufu,
sesame dumplings

©

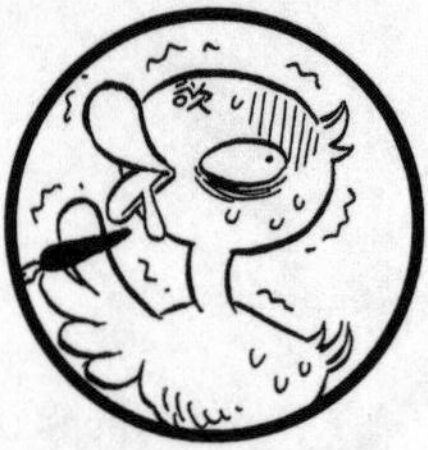

談

The tenshinhan
from Ohsho, with
Kyoto-style sauce

Captain Tabata

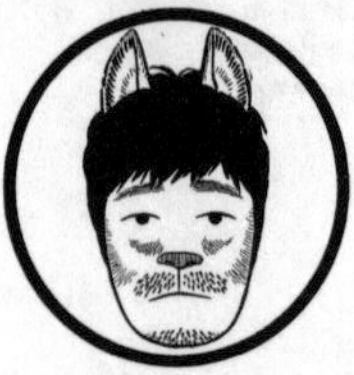

Spring rolls,
annin tofu

Comics
editor
Fujiwara

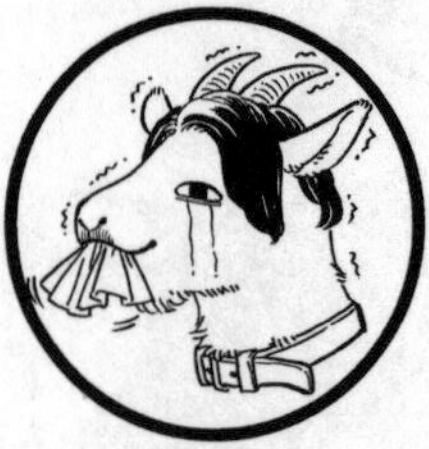

Ramen-
potstickers-
fried rice
set meal

Editor Toide

AFTERWORD

✽

Because I work so slowly, I ended up creating a raging torrent of stress, and right in the middle of that, Ms. Koshimura the graphic novel editor—for whom my raging torrent of stress had caused all sorts of trouble—was transferred elsewhere. Ms. Koshimura, I'm sorry for everything!! Thank you very much!!! Mr. Fujiwara, my new graphic novel editor, let me start apologizing now!! I'm really looking forward to working with you!!!

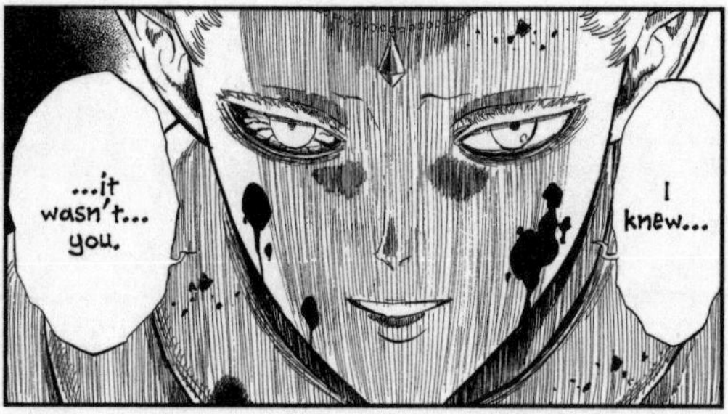
I knew...
...it wasn't... you.

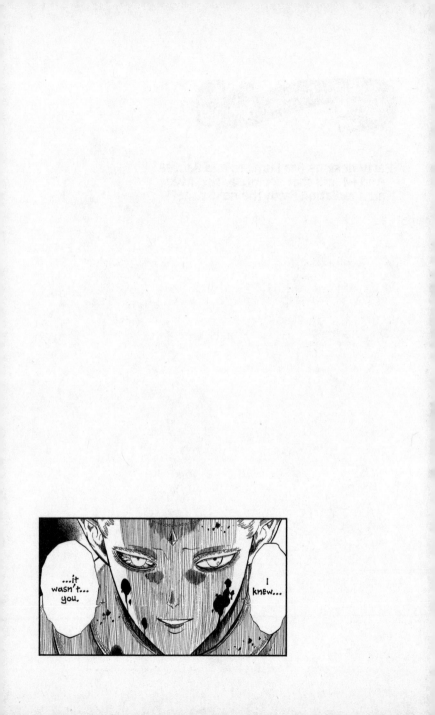

Special Bonus Materials

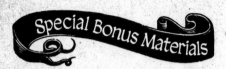

Early designs for Lumiere and Secre!!
And what's that seriously negative
aura radiating from the next page?!

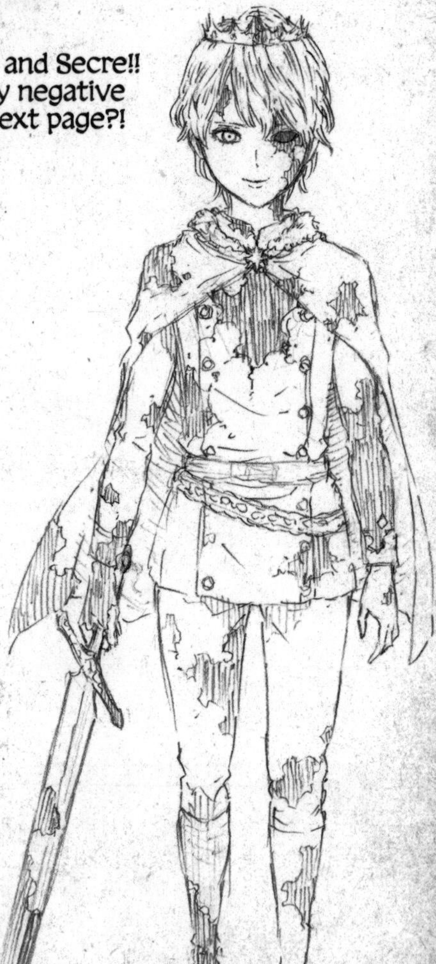

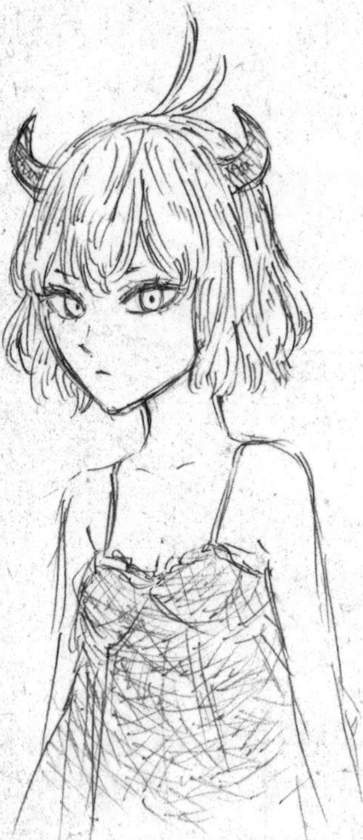

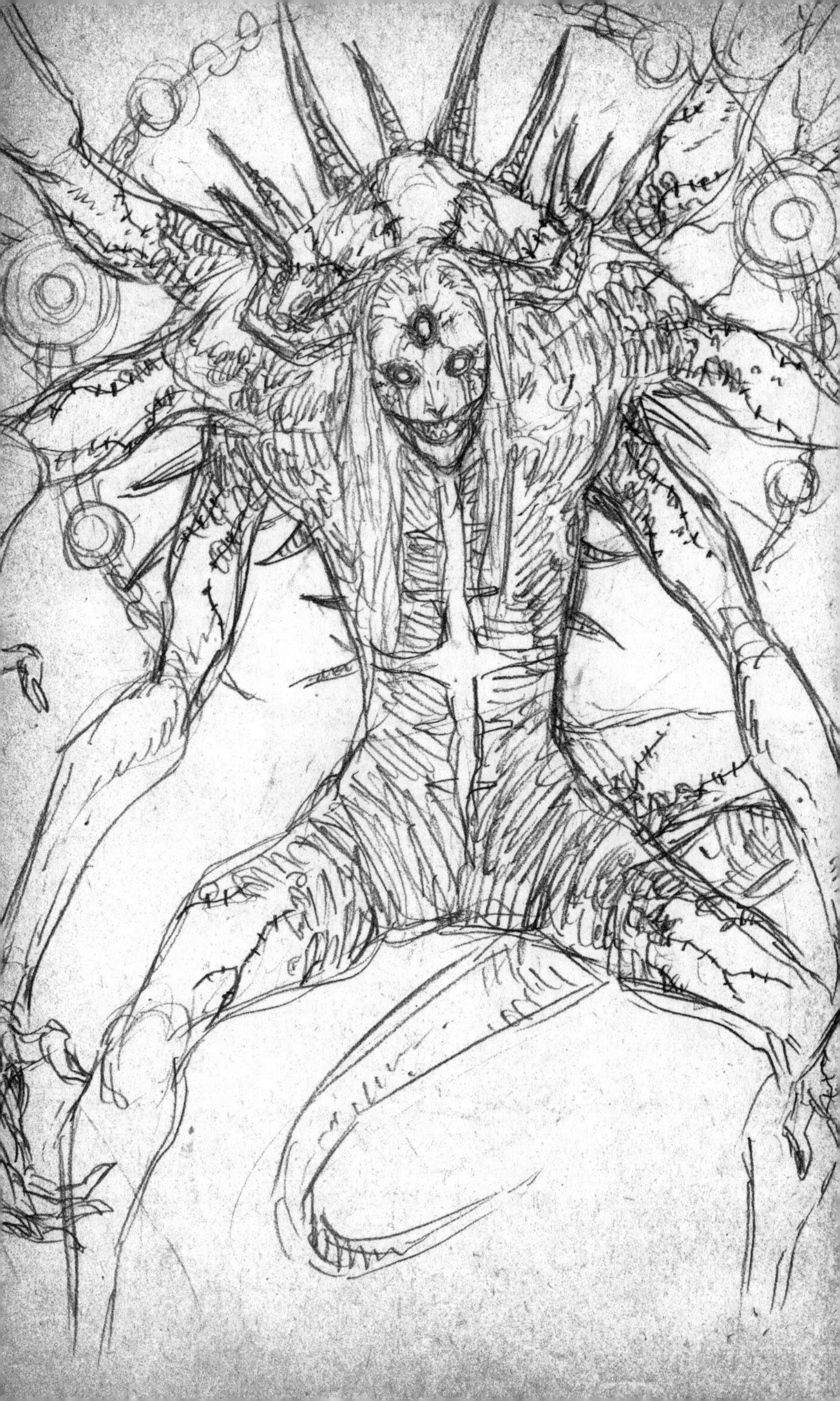

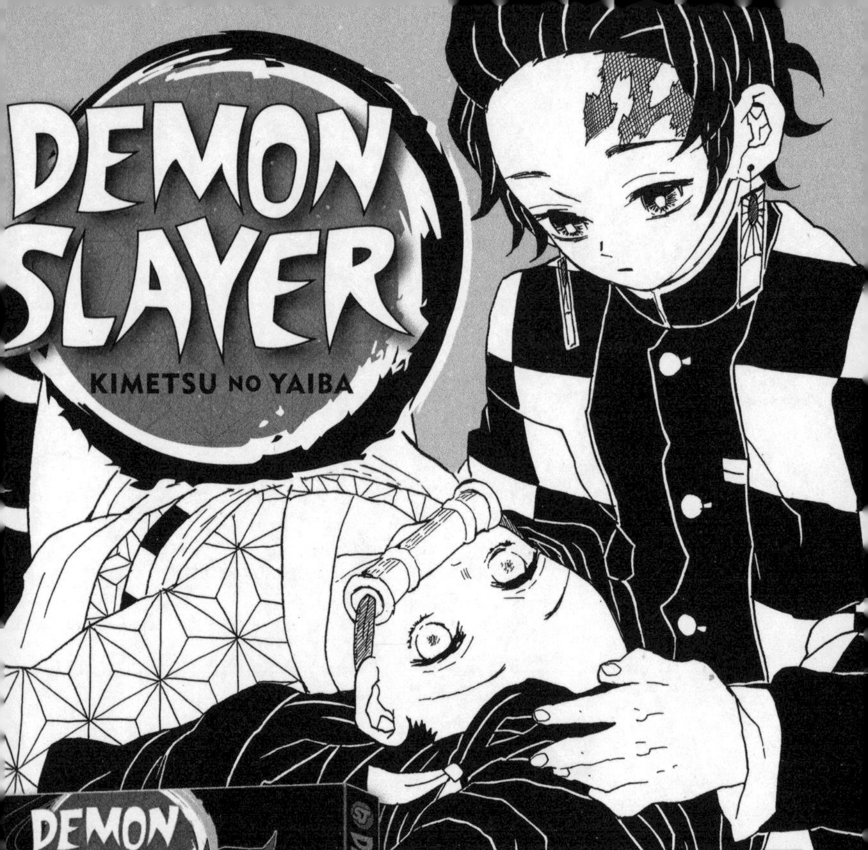

DEMON SLAYER

KIMETSU NO YAIBA

DEMON SLAYER
KIMETSU NO YAIBA

Story and Art by
KOYOHARU GOTOUGE

In Taisho-era Japan, kindhearted Tanjiro Kamado makes a living selling charcoal. But his peaceful life is shattered when a demon slaughters his entire family. His little sister Nezuko is the only survivor, but she has been transformed into a demon herself! Tanjiro sets out on a dangerous journey to find a way to return his sister to normal and destroy the demon who ruined his life.

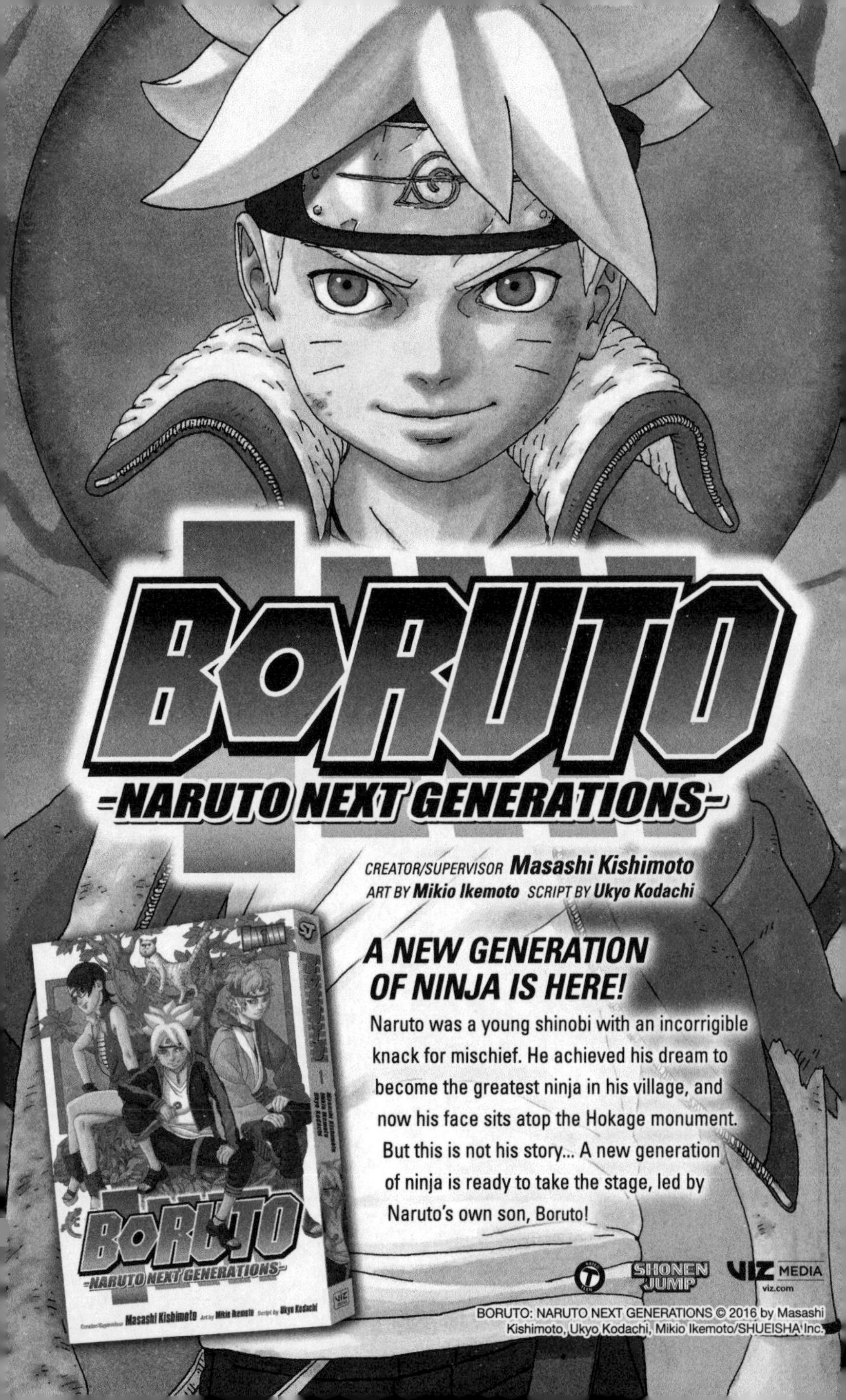
BORUTO
-NARUTO NEXT GENERATIONS-
CREATOR/SUPERVISOR Masashi Kishimoto
ART BY Mikio Ikemoto SCRIPT BY Ukyo Kodachi
A NEW GENERATION OF NINJA IS HERE!
Naruto was a young shinobi with an incorrigible knack for mischief. He achieved his dream to become the greatest ninja in his village, and now his face sits atop the Hokage monument. But this is not his story... A new generation of ninja is ready to take the stage, led by Naruto's own son, Boruto!
BORUTO
-NARUTO NEXT GENERATIONS-
SHONEN JUMP
VIZ MEDIA
viz.com
BORUTO: NARUTO NEXT GENERATIONS © 2016 by Masashi Kishimoto, Ukyo Kodachi, Mikio Ikemoto/SHUEISHA Inc.

ASTRA
LOST IN SPACE

CAN EIGHT TEENAGERS FIND THEIR WAY HOME FROM 5,000 LIGHT-YEARS AWAY?

It's the year 2063, and interstellar space travel has become the norm. Eight students from Caird High School and one child set out on a routine planet camp excursion. While there, the students are mysteriously transported 5,000 light-years away to the middle of nowhere! Will they ever make it back home?!

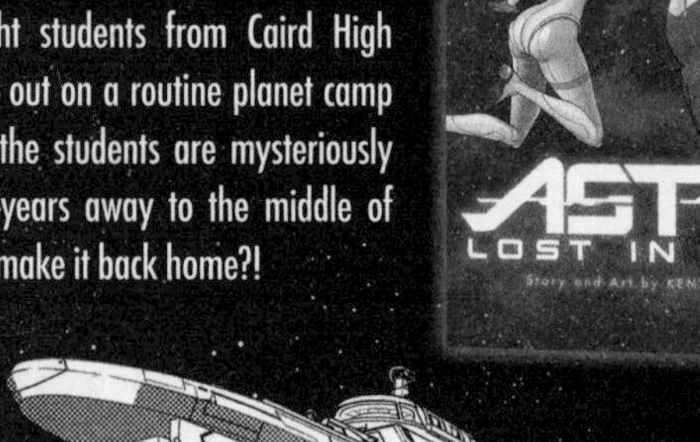

ASTRA
LOST IN SPACE
Story and Art by KENTA SHINOHARA

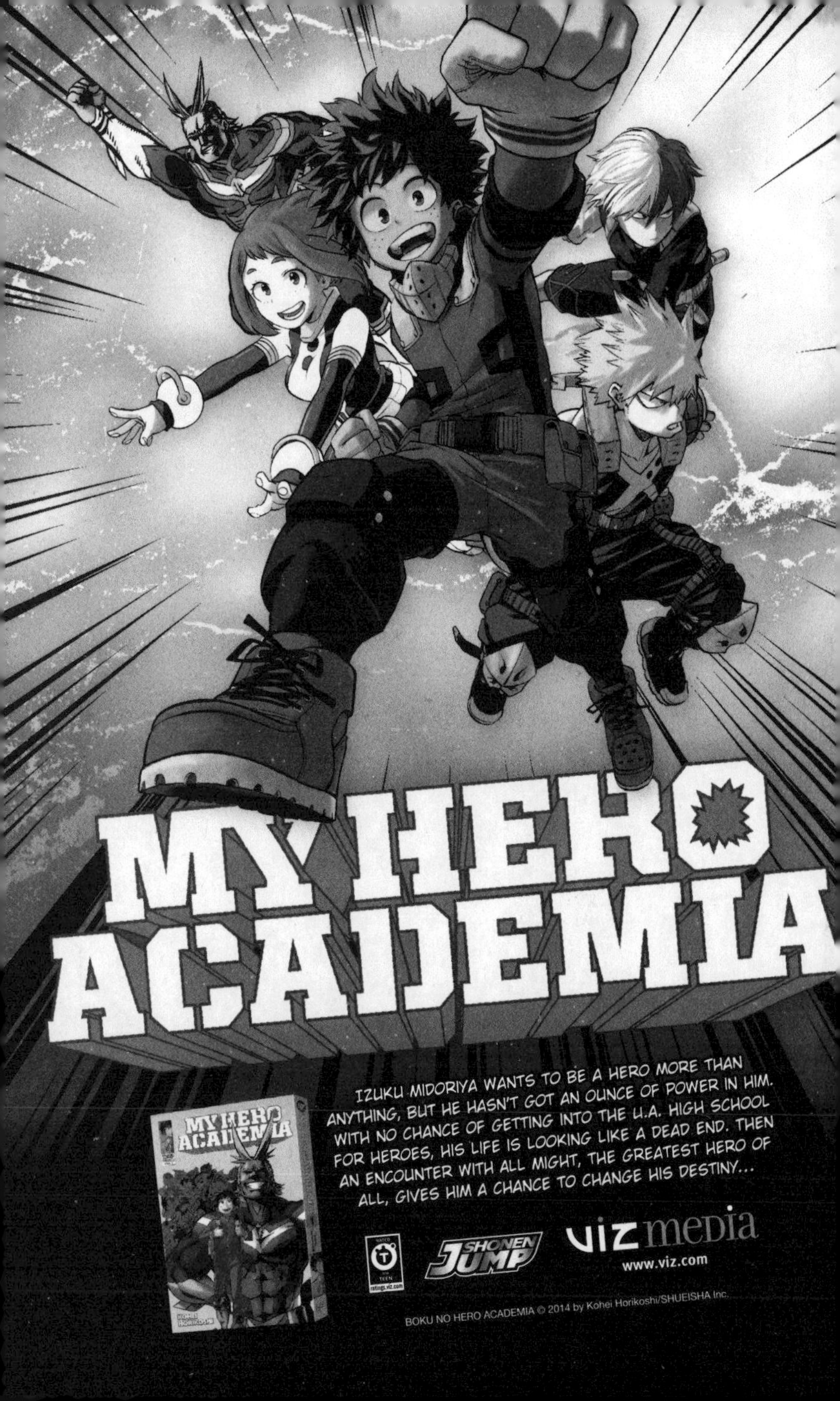

MY HERO ACADEMIA
IZUKU MIDORIYA WANTS TO BE A HERO MORE THAN ANYTHING, BUT HE HASN'T GOT AN OUNCE OF POWER IN HIM. WITH NO CHANCE OF GETTING INTO THE U.A. HIGH SCHOOL FOR HEROES, HIS LIFE IS LOOKING LIKE A DEAD END. THEN AN ENCOUNTER WITH ALL MIGHT, THE GREATEST HERO OF ALL, GIVES HIM A CHANCE TO CHANGE HIS DESTINY...
MY HERO ACADEMIA
TEEN
ratings.viz.com
SHONEN JUMP
VIZ media
www.viz.com
BOKU NO HERO ACADEMIA © 2014 by Kohei Horikoshi/SHUEISHA Inc.

Dr. STONE

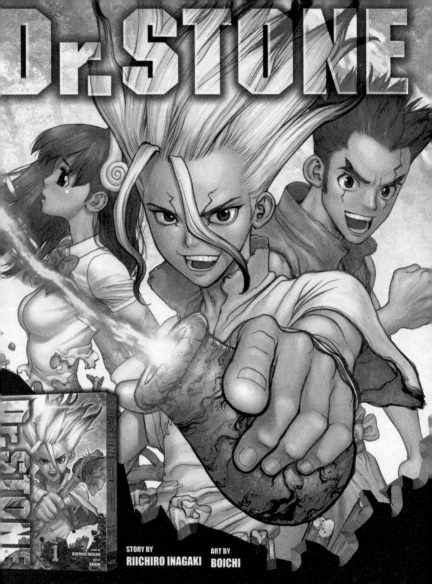

STORY BY
RIICHIRO INAGAKI

ART BY
BOICHI

ne fateful day, all of humanity turned to stone. Many millennia
ater, Taiju frees himself from petrification and finds himself
urrounded by statues. The situation looks grim—until he runs
to his science-loving friend Senku! Together they plan to restart

Stop

YOU'RE READING
THE WRONG WAY!

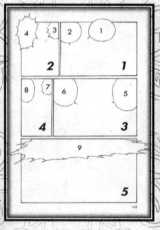

BLACK CLOVER
reads from right to left, starting
in the upper-right corner. Japanese
is read from right to left, meaning
that action, sound effects, and
word-balloon order are completely
reversed from English order.